His Majesty's Rebels

His Majesty's Rebels

Communities, Factions, and Rural Revolt
in the Black Forest, 1725–1745

David Martin Luebke

Cornell University Press
Ithaca and London

Copyright © 1997 by Cornell University

All rights reserved. Except for brief quotations in a review, this book, or parts thereof, must not be reproduced in any form without permission in writing from the publisher. For information, address Cornell University Press, Sage House, 512 East State Street, Ithaca, New York 14850.

First published 1997 by Cornell University Press.

Printed in the United States of America

Library of Congress Cataloging-in-Publication Data

Luebke, David Martin, 1960–
    His majesty's rebels : communities, factions, and rural revolt in the Black Forest, 1725–1745 / David Martin Luebke.
       p. cm.
    Includes bibliographical references and index.
    ISBN 0-8014-3346-0 (alk. paper)
      1. Black Forest (Germany)—History. 2. Black Forest (Germany)—Rural conditions. 3. Black Forest (Germany)—Economic conditions. 4. Black Forest (Germany)—Social conditions. I. Title.
DD801.B64L84   1997
943'.46—dc21   97-720

Cornell University Press strives to utilize environmentally responsible suppliers and materials to the fullest extent possible in the publishing of its books. Such materials include vegetable-based, low-VOC inks and acid-free papers that are also either recycled, totally chlorine free, or partly composed of nonwood fibers.

Cloth printing 10 9 8 7 6 5 4 3 2 1

Contents

	Preface	vii
	Abbreviations	xi
	Currency Equivalents	xiii
INTRODUCTION	*Faction and Community in the "Salpeter Wars"*	1
CHAPTER 1	*Power in the County* Lords and Subjects in Hauenstein	25
CHAPTER 2	*Uncivil War* A Chronicle of the Revolt	54
CHAPTER 3	*A House Divided* Dissension and the Geography of Fear	90
CHAPTER 4	*Big Shots versus Little People?* Social Dimensions of Factional Conflict	117
CHAPTER 5	*"Into the Devil's Jaws"* Patrolling the Boundaries of Community	147
CHAPTER 6	*The Practice of Rebellion*	180
CONCLUSION	*Peasant Factions in the Holy Roman Empire*	212
	Appendixes	233
	Selected Bibliography	249
	Index	265

Preface

WHEN THIS PROJECT BEGAN, I ENTERTAINED THE MODEST HOPE THAT it would confirm some hypotheses about the communalism of political life among early modern European peasants and, with a little luck, impart to them the depth and richness of local detail that case studies can provide. From a wealth of writing by historians and folklorists, I knew that the documentation on the "Salpeter Wars," a series of early eighteenth-century peasant rebellions in the Black Forest county of Hauenstein, was exceptionally rich. With such resources at my disposal, I expected to find peasants actively organizing themselves communally in the defense of the legal autonomies and immunities of their villages against the predations of seigneurs bent on reducing their independence of action. I also expected to find the peasants driven to action by collectively held but unspoken notions of "moral economy." Within days of my arrival in Germany for a preliminary survey of these sources, however, several of my expectations were dashed: among the first documents I encountered were long and exhaustive lists, enumerating families known to the compilers either as "peaceable" or "rebellious." At the outset, it seemed that the principal categories of political self-classification revolved around questions of obedience and displays of deference. This in itself came as no great surprise. Instead, the surprise lay waiting in the proportions: upon totaling the lists, I discovered to my dismay that in most villages, the sum membership of each group, "peaceable" and "rebellious," was about equal. More lists yielded similar results; slowly but surely, geographical patterns and chronological fluctuations in the distribution of factional loyalties began to appear.

Something had divided these people deeply and evenly. Clearly, I would have to adjust my anticipation of peasant communalism. This impression was confirmed as I read deeper. It became apparent to me that questions of obedience to authority were not, after all, the principal touchstone of political consciousness among these peasants. Rather, membership in one of two major political factions was decisive. Indeed, the very existence of my evidence reinforced this impression. In this connection, the survival of interrogation transcripts and other official records was not particularly revealing; but the fact that the rebels' correspondence and manifestos had been preserved suggested the snooping of factional rivals. Some set of eighteenth-century Hauensteiners had thought it worthwhile to intercept these letters, copy them down, and pass the copies along to the authorities. Peasants were denouncing other peasants; it was also surprising how many of these peasants could write, how much they wrote, and how dependent their activities were on writing. My first impulse was to attribute such espionage to opportunism or treachery, but it quickly became clear that this analysis merely took the rebels' view of factional politics at face value. Proof of this emerged from evidence that ostensibly "peaceable" peasants were also engaged in resistance, albeit by different methods. Finally, notions of "moral economy" seemed almost entirely absent from the political rhetoric of either of these groups. Thus commenced an inquiry into the political culture of factionalism among these Black Forest peasants, in which I eventually felt compelled to abandon many, if not all, of my original ideas. I returned from the archives of the Rhineland to Connecticut, tore up my initial prospectus for the book, and started over from scratch.

Fortunately, I received much encouragement along the way. I owe special thanks to Claudia Ulbrich, Wolfgang Ulbrich, Peter Blickle, and Renate Blickle, who extended their hospitality to me and offered invaluable advice on avenues of interpretation and the use of archival sources; Peter Blickle's doctoral students also gave my ideas an early, thoroughgoing, and constructive critique. In addition, I have profited greatly from the comments and suggestions of Thomas A. Brady Jr., Thomas Fox, Keith Luria, R. Emmet McLaughlin, Edward Muir, Thomas Robisheaux, David W. Sabean, Peter Sahlins, Winfried Schulze, James C. Scott, Robert W. Scribner, Peter K. Taylor, John Theibault, Henry A. Turner, Jr., Lee Palmer Wandel, Mack Walker, and Heide Wunder, all of whom took the time to read and critique my manuscript at various stages in its evolution. Above all, I wish to acknowledge Peter Gay, my doctoral mentor, who nurtured this project with his wise advice and support through all of its phases.

This book is partly the product of many years of study in graduate school. By their interest, forbearance, and lively readiness to discuss, Ruthanne Deutsch, Carolyn Kay, Kenneth Mayer, Helmut W. Smith, and Kali Tal, fellow travelers all, contributed to it in more ways than they know. Marc Forster, Tina Forster, Hans-Jürgen Kremer, and Rupert Kubon were amiable companions both in and outside the archives; as a result, they know more about Black Forest peasant rebellions than they ever wanted to, and I owe them thanks for indulging my questions and endless storytelling. On more than one occasion, Jeffrey Paul Burds rescued me from the calamitous results of my own of my computer illiteracy. My colleagues at Bennington College offered invaluable stylistic advice.

The research for this book was conducted at archives in the Federal Republic of Germany, mainly the Generallandesarchiv Karlsruhe, but also the Stadtarchiv Freiburg im Breisgau, the Erzbischöfliches Archiv Freiburg im Breisgau, the Stadtarchiv Waldshut-Tiengen, and the Gemeindearchiv Dogern am Rhein. My deepest gratitude goes to the staffs of all these institutions for their generosity and eagerness to help me. Without the generous support of the Deutscher Akademischer Austauschdienst (DAAD) and the Yale Council on West European Studies, the research for this book would never have been done.

Finally, I owe a special debt of gratitude to my parents, Frederick C. Luebke and Norma M. Luebke, both of whom are all too familiar with the life a fledgling historian leads and whose moral support was inexhaustible. This book is dedicated to them.

Bennington, Vermont   DAVID MARTIN LUEBKE

Abbreviations

Archives

EAF	Erzbischöfliches Archiv Freiburg im Breisgau
GAD	Gemeindearchiv Dogern am Rhein
GLA	Badisches Generallandesarchiv Karlsruhe
StAFB	Stadtarchiv Freiburg im Breisgau
StAWT	Stadtarchiv Waldshut-Tiengen

Other

KK	Kaiserliche Kommission (Imperial Commission); Kaiserlicher Kommissar (Imperial Commissar)
NF	Neue Folge (Second Series)
OÖKR	Oberösterreichische Kammerregierung (Upper Austrian Provincial Government, Innsbruck)
OVA	Obervogteiamt (Abbatial High Steward's Bureau, Gurtweil)
RP	Rechnungsprotokoll (Account Ledger)
VÖRK	Vorderösterreichische Regierung und Kammer (Outer Austrian Provincial Government, Freiburg)
WGP	Wochengerichtsprotokoll (Weekly Court Protocol)
WVA	Waldvogteiamt (Forest Steward's Bureau, Waldshut)

Periodical journals

AESC	*Annales: Économies, Sociétés, Civilisations*
ASG	*Archiv für Sozialgeschichte*
ARG	*Archiv für Reformationsgeschichte*

CEH	Central European History
GG	Geschichte und Gesellschaft
HJ	Historisches Jahrbuch
HZ	Historische Zeitschrift
JMH	Journal of Modern History
JPS	Journal of Peasant Studies
MIÖG	Mitteilungen des Instituts für Österreichische Geschichte
MÖS	Mitteilungen des Österreichischen Staatsarchivs
NBHK	Neujahresblätter der Badischen Historischen Kommission
NJLG	Niedersächsisches Jahrbuch für Landesgeschichte
PP	Past and Present
PS	Peasant Studies
PSN	Peasant Studies Newsletter
SVGBU	Schriften des Vereins für die Geschichte des Bodensees und seiner Umbgebung
VSWG	Vierteljahresschrift für Sozial- und Wirtschaftsgeschichte
ZAA	Zeitschrift für Agrargeschichte und Agrarsoziologie
ZBLG	Zeitschrift für Bayerische Landesgeschichte
ZfG	Zeitschrift für Geschichtswissenschaft
ZHF	Zeitschrift für historische Forschung
ZGO	Zeitschrift für die Geschichte des Oberrheins
ZWLG	Zeitschrift für Württembergische Landesgeschichte

Currency Equivalents

1 gulden (fl) = 60 kreuzer (xr) = 180 pfennig (d)

1 pfund (lb) = 40 kreuzer

Ratio of imperial to provincial gulden = approximately 1:0.73

His Majesty's Rebels

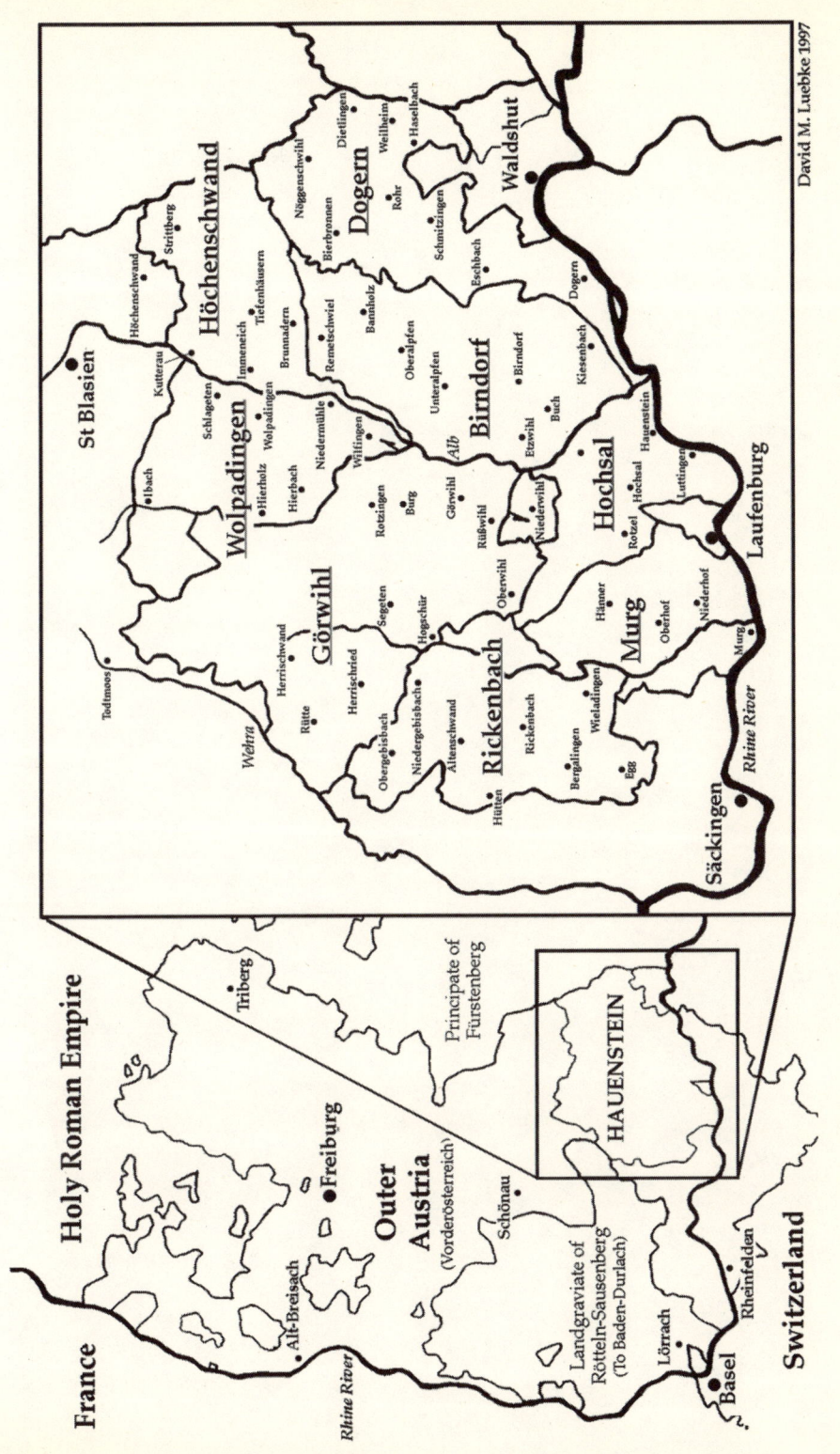

INTRODUCTION

Faction and Community in the "Salpeter Wars"

> However grievous the unrest [that rebels] foment may be, the poor and innocent must adhere to the others against their own will, and even contribute to it, otherwise they will banned from the barn and will be given no work, nor will anyone drink with them from the same jug. If they become recalcitrant, the village community will divide into two factions, and tumult, death, and murder will arise among them.
>
> *[Anon.] Der glückselige und unglückselige Bauernstand (Leipzig, 1711)*

ON A CHILLY FRIDAY IN EARLY NOVEMBER 1745, THE MILITIAS OF two peasant factions clashed near Schmitzingen, a tiny Black Forest village located just a few kilometers north of the Rhine River town of Waldshut. Several days before, the larger of the two forces had helped lay siege to Waldshut because its burghers had given refuge to leaders of the enemy faction. The smaller force—about seventy men—had marched through the previous night to relieve Waldshut and their leaders within its walls. As they approached the town, some two hundred of the besiegers ambushed, encircled, and routed them. Two members of the vanquished force died from wounds suffered in the melee, and many more were severely wounded.[1] These were only the latest casualties in a bitter internecine struggle that by 1745 was already two decades

---

1. GLA 113:260, 149r–150v, "Bitt wegen der Unruohigen verursachten Sterben des Michel Ebners seel. zu Immenaich, seiner hinderlassenen Witwee und Waissen betreffent," 23 December 1745.

old, and more fatalities were to come. Why were these peasants fighting each other? What had divided them so deeply that their differences had escalated to the point of bloodshed?

Peasants throughout Europe in the seventeenth and eighteenth centuries faced the difficult task of maintaining political cohesion against princes and seigneurs who, at the very least, seemed intent on expanding their powers at the expense of local leaders. For the most part, the large and relatively centralized polities of the Atlantic seaboard shared with the smaller states that made up much of the Holy Roman Empire a common determination to diminish the sphere of human activity traditionally regulated at the local level. The challenge to local autonomies came from many sources and could take many forms. Little by little, village institutions were transformed into tools of enforcement, just as village officials—headmen, jurors, elders—gradually became the supervised executors of state authority. Nowhere, to be sure, was this process simple, unbroken, or even complete. But on balance, state authority waxed as local autonomies waned. As one historian put it, a system of rule *with* peasants was replaced by one of rule *over* them.[2]

This book is about a group of Black Forest peasants who, roughly between 1725 and 1745, failed to stand together in opposition to such intrusions. They inhabited Hauenstein, a small county that straddled the exposed upland plateaus on the southeastern slope of the Feldberg massif in the southwestern corner of the Holy Roman Empire. Despite several points of widespread consensus, Hauensteiners debated every point of strategy and tactics; they formed political factions around competing visions of their collective past, present, and future; in time, each faction enlisted every available device to overcome the other. Luckily for the historian, their dissensions generated ample opportunities for village snoops to hoard politically damaging information on their enemies and pass it up the administrative ladder. The copious documentation produced by all this activity allows us to explore the inner workings of peasant politics and culture, topics for which historical evidence is often scant. These sources reveal a peasant society out of step with an increasingly authoritarian environment, and the behaviors this disorientation called forth cast new light on the political universe of rural Europeans

2. Heide Wunder, *Die bäuerliche Gemeinde in Deutschland* (Göttingen, 1986).

in the last preindustrial century, a universe that was in many ways as complex as our own.

These internecine quarrels played out in a harsh, mountainous environment in which agricultural pursuits occupied the lives of nearly all the inhabitants. Hauenstein was bounded to the north by dense forests, to the east and west by deep canyons cut by the Wehra and the Schwarza, and to the south by the Rhine. Its total area was small, about 360 square kilometers.[3] Although the peasants of Hauenstein shared an Alemannic dialect with their Swiss cousins across the Rhine, they were subjects of the Habsburg dynasty, denizens of a province in the hereditary Crown Lands called "Outer Austria" *(Vorderösterreich),* with its administrative seat in the city of Freiburg im Breisgau. But the Habsburg monarch was not the peasants' only lord: for centuries, they had fought off the encroachments of nearby St. Blasien, a powerful Benedictine abbey situated a few kilometers to the north which owned much of the land and many serfs within its borders and exerted numerous juridical prerogatives there as well. It was St. Blasien's slow encroachment on local autonomies that in the early eighteenth century divided the Hauensteiners into two opposed and often bloodily hostile camps.

Their discord is well known to folklorists and local historians as the Salpeter Wars, named for the founder of the rebellious faction, one Hans Friedle Albiez, an old and wealthy peasant in the village of Buch who supplemented his income by selling saltpeter, which he refined from manure smeared on livestock stalls. At the time of the Salpeter Wars, all parties to the conflict in Hauenstein recognized the centrality of factional divisions and developed a vocabulary to reflect it. For their part, provincial Austrian officials availed themselves of a set of ready-made political labels that arrayed peasants according to the measure of obedience they displayed: the more rebellious majority of Hauensteiners were described as *unruhig* ("restless" or simply "disobedient"), while the others were called *ruhig* ("peaceable" or "obedient"). This classification scheme oversimplified grossly the complexities of peasant politics, to the great annoyance of so-called restless Hauensteiners, who like their

---

3. Leopold Maldoner, "Aktenmäßige Beschreibung der Grafschaft Hauenstein," in Josef Bader, ed., "Nachträge zu den Mittheilungen über die Grafschaft Hauenstein," *ZGO* 12 (1861): 101–27; Alphons Johann Lugo, "Statistik der k.k. Vorlande (30 May 1797)," in Friedrich Metz, ed., *Vorderösterreich: Eine geschichtliche Landeskunde,* 2d rev. ed. (Freiburg, 1967), 797–818.

ancestors during the Peasants' War of 1525, recoiled at the suggestion that their behavior was at all rebellious.[4] Instead, they described themselves as *salpeterisch,* the followers of "Salpeter-Hans" Friedle Albiez. Their least incendiary adjective for the other faction was *müllerisch,* a term that likewise referred to the profession of its leader, one Joseph Tröndle, a miller in the village of Unteralpfen. Each of these factions offered profoundly different responses to challenges posed by St. Blasien. Although most peasants could agree on the identity of their common foe—St. Blasien—the two factions hotly disputed almost everything else: the ultimate nature of their troubles, the peasants were responsible for them, and the best strategy for mastering their common afflictions. The *müllerisch* faction was broadly reformist in outlook and generally nonviolent; its members tended to seek redress of collective grievances through officially sanctioned channels of litigation and judicial appeal. By and large, the *salpeterisch* faction rejected the existing order as corrupt and offered more violent means to correct it. In time, the dispute between the *salpeterisch* and *müllerisch* factions grew to overshadow the common concerns that had originally provoked it into being.

An acrid scent of fraternal strife lingers over the documents of these unrests. Indeed, the pattern of factional conflict they reveal calls into question the very idea of rebellion. There were, to be sure, many occasions of violent confrontation between peasants and lords that resemble stereotypes of agrarian uprising. But Hauensteiners devoted at least as much energy to fighting each other as they did to resisting the predations of St. Blasien and military interventions by the Austrian state. The Salpeter Wars were at once a conflict between peasants and lords and a kind of civil war *among* peasants. Yet peasant politics in Hauenstein were even more complicated than that: between the two main camps sat an uncommitted group of fluctuating size, who were referred to as *nederal* ("neutral") and somewhat later as *Sparrengücksler* (roughly, "those who gawk from the rafters").[5] Moreover, differences of opinion eventually

---

4. See Article 2 of the Twelve Articles of the Peasants (1525), reprinted in translation in Peter Blickle, *The Revolution of 1525: The German Peasants' War from a New Perspective,* trans. Thomas A. Brady Jr. and H. C. Erik Midelfort (Baltimore, 1981), 195–96. Among the rebels' complaints in 1743 was the charge that "one continually names and treats [us] as *unruhig* [rebellious]"; see GLA 65:11419 [Nachlaß J. L. Meyer], 60r.

5. The latter phrase was reported by Joseph Viktor von Scheffel in youthful observations of a nineteenth-century aftershock of the "Salpeter Wars"; see his "Aus dem Hauen-

emerged within the two main factions as well. Although the factional divide cut deeper than these finer distinctions, their mere existence underscores the surprising complexity of political discourse among early modern peasants. Clearly, then, these tumults cannot be described as a binary confrontation between lords and subjects. In what sense, then, were the politics of the peasants of Hauenstein primarily "rebellious"?

The pattern of factionalism also calls into question the very nature of community, especially village community, in early modern Europe. Peasant rebellions in preindustrial Europe are often said to have been communal in nature, because institutions of village government were often used to enforce solidarity among peasants against a common threat, penalizing individuals who defied the consensus. This view owes much to the pathbreaking work of Peter Blickle on southern German and of René Pillorget on Provençal revolts.[6] To simplify their arguments greatly, they hold that as noble landowners withdrew from direct participation in agricultural production during the thirteenth and fourteenth centuries, village communes emerged to regulate the agricultural calendar and to distribute scarce resources, eventually acquiring formal jurisdiction over their members. At the same time, peasants acquired more secure legal claims to land through innovations like hereditary leasehold *(Erblehen)*. The formal characteristics of late medieval and early modern agrarian rebellions can be traced to this transformation: peasant revolts were communal in the sense that village institutions were used as instruments of discipline against those who refused to participate actively. Because the recalcitrant were often punished with exclusion from the use of common pastures on the authority of communal assemblies of elders, villages are often described as the institutional "carriers" *(Träger)* of rebellion. Not all was coercion, however. The communal revolt hypothesis also holds that social distance from lords and the integrating tendencies of everyday village life combined to produce a communal ideology of freedom from seigneurial domination that offered a viable alternative to the aristocratic model of social order. This communalism also exerted a powerful integrating influence.

---

steiner Schwarzwald (1853)," in *J. V. von Scheffels Gesammelte Werke*, ed. Johannes Proelß (Stuttgart, 1907), 3:144.

6. See Peter Blickle, *Deutsche Untertanen: Ein Widerspruch* (Munich, 1981), and René Pillorget, *Les mouvements insurrectionnels de Provence entre 1596 et 1715* (Paris, 1975).

But political cohesion was perhaps the *first* casualty of the unrest in Hauenstein. In what sense, then, can the "rebellion" there be regarded as communal? How did Hauensteiners conceive of community when traditional solidarities were collapsing all around them? Factional divisions are often explained away as manifestations of social conflicts between well-to-do, officeholding peasants and others who defied these oppressors. But in Hauenstein, the leaders of the *salpeterisch* faction were just as wealthy, just as heavily employed as agents of domination as their more "peaceable" enemies were. By the same token, *müllerisch* peasants seem to have been almost as allergic to official encroachments on local autonomies as their *salpeterisch* foes. In what sense, then, can peasant factions be seen simply as the by-product of a collision between incompatible interests?

Finally, with respect to communalism, even a cursory glance at the evidence shows that virtually all peasants, regardless of factional stripe, identified first and foremost with the "Whole County" *(Landsgemeinde)* of Hauenstein, a concept that underscored the county's status as a corporate entity with distinctive origins, traditions, and relationships to the House of Habsburg.[7] Moreover, all but the most militant Hauensteiners were united in viewing themselves as loyal subjects of the Habsburg monarch and obedient to his true wishes. In view of the fact that this "naive monarchism" and allegiance to the "Whole County" coexisted with sharp factional rancor, can communalism be said to have had integrating power? If not, how can peasant unrest be seen as the clash of competing social ideals? Further, in what way was their monarchism consistent with resistance to abbatial and Austrian officialdom?

The list goes on and on. In the chapters that follow, I attempt to answer some of these questions through an investigation of the various forces—social, economic, cultural, political, geographical, and ideological—that caused and shaped the Salpeter Wars, as they relate to broader structures and transformations in popular politics throughout early modern Europe. That said, this book is not an exercise in iconoclasm: my main concern is to show that early modern peasants were political beings in every sense of the phrase: that they were conscious of the possibilities

---

7. Claudia Ulbrich, "Der Charakter bäuerlichen Widerstands in vorderösterreichischen Herrschaften," in Winfried Schulze, ed., *Aufstände, Revolten, Prozeße: Beiträge zu bäuerlichen Widerstandsbewegungen im frühneuzeitlichen Europa* (Stuttgart, 1983), 203.

and limitations of their environment and, conversely, that they were no more or less the slaves of such forces than are we moderns. As political beings, they were possessed of something resembling public opinion and were fully capable of articulating their own interests in diverse ways and of translating those articulations into a wide variety of strategies and tactics—even if, in the end, they were losers in the game of history. To view them as anything less, I believe, is to participate in what E. P. Thompson once called the "enormous condescension of posterity."[8]

This means taking these peasants—all of them—at their word. As a practical matter, it also demands treating the two factions as evenhandedly as possible. There is solid empirical reason for doing this. It is obvious that had the autonomist dreams of *salpeterisch* militants been realized, the peasants' hand against predatory seigneurs would have been strengthened. But leaders of the *müllerisch* party, too, achieved some notable successes in the collective interest, including the manumission of all serfs resident within the county. Moreover, they understood that the constant threat of renewed *salpeterisch* unrest could be put to good diplomatic use. *Müllerisch* leaders often claimed to be acting in the interest of the common good, and there is little reason to doubt them.

But there is a deeper theoretical issue at stake here. Because of the great complexity of political discourse in Hauenstein, I tend to shy from the view of agrarian revolt that organically links rebellious activity with the interest of all peasants in preserving a maximum of self-rule through communal institutions. An implicit (though certainly not inevitable) corollary of the communal revolt hypothesis is the proposition that non-rebels opposed these objective, collective interests. Andreas Suter, for example, defines non-rebels as officeholders and others "in the entourage of the state" and *its* interests, who were "integrated vertically" into state channels of command and who opposed their "horizontally integrated" fellows, whose interests lay in preserving the values and institutions of the village against the intrusions of the state.[9] It is easy to imagine situations in which personal allegiance and action flowed smoothly from individual relationships to the state. But if circumstance matters at all, then complex power relationships forbid so mechanistic

---

8. E. P. Thompson, *The Making of the English Working Class* (New York, 1966), 12.
9. Andreas Suter, *"Troublen" im Fürstbistum Basel (1726–1740): Eine Fallstudie zum bäuerlichen Widerstand im 18. Jahrhundert* (Göttingen, 1985), 107–8.

a connection between public personae and political loyalties. And in Hauenstein, circumstances muddied simple distinctions between "vertical" and "horizontal" forms of integration.

Chapter 1 surveys the institutional context in which factions formed and reveals a complex tug-of-war between forces of domination and peasant autonomy that played out in the behaviors of peasant officeholders. On the one hand, peasant elites were involved at almost every stage in the process of domination: as jurors, village headmen, annually elected cantonal magistrates, constables, or rent collectors, their services were vital to the smooth functioning of sovereign and seigneurial rule. On the other hand, they worked within a customary institutional framework constituted to maximize self-rule and to prevent the formation of an officeholding peasant oligarchy beholden to seigneurs and other non-peasants.

This mixture of roles suggests that it is misleading to distinguish all too strictly between "vertical" and "horizontal" integration; the lines of obligation simply were not so cleanly drawn. It is far more useful, I think, to see these officeholders as brokers of power between rulers and subjects.[10] Briefly stated, the interpretation offered here operates from the twin propositions that peasant societies, given the spatially diffuse character of agricultural production and of rural settlement patterns, are difficult to govern and that the organizational forms of peasant political life are, to some extent, a function of attempts by the state (in the broadest sense) to overcome that difficulty.[11] The point is not simply that Hauensteiners were an ungovernable people, although contemporary Austrian officials would have regarded this a truism. Rather, it is to suggest that in Hauenstein as elsewhere in Europe, state and seigneurial authorities could extend bureaucratic controls beyond the village fence into the everyday lives of individual peasants only by involving them in the process of their own domination. But this is not to suggest that peasant institutions were simply tools of oppression. On

---

10. On "brokers" as managers of meaning, see Anthony P. Cohen and John L. Comaroff, "The Management of Meaning: On the Phenomenology of Political Transactions," in Bruce Kapferer, ed., *Transaction and Meaning: Directions in the Anthropology of Exchange and Symbolic Behavior* (Philadelphia, 1976), 87–107.

11. Gerd Spittler, "Staat und Klientelstruktur in Entwicklungsländern: Zum Problem der politischen Organisation von Bauern," *Archives européennes de sociologie* 18 (1977): 77.

the contrary, the tendency of early modern states to make demands not of individuals but of geographically defined polities, while leaving those polities otherwise to regulate themselves, *encouraged* the emergence of unions *(Verbände),* with their own, cooperative political structures.[12]

Chapter 2, a chronicle of the revolt, shows how patterns of factional politics flowed from just this complex interplay of forces. At certain crucial intervals, for example, *salpeterisch* candidates were elected to public office throughout the county. If the relationship between officeholding and loyalty had ever been simple, events like this turned it upside-down: *salpeterisch* peasants found themselves in the awkward position of managing the county fisc *while in a state of open rebellion.* Similarly, *müllerisch* leaders found themselves allying with one legitimate authority (the imperial government) against another one (the peasant magistracy). Yet when the Austrian government proposed abolishing elective office and installing *müllerisch* leaders as salaried officials with lifelong tenure, the latter protested vigorously, fearing that such a move would deprive them any vestige of legitimacy. Clearly, the obligations of officeholding were multifaceted.

The evidence presented in these first two chapters recommends a view of peasant interest as having not one, but several possible, valid articulations. I believe that there is good empirical reason for this, too. Chapter 3 presents aggregate data on factional loyalties as they changed over time and space, and the variations that emerge from them show that the population tended to split its allegiances almost evenly. However one interprets the politics of *müllerisch* peasants, it is difficult to imagine a minority so large as this acting contrary to communal interests in any meaningful sense. Does all this mean we must jettison the idea of communal interest because of the quarrels of a few thousand Black Forest peasants? Not if one accepts the proposition that class interest can have multiple articulations and that it may be promoted in a variety of ways.

---

12. Karl S. Bader, "Grundlagen dörflichen Verfassungslebens im südwestdeutschen Raum," in Wolfgang Müller, ed., *Landschaft und Verfassung: Beiträge zur ländlichen Verfassungsgeschichte im deutschsprachigen Südwesten* (Bühl, 1969), 261–81; see also Peter Blickle, *Landschaften im alten Reich: Die staatliche Funktion des Gemeinen Mannes in Oberdeutschland* (Munich, 1973).

The reader might legitimately wonder how one explains the depth and ferocity of factional strife if most peasants were so committed to preserving the common good of the "Whole County." An answer, I think, may be found in the intersecting effect of changes in the structure of domination and social transformations on peasant political culture. In the first place, the transition from a system of rule *with* peasants to one of rule *over* them altered the complexion of agrarian social relations. Admittedly, this was a long process, spanning many centuries in most places, and Hauenstein was no exception. St. Blasien's attempts to undermine local autonomies went back at least as far as the mid-sixteenth century, but the ravages of the War of Spanish Succession (1698–1714) had temporarily halted the process. As the war wound down, however, the abbey revived its efforts. Beginning in the 1710s and 1720s, St. Blasien strove to centralize its juridical bureaucracy by removing decision-making authority from local tribunals to courts higher up the appellate ladder, to increase its exactions from serfs, tenants, and juridical subjects in Hauenstein, and to obstruct the influence that peasant magistrates could exert within its jurisdictions. At the same time, however, neither St. Blasien nor the provincial government possessed the personnel to govern at the village or cantonal level without the active cooperation of peasant elites. These elites therefore faced difficult choices: if they accommodated St. Blasien, they might benefit personally, but at the risk of alienating their electors. If they resisted centralization, St. Blasien or the provincial government might retaliate against the security of their tenancies. Worse, they risked the personal dangers of open rebellion. Factions formed around the horns of this tactical dilemma.

Second, the economic upswing of the early eighteenth century encouraged factionalism by exacerbating social stratification among peasants. Chapter 4 presents a social profile of the peasant elite in Hauenstein and shows how expanding markets, rising grain prices, and improved harvest yields mainly benefited lineages that could protect their holdings against fragmentation in an era of rapid population growth and in a region where partible inheritance customs prevailed. Their solution amounted to a subversion of inheritance customs: wealthier peasants devised a system of preferential endowment designed to circumvent the custom of egalitarian partibility. In matters of inheritance, the peasant elite subverted custom without much difficulty. By the same token, their efforts to preserve the county's *political* autonomies were a matter of economic self-preservation: in opposing St. Blasien's attempts to wrest control over real-estate exchange, peasant elites defended their own independence of action in matters of sale, trade, and inheritance. As wealth and prestige converged, the economic upswing enhanced the dominance of this peasant oligarchy. As power compressed within it, the St. Blasien's flint struck the iron of village friendship and alliance, enmity and vendetta. When their tactical dispute deepened and became more ideologically charged, peasant elites hauled their kin groups and clienteles into the factional struggle.

A third influence on the development of factions was political culture, a rather more slippery historical quantity. Both the centralizing tendencies of states and seigneurs and the social disruptions of economic expansion contrasted jarringly with certain organzining myths of peasant polity, among them a medieval vision of reciprocal obligation between sovereign and subject, a strong sense of corporate unity embodied in the notion of the "Whole County," and a stiff dose of social egalitarianism. St. Blasien's efforts were widely interpreted to veil an attempt to annex Hauenstein, or at least dismember it, which in turn threw into question the nature and meaning of community. Chapter 5 describes how the debate over tactics quickly transformed into acrimonious name-calling over suspect loyalties, which in time produced habits of factional allegiance as compelling as loyalties to the county as a whole. A succession of Austrian military interventions to suppress the tumult only drove the factional wedge deeper.

The point here is that the political culture of peasants offered a rich vocabulary for the construction of symbolic barriers between factions. *Salpeterisch* peasants proved particularly adept at using old corporate identities to erect a new, factional one in their place. To some extent, this was old wine in new bottles. But where the old myths served to unite, the new identities were meant to define and divide. The differences between them were more than functional as well. In time, militants in the *salpeterisch* cause carried Hauenstein's organizing myths to their logical extreme and elaborated a vision of "Swiss" freedoms in a future world without lords. Not all *salpeterisch* leaders went this far. But the mere fact that a few *did* also highlights the persistence of anti-aristocratic dreams of freedom that had never completely died out since the fifteenth century, when "turning Swiss" had been a tangible option for many southwest German polities.[13]

Chapter 6 describes how rebel ideology and the process of factional differentiation played out in the resistance practices that *salpeterisch* Hauensteiners used to further their cause. In choosing particular modes of collective action, they acted out their conception of right political and social order described in the previous chapter. Chapter 6 also shows how the construction of symbolic walls of community was actually achieved: publicly, in a succession of brilliantly stage-managed campaigns of rallies, fund-raising, and highly ritualized diplomatic delegations to petition the emperor in Vienna. The combined effect of these exertions was to tip the balance of power in the rebels' favor, which was reflected in their electoral successes. Finally, Chapter 6 demonstrates how *salpeterisch* activists succeeded not by exploiting institutions of village governance, but in spite of them.

These insights raise two theoretical issues. First, the rebels exhibited a pattern of appropriation that undermines the argument that peasants were the more-or-less passive objects of elite cultural hegemony.[14] In the words of one of its critics, this model of cultural interactions "suggests that elites escape[d] ancestral traditions sooner, adopt[ed] a critical point of view vis-à-vis these traditions, then impose[d] it."[15] Gradually, peasant culture was forcibly "acculturated" to that of elites. Without detracting from the power of this model to explain such transformations as the progress of the Reformation and Counter-Reformation, witchcraft persecution, or the suppression of popular entertainments, Chapter 6 suggests that peasants were active participants in cultural exchanges across social divides. Hauenstein's rebels adapted elements of elite culture to their *own* purposes, which more often than not entailed factional politics. If this was "acculturation," it was not hegemonic.

A second theoretical implication pertains to a view of peasant rebellion that conflates communal institutions with popular meanings of

---

13. See Thomas A. Brady Jr., *Turning Swiss: Cities and Empire, 1450–1550* (Cambridge, U.K., 1985).

14. This perspective has been articulated most thoroughly by Robert Muchembled, *Culture populaire et culture des élites dans la France moderne* (Paris, 1978).

15. Jean Wirth, "Against the Acculturation Thesis," in Kaspar von Greyerz, ed., *Religion and Society in Early Modern Europe, 1500–1800* (London, 1984), 66–78.

community. The idea that communal institutions and communal ideologies promoted political solidarity not only overstates the integrating potential of village institutions, it also favors a legalistic understanding of community to the neglect of its cultural aspects. To be sure, village institutions possessed identifiable histories, settlement patterns, and political structures that imparted to their members an equally identifiable set of rights and obligations. The evidence presented here, however, suggests that while village institutions surely aggregated people, they did not always integrate them. As David Sabean puts it, communal institutions functioned as a forum "in which alternative strategies, misunderstandings, conflicting goals and values are threshed out."[16] One might add that they are also a forum in which misunderstandings sometimes remain unresolved.

The case of Hauenstein suggests that as a symbolic construct, community served as easily to cleave as to combine. The reason, I think, is that in symbolic terms, a well-defined community needs an opposite: participating in a community means sharing in perceptions of what its members are *not*. Social anthropologists describe this as the "implicit negativity" of community, the idea that members of a community express their sense of distinction by erecting symbolic limits to define themselves.[17] Of course, community in this cultural sense is not all negations. Still, the crucial question remains: where does its boundary lie? Boundaries signify to those within them their "own sense of community as refracted through all the complexities of their lives and experiences."[18] Their contingency on, let us say, a critical mass of social relevance both exposes them to the shifts and turns of events and requires their frequent renewal. Small wonder that rebellious peasants throughout the early modern era relied on such rituals as oath-taking not only to create bonds of mutual obligation but also to renew and define the limits of community.[19]

---

16. David Sabean, *Power in the Blood: Popular Culture and Village Discourse in Early Modern Germany* (Cambridge, U.K., 1984), 29.

17. This interpretation follows the work of Anthony P. Cohen, *The Symbolic Construction of Community* (Chichester, 1985), 115, and "Of Symbols and Boundaries, or, Does Ertie's Greatcoat Hold the Key?," in Cohen, ed., *Symbolising Boundaries: Identity and Diversity in British Cultures* (Manchester, 1986), 1–19.

18. Cohen, "Of Symbols and Boundaries," 13.

19. See, for example, Winfried Schulze, *Bäuerlicher Widerstand und feudale Herrschaft in der frühen Neuzeit* (Bad Canstatt, 1980), 118–20.

Nor should it come as any great surprise that neither faction defined itself solely on its own terms, but always with reference to an Other. By 1745, indeed, Hauensteiners seemed to define themselves in almost exclusively negative terms: *salpeterisch* was as *müllerisch* was not. A rebel named Joseph Jehle neatly summarized this relationship when he wrote to a friend that "were it not for our opposite *(Gegentheil)* we would have to bicker amongst ourselves."[20] Jehle's half-serious gratitude acknowledged the dependency of his own identity on the existence of a clearly defined enemy. In twenty years' time, factionalism became a kind of *habitus,* a structure of beliefs about human relations that delimited and imparted meaning to specific practices.[21] Perhaps the poet Constantine Cavafy had something like this in mind when he wondered, "What shall become of us without any barbarians? / Those people were a kind of solution."[22]

Sooner or later, most writers of case studies face the awkward question: how representative is the example? Is it possible, let alone desirable, to generalize from a study so focused? In 250 years since the battle of Schmitzingen, answers have gone both ways. On the one hand, less responsible interpreters of the Salpeter Wars have seen them as antecedents for the widest variety of modern political movements. Johann Viktor von Scheffel, a romantic poet of homespun virtues, saw the *salpeterisch* rising as a yeoman defense of rural republicanism. For Nazi ideologues, the Salpeter Wars gave spurious depth to their doctrine of "blood and soil." More recently, German neo-nationalists have defamed the rebels as "predecessors" of the terrorist Baader-Meinhoff gang, while for others, the inspiring example of *salpeterisch* resistance has legitimated opposition to the construction of nuclear power reactors in the state of Baden-Württemberg.[23] Clearly, a little caution is in order.

On the other hand, historians of early modern Germany have tended to regard the rebellion as a rather freakish exception, unusual for its

20. GLA 113:267, Joseph Jehle to Bläsi Hottinger, 12 March 1746.
21. Pierre Bourdieu, *Outline of a Theory of Practice,* trans. Richard Nice (Cambridge, U.K., 1977), 78–95.
22. "Expecting the Barbarians," in *The Complete Poems of Cavafy,* trans. Rae Dalven (New York, 1976), 18–19.
23. Scheffel, "Aus dem Hauensteiner Schwarzwald"; *Deutsche Nationalzeitung,* 16 June 1972; Hubert Matt-Willmatt, "Die Hotzenwälder Freiheitsbewegung der 'Salpeterer' und ihre Vorgeschichte," in Heiko Haumann, ed., *Vom Hotzenwald bis Wyhl: Demokratische Traditionen in Baden* (Cologne, 1977), 80–97.

duration, for the dissension it generated, and for the point (serfdom) around which much popular resentment coalesced.[24] Most often, the Salpeter Wars are presented as the exception that proves the rule: that most rebellions were communal, not factional; that most were brief, not long-lasting; and, finally, that German uprisings were rarely directed primarily against serfdom.

Were the Salpeter Wars really so exceptional? The question, I think, has several answers. One is to challenge the demand that any valid case study must typify a broader phenomenon in all its particulars. Of course, it would be silly to refract the entirety of early modern peasant politics through any prism so tiny. That said, there is something a little disingenuous about the "desideratum of typicality." Some historians in my position have shrugged off the imperative to generalize, suggesting that comparison is inherently ambiguous and serves just as often to prove uniqueness as it does to demonstrate typicality.[25] But the very phenomenon of peasant rebellion lends itself to comparison, if for no other reason than that, as Marc Bloch noted, it was as endemic to the seigneurial order as strikes are to the industrial.[26] I have already suggested some lines of inquiry along which the topic of this book can be put to comparative use, and in the following chapters I hope to expand on them. In certain respects this is a simple matter: in fact, many rebellions displayed factionalism, though none perhaps as profound as Hauenstein's, and quite a few included serfdom among their concerns. Beyond this, I argue that the Salpeter Wars were, in a variety of ways, symptomatic of the manner in which transformations in the structure of domination played out at the local level. But it should always be borne in mind that every rebellion was unique in certain ways that confound the drawing of parallels.

Since the present discussion has been framed in relation to the communal revolt hypothesis, it might do well to point out some of Hauenstein's peculiarities, and how these relate to that theory of peasant revolt. For starters, the physical environment of the Black Forest was in many

---

24. See, for example, Peter Bierbrauer, "Bäuerliche Revolten im Alten Reich: Ein Forschungsbericht," in Peter Blickle, ed., *Aufruhr und Empörung? Studien zum bäuerlichen Widerstand im Alten Reich* (Munich, 1980), 55, 57.

25. David W. Sabean, *Property, Production and Family in Neckarhausen, 1700–1870* (Cambridge, U.K., 1990), 7–15.

26. Marc Bloch, *French Rural History: An Essay on Its Basic Characteristics,* trans. Janet Sondheimer (Berkeley, 1966).

ways unusually austere. Its forests and poor soils distinguished it from more fertile landscapes in surrounding regions, such as Alsace, the Aare basin in Switzerland, Upper Swabia, or the Neckar basin in the duchy of Württemberg. Hauenstein itself was well known in the eighteenth century for an "extremely harsh and uncomfortable" climate, even in relation to the rest of the Black Forest.[27] Oats made up about half of all cereal production, spelt and winter rye about a quarter each.[28] Even within the county, there was considerable ecological variation. According to an Outer Austrian provincial registrar, Leopold Maldoner, soil fertility was uneven: northern fields were less fecund than those along the Rhine.[29] To meet their nutritional needs, the peasants were compelled to import cereals from more fertile regions. Together, these ecological deficiencies encouraged a heavy reliance on animal husbandry.[30] Registrar Maldoner noted that the "subsistence [*Nahrung*] of Hauensteiners consists largely in animal husbandry," and indeed by 1777, the county contained one ox for every ten humans.[31]

Another element in this overwhelmingly agricultural economy was logging and charcoal production, which had a devastating effect on forest reserves.[32] Already by the late seventeenth century, provincial officials were troubled by the deforestation of Hauenstein. Peasants exploited their private woods to the limit; others less fortunate regularly pillaged royal forests in the north of the county.[33] "It would seem impossible that a shortage of wood should ever emerge in the Black Forest,"

---

27. Lugo, "Statistik," 797–818.
28. Ibid., 805; Gerhard Endriß, "Landschaft, Siedlung und Wirtschaft des Hotzenwaldes," in Friedrich Metz et al., eds., *Der Hotzenwald: Quellen und Forschungen zur Siedlungs- und Volkstumsgeschichte der Oberrheinlande* (Karlsruhe, 1941), 19, 22; Karl F. Wernet, "Die wirtschaftlichen Verhältnisse der Grafschaft Hauenstein zwischen den Burgunderkriegen und den Salpetereraufständen," *ZGO* 98 (1950): 115–46.
29. Maldoner, "Aktenmäßige Beschreibung," 126.
30. Wernet, "Wirtschaftlichen Verhältnisse," 146.
31. "Beschreibung der Österreichischen Vorlande," 126. The roughly seventeen thousand human denizens of Hauenstein in 1777 kept 1,733 oxen and 567 horses; compare GLA 113:198, "Seelen–Beschreibung in der kaiserl. königl. V:Öen Grafschaft Hauenstein pro Anno 1778" [includes data from 1777], and "Viehe–Beschreibung in der kaiserl. königl. V:Ö: Graffschafft Hauenstein pro Anno 1777."
32. Maldoner, "Aktenmäßige Beschreibung," 126.
33. For an assessment of the damage, see GLA 229:859, nr 3, "Anzeige des Schadens und Ruins in Waldungen, wovon Holz nach Albbruck geliefert werden könte," 15 June 1737.

lamented an anonymous eighteenth-century observer; a monk of St. Blasien added ruefully that "one never saves in the midst of plenty."[34]

This stark ecology need not have dictated poverty, if only the population had been small enough. Unfortunately, it was not. Census data were not collected systematically in the Crown Lands until 1754, so it is difficult to determine population levels exactly. The best guess for Hauenstein is about sixteen thousand at midcentury.[35] This made for low population density (roughly forty-five persons per square kilometer), at least in relation to the rest of Outer Austria.[36] The relevant comparison, however, was not geographical but ecological: in an agricultural economy, climate, fertility, and technology set the boundary of overpopulation, and contemporaries knew that Hauenstein was "a poor landscape, which is excessively populated in relation to the productive power of the soil."[37] In one key respect, however, Hauenstein was typical in ways that increased these ecological pressures: the population was growing. The oldest accurate data show a rapid demographic increase, 2.45 percent between 1777 and 1782 alone. After that, the annual rate more than trebled: in the decade after 1784, the rural population grew fully 17.51 percent, at an annual average rate of 1.6 percent![38] In all likelihood, this period of rapid growth was anticipated by a longer phase of slower expansion, and indirect evidence tends to support this view.[39]

Few if any of these environmental idiosyncracies are exceptional with respect to the communal revolt hypothesis, because it is not based on *which* resources peasants had available to them, but on *how* resource allocation provided the basis for collective resistance. Here, human geography is of central importance to the argument: communal institutions were typically strongest in large, nucleated "cluster villages"

---

34. "Beschreibung der Österreichischen Vorlande," 790; Endriß, "Landschaft," 12.

35. See GLA 113:198, "Graffschaft Hauwensteinische Seelen Beschreibung den 20tn 9bris 1754," which gives a total of 15,261 souls. On the history of census-taking in the Crown Lands, see P. G. M. Dickson, *Finance and Government under Maria Theresia, 1740–1780* (Oxford, 1987), 1:24–29.

36. This was about half the province's overall density; Dickson, *Finance and Government*, 1:24, 438–39.

37. GLA 113:13, Oberamt Waldshut to Kreisdirektion Lörrach, 1 July 1812.

38. GLA 113:198, "Seelen und Viehe Beschreibung," 1777–82, 1784–94.

39. Karl F. Wernet, "Die Bevölkerung der Grafschaft Hauenstein," *ZGO* 104 (1956): 245–57.

(Haufendörfer), a common village form typical of central Swabia, Franconia, and other parts of Germany. Yet this type of village was largely absent from Hauenstein. According to Registrar Maldoner, Hauenstein possessed "few real villages" except Dogern, a Rhine-bank village near Waldshut with about 650 inhabitants, and a handful of other settlements.[40] Rather, the predominant village-type in Hauenstein was the "swarm-settlement" *(Schwarmsiedlung)*, a loose configuration of farmhouses arrayed in little geometric order. The average population size of these settlements was small, usually between 150 and 200 inhabitants. Their number was correspondingly great, fully 130. Finally, social stratification in them was pronounced.[41]

The combined effect of "swarm-settlements" and social stratification within them was that communal institutions *in the village* were relatively weak. Each village had one or two elected headmen *(Dorfmeier)*, chosen annually at Easter or on St. Martin's Day by the assembled males of a village.[42] Apart from managing the village fisc, headmen served mainly as the local executors of higher authority: they reported crimes and misdemeanors, coordinated such official tasks as road repair, and were also required to proclaim decrees of the Eight, St. Blasien, and the imperial Austrian government.[43] Similarly, communal assemblies normally were convened at the headman's bidding, usually to hear decrees or to assist in the adjustment of seigneurial records.[44] On the other hand, the right of villages to sue indicates a corporate legal identity that included formal jurisdiction over their members. While it would be foolhardy to underestimate the informal coercive power of

---

40. Maldoner, "Aktenmäßige Beschreibung," 126.

41. See Willi A. Boelcke, "Wandlungen der dörflichen Sozialstruktur während Mittelalter und Neuzeit," in Heinz Haushofer and Willi A. Boelcke, eds., *Neue Wege und Forschungen der Agrargeschichte: FS Günther Franz* (Frankfurt, 1967), 80–103.

42. GLA 229:2336, "Actum Strittberg den 12ten April ao 1656: Aufstellung zwey Dorfmeyer und deren Verrichtung"; GLA 61:5776, 174–76, "Schadenbirndorf: Dorfmeyers Beeydigung," 7 May 1741; GLA 61:5777, 3–7, 12 January 1742.

43. See, for instance, GLA 61:10172, 341–42 [Hochamtsprotokoll St. Blasien], 14 October 1738. In some villages, the headman was assisted in his executive duties by a village constable *(Bannwart)*, who was also nominated by the commune for official appointment; GLA 61:5777, 19, "Nöggenschwiel: Bestell. und Beeyd. Bannwart," 3 March 1742.

44. See Günther Haselier, *Die Streitigkeiten der Hauensteiner mit ihren Obrigkeiten: Ein Beitrag zur Geschichte Vorderösterreichs und des südwestdeutschen Bauernstandes im 18. Jahrhundert* (Karlsruhe, 1940), 15.

male elders in small settlements, the fact remains that the majority of Hauenstein's villages were factionally divided, which bespeaks a failure to enforce solidarity. Do these peculiarities disqualify the Salpeter Wars as a basis for meaningful comparison to other peasant revolts? I think not, for three reasons.

In the first place, the relative weakness of village institutions did not mean that Hauenstein was lacking in institutions capable of providing a communal basis for rebellion. On the contrary: the county was unusually rich in institutions that involved ordinary peasants in the process of decision-making. In addition to its village institutions, Hauenstein was subdivided into eight regional cantons, or *Einungen,* which met annually to elect a presiding magistrate; the eight cantonal magistrates, in turn, met regularly to administer justice, to maintain public peace in the county, and to represent its interests in the provincial Estates of Outer Austria. These magistrates were called *Einungsmeister* or *Achtmannen,* which translates roughly as "canton-masters" (for simplicity's sake, I will refer to them individually as "Octovirs," collectively as "the Eight"). Through the institutions of cantons and the Eight, Hauensteiners possessed vehicles for the formation of public opinion and collective action above and beyond the local level. For these reasons, communal institutions were arguably more powerful in Hauenstein than elsewhere.

Not for nothing was Hauenstein situated in the very heart of what Peter Blickle has called the "communal-cooperative zone" of southwestern Germany, where communally based revolts were most frequent.[45] Nor was the separation of village and supralocal political institutions such as the *Einung* uncommon elsewhere in southern Germany. In his overview of agrarian political institutions in that region, Peter Bierbrauer notes that because of the coexistence there of powerful communal institutions with a wide variety of *non-nucleated* settlement patterns, "cluster villages" cannot be considered the norm. For example, in the Grissons, Tyrol, and Vorarlberg, communal institutions were organized around lower court districts comprising multiple scattered settlements, whereas in central and western Switzerland, the predominant form of peasant political

---

45. P. Blickle, *Deutsche Untertanen.*

organization was not the village but the "incorporated valley" *(Talschaft)*.[46] Bierbrauer concludes, in effect, that nucleated rural settlement patterns were no necessary precondition for communal institutions, least of all in Switzerland, the "summit of a broad mountain" of "communalism" in late medieval and early modern Europe.[47] Supralocal institutions of opinion formation and collective action were arguably as characteristic of the "communal-cooperative" zone as nucleated villages were.

The second reason is that inequality in "cluster villages" was as great as in the "swarm-settlements" of Hauenstein. Indeed, Hauenstein's village assemblies were arguably *less* stratified and more "democratic" than elsewhere. Typically, the formal structures of large, nucleated villages organized inhabitants in ways that defy simple divisions between agents of communal and official interests. As polities, they were a many-layered structure of cooperative associations that simultaneously included certain categories of peasant in and excluded others from consultative bodies of decision-making.[48] Especially after 1648, most villages developed large populations of landless, disenfranchised residents who were excluded from the use of common fields and forests.[49] Hauenstein's villages, in contrast, did not distinguish between enfranchised and nonenfranchised adult male inhabitants, and excluded only women, children, and priests from active participation in consultative assemblies.

The third and final reason for drawing comparisons between the Salpeter Wars and other rebellions is that factionalism could also occur in the context of revolts based on communal institutions characteristic of "cluster villages." At the time of the Salpeter Wars, rebellious villagers in the bishopric of Basel encountered grave difficulties in suppressing the so-called *Craichies*, an "intracommunal opposition" which may have comprised a third of the population in some villages. The factional split

46. Peter Bierbrauer, "Die ländliche Gemeinde im oberdeutsch-schweizerischen Raum," in Peter Blickle, ed., *Landgemeinde und Stadtgemeinde in Mitteleuropa: Ein struktureller Vergleich* (Munich, 1991), 169–90.

47. Peter Blickle, "Kommunalismus: Begriffsbildung in heuristischer Absicht," in P. Blickle, ed., *Landgemeinde und Stadtgemeinde*, 5.5.

48. K. S. Bader, *Dorfgenossenschaft und Dorfgemeinde: Studien zur Rechtsgeschichte des mittelalterlichen Dorfes* (Cologne, 1957–62), 2:21–29, 267–321.

49. Heide Wunder, "Peasant Communities in Medieval and Early Modern Germany," in *Les communautés rurales/Rural communities* (Paris, 1987), 5:20–21; Rudolf Endres, "Ländliche Rechtsquellen als sozialgeschichtliche Quellen," in Peter Blickle, ed., *Deutsche Ländliche Rechtsquellen: Probleme und Wege der Weistumsforschung* (Stuttgart, 1977), 165–68.

weakened village solidarities as the rebellious majority banned the peaceful *Craichies* from communal assemblies.⁵⁰ Although factional divisions never dominated internal peasant politics in the Wetterau region of Hessen in central Germany, most villages there were forced to contend with "peaceable" *(ruhig)* peasants, who were unwilling to undergo the risks that resistance entailed and who comprised half the population of a few districts.⁵¹ In neither of these regions, could the forces of communal cohesion always prevent the development of factional rifts.

None of this necessarily disproves the communal revolt hypothesis. On the one hand, it remains true that the cantonal structure distinguished Hauenstein from regions where peasant institutions were concentrated in "cluster villages," such as Franconia. This difference severed the connection between police powers and the administration of communal resources. As far as I have been able to determine, the Eight could not exclude a particular villager from the use of common fields or pastures as punishment for refusing to participate in agreed-upon resistance actions. Nevertheless, this comparison highlights a neglected factor that is central to the problem of interpreting relationships between peasant institutions and rebellion: public opinion, and how it formed in the first place. Hauenstein and other polities like it had the comparative advantage of regional institutions that made supralocal opinion formation a relatively easy affair. Polities lacking in supralocal consultative institutions arguably had a harder time of it. In such situations, the broader role of villages as places where people meet to buy, trade, eat, drink, and discuss might better explain the communal basis of peasant revolts.⁵²

The question of public opinion returns us finally to the effects of "vertical" and "horizontal" integration. Instead of viewing factional loyalty mechanistically as a function of personal, material, or political dependence on state or seigneurial authorities, a more elastic approach might take cognizance of another major theory of peasant revolts in early modern Germany, Winfried Schulze's theory of the "juridification of

---

50. Suter, *"Troublen,"* 117–20.
51. Werner Troßbach, *Soziale Bewegung und politische Erfahrung: Bäuerlicher Widerstand in hessischen Territorien, 1648–1806* (Weingarten, 1987), 82, 84.
52. David W. Sabean, "The Communal Basis of Pre-1800 Peasant Uprisings in Western Europe," *Comparative Politics* 8 (1976): 355–64.

social conflict."⁵³ Among the chief effects of the Peasants' War of 1525 was that peasants gained new opportunities to sue their lords through imperial tribunals of justice in Wetzlar and Vienna. The same phenomenon recurred on a smaller scale within principalities, such as the Habsburg Crown Lands, where in 1579 all subjects were granted the right to present grievances before provincial administrations.⁵⁴ Thus, so the argument goes, social tensions were channeled into legal disputes. While the evidence presented here suggests that litigation did not defuse these conflicts, it is safe to say that early modern German peasants had many more options than their medieval ancestors had had, and one can assume that occasions for tactical disagreement increased with the expanded range of options available to them. In perhaps the majority of agrarian unrests in the early modern empire, peasants combined litigation with "illegal" actions along a continuum of resistance practices that continued to include older, unsanctioned actions such as rent boycotts, poaching, village desertions, and armed resistance. The Wetterau peasants, for example, managed to combine lawsuits with violence without succumbing to debilitating factional strife.⁵⁵ In Hauenstein, peasant leaders could not agree on which approach to take. To some extent, then, their factionalism was nothing more than a crisis of too many choices.

Prosaic though this sounds, its implications are weighty and return us to E. P. Thompson's lively defense of the autonomies of popular political experience. It suggests, as I have noted already, that as political beings in the fullest sense, early modern peasants deserve the generous assumptions historians routinely bring to bear in the study of elites and *their* politics without so much as the blink of an eyelash. Historians of great politics do not hesitate to admit that elites, while acting in broad terms out of class-specific interest, articulate them in a variety of ways, and that their partings of company are determined as often by upbringing, kinship, patronage, or even idiosyncratic moral or ethical inclina-

---

53. See Winfried Schulze, "Die veränderte Bedeutung sozialer Konflikte im. 16. und 17. Jahrhundert," in Hans-Ulrich Wehler, ed., *Der Deutsche Bauernkrieg 1524–1526* (Göttingen, 1976), 277–302.

54. On the possibilites of litigation within Austrian Crown Lands, see Helfried Valentinisch, "Advokaten, Winkelschreiber und Bauernprokuratoren in Innerösterreich in der frühen Neuzeit," in Schulze, ed., *Aufstände, Revolten, Prozeße*, 183–201, and Schulze, *Bäuerlicher Widerstand*, 77.

55. See Troßbach, *Soziale Bewegung*, 101–54, 179–90.

tions as they are by the ostensibly objective dictates of class necessity. As William Reddy recently put it, the effect of recent research into the social origins of the French Revolution "has been to sharpen and refine our awareness of class . . . to such an extent that we must put into question the notion that classes can be neatly identified with national-level political factions."[56] To cite a German example: if Schulze is right, the majority of delegates to the Imperial Diet of Speyer in 1526 was acting in a conservative and self-interested manner when in the wake of the Peasants' War it *expanded* opportunities for the legal redress of peasant grievance against lords and sovereigns—an improvement of conditions for peasants, to be sure, but one intended to prevent future fundamental challenges to the dominance of feudal-aristocratic elites. Simultaneously, however, Germany's ruling elites pursued a contradictory policy toward the recent rebels: that of repression, through executions, the confiscation of weapons, and the imposition of heavy reparations *(Brandschatzungen)*. Which device—carrot or stick—more accurately advanced the interests of the noble class? Surely both did.

Seeing peasant factions as variations on a theme of collective interest should not lead one to deny the possibility of mendacity, or that individual peasant magistrates could not betray their fellows. "Vertical integration" was not without consequences, one of which was that it placed certain peasants in a position to benefit personally from their roles as arbiters of conflict between lord and subject. It would be naive to think that a figure such as the *müllerisch* Octovir Joseph Tröndle of Unteralpfen might have sustained his family's enormous local influence solely on the strength of his incomes from farming and milling. Tröndle could and did exploit his position for personal gain. By the same token, political activists of both factions proved capable of economic egoism, if they had the wherewithal to do so. Still, the "vertical integration" of *müllerisch* peasant-magistrates also enabled them to achieve a great many legal victories (by the standards of the day), while their more hot-headed *salpeterisch* rivals accomplished little more than to provoke a succession of violent and destructive military interventions that culminated in the elimination of their cherished voting rights and

---

56. William M. Reddy, "The Concept of Class," in M. L. Bush, ed., *Social Orders and Social Classes in Europe since 1500: Studies in Social Stratification* (New York, 1992), 16.

corporate autonomies. Is it not an "enormous condescension" to suggest that *either* faction betrayed the common peasant weal? Surely it is.

This conclusion need not, however, diminish the causative powers of social forces *per se* (let alone of economic or cultural ones) in forming the political lives of ordinary people. In a rather backhanded way, this book reconfirms the subtle, motivating power of common, peasant interests on the actions of peasant elites. The balance of evidence presented here suggests that, notwithstanding the progress of social stratification in rural Germany, the common life-experiences and material exigencies of all Hauenstein peasants united them in the political cause of defending the institutional autonomies of the "Whole County" against seigneurs and state officials whose power to undermine them derived ultimately from their ability to appropriate ever greater proportions of surplus agrarian production. The fact that *müllerisch* leaders were sufficiently adept at manipulating the practical dependence of St. Blasien and the Austrian state on peasant complicity in the management of expropriation to expand—if only temporarily—the scope of peasant political autonomy in Hauenstein only reveals them as more clever and realistic than their militant *salpeterisch* detractors as representatives of interests shared by all peasants.

CHAPTER I

Power in the County

Lords and Subjects in Hauenstein

OF ALL THE LOCAL MYTHS ABOUT THE COUNTY OF HAUENSTEIN, perhaps the most persistent is that it was once a republic of free yeoman farmers, subject only to the Holy Roman Emperor. As myths often do, this one contains a kernel of truth. Hauenstein's system of eight cantons involved large numbers of peasants in decision-making over a wide range of issues in the common interest. But the Salpeter Wars and their institutional setting were more complex than the myth suggests. In the first place, the canton system was not unusual in the institutional context of southern Germany. Of course, several Swiss cantons sustained important roles for representative assemblies and the magistrates they elected. Even the duchy of Württemberg—the largest and most centralized of the southwest German polities—preserved vestiges of local representation in the management of its administrative districts.[1] Second, a fairly large number of principalities in southern parts of the Holy Roman Empire included peasant delegates in territorial diets, which involved them in the fiscal decision-making and in

---

1. Walter Grube, "Dorfgemeinde und Amtsversammlung in Altwürttemberg," *ZWLG* 13 (1954): 194–219.

the machinery of tax collection. In a few small territories, parliaments consisted *only* of peasant delegates.[2]

The third point may seem obvious, but it is worth stating for reasons that will become clear. It is simply that Hauenstein lacked none of the major institutional forms of domination *(Herrschaft)* typical of *ancien régime* Germany: seigneurs (both lay and ecclesiastical) owned most of the land, exercised patrimonial jurisdiction in parts of the county, and held the majority of Hauensteiners in bonds of personal serfdom. Paradoxically, perhaps, seigneurs relied on the services of peasants recruits to administer these authorities. There was a practical reason for this: states and seigneurs—in Outer Austria as elsewhere—lacked the wherewithal to rule without the active participation of their subjects. The decentralized nature of agricultural production and peasant settlements made the cost of governing them directly prohibitive; the great number and small size of villages placed narrow limits on the ability of provincial and seigneurial officials to maintain regular and systematic checks on the behavior of subjects.[3] Its clearest manifestation was a nearly total absence of non-peasant officials in the countryside. At the time of the Salpeter Wars, only two non-peasant officials managed royal affairs in Hauenstein, yielding a ratio of non-peasant functionaries to peasants on the order of one to eight thousand.[4]

In view of such constraints, effective rule required a "minimum of voluntary compliance" (as Max Weber put it), which was achieved by maintaining at least the symbolic trappings of reciprocity and by recruiting subjects into the machinery of domination.[5] The symbolic

---

2. Peter Blickle, *Landschaften im alten Reich: Die staatliche Funktion des Gemeinen Mannes in Oberdeutschland* (Munich, 1973).

3. See Gerd Spittler, "Staat und Klientelstruktur in Entwicklungsländern: Zum Problem der politischen Organisation von Bauern," *Archives européennes de sociologie* 18 (1977): 67, 73–81, and *Verwaltung in einem afrikanischen Bauernstaat: Das koloniale Französisch-Westafrika, 1919–1939* (Freiburg, 1981), 13–19; and Sharon Kettering, "The Historical Development of Political Clientelism," *Journal of Interdisciplinary History* 18 (1988): 419–47.

4. See Franz Quarthal and Georg Wieland, *Die Behördenorganisation Vorderösterreichs von 1753 bis 1805* (Bühl, 1977), 308–9. For purposes of comparison, the ratio for the Crown Lands was on the order of 1:800 in 1762 (excluding city officials); see P. G. M. Dickson, *Finance and Government under Maria Theresia, 1740–1780* (Oxford, 1987), 1:36, Table 2.5, and 1:307, Table 11.2.

5. Max Weber, *Economy and Society*, ed. Guenther Roth and Claus Wittich (Los Angeles, 1978), 1:53–54.

imperative of reciprocity vested subaltern groups with legitimate claims against lords, and within these bounds, *Herrschaft* was partly a matter of barter and negotation. At the same time, peasants were involved in the management of state and seigneurial administration at nearly every stage. Peasant officeholders, therefore, cannot be seen simply as agents of lord *or* subject. Rather, they were brokers, ensnared between the two; they were both enforcers of royal authority *and* the peasants' chief line of defense against bureaucratic meddling in communal affairs. On balance, the institutional structure of Hauenstein presents a complex mixture of cooptations and coercions.

Sources of Peasant Power

Situated as it was in Outer Austria, Hauenstein's relationship to surrounding territories and to the Holy Roman Empire was like that of other Habsburg dominions. Despite its isolation from the principal Crown Lands, Outer Austria ranked among the oldest Habsburg possessions. Parts of it had been added to the oldest Habsburg estates in the Aargau and Sundgau regions in the thirteenth century.[6] Even after the Aargau was lost to the Swiss Confederation in 1415 and the Sundgau to France in 1648, Outer Austria remained in Habsburg possession until its absorption by the grand duchy of Baden in 1805.

Until that year, Hauenstein remained subject to Habsburg sovereign rule *(Landherrschaft)*, which placed it in the great, unwieldy administrative hierarchy of the hereditary Crown Lands. As a salaried representative of the crown, the Forest Steward *(Waldvogt)* answered to the provincial government in Freiburg, known officially as the "Outer Austrian Government and Chamber" *(Vorderösterreichische Regierung und Kammer)*. The provincial government, in turn, was subordinate to the government of Upper Austria *(Oberösterreichische Kammer-Regierung)*, seated in Innsbruck, which also oversaw the affairs of Tyrol and Vorarlberg, as well as those of an archipelago of smaller possessions scattered across Upper

---

6. On the early evolution of Habsburg possessions, see Hans E. Feine, "Die Territorialbildung der Habsburger im deutschen Südwesten vornehmlich im späten Mittelalter," *Zeitschrift der Savigny-Stiftung für Rechtsgeschichte, Germanische Abteilung* 67 (1950): 176–80.

Swabia.⁷ From Innsbruck, the next and final step up the bureaucratic ladder was the Court Chancellery *(Hofkanzlei)* in Vienna and its two chancellors, one for each "senate" responsible for external and internal affairs, respectively.⁸

Because it also lay within the Holy Roman Empire, however, Hauenstein was formally subject to the Habsburg dynast in his capacity as emperor. Because the imperial office was elective, this dual subjection was to some extent fortuitous. But ever since the fifteenth century, members of the Habsburg dynasty had been the only magnates capable of securing enough votes. The one, brief exception was the reign of Bavarian elector Charles Albert, who reigned as Charles VII from 24 January 1742 to 20 January 1745. Otherwise, a Habsburg was doubly sovereign in the county. Regardless of the throne's occupant, moreover, Hauenstein (indeed, all the Crown Lands) was technically subject to decisions of the empire's quasi-parliamentary body, the Imperial Diet *(Reichstag)*, which after 1663 sat in permanent session in the city of Regensburg. But the Diet had little direct impact on political life in the Crown Lands, mainly because after Thirty Years' War, its principle function was no longer to legislate, but to serve as a diplomatic forum for the resolution of conflicts between the empire's sovereign, constituent states.⁹

---

7. The administrative terminology used here reflects subordination of the provincial governments in the archduchy of Austria, Styria, Carinthia, and Carniola to a "Lower Austrian" regime seated in Vienna and the remaining lands (including Outer Austria) to an "Upper Austrian" regime in Innsbruck. These are not to be confused with the Austria "above the Enns" and Austria "below the Enns," two parts of the archduchy of Austria, often called Upper and Lower Austria. My use of "Crown Lands" refers to all these lands plus Bohemia, Moravia, and Silesia (declared hereditary possessions by Emperor Ferdinand II in 1627, 1628, and 1652), but *not* the Habsburg possessions beyond the imperial frontiers in Croatia, Slovakia, Hungary, and Transylvania. On the chaos of Austrian regional nomenclature, see R. J. W. Evans, *The Making of the Habsburg Monarchy, 1550–1700: An Interpretation* (Oxford, 1979), 157, 160–61.

8. For a full discussion of its central institutions, see Thomas Fellner and Heinrich Kretschmayr, *Die österreichische Zentralverwaltung, pt. 1, Von Maximilian I. bis zur Vereinigung der österreichischen und böhmischen Hofkanzlei (1749)* (Vienna, 1907), 1:165–67, 231–33, and 3:351–75. On the relationship between Outer Austria and the Upper Austrian government in Innsbruck, see Otto Stolz, "Das Verhältnis der vorderösterreichischen Lande zu den landesfürstlichen Regierungen in Innsbruck und Wien," in Friedrich Metz, ed., *Vorderösterreich: Eine geschichtliche Landeskunde*, 2d rev. ed. (Freiburg, 1967), 111–12.

9. See Karl Otmar von Aretin, *Das Reich: Friedensgarantie und europäisches Gleichgewicht* (Stuttgart, 1986), 20–38, 55–75.

But there was a more important reason for the impotence of imperial institutions in Hauenstein: the two supreme imperial courts had no jurisdiction over the Habsburg Crown Lands. The latter, like many estates of the empire, enjoyed exemptions from the authority of the Imperial Chamber Court (*Reichskammergericht,* or RKG), the Diet's juridical organ. Moreover, the RKG was all but lamed by confessional disputes throughout the central third of the seventeenth century, a crisis from which it never fully recovered. Like the RKG, the Imperial Aulic Council (*Reichshofrat,* or RHR), an arm of the emperor's authority as suzerain, exercised formal jurisdiction over all territory within the imperial borders. But since the late seventeenth century, Habsburg dynasts had diminished the RHR's authority over cases arising in the Crown Lands, which were reserved instead for the Court Chancellery. This state of affairs was codified in 1720 with the "Court Chancellery Ordinance" *(Hofkanzleiordnung)* of Emperor Charles VI.[10] For Hauenstein, the practical effect was that court decisions reached in the county could only be appealed up the Austrian administrative chain. With respect to the Salpeter Wars, this was a crucial distinction: throughout the early modern era, both the RKG and RHR played important, often decisive roles in the resolution of agrarian conflicts in those smaller territories of the empire which were not privileged with immunity from their jurisdiction.[11] Not so Hauenstein.

Top-heavy though it appeared, however, the administrative pyramid of the Crown Lands left wide room at the bottom for institutional idiosyncracies. All provincial diets, for example, were made up of the clergy, nobility, and an estate of commons, usually consisting exclusively of townsmen. The diet of Tyrol, however, included representatives from court districts with jurisdiction over royal peasants *(Pflegegerichte),* while in Vorarlberg peasant delegates had a say in approving tax levies, which they would not give without the approval of their constituents.[12] Similarly, the common estate of the Outer Austrian Diet included the Eight

---

10. Fellner and Kretschmayr, *Österreichische Zentralverwaltung,* pt. 1, 1:165–67, 1:231–33, and 3:351–75.

11. Werner Troßbach, "Bauernbewegungen in deutschen Kleinterritorien zwischen 1648 und 1789," in Winfried Schulze, ed., *Aufstände, Revolten, Prozeße: Beiträge zu bäuerlichen Widerstandsbewegungen im frühneuzeitlichen Europa* (Stuttgart, 1983), 233–85.

12. Dickson, *Finance and Government,* 1:299–301; P. Blickle, *Landschaften,* 54–59, 74–75, 159–315.

of Hauenstein as one among eighteen voting members. Moreover, the administrative structure of the Crown Lands also allowed the customary political structure of Hauenstein to leave wide-ranging powers in the hands of peasants. Above all, it was electoral custom that engaged the largest number of inhabitants in the political process, restrained the influence of lords, and prevented the formation of peasant oligarchies. Similarly, the traditional structure of judicial appeal involved peasants in a wide range of official capacities. Of course, these arrangements were vulnerable to seigneurial manipulation; by the eighteenth century, moreover, an elite within the peasantry threatened to assume a monopoly over public office. Nevertheless, officeholding remained contingent on popular approval, and during the Salpeter Wars, rebel activists strove to make elections more inclusive, for the dual purposes of excising lordly influence and of ousting their *müllerisch* rivals.

The Eight had so much power that contemporaries likened Hauenstein to the Forest Cantons of Switzerland.[13] As ministers of public finance in Hauenstein, the Eight levied all regular and occasional taxes; they also supervised the rent collection on royal Habsburg seigneuries and performed several autonomous juridical functions. In return for their services, the Eight received only paltry compensation—less than the pay of a mere day laborer.[14] Each of the eight cantons contained twelve to fifteen settlements and was usually named for the largest one among them. Every year on St. George's Day (23 April), all adult males in each canton assembled to elect their Octovir for the coming year. Voting was public: electors formed a crowd around their favorite candidate, and the larger crowd won.[15] One week after St. George's Day, the newly elected Eight met with their predecessors in office in the village of Görwihl to elect a Speaker *(Redmann)* from among the new crop, who would serve as county treasurer and preside over the Eight as *primus inter pares*.

13. Günther Haselier, *Die Streitigkeiten der Hauensteiner mit ihren Obrigkeiten: Ein Beitrag zur Geschichte Vorderösterreichs und des südwestdeutschen Bauernstandes im 18. Jahrhundert* (Karlsruhe, 1940), 6, 17.

14. GLA 113:269, 59r–66v, "Synoptischer Entwurff des Ursprungs und alten Verfassung der Graffschafft Hawenstein," [1751?]. Octovirs received twenty kreuzer for each day spent in public service, plus an annual bonus of ten gulden.

15. For a detailed description of an actual election (albeit one disrupted by rebellion), see GLA 113:263, no. 37, "Ohngefährliche Beschreibung, waß sich bey der Einungsmeisterwahl am Tag des Hl. Ritters Georgy zugetragen," 28 April 1745.

The origins of this arrangement are difficult to reconstruct. Joseph Merk, a nineteenth-century historian, speculated that the system of cantons began as a defensive military pact, perhaps as early as 1333, after the turmoil that had ensued from the double election of Ludwig the Bavarian and Friedrich the Fair to the imperial throne in 1314.[16] The vestigial military functions of the canton system seem to bear this out: the Eight commanded a county militia *(Landfahnen)*, which over the years had been mustered for local defense against invaders, although by the eighteenth century it had lapsed into disuse.[17] Recent research, however, indicates that defense against St. Blasien's introduction of serfdom to Hauenstein in the late fourteenth and fifteenth centuries played the decisive role in perpetuating what had been a temporary military alliance as a durable political formation. In any case, the rights and authorities of the Eight were more or less fixed by the mid-fifteenth century.[18]

On paper, at least, the electoral customs of Hauenstein seemed designed to inhibit inteference by outsiders, to minimize corruption, and limit the formation of political oligarchies within the peasantry. In the first place, Octovir elections were to be held "in the open air" *(unter freiem Himmel)* and non-peasants were forbidden to attend.[19] Official interference was inhibited in other ways as well. By law, the Forest Steward could only cast a nominating ballot in the election of a Speaker and invest the Eight with the oaths and symbols of office.[20] He might, of course, withhold his approval, but only at great risk, as events during the Salpeter Wars would prove. To minimize corruption by the Eight,

---

16. Joseph Merk, "Geschichte des Ursprunges, der Entwickelung und Einrichtung der Hauensteinischen Einung im Mittelalter," *Jahrbücher der Geschichte und Staatskunst* 2 (1833): 132–33.

17. Karl F. Wernet, "Der Hauensteiner Landfahnen: Entstehung, Entwicklung, und Bedeutung der Hauensteiner Wehrorganisation bis zum Beginn der Unruhen in der Grafschaft im Jahre 1726," *ZGO* 95 (1943): 301–3.

18. See Claudia Ulbrich, *Leibherrschaft am Oberrhein im Spätmittelalter* (Göttingen, 1979), 60–65.

19. On the electoral system, see GLA 113:231, 11r–14v, [Joseph Tröndle of Rotzel], "Ohngefehrlicher Bericht wie die Redtmann undt Einungsmeister, auch Vögt, Steurer undt Geschwohrene ins Ambt genohmen werdten undt was der ein oder der andere zue thuen undt zue verrichten habe," n.d., and GLA 113:269, "Pro memoria wie in der Herrschaft Hauenstein die Ruhe für das khünftige hergestellet . . . werden könte," n.d.

20. Karl F. Wernet, "Der Umfang der Grafschaft Hauenstein," *ZGO* 104 (1956): 455. The symbols of office included a blue sash *(Tschoben)*, and a hunting knife. At religious observances, the Eight were accorded precedence. Furthermore, tradition entitled each Octovir to carry the symbols and prestige of office for life.

second, a public review of all fiscal transactions *(Landsrechnung)* was held immediately after the annual inaugural ceremonies. Finally, electoral custom hindered the concentration of power in the hands of the few: no Octovir-elect could be related "all too closely" to any other, nor could anyone serve consecutive terms.[21]

At the time, everyone agreed that Octovir elections were a genuinely popular affair. When the provincial government tried to ban them in 1714, the incumbent Eight objected vehemently, insisting that "since time immemorial the peasantry has had the right to elect the Eight . . . in such a way that each and every [adult male] subject in a canton may vote."[22] Elite observers acknowledged this, albeit grudgingly. Just as electoral customs exposed politics to popular "whims," the customary juridical structure of Hauenstein also engaged common folk in ways that compromised the authority of royal officials.[23] By the eighteenth century, it had become common practice for the Forest Steward to hold a weekly court in the company of two Octovirs. Judgments were reached by majority so that technically, the Eight could overrule their governor. Nor was that all. The traditional route of judicial appeal within Hauenstein extended from the Forest Steward's weekly tribunal to annual "courts of the twelve" in each canton, consisting of an Octovir plus ten peasant jurors appointed by the Forest Steward.[24] *Their* decisions, in turn, could be appealed to an annual "court of sixteen" in May, consisting of the old and new Eight. Thus *two* stages of judicial appeal intervened between the Forest Steward and his superiors in Freiburg. An imperial investigator only stated the obvious when he suggested that this route of appeal "caused no small diminution of . . . the Forest Steward's authority."[25]

The Forest Steward was limited in other ways as well. For one thing, he was a salaried official; other governors of Outer Austrian lordships leased the right to rule and pocketed as much as they could squeeze from

21. GLA 113:231, 11r–14v, "Ohngefehrlicher Bericht."
22. GLA 113:98, Eight to OÖKR, 11 July 1714.
23. The legal basis for Hauenstein's traditional juridical structure was the so-called *Waldvogteiordnung* of Emperor Maximilian I, dated 15 March 1507; see "Ordnung von Kaiser Maximiliano, wie sich die Waldvögt im Schwarzwald in gerichtlichen Handlungen, Bueßen, Freveln, Straffen und andern Sachen zu verhalten," 15 March 1507, reprinted in Josef Bader, ed., "Nachträge zu den Mittheilungen über die Grafschaft Hauenstein," *ZGO* 12 (1861): 111–18.
24. *Waldvogteiordnung*, 15 March 1507, §6; see also Haselier, *Streitigkeiten*, 5, 20.
25. GLA 113:229, 261r–72v, KK Beaurieu to VÖRK, 11 August 1728.

the peasantry.²⁶ Worse, the Forest Steward had but one assistant, the "Stattholder."²⁷ Together, these limits forced him to rely on the Eight, without whom adjudication and tax collection were impossible. Granted, the Forest Steward also commanded six royal bailiffs *(herrschaftliche Vögte)*, all of them peasants, who published royal decrees, enforced debts, and helped with tax collection. But the bailiffs were not entirely of the Forest Steward's choosing, either: according to custom, three bailiffs were nominated annually by popular election in each canton, for a total of twenty-four, from whom the Forest Steward chose his six.²⁸ Finally, custom restricted the Forest Steward's authority symbolically by requiring each new incumbent to swear an oath to preserve the customs of Hauenstein and to defend the county against "foreign courts of law" *(fremde Gerichte)*.²⁹ By making his authority contingent on the defense of custom, the Forest Steward's vow underscored the assumption of reciprocity that underlay all relationships of subordination.

All this sounds suspiciously like the republican myth, and no wonder: like any legal representation of reality, custom "propounds the world in which its descriptions make sense."³⁰ But the procedural reality of elections often departed from customary norms. First, electoral practice in several eastern cantons secured the influence of incumbents, where the outgoing Octovir nominated a successor, while the assembly nominated another by means of a preliminary balloting variously called the "query" or the "proposal" *(Umfrag* or *Vorschlag)*. Second, in two western cantons electoral assemblies chose from two candidates nominated

---

26. See Haselier, *Streitigkeiten*, 4–6, and Wernet, "Der Umfang der Grafschaft Hauenstein," 431–66.

27. A scrivener was assigned to the Forest Steward's bureau only in 1731; GLA 113:229, 261r–72v, KK Beaurieu to VÖRK, 11 August 1728; GLA 227:39, "Ernennung von Johann Valentin Speth zum Amtsschreiber des Waldvogteiamtes," 1731. The appointment came none too soon: minutes had not been maintained since 1721; see GLA 61:13148 [WGP WVA].

28. GLA 21:219, "Vergleich zwischen Hauenstain und der Waldvogtey wegen zerschidenen Puncten, sonderlich des Taxes," 5 December 1670, §2; excerpted in J. Bader, ed., "Urkunden und Regeste aus dem Archive der ehemaligen Grafschaft Hauenstein," *ZGO* 11 (1860): 484–86; and GLA 113:16, "Erinnern von Reedman und Einungsmeister ... über die ... Dienst Instruction für die Vögte," January 1784.

29. "Des Schwartzwalds Fryheiten," [1484], §8; *Waldvogteiordnung*, 15 March 1507, §2, and "Landsordnung des Schwartzwalds," 19 December 1552, §9, reprinted in Bader, ed., "Nachträge," 118–23.

30. Clifford Geertz, "Local Knowledge: Fact and Law in Comparative Perspective," in his *Local Knowledge: Further Essays in Interpretive Anthropology* (New York, 1983), 173–74.

by the royal bailiff.[31] Third, abbatial officials influenced the outcome of elections in the two northernmost cantons of Höchenschwand and Wolpadingen, where the chamberlain of St. Blasien cast the first vote.[32]

These messy exceptions tended to entrench the power of a magisterial elite within the peasantry. The surviving evidence indicates that by the eighteenth century, public office was coming under the control of relatively few families. The most egregious example of this trend was Birndorf Canton, where several generations of the Tröndle clan dominated public office throughout the eighteenth century.[33] Sometimes public office oscillated between two dominant families, as in Wolpadingen Canton, where Hans Denz and Friedle Albiez succeeded each other almost without interruption from 1714 to 1726.[34] The office of royal bailiff, too, rarely changed hands. What few records survive suggest that they were habitually reelected; with no customary ban against self-succession, bailiffs often occupied their posts for many years on end. In addition, the Eight sometimes used the position as a proving ground for new initiates to the inner circle of officeholders.[35] Hauensteiners were sufficiently aware of these tendencies to accuse the Tröndle clan of wishing to "make their offices hereditary."[36]

Resentment against this elite proliferated during the rebellion. In *salpeterisch* opinion, the Eight were even more "proud and arrogant" than the royal heir-apparent, Maria Theresa herself.[37] *Salpeterisch* peasants knew that power, especially *müllerisch* power, corrupts: among many slanders reported in 1738, for instance, was the claim that since his election, the *müllerisch* Baptist Zimmermann had become "like all the old Octovirs; people say that as soon as one feeds from the Octovir's plate,

---

31. GLA 65:11426, 137r–39v, "Wahl der Einungsmeister," n.d.
32. GLA 113:263, no. 37, "Ohngefehrliche Beschreibung."
33. Beginning with Adam Tröndle (1655–1714), the office passed to his son Joseph (d. 1748) and grandson Johann Michael (1715–80), who held it continuously for twenty-nine years; see Jakob Ebner, *Eine Müllerdynastie im Schwarzwald* (Radolfzell, 1908).
34. GLA 229:43925 and GLA 61:13148 [WGP WVA].
35. Such a person was Joseph Tröndle of Rotzel, who was royal bailiff in Hochsal canton in 1715, before his election as Octovir in 1718; see GLA 229:1327, "Abrechnung mit Joseph Tröndlin Vogt zue Rotzel," 1715.
36. GLA 65:11419 [Nachlaß J. L. Meyer], 60r.
37. GLA 113:255, 265r–68v, Interrogation of Hans Strittmatter of Görwihl, WVA, 7 January 1744.

then he must act like them."³⁸ Such disaffection was compounded by accusations that the Eight abused their authority. One of the few points on which *salpeterisch* peasants and provincial officials could agree concerned the Octovir's administration of public finances. The latter charged that the Eight kept their fiscal accounts secret, even from the Forest Steward; tax collection was arbitrary and public accounts were sloppy, if they were maintained at all.³⁹ The annual settling of accounts was dismissed as an occasion for eating and drinking at public expense, and *salpeterisch* peasants added the charged that the Eight met four or five times each week to "gorge and guzzle, dance and jump, for which the subjects must afterwards pay the tab."⁴⁰ For *salpeterisch* peasants, the problem was not simply mismanagement, but outright graft. Some said, for example, that in 1743, Speaker Hans Jacob Bächle had absconded with eight thousand gulden levied in excess of the Estates' tax appropriation for that year.⁴¹ Yet despite such attacks, *salpeterisch* peasants never questioned the validity of elective office. Rather, their scorn was aimed at abuse: the Eight had "perjured" their oath, which enjoined them to act impartially toward all peasants, rich and poor alike.⁴² Until elections were effectively banned in 1745, officeholding remained formally contingent on popular approval.

Forms of Domination

If oligarchic trends often flowed at cross-currents with custom, peasant autonomies were also compromised by the rights and powers of seigneurs. The two most powerful lords in Hauenstein—St. Blasien and the

---

38. GLA 113:242, 304r–6v, Interrogation of Hans Ebner of Hechwihl, Unteralpfen, 23 August, 1738.
39. GLA 113:269, 59r–66v, "Synoptischer Entwurff"; GLA 113:195, "Beschreibung des V:Ö: oberen Rheinviertels," n.d.; GLA 99:1037, 3r–8v, Amtsschreiber Beck to Marquard Herrgott, 5 March 1735.
40. GLA 113:252, 20r–23v, Interrogation of Joseph Ebner of Hottingen, Unteralpfen, 6 March 1739.
41. GLA 113:222, 13r–14v.
42. GLA 113:232, 60r–v, Martin Thoma of Haselbach to Joseph Tröndle of Schmitzingen, 21 April 1728.

noble convent *(Damenstift)* of St. Fridolin in Säckingen—employed all the major forms of domination to extract a share of surplus peasant production and to compel obedience to their commands. At the same time, however, seigneurs *also* required the help of peasants to rule effectively, just as the Forest Steward did. Furthermore, the terms of their domination were likewise set by negotiation and contract, which legitimized peasant claims in the process of political barter. Here too, then, the processes of domination were interactive.[43]

Of the two principal seigneurs in Hauenstein, St. Blasien was by far the stronger. Situated five kilometers north of the county in a narrow valley along the upper reaches of the Alb river, St. Blasien was one of the wealthiest monasteries in the empire. In the late Middle Ages, the abbot enjoyed incomes from seigneuries in Outer Austria, upper Swabia, Alsace, the upper margraviate of Baden, and several Swiss cantons that exceeded those of his immediate ecclesiastical superior, the bishop of Constance.[44] St. Blasien also owned large numbers of serfs throughout southwestern Germany.[45] Within Outer Austria, the abbot exerted various forms of jurisdiction over the lordships of Schönau and Todtnau, Oberried (after 1725), and Staufen-Kirchhofen (after 1738), and inside a zone immediately surrounding his abbey called the *Zwing und Bann,* not to mention its prerogatives in Hauenstein (see Map 2). Finally, the abbot also wore the hat of imperial count of Bonndorf from 1613 on. One can only guess how much these prerogatives delivered in revenues; the Prussian philosopher Friedrich Nicolai, who visited St. Blasien in 1781, speculated that the abbey collected in excess of eighty

---

43. In addition to St. Blasien and St. Fridolin, two other lords exercised minor powers of *Gerichtsherrschaft* in Hauenstein. One was the Baron von Zweyer, juridical lord over the village of Unteralpfen, who also owned scattered lands in Birndorf, Görwihl, and Hochsal cantons. The other was a prebend of the Teutonic Knights in Beuggen, which owned a few small estates in the southwest. Both lords also claimed serfs, but by the eighteenth century their numbers were negligible. Because their powers were so few, however, I have omitted them from the present discussion. On Beuggen prebend, see Peter Heim, *Die Deutschordenskommende Beuggen und die Anfänge der Ballei Elsass-Burgund* (Bonn, 1977). A host of small-time seigneurs owned bits of land here and there in Hauenstein; for a full listing, see GLA 113:193, [18th cent.].

44. On the late medieval extent of St. Blasien's seigneuries, see Hugo Ott, *Die Klostergrundherrschaft St Blasiens im Mittelalter* (Stuttgart, 1969).

45. See Jürgen Tacke, "Studien zur Agrarverfassung der oberen badischen Markgrafschaft im 16. und 17. Jahrhundert," *Das Markgräflerland* 2 (1956).

thousand gulden annually.⁴⁶ St. Fridolin, by contrast, had far fewer resources at its disposal, despite its great age (the convent was founded in the 600s) and despite its high rank (it had enjoyed princely status since 1307).⁴⁷ This was not due to any lack of formal rights of domination. Like St. Blasien, the convent exerted legal jurisdiction over the churches and owned land, serfs, and patronage in several parishes in Hauenstein (see Map 3). But the specific terms of these prerogatives allowed fewer claims against the obedience of individual peasants, much less their pocket books.

This imbalance was evident in every category of domination. St. Blasien's juridical powers *(Gerichtsherrschaft)* in Hauenstein were considerable. The abbey held juridical sway over two entire cantons (Höchenschwand and Wolpadingen) and over large portions of Dogern, Birndorf, and Görwihl cantons in central and eastern Hauenstein. Together, these zones comprised about 30 percent of the county and roughly 23 percent of its total population.⁴⁸ Although the abbey claimed to own these courts outright, their juridical competence was in fact subject to ongoing negotiation with Hauenstein and the provincial government.⁴⁹ Generally speaking, St. Blasien regulated conflicts over property, inheritance, and debt, judged misdemeanors, and enjoyed a handful of privileges normally associated with sovereign authority, such as the right to impose frontier tariffs.⁵⁰ By contrast, the convent's juridical authorities comprised only two small zones around the villages of Herrischried and Murg. Like St. Blasien's courts, these courts regulated cases involving property, debt, and inheritance, but exercised no "sovereign" authority. In part, this juridical weakness was the result of neglect. The sisters realized this, and in 1713 resolved "to take better heed of [our] rights of

46. Friedrich Nicolai, *Beschreibung einer Reise durch Deutschland und die Schweiz im Jahre 1781* (Berlin, 1796), 12:54.
47. Fridolin Jehle, *Die Geschichte des Stiftes Säckingen* (Säckingen, 1969). The convent belonged to no monastic order, but followed its own rule.
48. Percentages are extrapolated from GLA 113:194, "Die Verzeichnung der in der Grafschaft Hauenstein gelegenen Ortschaften," a summary population roster that probably dates from the 1760s.
49. See Karl F. Wernet, "St Blasiens Versuche, sich der Grafschaft Hauenstein pfandweise zu bemächtigen," *ZGO* 107 (1959): 161–82.
50. GLA 99:79, "Verzeichnus der Gerichten, so man von St Blasmischer Cantzley zu verwalten . . . hat," [1638]; and GLA 65:11398, "Urkundlicher Außzug deren Rechten und Freyheiten des uralten löbl. Stiffts St Blasien am Schwartzwaldt," [18th cent.].

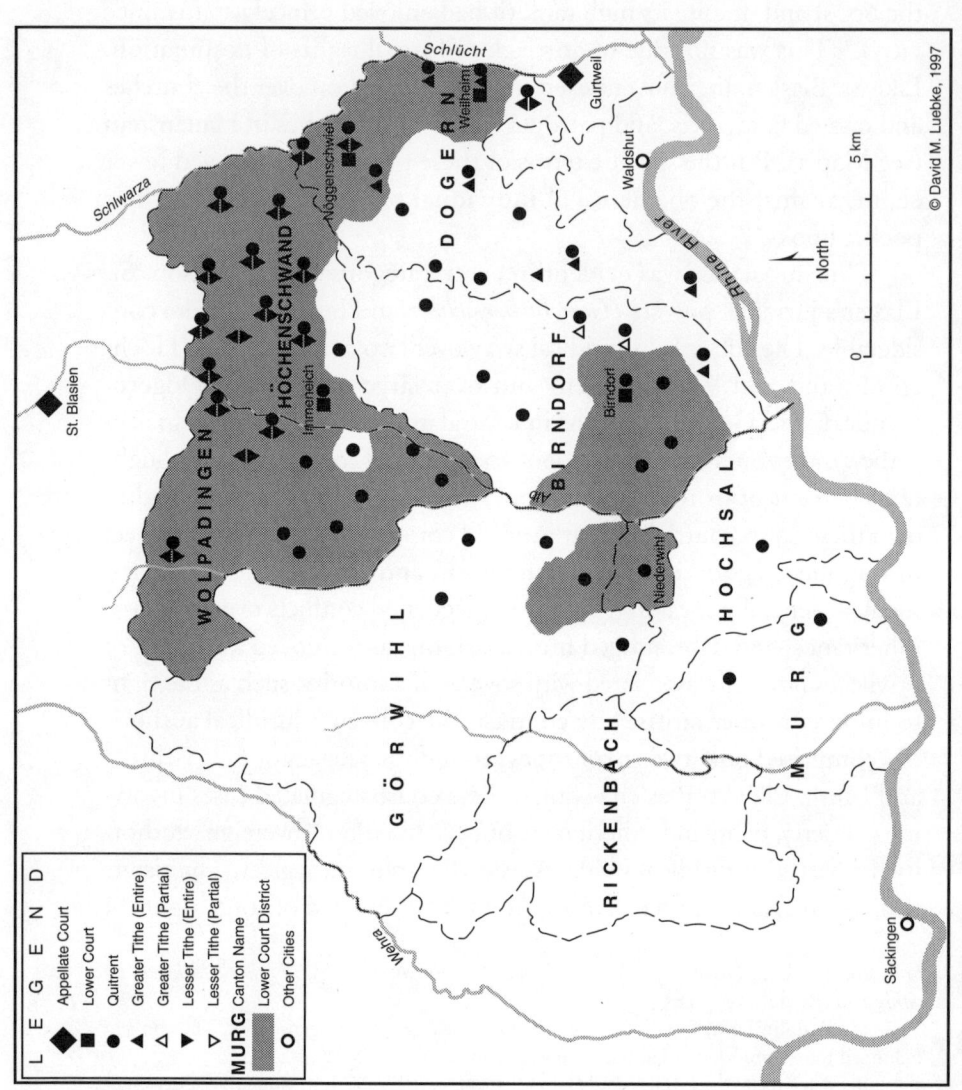

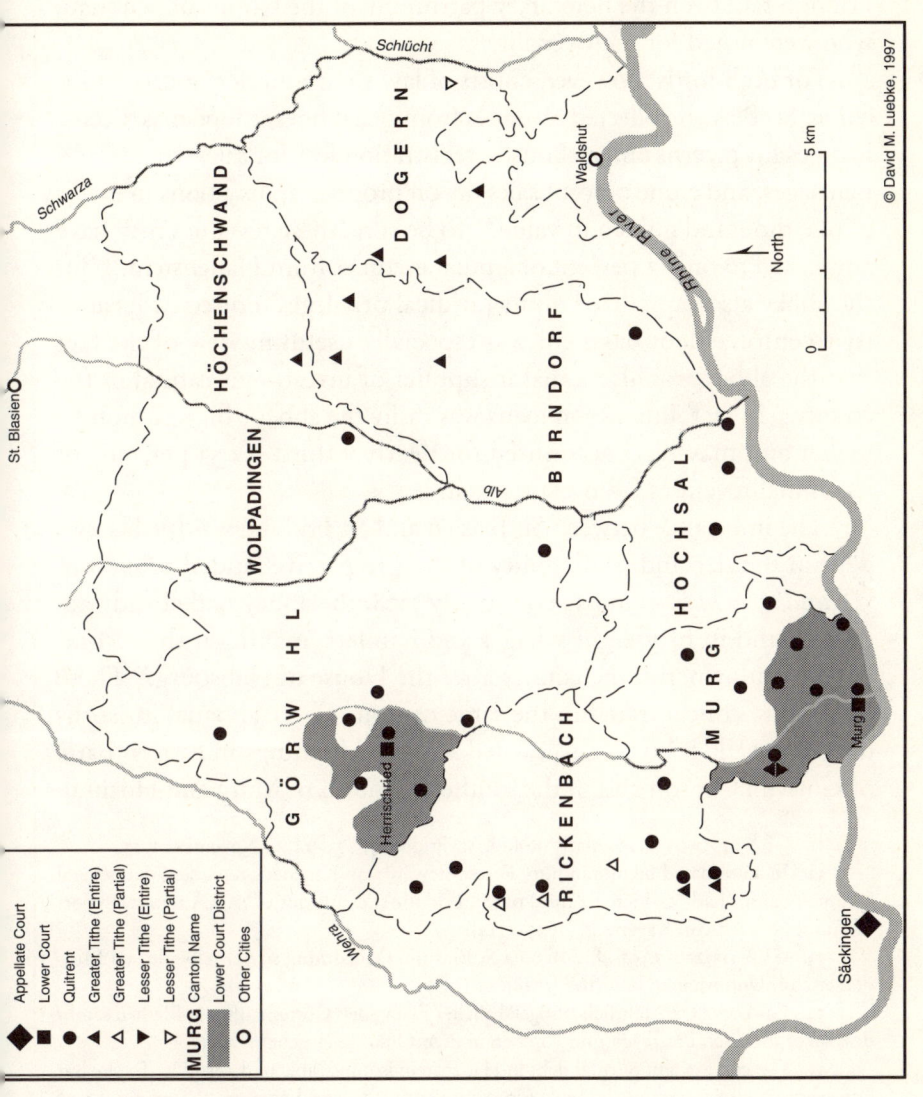

The Dominions of St. Fridolin

jurisdiction" lest they "suffer from lack of use."[51] But the matter was not entirely under their control: since 1365, the fiscal administration of St. Fridolin had been the hereditary patrimony of the barons of Schönau, who were noted for their venality.[52]

For both lords, however, courts of law were a modest source of income. St. Blasien collected revenues from penal fines, subpoenas, licensing fees for taverns and alehouses, registration fees for sales, trades, and marriages, and a one percent sales tax on property transactions in excess of one thousand gulden in value.[53] To be sure, these revenues may have amounted to only 2 percent of annual incomes from Hauenstein.[54] But the abbey also capitalized on its juridical privileges indirectly. Its ability to enforce debt payment was especially useful in view of the fact that the abbey was also a major supplier of investment capital in the county.[55] In fact, interest on loans was easily the abbey's biggest moneymaker and may have accounted for nearly a third (32.53 percent) of its annual revenues from Hauenstein.[56]

The imbalance between St. Blasien and St. Fridolin was further evident in the size and profitability of their respective landed properties *(Grundherrschaften)* in the county. By 1328, the abbey had already acquired land in fifty-eight villages and hamlets, making it the second largest landowner in the county after the House of Habsburg.[57] These lands were concentrated in the same cantons where abbatial jurisprudence prevailed, but it also owned scattered holdings in eastern parts of Görwihl Canton and in the southern cantons of Murg and Hochsal.

51. GLA 61:10505 [Kapitularprotokoll St. Fridolin], 273–74, 15 November 1713.

52. In an undated memorandum, Forest Steward von Kageneck remarked that several Schönau barons had "cashiered a third of [St. Fridolin's] death-duties"; GLA 113:112, Report of Forest Steward von Kageneck, [1693–1714].

53. GLA 113:228, 145r–48v, "Copia St Blasml: Taxordnung soviel selbe dessen Mindergerichtl: Unterthanen betrifft," [1728].

54. GLA 79:2875, "Jährlich-ohngefährlicher Ertrag deß Gotteshaußes St Blaßien sambt dess incorporierten Pfarreyen und Kirchen in dem Oesterreichischen," 1716.

55. The exact extent of rural debt in Hauenstein is impossible to determine. To cite but one example, the church of the Holy Cross in Birndorf received an average annual interest of 125 gulden on an average loaned capital of 2,143 gulden between 1727 and 1750, a rate of 5.82 percent; see GLA 62:34, "Kirchenrechnung löbl. Gottßhauß S. Crucis in Birendorf, Martini 1727–Martini 1747."

56. GLA 79:2875, "Jährlich-ohngefährlicher Ertrag," 1716.

57. This according to the 1328 *Waldamtsrodel* (GLA 11:27).

This overlapping of authorities meant that many of St. Blasien's tenants were *also* subject to its juridical rule. Incomes from these lands were substantial, and comprised about 18 percent of St. Blasien's total revenues from Hauenstein.[58] If St. Blasien's estates were concentrated and reasonably lucrative, St. Fridolin's ongoing inability to enforce its prerogatives meant that by the eighteenth century, it had lost control of extensive lands over which it could no longer prove ownership. In stark contrast to St. Blasien, moreover, St. Fridolin stopped acquiring new estates in the fourteenth century.[59] Without adequate record keeping, receipts dwindled, such that by 1724 its incomes from one village threatened "soon to disappear" entirely.[60] As a consequence, quitrents represented only a small portion of the convent's revenues, around 10 percent of total incomes from all its lands in Habsburg territories.[61]

In the late Middle Ages, tenants of St. Blasien and St. Fridolin had held land under a dizzy variety of terms. After a reorganization of its seigneurial administration in 1610, however, St. Blasien only distinguished between two main types of tenancy, "quitrent-estates" *(Zinsgüter)*, and "manses" *(Fronhöfe)*.[62] This distinction allowed the greatest feasible control over the largest parcels. Both quitrent-estates and manses were held under secure, hereditary tenures similar to the English copyhold. Whereas the tenants of quitrent-estates could sell their lands more or less freely, manses were subject to the terms of tenancy contracts with St. Blasien, which typically forbade partition through sale or inheritance.[63] To be sure, such constraints could not always be enforced, and nearly all manses

---

58. GLA 79:2875, "Jährlich-ohngefährlicher Ertrag," 1716.

59. Franz J. Mone, "Die Einkünfte des Klosters Säckingen in Glarus im 14. Jahrhundert," *ZGO* 18 (1865): 420–33.

60. GLA 229:882 [Quitrent Renovation], 16 May 1725.

61. GLA 79:2875, "Auf verlangen würdet daß von dem Stüfft Seckhingen besitzende Vermögen und hiervon jährlich genießende Fructus, Ohngelt, Getreydt, und Wein, dargegen aber auch die obhabendte Schulden, undt nothwendige Außgaben hinauß nachfolgendermaßen außgeworffen," [1716].

62. On the earlier forms of land tenure in St. Blasien's properties in Hauenstein, see Karl F. Wernet, "Die wirtschaftlichen Verhältnisse der Grafschaft Hauenstein zwischen den Burgunderkriegen und den Salpeteteraufständen," *ZGO* 98 (1950): 115–46.

63. On the number and location of abbatial manses in Hauenstein, see GLA 99:157, "Kurzer Bericht über deß löbl. Gottshauses St Blasien Lehen- und Frohn-Hoff auch Widumb," 1665, and GLA 229:37289, "Verzaichnus deren, in denen St Blasmischen Reichsherrschafften ligenten Lehen welche Ehrschätzig seyendt," 1701.

had been subdivided at least once since the sixteenth century.[64] But the geographical overlap of juridical and seigneurial authority imparted to St. Blasien a degree of control that St. Fridolin lacked.

Like land ownership, church patronage *(Kirchenpatronat)* entitled lords to an additional share of peasant production. St. Blasien levied all or part of the tithe in twenty-seven villages and hamlets in the northern and western cantons.[65] Typically, tithes were of two varieties. The greater tithe *(Großzehnt)* was levied against harvests of major cereal crops; the lesser tithe *(Kleinzehnt)* was comprised of "blood tithes" *(Blutzehnt)* on newborn livestock and the "straw" or "hay tithe" *(Heuzehnt)*. Not everywhere did the abbey enjoy claims to both sorts: in eight of the twenty-seven villages, for example, St. Blasien drew only the greater tithe.[66] Tithes, of course, were roughly proportional to harvest yields, and their market value did not fluctuate with cereal prices, as fixed payments *in natura* did; the abbey could therefore compensate for meager harvests by selling tithe yields at high prices. The relatively stable incomes of tithes probably delivered about 30 percent of its annual revenues from Hauenstein.[67]

Tithes were resented, but by far the most contentious tool of domination was serfdom *(Leibherrschaft)*. Originally, servile status came with tenancy, but since the late fifteenth century, St. Blasien had severed this link. Henceforth, serfdom became a personal status independent of other forms of domination, with its own set of rules, legal disabilities, and fiscal obligations. In southwestern Germany generally, peasants inherited servile status from their mothers, but St. Blasien claimed that the status of its serfs was heritable through both mothers and fathers alike, a rare form of bondage known as "serfdom of the baser hand" *(Leibeigenschaft der ärgeren Hand)*. According to these rules, mixed marriages between abbatial serfs and free persons or the serfs of other lords inevitably pro-

---

64. See GLA 11:159, nr. 1553, "Lehenrevers für Friedle Strittmatter Vogt von Birndorf," 24 December 1660, and GLA 229:9112, no. 2, "Bericht wie der St Blas: Lehen-Frohn-Hoff zu Birndorff seit vor Hundert Jahren hero vertheilet und von welchen Lehen-Leuthen solcher theilbar biß hero besessen worden," 1763.

65. GLA 113:193, "Die Beschreibung der Grafschaft Hauenstein," [18th cent.].

66. GLA 229:37381, III, "Zehents-Notanta über Waldt," July 1719. In a few villages along the Rhine, St Blasien also collected a tithe on wine (the *Weinzehnt*); see GAD Urkunden 16, "Beschwerdeschrift der Gemeinden Dogern, Espach, Gaise [und] Kiesenbach gegen das Stift St Blasien, die Schatzung des Weinzehendts betreffend," 10 September 1729.

67. GLA 79:2875, "Jährlich-ohngefährlicher Ertrag," 1716.

duced children born in bondage to the abbey.⁶⁸ This arrangement had two principal side effects. One was double serfdom: marriages between male abbatial serfs and the female serfs of other lords produced children simultaneously bound to *two* serf lords. Second, the mechanism of "baser hand" serfdom also guaranteed that the total number of abbatial serfs would always grow, and because it was unconnected to land tenure, abbatial serfdom passed without hindrance from one village to the next every time a serf changed residence or tenancy. By the eighteenth century, St. Blasien's serfs lived in every village and hamlet of Hauenstein. Contemporary estimates vary, but it is probable that by 1738 just under 70 percent of Hauensteiners were abbatial serfs (see Table 1).

TABLE I. The serfs of St. Blasien, by canton (28 February 1738)

Canton	Men	Women	Children	All serfs	Total pop.	% Servile
Dogern	398	436	1543	2377	2609	91.11
Birndorf	398	442	1522	2362	2659	88.83
Höchenschwand	199	210	578	987	1222	80.77
Wolpadingen	184	188	573	945	1163	81.26
Görwihl	328	365	1158	1851	2822	65.59
Rickenbach	246	250	878	1374	2492	55.14
Hochsal	86	73	169	328	1353	24.24
Murg	72	68	138	278	941	29.54
Total:	1911	2032	6559	10,502	15,261	68.82

Sources: GLA 113:116, 26r-v, "Ohngefährlicher Auffsatz der fallbaren Leüthen in der Graffschafft Hawenstein," 28 February 1738; GLA 113:198, "Graffschafft Hawensteinische Seelenbeschreibung den 20tn 9bris 1754."

These totals also show that the highest percentages of serfs obtained in cantons where other forms of abbatial domination were dense: Höchenschwand, Wolpadingen, Birndorf, and Dogern. A rough overlap between various forms of domination characterized the spatial geographical scope of servitude.

The fairly light annual dues and services connected with serfdom were not their principal grievance: according to the 1467 charter, each servile household paid two annual dues (a "shrove chicken" or *Fastnachtshuhn* on Shrove Tuesday and three days of corvée labor, called

68. GLA 99:459, 6r–29v, "Aigenschaft"; GLA 67:1181, 189r–90v, "Ungenossame." See also Ulbrich, *Leibherrschaft*, 109–10.

Ehrtawen or *Frohntawen*). Revenues derived from serfdom averaged only 395 gulden between 1723 and 1732; according to a summary account compiled in 1716, these revenues represented a mere 11.5 percent of the total incomes from Hauenstein.[69] More contentious were occasional dues triggered by changes in the serf's personal or legal status. The heaviest of these came in the form of death duties *(mainmorte* or *Todfall)*, essentially an inheritance tax, which compensated the abbey for the loss of a dues-paying subject. The survivors of a deceased female serf were required to surrender her finest item of clothing *(Bestkleid)*; a male paid with his largest head of livestock *(Bestvieh)*. Matrimonial taxes (analogous to the *formariage* in France) marked the passage of young serfs into the procreative stage of their lives. Also, male serfs over the age of fourteen were required to perform an oath of loyalty and obedience to the abbey. Finally, each adult male serf was to attend a biennial court *(Dinggericht)* in the village of Remetschwiel, where the list of servile obligations was recited and where the Eight negotiated disputes with St. Blasien on the serfs' behalf.[70] By the eighteenth century, nearly all of these dues had been converted into fixed money payments, but they remained linked to a series of legal disabilities that restricted the ability of serfs to alter their social or legal standing and to dispose of property freely. *Formariage*, for example, reflected the requirements of servile endogamy: serfs were allowed only to marry among serfs of the same lord, or else suffer a penalty. Of course, serfs could not emigrate without the lord's consent and the payment of a manumission fee; if they "deserted" anyway, St. Blasien claimed a "right of pursuit" *(Nachjagerecht)*, which in theory permitted the abbey to hunt down serfs in foreign jurisdictions.[71]

The convent of St. Fridolin also laid claim to serfs in Hauenstein, but their obligations were far less stringent than those of St. Blasien. Unlike the abbey, St. Fridolin demanded no oath of obedience, no labor

---

69. GLA 79:2875, "Jährlich-ohngefährlicher Ertrag," 1716; GLA 99:1038, 26r–27v. The majority of these revenues came from death duties, an average of 217 gulden annually, roughly 55.2 percent of the total.

70. For transcripts of these courts held in 1701 and 1719, see GLA 229:5658, "Bericht aus dem Archiv gezogen, über ds Dinggericht zue Rometschwil," n.d., and "Actum Römetschwyl den 4ten May 1719."

71. Haselier, *Streitigkeiten*, 34–35.

services, and no shrove chickens; the sole obligations were *formariage* and *mainmorte*.⁷² Moreover, these dues proved difficult to collect. In 1740, for example, one official noted that St. Fridolin's serfs in the northern and eastern cantons of Hauenstein had not paid *mainmortes* since the turn of the century, and certain evidence suggests that this was due to obstructionism on the part of the Eight.⁷³ Finally, conventual serfdom was strictly matrilineal, with the result that the number of St. Fridolin's serfs gradually shrank in proportion to abbatial bondsmen. By the eighteenth century, St. Blasien's serfs far outnumbered St. Fridolin's, even in districts where the convent's courts and seigneuries were concentrated. In Rickenbach Canton, for example, abbatial serfs outnumbered St. Fridolin's bondmen by over two to one; in Görwihl Canton the ratio was four to one. In all probability, there were only a few villages where conventual serfs outnumbered abbatial ones.⁷⁴

The inability of St. Fridolin to enforce its authority effectively poses the question of St. Blasien's success, and part of the answer lies in the abbey's attempts to centralize bureaucracies of rule. Indeed, St. Blasien was an early innovator in bureaucratic technique. By the fourteenth century, the abbey had already centralized its administration into territorial bureaus *(Ämter);* by 1383, abbatial authorities in Hauenstein were under the supervision of the so-called Forest Bureau *(Waldamt),* headed by a Forest Provost *(Waldprobst).* ⁷⁵ At the local level, this process of consolidation passed through several stages. Initially, St. Blasien placed its courts in the villages of Nöggenschwiel and Weilheim under the authority of a

72. GLA 67:1877, "Vahlbüech darüver alle Vähl, Ungenossame und Ledigstellung," n.d.; Haselier, *Streitigkeiten,* 35–36.
73. GLA 61:10507 [Kapitularprotokoll St Fridolin], 428–35, 10–14 November 1740. On obstructionism, see GLA 113:108, "Gegenanthworth wider die Klag so ds . . . Stifft Säckhingen bey löbl. V.Ö. Regierung wegen der Fahlbohrkeith halber . . . angebracht," [1727?].
74. These data are based on a comparison between GLA 113:108, "Verzeichnus der fahlbar Leüthen auff Seggingen zue Rickenbacher Einung 1740 ersuocht," [30 December 1740], "Specification der sekhingische fahlbaren Leüthen so sich in der Graffschafft hin und wider befinden so den 12tn & 13tn und 14tn Feburary 1742 undtersucht worden"; GLA 113:111, "Specification wievill Männer Weiber undt Kindt so nacher St Blasien fahlbar seindt," 28 July 1739; and GLA 113:116, "Ohngefehrlicher Auffsatz," [1738]. Population totals are from the same source as in Table 1. It was impossible to ascertain the numbers of conventual serfs living in cantons other than Rickenbach and Görwihl.
75. See GLA 65:11398, 1r–49v, "Urkundlicher Außzug deren Rechten undt Fre–heiten des uralten . . . Stifts St Blasien im Schwartzwaldt," [18th cent.]. For the founding 1383 charter of the Waldamt *(Waldamtsöffnung),* see Jakob Grimm, *Weisthümer* (1840–78), 4:487–96.

new bureau in Gurtweil, headed by a High Steward, or *Obervogt*.[76] Then in 1601, the abbot consolidated its jurisdictions over Höchenschwand and Wolpadingen cantons in a single court, located in the village of Immeneich, which was subjected directly to the chancellery in St. Blasien.[77] Finally during the late seventeenth century, the abbey transferred virtually all decision-making from local tribunals to administrative offices higher up the bureaucratic ladder.

Originally, these local courts had been maintained by abbatial bailiffs *(sankt-blasische Vögte)* recruited from among the peasantry, one for each of its lower courts in Immeneich, Nöggenschwiel, Weilheim, and Birndorf.[78] But as St. Blasien eroded their ability to make judgments on their own, bailiffs were gradually transformed from justices into policemen.[79] Village tribunals grew rare, although the Immeneich court met as late as 1712 to register and enforce payment on loans.[80] By minimizing their involvement in judicial decision-making, St. Blasien robbed peasants of their few formal controls over the mechanics of *Gerichtsherrschaft*, which only heightened the contrast to other jurisdictions, where peasants played a more active role.

Still, ordinary peasants retained some influence in the choice of abbatial bailiffs. Candidates were nominated by majority vote of subjects in a given court district, then rejected or approved by the High Steward or the abbatial chancellor.[81] Technically, candidacy was limited to manse-holders, but in practice all kinds of tenants were approved for the job.[82] The abbots seem to have realized that peasants would more likely

---

76. See GLA 229:37331, I, "Deduction ex archivo S. Blasiano über das St Gallische Lehen deß Thurn Guttenburg und Gerichts Weylheimb," 19 January 1723.

77. GLA 67:644, 127r–35v, "Verzeichnis der Gerichten, so man von St Bläsmischer Cantzley zu verwalten . . . hat," 3 November 1638.

78. On the duties of abbatial bailiffs, see GLA 229:74944, "Besetzung des Vogtsamts zu Niederwihl," 30 March 1699; and GLA 61:5775, 78–80, "Bürdorf: Bestellung und Beeidigung der Vogt," 22 January 1740.

79. See "Vögt unndt Waibels Verrichtungen" in GLA 99:79, "Verzeichnus der Gerichten," [1638].

80. GLA 229:49016, "Actum Immeneich," 9 November 1712.

81. GLA 229:75480, 9r–10v, 20 September 1751.

82. For the stipulation that bailiffs be manse-holders, see GLA 61:10648, 45r, "Wyhler Denominierung eines Vogten . . . die Frohnhoff Meyere haben das Vorrecht darzue," 13 May 1713. But none of the bailiffs of Birndorf court between 1695 and 1740 held manses; compare GLA 229:9112, no. 2, "Lehen-Frohn-Hoff zu Birndorff," [1763], and GLA 61:5775, 75–81, "Bürdorf: Bestellung und Beeidigung der Vogt," 22 January 1740.

obey an official of their own choosing, and the same thinking probably informed the organization of seigneurial quitrent-collection. Here too, St. Blasien made quitrent-collection the responsibility of the tenants themselves. In each village, a certain number of "carriers" *(Träger)* were assigned to assemble annual dues from a specified number of "contributors" *(Einzinser)*. The abbey spread these duties wide and thin: on average, each carrier collected rents from only eight other contributors.[83] In other words, some 12 percent of all tenants on abbatial quitrent-estates collected quitrents! While this system spared the abbey considerable administrative outlay, it also exposed St. Blasien to risks. For example, the subdivision of quitrent-estates through sale and inheritance made quitrents increasingly difficult to calculate, which resulted in administrative chaos. By 1728, the confusion had so soured relations between contributors and carriers that the latter "refused to pay quitrents any more until [the land] had been inventoried, because the contributors [could] no longer be identified."[84] Few episodes described so well the long-term effects of decentralized agricultural production on political relations between peasants and their lords. Originally, St. Blasien's manors in Hauenstein had formed organizational unities for the purposes of quitrent-collection and the exploitation of corvée labor. But since St. Blasien began centralizing its seigneurial administration into *Ämter* during the late fourteenth century, manors gradually disappeared except as record-keeping anachronisms. Increasingly, villages displaced manors as the basic organizational units of quitrent-collection, as carriers collected from contributors in their own villages. But manors and villages were not coterminous—the village of Dogern, for example, contained lands attached to four different abbatial manors within its boundaries.[85] One practical result of St. Blasien's efforts to centralize the administration of its seigneuries, therefore, was severe administrative confusion at the village level. Small wonder that St. Blasien was so concerned to assert a right to arbitrate property exchanges. In sum, then, bureaucratic centralization enhanced abbatial reliance on its peasant agents, but because village politics constrained carriers no less than other peasants, village

83. GLA 66:7296, "Zinsrodel deß Waldamts," 1709, and GLA 66:7326, "Berein," 1731.
84. GLA 227:71, Abbatial Schaffner to St. Blasien, 8 February 1728.
85. GLA 229:19644, "Specification was, und wohin jedes Ort in der Dogemer Einung ihren Bodenzinß an Früchten, und Geld jährlich zu lüferen seye," [18th cent.].

politics indirectly constrained St. Blasien, too. The upshot is that, as Thomas Robisheaux has argued, "village society itself left its imprint on the practice of ... power almost as much as the state shaped the village."[86]

Conclusions

How does any of this compare with circumstances elsewhere in the Holy Roman Empire, and what does it tell us about the formation of factions during the Salpeter Wars? With respect to the first question, I have already suggested that unequal reciprocities and interdependencies were inherent in the structure of domination under the pre-Revolutionary social and political order. But so broad a generalization still leaves plenty of room for local variation in the balance of power and dependence between lords and subjects. What was the norm, and was Hauenstein typical?

To begin with, St. Blasien was an unusually powerful lord within the Habsburg lands and had a reputation for harshness with its subjects.[87] The abbey was easily the wealthiest ecclesiastical estate in Outer Austria and compared favorably with the incomes of other monasteries and convents in the Crown Lands. According to a survey taken in 1781, the average revenue of religious houses in Lower Austria was 10,644 gulden, which St. Blasien exceeded seven-fold, if Friedrich Nicolai's estimate of 80,000 gulden can be believed. Setting aside the fabulously wealthy Bohemian magnates, it is safe to say that the abbey enjoyed wealth on a par with the best-endowed barons in the Crown Lands. Moreover, the abbot's claim to certain "sovereign" rights over the *Zwing und Bann*, his prerogatives as count of Bonndorf, and his pretensions to the status of imperial prince were uncommon and made for long-winded bickering with the imperial chancellery in Vienna.[88] Only a few other ecclesiastical corporations in the Habsburg territories could lay claim to status so lofty, and the abbey's wealth made it a formidable opponent.

---

86. Thomas Robisheaux, *Rural Society and the Search for Order in Early Modern Germany* (Cambridge, 1989), 258.

87. As Eberhard Gothein once remarked, the abbots "were in no way indulgent lords"; "Der Breisgau unter Maria Theresia und Joseph II," *NBHK* 10 (1907): 7.

88. See Josef P. Ortner, *Marquard Herrgott (1694–1762): Sein Leben und Wirken als Historiker und Diplomat* (Vienna, 1972), 46–47.

Nevertheless, the interposition of St. Blasien's patrimonial authorities between peasants and the state was altogether commonplace. Unlike the large number of medium-sized German principalities such as nearby Württemberg, which over the centuries had managed to eliminate the indigenous territorial nobility, the vast Habsburg domains all contained large landed aristocracies, both secular and ecclesiastical. In a 1762 census, for instance, the archduchy of Austria showed a combined total of 5,327 male nobles (although this included sons and *parvenus*); according to a 1759 tax assessment, the province of Styria alone had 1 prince, 100 counts and countesses, 51 barons and baronesses *(Freiherren* and *Freiinnen)*, 10 gentry *(edle Herren)*, and 49 persons bearing the noble predicate "von," a total of 213 lay nobles, male and female.[89] In the diet of the relatively tiny province of Outer Austria, the prelacy had 18 members and the nobility 35.[90]

With so large a landed aristocracy, it was commonplace for state authorities to mediate conflicts between seigneurs and peasants, and when the former were as powerful as St. Blasien, the state often pursued decidedly "peasant-friendly" policies. In the early stages of the Salpeter Wars, even the Court Chancellery in Vienna was ill disposed toward St. Blasien. More broadly, the Austrian state afforded ample opportunity for peasants to petition against seigneurs, opportunities they used heavily; by the eighteenth century, a whole industry had grown up around the business of litigating the grievances of peasants against their seigneurs in Vienna and the provincial capitals. The trend toward a "peasant-friendly" stance only increased with the reforms of Maria Theresa and reached its apogee with the 1781 "Decree on Subjects" *(Untertanenpatent)* of Emperor Joseph II. On balance, then, the stance of state officials was determined more by the subjects and objects of peasant unrest, rather than by the fact of unrest itself, and in this respect, the Salpeter Wars were unexceptional.

Most of the specific terms of abbatial domination were conventional, too. It is notoriously difficult to assess the weight of seigneurial dues and services, but if the near complete absence of complaints about them is any indication, they were not perceived as particularly burdensome. Nor were St. Blasien's patrimonial jurisdictions unusual, even if the abbey

---

89. Dickson, *Finance and Government*, 1:43, Table 5.12, 1:101, and Table 3.2, 1:444–445.
90. P. Blickle, *Landschaften*, 132.

strove to attach some "sovereign" status to them: though lacking in Württemberg and elsewhere, patrimonial jurisdiction flourished in Habsburg lands just as its aristocracy did. Most of these courts judged only lesser civil suits, as St. Blasien's did, although some had the power of life and death in criminal cases until the legal reforms of Empress Maria Theresa (the so-called *Nemesis Theresiana*) subjected them to sovereign judicial review in 1768.[91]

With respect to serfdom, St. Blasien's rules governing "baser hand" heritability were, to be sure, out of the ordinary and generated unusual animosity between St. Blasien, serfs, and other serf lords. In particular, "double serfdom" caused the contradictory demands of competing serf lords to clash, and the need to avoid such conflicts resulted in periodic exchanges of serfs. Such trades occurred in Hauenstein on at least thirteen occasions between 1325 and 1728, on average once a generation.[92] Moreover, these exchanges were the source of considerable dissatisfaction among serfs who were traded into the hands of stricter lords.[93] But otherwise the material obligations and legal disabilities of abbatial servitude were not exceptional. In Hauenstein as in most other lordships, the regular dues of serfdom ("shrove chickens" and corvées converted to cash payments) were slight, only a few coins per year. *Mainmortes* rarely exceeded 5 percent of the assessed value of an inheritance, in Hauenstein or anywhere else.[94]

What, then, of the wide-ranging political powers that Hauenstein's peasants enjoyed? Thanks to the exhaustive researches of Peter Blickle, we now know that the late medieval and early modern laws and customs *(Landrechte)* of several principalities, including a few Habsburg provinces, enabled peasants to participate in public administration throughout a region extending from the Black Forest across the northern Alpine foot-

91. Edith Murr Link, *The Emancipation of the Austrian Peasant, 1740–1798* (New York, 1949), 18; on private jurisdiction in Bohemia, see William Wright, *Serf, Seigneur and Sovereign: Agrarian Reform in Eighteenth-Century Bohemia* (Minneapolis, 1966), 14–15.
92. See GLA 96:458, "Memoriale nacher St Blasien," 2 November 1718.
93. See, for instance, the case of Bläsi Hottinger of Niedergebisbach, whose ancestors had been traded to St. Blasien in the seventeenth century; GLA 113:108, "Ungefehrlicher Auffsatz worin ds abgetauschte einsidtlerische Geschlecht sich beschweret befinde," n.d..
94. See Werner Troßbach, "'Südwestdeutsche Leibeigenschaft' in der frühen Neuzeit: eine Bagatelle?" *GG* 7 (1981): 81–83, and Claudia Ulbrich, "Freiheit und Eigenschaft in spätmittelalterlichen ländlichen Rechtsquellen des Oberrheins," in Peter Blickle, ed., *Deutsche Ländliche Rechtsquellen: Probleme und Wege der Weistumsforschung* (Stuttgart, 1977), 187–91.

hills of the Allgäu to Tyrol and Salzburg. Just to the west of Hauenstein, for example, in the lordship of Rötteln-Sausenberg (an appendage of the margraviate of Baden-Durlach), *any* subject had the right to attend territorial diets, although for convenience' sake delegates were elected from each of four military districts. Similarly in the imperial abbey of Kempten, the territorial diet consisted only of peasant delegates, elected by a patchwork of districts, parishes *(Kirchenpatronate)*, and village communes. From 1732 on, it comprised seven committees *(Ausschüsse)* consisting of ten communally elected delegates each, which voted tax levies and exerted pressure on the abbey in matters relating to fiscal and social policy. Subjects of Toggenburg, a Swiss county belonging to the great Benedictine abbey of St. Gallen, formed a defensive union in 1436 that remained the basis for the political representation of peasants until the late 1700s. Territorial assemblies comprising every adult male can be dated to 1683, and after 1718, a council of communally elected delegates met annually to deliberate issues in the common interest. At various times and to varying degrees, peasants enjoyed forms of electoral representation in the territorial diets of Württemberg, the margraviates of Baden-Baden and Baden-Durlach, the imperial city of Rottweil, the abbeys of Ochsenhausen and Schüssenried, most Swiss cantons, Rötteln-Sausenburg, Outer Austria, Vorarlberg, Tyrol, and the Habsburg possessions in Upper Swabia, Kempten, the provostry of Berchtesgaden, and the archbishopric of Salzburg, and in the territories of a host of Swabian imperial knights and religious houses. For all their structural idiosyncracies, these political formations played important roles in fiscal administration, and many had more functions even than that.[95]

In most of these cases, representatives were drawn from the rural political elite of bailiffs, village headmen, and other magistrates, just as in Hauenstein. For instance, the majority of peasant delegates to the diet of Baden-Baden were officeholders, while 50 to 75 percent of the representatives in Kempten were large-scale farmers. For the purposes of comparison, the crucial question is: how were these magistrates chosen? Apart from plenary assemblies of all male subjects, most diets consisted of magistrates serving *ex officio,* as was the case in Hauenstein. The answer, therefore, depends in part on how officeholders were selected. It is likely that

---

95. P. Blickle, *Landschaften,* passim.

procedures as diverse as these institutions were idiosyncratic, but if Toggenburg is any indication, the degree of popular involvement was considerable. There, several villages had the right to choose four candidates for district headman *(Amtmann)*, from whom the abbot of St. Gallen chose one. According to Blickle, the balance of evidence suggests that nomination by election was the norm.

To be sure, such elections were rarely as "democratic," or the authorities of peasant magistrates as wide-ranging, as in Hauenstein. In several other Outer Austrian lordships, for example, peasant delegates to the territorial diet were chosen by village elders, not by majority vote of all electors; however, these comparisons suggest that the difference was one of degree, not kind, and although the zone in which such forms of representation occurred was relatively small, Hauenstein's institutional structure not exceptional within it. All of them imparted a high measure of political experience to ordinary peasants; the whole zone was populated by people accustomed to choosing their own leaders, disputing which candidates might serve them best, and holding them to account. All this compounded a phenomenon that historians of early modern Germany have recognized for some time already, namely that nowhere were the forms and functions of domination wholly beyond question.[96]

These patterns suggest some of the ways in which the complex interplay of forces between peasant, seigneur, and sovereign affected the growth of factions during the Salpeter Wars. As brokers between lord and subject, peasant magistrates, for example, were "amphibians" in the institutional taxonomy of early modern Germany. Of course, a deep social chasm separated rulers from ruled: no peasant, even an Octovir, could realistically aspire to noble status, just as no lord or bureaucrat could hope for genuine acceptance among peasants. The social divide made oppressors like the abbot easy to identify. But in political terms, the location of the Eight and bailiffs was harder to define. Whom did they serve?

In fact they served *both* lord *and* subject. While administration was impossible without them, the Eight also amounted to a standing resistance committee. Certainly, bonds of dependence and mutual interest tied abbatial bailiffs and other functionaries to St. Blasien, St. Frido-

---

96. Winfried Schulze, *Bäuerlicher Widerstand und feudale Herrschaft in der frühen Neuzeit* (Bad Canstatt, 1980), 115–27.

lin, or the Forest Steward. But these ties were not incompatible with the Octovirs' role as the embodiment of peasant self-rule. Such ambiguities exposed all officeholders to the same pressure to legitimate their actions that seigneurs experienced. Some of the popular fear about oligarchy can be reduced to a generalized suspicion that the officeholders' loyalties could at any time tip in favor of seigneurs. This circumstantial reality made it imperative that officeholders manage popular perceptions in such a way that their behavior remained both intelligible and acceptable within the terms of their electors' experience.[97] The advent of rebellion only enhanced this need to control public opinion carefully. *Salpeterisch* leaders proved adept at this, while *müllerisch* Octovirs often failed dismally. Nevertheless, both factions continued to rely on the legitimating effect of elections to sustain their ability to make claims against the obedience of ordinary peasants. Perhaps this explains why the *de facto* ban on elections in 1745 transpired against the explicit wishes even of haughtier *müllerisch* Octovirs like Josef Tröndle of Birndorf Canton.

For these reasons, the Octovirs' function as a defense against intrusions into peasant affairs was easily the most compelling of their various roles. As the events of the Salpeter Wars would show time and again, a population trained by electoral custom in the ways and means of public political discourse could be counted on to make its wishes felt. By the same token, Hauenstein's electoral customs nurtured the growth of a political elite that was reasonably familiar with the Austrian bureaucratic hierarchy and aware of the multiple possibilities available to peasants for the redress of their grievances. However much they disputed the sources and solutions of Hauenstein's malaise, the fact remains that Octovirs on both sides of the factional divide continued to promote the common good, as they saw it, with the tools they thought best adapted to the task. Arguably, it was the ambiguity of their position, with one foot in the world of state bureaucrats and seigneurial officers, the other foot squarely in the everyday world of peasant life, that made them such effective politicians, in their dealings both with seigneurs andsovereigns and against one another.

97. See Anthony P. Cohen and John L. Comaroff, "The Management of Meaning: On the Phenomenology of Political Transactions," in Bruce Kapferer, ed., *Transaction and Meaning: Directions in the Anthropology of Exchange and Symbolic Behavior* (Philadelphia, 1976), 87–107.

CHAPTER 2

Uncivil War

A Chronicle of the Revolt

> They stole our horses,
> And deceived almighty God,
> Get out, get out, scoundrels! Get out!
>
> They stole our butter,
> And brought in their great lords,
> Get out, get out, scoundrels! Get out!
> *Salpeterisch* jingle, ca. 1745

THE PROXIMATE CAUSE OF CIVIL STRIFE IN HAUENSTEIN WAS A quarrel among members of a peasant elite over the most effective defense against St. Blasien's campaign to expand its age-old powers of domination in the county. For several reasons, it escalated into factional strife as positions hardened, animosities deepened, and as ever-larger numbers of ordinary peasants were drawn into the controversy. For its part, the abbey of St. Blasien adopted an increasingly harder line, while the Habsburg state played peasant against seigneur and turned peasant against peasant. As if to muddle the lines of confrontation even more, each faction sought in its own way to do the same, pitting the state against the abbey. Finally, both factions attempted to enlist the state against *each other*. The particular characteristics of each phase in the Salpeter Wars unfolded from this ever-changing, four-way scramble to seize the initiative and maximize advantage. Thus the Salpeter Wars were no irrational outburst of peasant rage, but an obscure ballet of alliances and hostilities performed by many skilled and calculating dancers.

But what were its long-term political causes? How did the Salpeter Wars emerge from the institutional structures and power relations described in Chapter 1? Was factionalism the inevitable symptom of a political organism that so broadly engaged peasants both in self-governance and in the process of their own domination? This chapter shows how factional strife flowed from the complex roles played by officeholders in Hauenstein and suggests some of the ways that these patterns compared with broader transformations in the character of agrarian revolt in central Europe. Superficially at least, the question of comparisons is easiest to answer: like most peasant rebellions in early modern Germany, the Salpeter Wars were the latest in a long chain of antiseigneurial conflicts that spanned several centuries and were carried out by various means, some violent, others not.

To show this it is necessary to go beyond the institutional analysis in Chapter 1 to describe how peasant elites actually behaved during the critical period between 1719 and 1728, when profound disagreements over proper defenses against St. Blasien took form. In part, these disputes reflected the development of two concepts of order within the peasant elite: one that understood the legitimacy of power relations in legalistic terms, and another that defined legitimacy in "traditional" terms of mutual obligation between sovereign and subject. As factions coalesced around these tactical and ideological poles, both Hauenstein's electoral custom and the equivocal stance of the Austrian state toward St. Blasien exerted decisive influences: a population habituated to expressing its opinions in the choice of magistrates sided initially with "Salpeter-Hans" Albiez against his principal rival, the miller Joseph Tröndle of Unteralpfen. Meanwhile, the diplomatic exertions of both Albiez and the abbey provoked the intervention of the imperial Habsburg Court Chancellery in Vienna, which opted both to thwart St. Blasien's expansionist designs and to suppress the *salpeterisch* movement. Even in its incipient phases, then, the uprising was not simply a binary conflict between lords and subjects but a complex transaction among many participants.

One effect of all this politicking was to bring about a *müllerisch* ascendancy imposed by Austrian authorities from 1728 to 1737. But even Austrian intervention was unable to restore order without exacerbating factional strife. Specifically, the punishment of "rebellious" peasants served to deepen and perpetuate factional enmities; more important, such interventions exposed the ongoing dependence of domination

(Herrschaft) both on the cooperation of peasant officeholders and on the successful maintainance of political unanimity within peasant communes. Factional animosities, then, were symptomatic of the transition from a system of rule with peasants to one of rule over them.

These enmities again boiled over between 1737 and 1745. Because in part of the disruptions attending of the wars of Polish and Austrian succession, it took two Austrian military interventions to put down a *salpeterisch* resurgence, interventions that no more simplified lines of confrontation between peasant, seigneur, and sovereign than earlier ones had. In the first place, a 1738 manumission of all abbatial serfs diminished St. Blasien's role in the whole affair, which only enhanced the rebellion's factional aspect. Second, *salpeterisch* leaders were able in early 1745 to persuade authorities in Innsbruck that theirs was a patriotic, pro-Austrian rising against a Franco-Bavarian occupation of Outer Austria. Briefly and unwittingly, the Habsburg state supported a brutal campaign of *salpeterisch* retribution against *müllerisch* peasants. By 1745, factional identities were so deeply ingrained in the political culture of Hauenstein that the Austrian state could suppress the conflict only by turning factional hostility to the service of military repression and authoritarian reform. It is tragically fitting that a principal casualty of factionalism was the custom of free peasant elections.

A Rebellious Tradition

At the time, provincial bureaucrats tended to view the unrest in stereotypical, psychopathological terms that belittled peasant mentality as inherently ignorant, perverse, and obstinant. Soon after Austrian arms had effectively ended the Salpeter Wars, for example, one official observer dreamt up a cyclical theory to explain Hauenstein's long history of intermittent political turmoil.[1] Every century or so, he reasoned, the peasants of Hauenstein vented their "rebellious spirit" *(Unruchs-Geist)* against the House of Habsburg. And sure enough: Hauensteiners had

---

1. The author was probably the Outer Austrian provincial president, Anton Thaddäus von Sumerau; GLA 65:11223, 1r–57v, "Summarischer Außzug deren in Annis 1525, 1612, 1626, 1728, 1729, 1744 undt 1745 in der Graffschafft Hawenstein vorgeganene Landtsunruehen, Auffstandt u[nd] Empörung gegen u[nd] wider allergnädige Herrschafft zue Österreich," [ca. 1751].

joined in the German Peasants' War of 1525; about a century later, in 1612–14, their agitations against a new tax had ignited the "War of the Penny," an uprising that eventually spread to several districts in Outer Austria.[2] With the Salpeter Wars in 1725, they had rebelled once more.

Although his interpretation fundamentally misread the causes and objects of unrest in Hauenstein, the analyst was certainly correct to note Hauenstein's long tradition of resistance. As Chapter 1 indicated already, the canton system originated as a defensive alliance against the extension of abbatial serfdom and the authority of the courts St. Blasien had acquired in the 1270s. Long before the Peasants' War of 1524–25, then, the county had disputed many of the abbey's seigneurial powers.[3] Such struggles were often attended by violence, as in 1369–71 and 1412, when peasants plundered St. Blasien.[4] After an abortive attempt to regulate them in 1522, these conflicts over jurisdiction and serfdom added fuel to the fires of unrest that swept across southwestern Germany in 1524–25.[5] In January of 1525, Hauenstein added its grievances to those of the confederation of Black Forest peasants.[6] As before, these protests soon took a violent turn: on 27 April 1525, a militia of some five hundred peasants invaded the abbey, smashed its sacred images, and robbed its stores of food, drink, and clothing.[7]

After a summer of antifeudal experiments, the great uprising was crushed, and in November 1525, Hauenstein laid down its arms.[8] Although the Peasants' War had altered the formal relationship between

2. On the "War of the Penny," see Peter Steuer, "Der vorderösterreichische Rappenkrieg (1612–1614)," *ZGO* 128 (1980): 119–65.
3. In 1370, for instance, Hauenstein put up two thousand gulden to purchase certain juridical authorities which the abbey had leased from the Habsburg crown; Claudia Ulbrich, *Leibherrschaft am Oberrhein im Spätmittelalter* (Göttingen, 1979), 60–65.
4. Karl F. Wernet, "St Blasiens Versuche, sich der Grafschaft Hauenstein pfandweise zu bemächtigen," *ZGO* 107 (1959): 170–72.
5. See GLA 67:1816, 75r–79v; excerpted in Josef Bader, ed., "Das Stift St Blasien und seine hauensteinischen Unterthanen," *ZGO* 7 (1856): 114–19. On the Peasants' War in Hauenstein, see Tom Scott, "Reformation and Peasants' War in Waldshut and Environs: A Structural Analysis," *ARG* 69 (1978): 82–102; 70 (1979): 140–68.
6. "Die Beschwerden der Grafschaft Hauenstein und der Täler Schönau und Todtnau gegen den Abt zu St Blasien [January 1525]," in Günther Franz, ed., *Quellen zur Geschichte des Bauernkrieges* (Munich, 1963), 98–101, no. 24, §§1–2, 5.
7. For narratives of these occupations, see "Chronik des Andreas Letsch" and "Stiftungsbuch von S. Blasien, vom Abte Caspar I. von 1323 bis 1571," in Franz J. Mone, ed., *Quellensammlung der badischen Landesgeschichte* (Karlsruhe, 1854), 2:47, 48, and 2:61–64.
8. GLA 67:1809, 198r–204v [Terms of Surrender], 13 November 1525.

Hauenstein and St. Blasien very little, in three key respects, its consequences set the tone for their future interaction. First, the county remained largely free of violent outbursts after 1525, in part because German princes subsequently widened avenues for the orderly redress of peasant grievances in order to prevent a recurrence of conflagrations on so grand a scale. These reforms had the effect of transforming conflicts between lords and peasants into legal disputes, defusing and localizing them in the process.[9] Archduke Ferdinand's speedy restoration of Hauenstein's corporate privileges in 1527 reflected this same desire to find a more proactive approach to social tensions in the countryside.[10] Second, Hauensteiners preserved the memory of 1525, just as other German peasants did. For some, this legacy was negative; one *müllerisch* leader publicly warned his fellow countrymen that a repeat of 1525 might result if the arrogance of the rebel agitators were not checked.[11] But for others, the Peasants' War remained an object lesson in the possibilities of militant collective action.

Finally, several long-winded litigations following the Peasants' War established the terms of political discourse during the Salpeter Wars. Although these conflicts touched on virtually every aspect of peasant-lord relations, controversy focused on the extent of St. Blasien's right to command the obedience of people who lived within the territory of its lower courts inside the county and on the character of material obligations and legal disabilities associated with abbatial serfdom. But this seeming preoccupation should not distract from the real issue at stake. Jurisdiction and serfdom were, to some extent, metaphors for a more profound question: would St. Blasien succeed in annexing Hauenstein, or would the county remain free?

The abbey's repeated attempts to lease sovereign jurisdiction over the *Zwing und Bann*—that area immediately surrounding the abbey, just north of Hauenstein—provided the occasion for most altercations with the county. Between 1596 and 1705, St. Blasien obtained five such leases,

---

9. Winfried Schulze, "Die veränderte Bedeutung sozialer Konflikte im 16. und 17. Jahrhundert," in Hans-Ulrich Wehler, ed., *Der Deutsche Bauernkrieg 1524–1526* (Göttingen, 1976), 277–302.

10. GLA 67:644, "Hauensteinische Landtsordnung, Freyheit und Begnadigungsbriefe de ao 1517, 1527, 1530, 1542, 1563"; Wernet, "St Blasiens Versuche," 163.

11. GLA 113:221, 503r–v, [Joseph Tröndle von Rotzel], "Notanta."

and each sparked indignation among the peasantry.[12] The principle reason for this was that each lease contract also regulated both the competence of St. Blasien's jurisdictions inside Hauenstein and the obligations of abbatial serfs. Hauensteiners were right to fear that St. Blasien might use the contracts to subject the entire county to its rule: between 1541 and 1574, Abbots Caspar I and Caspar II had attempted to annex Hauenstein outright.[13] Moreover, the sequence of leases coincided with St. Blasien's gradual removal of decision-making authority from local jurors to higher courts. Understandably, peasants feared losses of territory and autonomy.

Of course, St. Blasien's success in obtaining new leases depended partly on the balance of its power relative to the Eight, the Forest Steward, and the Austrian government. Until about 1670, the Forest Steward's powers were ascendant, which inhibited St. Blasien's policy of encroachment.[14] But the effects of chronic state deficits proved a weightier influence and ultimately, the promise of substantial payments for leased authorities persuaded the Habsburg government in every instance.[15] In 1655, the debt-burdened Austrian government granted St. Blasien a sixty-year lease in return for a payment of 48,000 gulden; similar pressures favored the abbey as the old lease neared its term, when the War of Spanish Succession was stretching Austrian finances once again. St. Blasien seized this opportunity to bargain for an "eternal perpetuation" *(Verewigung)* of its lease.[16]

This move sparked conflicts that would lead eventually to the Salpeter Wars. As any peasant knew, a perpetual lease was tantamount to outright ownership; the "eternal perpetuation" therefore threatened to destroy Hauenstein's institutional integrity. To combat it, the Eight lodged a grievance and withheld homage from Abbot Augustine Fink

---

12. For a narrative of these conflicts, see Wernet, "St Blasiens Versuche," passim.

13. Ibid., 164–72.

14. Ibid., 176–79; Günther Haselier, *Die Streitigkeiten der Hauensteiner mit ihren Obrigkeiten: Ein Beitrag zur Geschichte Vorderösterreichs und des südwestdeutschen Bauernstandes im 18. Jahrhundert* (Karlsruhe, 1940), 42.

15. Wernet, "St Blasiens Versuche," 179–81. On the financial situation, see Jean Bérenger, *Finances et absolutisme autrichien dans la seconde moitié du XVIIème siècle* (Lille, 1975), 1:88–151.

16. Wernet, "St Blasiens Versuche," 180. For the text of the 1655 lease, see GLA 67:644, 140r–56v; excerpted in J. Bader, ed., "Urkundenregeste über die ehemaligen sankt-blasischen Niedergerichte," *ZGO* 7 (1856): 253 (for the 1705 "eternalization," see 329).

in 1698, pending the outcome of their dispute.[17] When that tactic failed, an embassy was sent to Vienna in 1704 headed by a former Octovir, Adam Tröndle of Unteralpfen. At court, Adam Tröndle and his associates sought imperial confirmation of Hauenstein's corporate privileges, promises that the county would never be alienated from Habsburg rule, and the abolition of servile nomenclature in the homage oaths of abbatial bondsmen.[18] In the end, however, the abbey prevailed: on 1 October 1705, Emperor Joseph I renewed the lease in perpetuity in return for a "subsidy" of 24,000 gulden.[19] The treaty also confirmed St. Blasien's juridical powers within the county, thereby fixing the jurisdictional relationship between Hauenstein and the abbey for the next half-century.

Emperor Joseph's "perpetuation" decree settled the matter of jurisdiction, but only sharpened disagreements among peasants about definitions of right order. Here, the touchstone of this discord was serfdom, and to understand why, it is necessary to step back to the mid-seventeenth century, when St. Blasien introduced a new nomenclature for its bondsmen. Until that time, St. Blasien had described serfdom under the rubric of *Eigenschaft*, a term with late medieval roots.[20] During the Thirty Years' War, however, abbatial pronouncements introduced a new label, which included the prefix *Leib-* ("body" or "belly"). Thus *Eigenschaft* became *Leibeigenschaft*. It is unclear whether the monks hoped to use this new designation to further weaken the position of serfs, and the matter may simply have been one of administrative fashion. Either way, the addition of *Leib-* to *Eigenschaft* underscored the hereditary quality of unfreedom, the corporeality of bondage, and the symbolic connection between servile dues and the abbey's legal dominion over the physical person of each serf.

---

17. On the homage controversy of 1698–1701, see Haselier, *Streitigkeiten*, 43–52, and Wernet, "St Blasiens Versuche," 182.

18. See GLA 67:1809, 323–89, Abbot Augustine Fink to [Leopold I?], [1704?], which enumerates the peasants' grievances; 414–20, which contains an account by Joseph Tröndle of Unteralpfen of the 1704 deputation, written in 1723; and finally 422–27, an account of the deputation written by Adam Tröndle of Unteralpfen.

19. See Bader, ed., "Urkundenregeste," 329 (Emperor Charles confirmed the "perpetuation" with a decree of 19 July 1715), 330, and Wernet, "St Blasiens Versuche," 182.

20. To be sure, this term also had a late medieval antecedent in the phrase *aigen von dem lîpe*. Claudia Ulbrich notes that in the late Middle Ages St. Blasien employed a great variety of terms to describe conditions of dependence, none of them precisely; among the adjectival forms of servile nomenclature were *bläsiseigen* and *gotteshauseigen;* a male serf might also be called a *Gotteshausmann*. See Ulbrich, *Leibherrschaft*, 31–33.

By a logic of synecdoche, many peasants linked the change in terminology with St. Blasien's designs on Hauenstein. To fight it, they developed a belief that their county was inherently free, a historic and privileged condition that was incompatible with the presence of abbatial serfs within its borders. Around 1660, Hauensteiners began affixing pejorative meanings to servile labels; in September 1664, for example, nearly all abbatial subjects refused homage to Abbot Otto III Chübler, insisting that they were "not serfs of St. Blasien."[21] Similarly at homage ceremonies for Abbot Romanus Vogler in 1673, they claimed that servility "could not forcibly be derived" from the obligation to pay dues and services conventionally associated with serfdom; again in 1698, Hauensteiners objected to what they perceived as St. Blasien's attempt to drag the county from its condition of "inherited freedom" into a "hitherto unheard-of serfdom."[22] Most peasants seemed to believe that the new terms concealed a reduction of their collective status to that of slaves; abbatial officials insisted in vain that *Leibeigenschaft* was not instituted, "as the peasants assume, so that a slavery such as exists in Bohemia and elsewhere might arise" in Hauenstein.[23] Shortly before his death, however, Emperor Leopold in 1704 erased this "intolerable nomenclature," instructing St. Blasien to use the original term *(Eigenschaft),* but left all servile obligations and legal disabilities intact.[24] The material impact of his decree, therefore, was nil.

There is sound reason to dwell on these seemingly arcane distinctions, because Leopold's decision also sowed the seeds of ideological dissension. The heavy cost of Adam Tröndle's 1704 delegation could be justified only if the distinction between *Leibeigenschaft* and *Eigenschaft* was meaningful, but to accept that difference was to acknowledge the historic validity of St. Blasien's powers as a serf lord *(Leibherr).* Many Hauensteiners were unwilling to do this and instead took Leopold's

---

21. GLA 113:77 and GLA 229:9138; see also Wernet, "St Blasiens Versuche."
22. GLA 99:458, nr. 2, "Rationes rusticorum warumb sye nit leibeigen sein wollen," 25 February 1673; GLA 113:455, "Extract einer kayl. Lantsfürstl. Commission von sämbtl. V.Ö. Lantsständten übergebenen Gravaminen ao 1698."
23. GLA 113:226, 97r–102v, "Copia Extractus prothocolli über die von Abbate Augustino eingenohmene Huldigung," 13 June 1701.
24. GLA 11:71, 16 August 1704; Bader, ed., "Urkundenregeste," 328–29. Emperor Joseph I ratified Leopold's decree on 15 April 1705 (GLA 67:1809, 528–29) and Hauenstein's privileges on 3 February 1706 (GLA 21:215).

decree to abolish not only certain servile *labels,* but servile *status* in general. His decree, therefore, opened a rift between those who did and did not accept the basic legitimacy of servitude. Later on, the Adam Tröndle's 1704 embassy provided *salpeterisch* peasants with the earliest evidence of an Octovirs' plot to sell Hauenstein "into eternal serfdom."[25]

The Factions Form (1719–1728)

For reasons that are not entirely clear, peasant dissension lay dormant until about 1719. During the period that followed, renewed conflict with St. Blasien exposed widespread dissatisfaction both with the treaties that governed Hauenstein's relations with the abbey and with the policies of the Eight. As the previous chapter showed, St. Blasien had exploited the return of peace in 1714 to consolidate its powers in Hauenstein. This restoration took three forms. First, the abbot and his agents sought and received confirmation of the "eternal perpetuation" from Emperor Charles VI in 1715.[26] A second move was to hold a session of the serf court *(Dinggericht)* at Remetschwiel on 4 May 1719, where abbatial serfs would be reminded of their obligations to the abbey. The third was a census in 1725 of all abbatial serfs residing in the county.

Each of these moves heightened tensions between St. Blasien and Hauenstein. For the most part, the pattern of conflict developed along familiar lines, with the important difference that now, Octovir policy sparked dissension among the peasantry. At the 1719 court session at Remetschwiel, for example, a group of five Octovirs allied with Adam Tröndle's son Joseph, the miller of Unteralpfen, committed what were soon afterwards interpreted as crimes of *müllerisch* treason. The abbatial serfs, represented by the Eight, objected to new and higher levels of subpoena fines in abbatial courts, the monetized value of shrove chickens, and several technical points in the law of serfdom. The abbot's representative conceded nothing, so the Octovirs appealed his verdict to the next highest court—the chancellery in St. Blasien.[27] This appeal,

25. GLA 113:99, 1r–2v.
26. GLA 67:644, 213r–22v, "Kayser Karl des Sechsten Vierte Pfandtshandlung ddo Wien den 19. July 1715"; excerpted in Bader, ed., "Urkundenregeste," 330.
27. GLA 229:5658, "Bericht aus dem Archiv gezogen, über ds Dinggericht zue Rometschwil," n.d., and "Actum Römetschwyl den 4ten May 1719."

however, recognized the abbot's competence to judge the case, in conformity with the terms of St. Blasien's much-disputed lease "perpetuation" of 1705. But a group of eleven incumbent and retired Octovirs led by "Salpeter-Hans" Albiez objected that the appeal compromised imperial jurisdiction over Hauenstein; as Albiez's colleague Friedle Hottinger later wrote, Joseph Tröndle and his cohorts had violated their sacred oath of office to protect "the interest of the county," acted against the will of the "Whole County," and abrogated customs and freedoms which "seven emperors had . . . donated and confirmed."[28] Thus while Tröndle followed the letter of laws and treaties, Hottinger spoke of ancient traditions and broken promises. Both were concerned to thwart the abbey, but in ways that seemed increasingly incompatible.

Interpretations of another event at Remetschwiel exposed the depth of disagreement over concepts of legitimate order. During the proceedings, an abbatial scribe had recited the text of the 1467 charter of servile obligations, but neglected to omit the prefix *leib-* from his reading. Another abbatial official quickly conceded that Leopold had indeed abolished the term *Leibeigenschaft* and replaced it with *Eigenschaft*, but added that "it is all the same to the abbot."[29] *Salpeterisch* and *müllerisch* peasants later ascribed vastly different meanings to this remark. The legalistically minded Joseph Tröndle of Unteralpfen later wrote that the abbot had meant only that he "does not care how one labels [servile status], if only the subjects deliver the dues they owe to the . . . monastery."[30] Albiez, on the other hand, confessed that in his opinion, the statement amounted to an admission that *both* designations equally burdened Hauensteiners with the "intolerable nomenclature" of serfdom.[31] In the wake of this event, all consensus collapsed: rumors spread that the "abbot-lover" Joseph Tröndle and others had "sold the county and

28. GLA 113:244, 14r–15v [Open Letter of Friedle Hottinger of Niedergebisbach, ca. 1730]; see also GLA 99:983, "Copia was Hans Fritlin Albüöz der sogenante Salbeter dn 6 Jener 1727 in dem löbl. Regemenz-Haus Freyburg, den Adam Schmitlin Müller von Nitermühle für ein Schreiben . . . hinaugeben hat," §1.

29. Joseph Tröndle of Unteralpfen, "Grundlicher Bericht von dem in der Gravschaft Hauwenstein entstandenen Unruhhandel von 1720 bis 1730," reprinted in Josef Bader, *Briefe über das badische Oberland* (Freiburg, 1833), 88.

30. Ibid.

31. GLA 113:224, 3r–6v, Interrogation of Hans Friedle Albiez of Buch, Freiburg, 22–26 October 1726, and GLA 99:983, "Copia was Hans Fritlin Albüöz der sogenante Salbeter dn 6 Jener 1727 zuo Freyburg für ein Schreiben . . . hinausgeben."

made everyone into a serf, for which they received . . . silver goblets filled with gold."[32]

Clearly, Tröndle and his fellow Octovirs were in grave danger of losing public confidence as brokers between lord and subject. They had failed to present themselves as lacking self-interest in their dealings with dominant powers outside the polity, an essential challenge in any political system based on popular election. Albiez, by contrast, had succeeded in presenting his actions in altruistic terms with which peasants could identify.[33] This placed Tröndle's party in a difficult position: on the one hand, any alternative to his policy of litigating through officially sanctioned channels bore the risk of a military confrontation from which Hauenstein could not emerge the winner. On the other hand, criticism against their legalistic policies continued to multiply.[34] The Eight pressed on all the same. In 1720, they tried to resolve disputes with St. Blasien in the so-called Accord of Dogern, a treaty that fixed the monetized value of shrove chickens and lessened the severity of death duties levied against unmarried male serfs. But the Eight failed to gain any concessions from St. Blasien on subpoena rates or on the abbey's claim to own its lower courts outright.[35] Predictably, the Dogern Accord failed to assuage Albiez and his followers.[36] Discontent with Joseph Tröndle's camp was manifested in the April elections of 1725, which returned Albiez and a number of his followers to public office.

The abbot's third measure to reassert his powers—a census of all his hereditary serfs—transformed Albiez's dissidence into a full-blown political movement. From January to March 1725, abbatial agents went

32. GLA 99:979, Interrogation of Abbatial Bailiff Lorenz Baumgartner of Niederwihl, 31 August 1726. Joseph Tröndle recorded the epithet "abbot-lover" in a letter to the abbatial High Steward in Gurtweil; GLA 99:975, Tröndle to Obervogteiamt, 18 October 1728.

33. See Anthony P. Cohen and John L. Comaroff, "The Management of Meaning: On the Phenomenology of Political Transactions," in Bruce Kapferer, ed., *Transaction and Meaning: Directions in the Anthropology of Exchange and Symbolic Behavior* (Philadelphia, 1976), 93–94.

34. The denizens of Todtmoos, for example, complained that abbatial tax collectors unfairly demanded shrove chickens from both serfs and tenants, even though the impost was supposed to apply only to the former; GLA 229:106056, "Protocollum yber dasjenige, so wegen denen strittigen Leibhennen mit der Gemeind Todtmos abgehalten worden," 20 July 1723, especially §2.

35. GLA 113:225, "Protocoll und freundnachbarl. Verabschiedung vom 22. März, 1720."

36. See, for example, GLA 113:224, 40r–43v, Interrogation of Joseph Scheuble of Wolpadingen, St. Blasien, 6 November 1726, and GLA 113:248, A1, Interrogation of Leonzi Brutschi of Dogern, Vienna, 6–27 April 1739.

from village to village, updating lists of bondsmen and women.[37] By drawing large numbers of serfs into face-to-face encounters with the fact of their own unfreedom, the procedure had a powerful politicizing effect. Even at this late stage, however, not all hope of united peasant resistance was lost. On 19 June 1725, for example, Albiez joined with Tröndle and other ex-Octovirs in an attempt to negotiate the elimination of patrilineally heritable serfdom of the "baser hand." Unfortunately for Tröndle, St. Blasien refused to budge.[38] Meanwhile, the belief that Emperor Leopold had abolished *all* serfdom gained popularity. Thus the serf-census helped create a broad opposition to both the abbey and the Octovirs tied to the miller Tröndle of Unteralpfen.

Absent the personal energies of "Salpeter-Hans" Albiez himself, however, this transformation might never have occurred. Albiez was exceptionally well positioned to articulate peasant grievances against both St. Blasien and the Eight. Born in about 1654, Albiez was a veteran Octovir, having been elected to that office in 1715, 1717, and 1725.[39] After his third term as Octovir lapsed in April 1726, Albiez departed on a mission to Vienna, where he attempted to enlist the emperor's aid against the "introduction" of serfdom, just as Adam Tröndle had done in 1704. On 1 August, Albiez delivered his petition to Emperor Charles, but on 20 August, Chancellery officials instructed him to return home and present his case before the provincial government in Freiburg as the proper appellate instance. Albiez returned with nothing, save the certainty that "all will come to rights."[40] Back home, he began to rally support for another trip to Vienna, assembling money and signatures from his followers.[41] The provincial government in Freiburg intervened to stop him only after he had disrupted a session of the Forest Steward Franz Leopold von Beck's weekly court, held in the village of Görwihl.

37. The protocols of these censuses are preserved in GLA 113:110. See also Haselier, *Streitigkeiten*, 56.
38. Protocols of the meeting may be found in GLA 113:110 and GLA 113:89, n.p.
39. For Albiez's age, see GLA 113:224, 1r–26v; on his land tenures, see GLA 67:1739, 143r, and GLA 66:7296, "Zinsrodel deß Waldambts," 1709; and on his activities as Octovir, see GLA 62:10170 [RP Grafschaft Hauenstein], 1715, and GLA 61:13148 [WGP WVA], 1717.
40. GLA 113:224, 403r–4v, Hans Friedle Albiez to Conrad Binkert of Dogern, 9 August 1726.
41. See, for example, GLA 99:979, Interrogation of Adam Schmiedle of Niedermühle, St. Blasien, 4 September 1726.

On 20 October, Albiez was imprisoned in Freiburg, where he remained until his death almost a year later, on 29 September 1727.[42]

The movement might have perished with him if two events had not propelled the conflict to a crisis. First, Abbot Blasius III Bender died and his successor, Franz II Schächtelin, demanded the customary oath of homage that inaugurated the reign of each new abbot. Second, the arrival of Octovir elections in April 1727 radically transformed the face of peasant politics: Albiez's allies were elected to head all but one canton, transforming Albiez's dissident program into formal policy of the Eight.[43] Prompted by Albiez's instructions smuggled from prison, these magistrates withheld homage from Franz II until their dispute was resolved. As a result, the homage ceremonies were symbolic disasters: only 183 peasants gave the oath and the refusing peasants' spokesman announced that abbatial serfs were "simply not willing or inclined to swear" an oath of allegiance that included the term *Eigenschaft,* because Emperor Leopold (so they thought) had already abolished it.[44]

This homage boycott solidified the leadership of Albiez's sympathizers, who by now were already being called the *"salpeterisch* party."[45] But the boycott was an entirely conventional tactic. Homage rites were structured to restore the symbolic continuity of rule, hierarchy, and reciprocities between lord and subject after the death of a lord or prince. The transaction was widely regarded as having a contractual character, an understanding reflected in the fact that most jurists considered homage given under duress to be invalid. This symbolic rupture offered peasants an opportunity to present grievances and bargain for concessions from their new lords in exchange for homage. In this way, homage boycotts straddled the formal divide separating sedition from legitimate forms of resistance, such as litigation. The exhaustive studies of André Holenstein have shown that peasants all over the Holy Roman Empire and Switzerland commonly used homage boycotts both as a tactical device

---

42. Haselier, *Streitigkeiten,* 62.
43. Birndorf Canton went so far as to elect the already imprisoned "Salpeter-Hans" Albiez himself; see GLA 113:225, 168r–69v, Birndorf Canton to VÖRK, 29 April 1727.
44. GLA 99:433, 6r–77v, "Huldigungsprotokoll über die Huldigung in der Graffschafft Hawenstein," 13–15 May 1727.
45. GLA 113:229, 9r–10v, Martin Thoma of Haselbach to Speaker Joseph Tröndle of Schmitzingen, [21? May 1728].

and as a vehicle to criticize domination *(Herrschaft)* in general.⁴⁶ In this, Hauenstein was no exception. The principle difference was that here, peasant elites were sharply divided over the wisdom of this tactic.

Since the homage boycott implicitly challenged the fundamental assumptions of a hierarchical social and political order, the Austrian government could not remain neutral for long. In May 1727, the imperial government in Vienna had recommended that St. Blasien accept a lesser form of homage—a vow signified with raised fingers *(Handgelübde)*—which omitted the controversial, servile language in customary oaths. But both the abbot and the *salpeterisch* Eight refused to accept this compromise. Confronted with such intransigence, the Austrian state sided with Abbot Franz, and on 28 June, an imperial decree commanded the *salpeterisch* Eight to abandon their resistance.⁴⁷ But these attempts to browbeat the peasantry failed: the Eight refused a second command of 5 July to perform homage, and according to the miller Tröndle, public announcement of this decree produced "such shrieks, lamentations, and loud complaints . . . that one could not hear one's own words."⁴⁸

By the time "Salpeter-Hans" Albiez died in September 1727, events had escaped the provincial government's control. In October, a *salpeterisch* delegation headed by the blacksmith Conrad Binkert of Dogern departed for Vienna to petition the emperor once again, and like Albiez, Binkert also seems to have received an imperial hearing.⁴⁹ Meanwhile, an incendiary "Salpeter-Song" inspired popular outrage against *müllerisch* Octovirs, who were violently attacked in several villages throughout the county.⁵⁰ Blind to these incidents, Abbot Franz sabotaged a last-ditch *müllerisch* effort to prevent further escalation, when he refused to budge on disputed homage terminology.⁵¹ If Abbot Franz supposed that intransigence would strengthen his position, the events of December proved

---

46. André Holenstein, *Die Huldigung der Untertanen: Rechtskultur und Herschaftsordnung (800–1800)* (Stuttgart, 1991), 385–432.

47. GLA 113:235, 28r–30v, Imperial Patent of 28 June 1727.

48. GLA 99:984, 5r–6v, Joseph Tröndle of Unteralpfen to OVA, 6 July 1727.

49. GLA 99:985, 171r–v, Interrogation of Joseph Wagner of Unteralpfen, 7 December 1727.

50. For the text of the "Salpeter Liedt," see GLA 113:221, 10r–11v.

51. GLA 99:985, 59r–60v, Joseph Tröndle of Unteralpfen to [OVA?], 30 October 1727.

him mistaken, for Binkert's delegation succeeded in moving the Vienna government into action. To be sure, the latter forbade all "rebellious activities" in a decree of 6 December 1727. But the same decree reiterated Emperor Leopold's ban against the terms *leibeigen* and *Leibeigenschaft* and instructed all parties to submit their claims before a special imperial commission.[52] In effect, Vienna challenged St. Blasien to defend itself in court.

Still, an abbatial diplomat had convinced the imperial government to enforce the homage oath. Already in March 1727, Abbot Franz had dispatched an emissary, the historiographer Marquard Herrgott, to provoke the Chancellery's intervention.[53] Herrgott initially met with suspicion from several imperial privy councillors, perhaps because of his suggestion that the best solution to the homage crisis lay in giving St. Blasien the power to control Octovir elections—in other words, precisely the annexation of powers that Hauensteiners feared most.[54] Few in Vienna could stomach so complete a surrender to an abbey they already regarded as overly presumptuous. In the end, however, Herrgott's warnings against the disastrous consequences of any show of weakness convinced the Chancellery to enforce the homage, militarily if need be.[55] On 15 April 1728, an imperial decree suspended Octovir elections, renewed its call to homage, and established an *ad hoc* imperial commission headed by an Innsbruck official named Franz Edmund von Beaurieu to investigate the grievances of Hauenstein.[56] When *salpeterisch* peasants continued to refuse homage and held elections anyway, Beaurieu sent in the troops: on 12 May, nine hundred Austrian soldiers

---

52. GLA 113:225 Beilagen, 391r–92v, 406r–11v, Imperial Patent of 6 December 1727. The decree apparently added to the confusion among the peasants, many of whom understood it to mean that "all homage is completely abolished." "If that is not the case," Bläsi Hottinger reasoned, "why then is the word 'abolished' expressly contained in the decree?"; GLA 99:986, "Actum St Blasien," 15 March 1728.

53. On Herrgott's embassy, see GLA S IV 737–38, Stiftsarchiv St Paul im Lavantal, Kloster St Blasien Handschriften 166/2, "Diaria R. P. Marquardi Hergots über seine Wienner Geschäfften de anno 1728–1729" [hereafter "Diaria Marquardi Hergots"], and Joseph P. Ortner, *Marquard Herrgott (1694–1762): Sein Leben und Wirken als Historiker und Diplomat* (Vienna, 1972).

54. "Diaria Marquardi Hergots," 4v–6v, entry for 11 March 1728.

55. Ortner, *Marquard Herrgott*, 33–40.

56. GLA 113:235, 36r–37v, Imperial Patent of 15 April 1728.

invaded Hauenstein via St. Blasien and Todtmoos and began to enforce the homage at gunpoint. *Salpeterisch* activists mustered an armed confrontation on 17 May outside Dogern, but the standoff ended without bloodshed, and by 20 May the county had capitulated.[57]

The unfolding of events from 1719 to 1728 exposed the systemic contradictions of Hauenstein's political system in an environment increasingly hostile to autonomous decision-making by peasants. Specifically, the election of *salpeterisch* Octovirs in 1725 and 1727 revealed the growing incompatibility of peasant self-rule with an increasingly authoritarian sociopolitical order. Thus when the *salpeterisch* homage boycott became Octovir policy, the Austrian government again found itself confronting a duly constituted authority that was openly defiant of its commands. But this clash of prerogatives did nothing to alter the state's dependence on the Eight to publish decrees and collect rents. By the same token, it presented the ousted *müllerisch* leaders with the alternatives of opposing magistrates whose legitimacy had rested on the same electoral basis as their own had one year before, or of siding with them against the Habsburg state. They chose the former path, but at no small cost: the imperial ban against Octovir elections in 1727 allied them in public perceptions with the very forces that seemed determined to destroy the basis of Hauenstein's "historic freedoms." This crisis left little maneuvering room for peasant officeholders: it thrust the burden of proving good faith on local representatives of Habsburg authority, the Forest Steward and, more important, the Eight, now deprived of access to traditional modes of legitimation.

The upshot is that to some extent, effective rule had always depended on maintaining consensus among peasants through communal institutions. The reliance of state and seigneurial authorities on the services of peasant officeholders was so great that the emergence of political divisions threatened to disrupt the continuity of domination. To be sure, this reliance was waning in most places: generally speaking, communal autonomies slowly deteriorated throughout the empire after the sixteenth century, as bureaucracies of state and seigneurie became more

---

57. GLA 99:1012, no. 3, Beaurieu to OÖKR, 19 May 1728; see Haselier, *Streitigkeiten*, 70–71. On the 1728 elections, see GLA 113:229, 181r–87v, Interrogation of Joseph Tröndle of Schmitzingen, Waldshut, 24 July 1728.

centralized and professional.[58] By the same token, communal institutions had always rested on certain sociopolitical norms, such as the "common good" *(Gemeinnutz),* "brotherly love," and the need to preserve a minimum economic basis for each household (expressed in the idea of "domestic necessity" or *Hausnotdurft*), all of which were at least partially at odds with the authoritarian ideological underpinnings of feudalism, let alone absolutism.[59] But however antithetical "communalism" and "feudalism" may have been, the actual executors of seigneurial and communal power remained mutually interdependent. The advent of factionalism exposed an increasingly uneasy symbiosis between communal institutions and structures of domination in transition.

The Müllerisch *Ascendancy (1728–1737)*

Once Beaurieu had pried homage from the abbot's subjects in May 1728, he set out to accomplish the dual tasks of punishing the rebels and adjudicating their grievances.[60] As judge, Beaurieu contented himself with minor modifications in rules governing serfdom and St. Blasien's juridical competence. Hauenstein presented thirty-nine grievances in June, and in November Beaurieu submitted his recommendations, which were eventually incorporated into a series of imperial resolutions.[61] The abbot would surrender extraordinary death duties demanded of unmarried male serfs (the so-called *Hagstolzenrecht*) and accept minor modifications to homage oaths and in the competence of his lower courts. For its part, Hauenstein lost the customary "right of withdrawal," an aspect of inheritance law which regulated land sales within

---

58. Heide Wunder, *Die bäuerliche Gemeinde in Deutschland* (Göttingen, 1986), 80–92.

59. See Renate Blickle, "Hausnotdurft: Ein Fundamentalrecht in der altständischen Ordnung Bayerns," in Günter Birtsch, ed., *Grund- und Freiheitsrechte von der ständischen zur spätbürgerlichen Gesellschaft* (Göttingen, 1987), 42–64, and "Nahrung und Eigentum als Kategorien der ständischen Gesellschaft," in Winfried Schulze, ed., *Ständische Gesellschaft und soziale Mobilität* (Munich, 1988), 73–93.

60. The abbatial subjects paid homage in accordance with an imperial decree dated 22 May 1728; see Bader, ed., "Urkundenregeste," 330–33.

61. For Hauenstein's brief, see GLA 65:11419, 5r–6v, "Gravamina des Schwarzwaldes gegen St Blasien," 8 June 1728; for Beaurieu's report, see GLA 113:84 C, "Ohnmaassgebliche Commissions-Gutachten über die von der Graffschafft Hauwenstein eingeklagte Beschwärden," 4 November 1728.

kin groups.⁶² But measured against the great turmoil that preceded it, the Beaurieu Commission altered little.

By the same token, however, state intervention unmasked the contradictions of official attitudes toward factional politics. Beaurieu had arranged that in his hearings, Hauenstein should be represented by a "grievance committee" that included equal numbers of *müllerisch* and *salpeterisch* Octovirs, including the Eight of 1727. Because the latter had been elected illegally, Beaurieu's policy placed at the bargaining table peasant magistrates who had openly defied imperial authority only a few months earlier. More paradoxical still, his arrangement confirmed the common interest that both factions had in combating St. Blasien, as litigation became matter of collaboration across factional lines.⁶³

Beaurieu's approach reflected the elite belief that legitimate grievances underlay most rebellions, even if sedition itself was criminal. A corollary of this outlook was that the bulk of peasants were the dupes of "ringleaders" who bore the brunt of punishment after revolts were suppressed. But the process of identifying and punishing "rebellious" peasants deepened and defined factional divisions. Thus prosecution along Beaurieu's lines could succeed only at the cost of exacerbating precisely the tensions his otherwise inclusive approach to peasant politics was designed to ameliorate. Of course, leaders of the *salpeterisch* faction were punished severely: the "arch-ringleader" Martin Thoma of Haselbach was sentenced to death (his sentence was later commuted to six years' hard labor in the Hungarian mines, where he died in 1736); Bläsi Hottinger of Niedergebisbach and Johannes Marder "the Prussian" of Eschbach received sentences of hard labor in Belgrade plus lifelong exile. Thirty-eight lesser figures also received hard-labor sentences in the fortress of Breisach, and a large number of the *salpeterisch* rank and file were compelled to perform public corvées, mostly in road repair.⁶⁴ In connection with factional politics,

62. See Bader, ed., "Urkundenregeste," for excerpts of the imperial resolutions of 22 May 1728 (330–32), 8 August 1731 (335), 18 February 1733 (335–36), 25 February 1733 (336), and 26 March 1733 (336–38).

63. As the summer of 1728 wore on, however, *müllerisch* Octovirs on the committee grew increasingly dominant. See, for example, Beaurieu's analysis in GLA 113:229, 261r–72v, Beaurieu to Charles VI, 11 August 1728, which drew heavily on the advice of *müllerisch* Octovirs.

64. GLA 65:11419, 14r, "Relation über das Strafenurtheil," 4 April 1730; GLA 113:238, 121r–122v, "Specification prod. in Conf. den 19tn Aug. 1730 deren pro Resolutionem Caesaream de dato Wienn den 8tn Jul. 1730 ad operas publicas condemnierte hauwenstein. Unterthanen."

however, monetary fines were more influential. From the start, Beaurieu intended to cover his expenses with imposts on Hauensteiners found guilty of sedition—a decision which provoked yet another "great lamentation."[65] In the end, a fine of 7,800 gulden was distributed among 233 activists, and another 4,200 gulden among rank-and-file rebels.[66] The process of identifying them and the stigma of penalization publicized factional difference to all.

This was a source of great concern to the *müllerisch* Eight. In a letter that otherwise bubbled with praise for Beaurieu's justice, the miller Tröndle begged that penalties be kept to a minimum: "Only if nobody demands anything more of the rebellious [peasants]," he argued, would Hauenstein remain at peace.[67] Tröndle seemed to comprehend that the mass penalization of "rebellious" peasants would entrench factionalism permanently. But if the severity of Beaurieu's punishments were a source of concern to the *müllerisch* Eight, his authoritarian political reforms were even more troubling. Specifically, Beaurieu bolstered the *müllerisch* faction in a manner so ham-handed that he further undercut its access to traditional sources of the legitimacy. After the forced homage of May 1728, Beaurieu had intended to abolish elections entirely, but *müllerisch* leaders convinced him that this was too hazardous.[68] Still, Beaurieu could hardly allow *salpeterisch* Octovirs to control the county, and to prevent any future *salpeterisch* victories, he suspended Octovir elections until 1730, forever barred the *salpeterisch* Eight of 1727 from holding public office, and deprived 108 rebels of voting rights.[69] But these measures only encouraged anti-oligarchic suspicions on the *salpeterisch* side and seemed to confirm their charge that *müllerisch* Octovirs were nothing but the pawns of "great lords."[70]

During the period of *müllerisch* ascendancy, the *salpeterisch* faction was forced to go underground. *Müllerisch* peasants spied on *salpeterisch*

65. GLA 113:81, 15r–20v, Beaurieu to OÖKR, 12 May 1728.
66. Ibid., 70r–83v, Beaurieu to OÖKR, 2 June 1728, and 130r–48v, "Repartition deren Kösten, so auß die Miliz-Commission auch anderwärthig aufgegangenen, so sich ohngefehr ad 10000 fl Reichswehr. oder 12000 fl Rauchwehr. belaufen," 7 July 1728.
67. GLA 99:1031, 306r–v, Joseph Tröndle of Unteralpfen to OVA, 23 April 1730.
68. GLA 113:226, 184r–86v, "Actum Togeren den 20ten Aprill, 1728"; GLA 113:229, Beaurieu to Charles VI, 11 August 1728.
69. GLA 113:237, 83r–84v, "Specification deren jenigen in der letzten vorgewesten... Ohnruhe interessierten Unterthanen welche... ddo Wienn den 28tn Mar. von activâ et passivâ bey denen Ämbter Wahlen perpetuò vel ad tempus priviert."
70. GLA 113:267, Interrogation of Joseph Ebner of Segeten, 24 December 1745.

activities and passed the information on to Austrian or abbatial officials. Thus news of rebel delegations to Vienna in 1730, 1730–31, and 1737 reached official ears almost immediately.[71] Such espionage recorded hushed discontent throughout the period, but the imprisonment or exile of most *salpeterisch* activists temporarily left their faction without effective leaders. By courier, the exiles frequently exhorted their fellows to take action, but for several years the faction undertook nothing.[72] The risks were simply too high: when the *salpeterisch* activist "Schwarzmichel" Tröndle of Bergalingen returned from Vienna in 1737, for example, he was quickly apprehended, whipped, pilloried, and banished from Hauenstein.[73]

Meanwhile, the Austrian government introduced reforms designed to strengthen the Forest Steward at the Octovirs' expense. An imperial resolution in 28 March 1730, for example, adjusted the public symbolism of his office: from 1730 on, new Forest Stewards would no longer swear loyalty to Hauenstein, but obedience to the Outer Austrian government instead. Another decree banned appeals of the Forest Steward's court rulings to the cantonal "courts of the twelve" and to the annual "court of the sixteen" at Görwihl. Thus the first wave of rebellion produced limits on popular involvement in the appellate process. Moreover, in 1735 a commission headed by an Outer Austrian official named von Reischach proposed reforms that would extend the Forest Steward's jurisdiction over credit, property exchanges, and communal orphan funds.[74] Indirect evidence suggests, however, that these changes proved virtually impossible to enforce, and fault probably lay with the obstructions of foot-dragging *müllerisch* Octovirs.[75]

71. GLA 113:235, 81r–85v, WVA to VÖRK, 22 February 1730, and WVA to VÖRK, 5 March 1730; GLA 113:239, 2r–3v, WVA to VÖRK, 25 March 1731, and 24r–25v, WVA to VÖRK, 15 April 1731; GLA 99:1038, 84r–v, Joseph Tröndle of Unteralpfen to St. Blasien, 22 April 1737; GLA 113:241, 71r–72v, WVA to VÖRK, 28 July 1737.

72. GLA 113:221, 300r–310v, "Ohngefehrlicher Bericht über den gottlosen leichtfertigen Brieff so die Unruehige Hawensteiner 15 Mann aus dem Arest aus Wienn den 10 Jener 1739 ahn einige Ohnruehige jns Landt der Graffschafft Hauenstein geschriben."

73. GLA 99:1039, 9r–v, Joseph Tröndle of Unteralpfen to OVA, 2 November 1737.

74. GLA 113:16, "Copia Baron Reischachischer Landseinrichtung," 18 May 1756; Haselier, *Streitigkeiten*, 79–80.

75. An administrative report of 1783 indicated that little had come of them since 1735; see GLA 113:16, "Wie und von wem die hochheitl. Jurisdiction in der Grafschafft Hauenstein ausgeübet werde," 26 May 1783.

A reform initiated by the *müllerisch* Eight proved more effective—and, in the end, more disruptive. This was the proposal to purchase freedom for all abbatial serfs in Hauenstein. The idea of collective manumission *(Loskauf* or *Auskauf)* had been debated in official circles since 1728, but only in 1737 did the Austrian government press St. Blasien to consider the matter seriously.⁷⁶ While Austrian pressure induced the abbey to agree in principle, *müllerisch* Octovirs threatened that another *salpeterisch* rising might erupt unless St. Blasien reduced the manumission fee to 45,000 gulden.⁷⁷ This proposal was much more reasonable, the miller Tröndle suggested, especially in view of "so many ill-spirited subjects."⁷⁸ Ultimately, the parties agreed to a comprehensive fee of 58,000 gulden. This was considerably higher than the Octovirs' initial offer, but, as Speaker Joseph Tröndle of Rotzel argued to gatherings of serfs held in every canton after the treaty was announced, it was cheaper by almost half than the 92,000 gulden that St. Blasien had originally demanded.⁷⁹

Thus *müllerisch* diplomacy banished forever the social taint of servility from Hauenstein. The manumission treaty was signed on 15 January 1738 and ratified by imperial edict six months later; the fee was paid in full by the end of 1742.⁸⁰ But the treaty was rife with paradox-

76. The final report of abbatial ambassador Herrgott notes that officials in Vienna had recommended collective manumission as early as the spring of 1728; GLA S IV 738, Stiftsarchiv St Peter im Lavanttal, Kloster St Blasien Handschriften, 166b/2, "Untertänigstes Referat oder Finalrelation über die bei dem Wiennerischen Hoff in verschiedenen, hauptsächlich in hauwensteinischen Geschäfften gehabten Verrichtungen von anno 1728 bis 1731," Vienna, 8 August 1731; and see Ornter, *Marquard Herrgott,* 43, 80–86. On the negotiations preceding the manumission, see Haselier, *Streitigkeiten,* 85–87. Noting a recent increase in factional violence, Joseph Tröndle of Unteralpfen urged this solution on Forest Steward Schönau in September; GLA 113:241, 180r–81v, Joseph Tröndle of Unteralpfen to WVA, 19 September 1737.

77. VÖRK to St. Blasien, 29 July 1737, in Bader, ed. "Urkundenregeste," 338. "I know of no other means to maintain the peace," Tröndle wrote to the Forest Steward, "than to purchase release . . . from the serfdom and servile dues of St. Blasien"; GLA 113:241, 180r–81v, Joseph Tröndle of Unteralpfen to WVA, 19 September 1737.

78. GLA 113:241, 180r–81v, Joseph Tröndle of Unteralpfen to WVA, 19 September 1737.

79. GLA 113:79, [Joseph Tröndle of Rotzel], "Ungefehrliche Vorstellung des Fallbarke[its]-Geschäffts so jeder Einungsmeister seinen Leüthen in dem Einung hinderbringen undt darüber einen audentischen Bescheidt wehr sich darzue verstehen wolle oder nit obbegehren solle," [January? 1738].

80. For the text of the manumission treaty itself, see Bader, ed., "Urkundenregeste," 338–48. For the original document, see GLA 11:3135, "Receß zwischen St Blasien und Hauenstein wegen Befreiung von der Leibeigenschaft und der Fallbarkeit," 15 January 1738. The receipt is preserved in GLA 11:3140, 2 October 1742; excerpted in Bader, ed., "Urkundenregeste," 350.

ical consequences. Surely the most bizarre was that the manumission treaty transformed the "Whole County" of Hauenstein into a serf lord. For a variety of complex legal technicalities, the treaty's authors had been vexed by the problem of what to do with a small number of abbatial serfs living in Indlekofen, a hamlet within the territorial limits of Hauenstein but under the civil administration not of the Eight, but of the town of Waldshut. For the purposes of emancipation, this peculiarity placed Indlekofen outside the county. A convenient solution to the problem was found in transfering serf-lordship *(Leibherrschaft)* over the Indlekofen serfs to Hauenstein as a corporation; thus one group of peasants became enserfed to another.[81]

A far more important paradox, however, lay in *salpeterisch* opposition to the treaty. Indeed, their antagonism proved so keen that it brought the period of *müllerisch* ascendancy to an abrupt end, unleashing the third and by far the most violent phase of the Salpeter Wars.

Salpeterisch *Dominance and Civil War (1737–1745)*

It has been suggested that the reasons for *salpeterisch* opposition to the manumission treaty lay in a resurgence during the 1730s of the idea that serfdom contradicted the "ancient customs" *(Altes Recht)* of Hauenstein.[82] But this interpretation is misleading on two counts: first, serfdom and manumission alike had been recognized, albeit resented, dimensions in the relationship between Hauenstein and St. Blasien for nearly four hundred years. The legal precedent for serfdom as such was rock-solid. On the other hand, the idea that servile status was incompatible with Hauenstein's corporate liberties was no invention of the 1730s, but went back at least to the 1660s. In this respect also, *salpeterisch* opposition to the manumission treaty illustrated the divergence of two concepts of order that had been emerging since 1719.

The new element in public discourse on serfdom was that now, unlike during earlier phases in the debate, peasants began openly to deny

---

81. To judge by their attempts to track the genealogy of serfs in Indlekofen, the Eight made good on their prerogatives as a serf lord; see GLA 113:109, n.p., "Specification was zu Inglikhoffen von Jörgy 1745 bis Jörgy 1746 ahn Fohll undt Manumission ihn Gelt gefohlen ist."
82. Haselier, *Streitigkeiten,* 88.

all the *appurtenances* of serfdom, including its dues and legal disabilities. Until 1738, even *salpeterisch* leaders had at least feigned acceptance of *dues* associated with serfdom, even while they rejected the attribution of servile *status*. In the course of public debates surrounding the manumission treaty, rebel leaders concluded that servile dues were also perverse and always had been. And because the *salpeterisch* peasants now rejected serfdom fundamentally, they were loathe to purchase liberties which they believed were already theirs. When the manumission was publicly announced at Waldshut, the militant "Gaudihans" Wasmer of Segeten protested that because the people had not been consulted, the treaty was null and void. In any case, he argued, the abbatial serfs were too poor to pay the fee.[83] Manumission enlivened other *salpeterisch* activists as well, who spent the late winter months converting people "to the rebellious side."[84] Despite the efforts of *müllerisch* Octovirs to persuade voters of the virtues of their treaty, the *salpeterisch* argument that manumission was a sham and that the 58,000 gulden fee amounted to robbery seems to have been more persuasive.[85] Indeed, some militants turned this logic on its head and argued that manumission was tantamount to the *purchase* of slavery![86] As Chapter 3 will show, the result was a decisive shift in the balance of factional power to the *salpeterisch* side.

The Octovir elections of 1738 reflected these changes. In defiance of yet another imperial ban, *salpeterisch* candidates were elected in half of the cantons.[87] The result was schism: because Forest Steward Franz Anton von Schönau refused to swear them into office, two sets of Octovirs now lay simultaneous claim to public authority in Hauenstein.[88] Predictably, this played havoc with the smooth running of affairs: while the *müllerisch* Eight generally retained control of the county's admin-

---

83. GLA 99:1040, 120r–27v, "Copia Actum Waldshut," 21 Feburary 1738.

84. GLA 99:1040, 184r–85v, Joseph Tröndle of Unteralpfen to Joseph Tröndle of Rotzel, 2 April 1738.

85. GLA 113:79, "Ungefehrliche Vorstellung des Fahlbarke[its]-Geschäffts," [January? 1738].

86. As Hans Wasmer of Segeten testified in 1739, for example, "word had it that we were to acknowledge the prelate of St. Blasien as our serf and liege lord, which words I understood to mean that we were to become serfs"; GLA 113:248, A4, no. 7, Interrogation of Hans Wasmer of Segeten, 20 April 1739.

87. GLA 113:242, 14r–15v, Imperial Resolution of 16 April 1738; GLA 113:241, 319r–21v, 324r–26v, WVA to VÖRK, 25 April 1738; Haselier, *Streitigkeiten*, 89.

88. GLA 113:242, 23r–26v, WVA to VÖRK, 18 June 1738.

istrative apparatus, the *salpeterisch* Eight organized a tax strike against them.[89] It also hampered collecting the manumission fee, which gave this phase of the Salpeter Wars the appearance of a tax revolt.[90]

During the summer of 1738, the *salpeterisch* leadership mounted a vigorous campaign to oust their opponents, despite an imperial edict banning unauthorized gatherings.[91] In June and July, one Hans Friedle Gerspach of Bergalingen organized numerous *salpeterisch* rallies to protest the manumission, while several *salpeterisch* delegations protested in Vienna against Forest Steward Schönau's *de facto* ban on elections. By August, tensions had reached the breaking point. On 13 August, Gerspach and an armed crowd of about six hundred gathered in Dogern to demand formal approval of the April election results.[92] When imperial ratification of the manumission treaty was publicly announced on 28 August, another large gathering demanded that the *müllerisch* Eight give "account before the emperor" for their crimes, and during an ensuing fracas "various youths" from Rickenbach Canton roughed up not only the Eight, but Forest Steward Schönau as well.[93]

Factional tensions finally snapped in the following spring. Partisan violence had escalated in January, and in February, the ongoing tax strike finally impelled Vienna to authorize another military intervention under the command of Ferdinand Sebastian Freiherr von Sickingen.[94] His force of six hundred grenadiers arrived in Hauenstein on 7 March, but Sickingen hesitated to attack, hoping instead to restore calm without bloodshed.[95] His hopes for a peaceful resolution were dashed when the *salpeterisch* Eight mustered the county militia, or *Landfahnen*.

89. GLA 113:253, 96r–87v, *Salpeterisch* Eight to Ferdinand Sebastian von Sickingen, 9 March 1739.

90. In October 1738, the miller Tröndle pleaded with abbatial officials that unless intervention were forthcoming soon, not a single gulden of the manumission fee would be paid on time; GLA 99:1040, 345r–v, Joseph Tröndle of Unteralpfen to OVA, 5 October 1738.

91. GLA 113:221, 26r–27v, Imperial Resolution of 19 April 1738.

92. GLA 113:242, 259r–61v, WVA to VÖRK, 20 August 1738.

93. GLA 99:1040, 330r–v, Joseph Tröndle of Unteralpfen to St. Blasien, 28 August 1738.

94. According to Forest Steward von Schönau, *müllerisch* bailiffs were attacked "on the open street"; GLA 113:242, 376r–79v, WVA to VÖRK, 7 January 1739. On the tax strike, see GLA 113:242, 367r–68v, Joseph Tröndle of Rotzel to WVA, 20 December 1738. On the Sickingen commission, see GLA 113:242, 217r–24v, Imperial Mandate of 3 February 1739.

95. GLA 113:253, 301r–28v, "Ahn löbl. V:Ö: Weesen gezimmend und gehorsambe Relation des V:Ö: Statthalteren Freyh. v Syckhingen," 26 June 1739.

Once the it had assembled in Görwihl on 15 March, *salpeterisch* leaders attempted a systematic persecution of *müllerisch* peasants. On the night of the 15 March, a company of seventy-eight militiamen equipped with "cudgels and firearms" marched through several villages in northern Birndorf and Dogern cantons, plundering *müllerisch* households, arresting and beating *müllerisch* peasants.[96] This "disciplinary campaign" *(Hatschierzug)* was aborted, however, by the outcome of a pitched battle with Sickingen's troops the following day. In a field outside the village of Etzwihl, an Austrian battalion routed a force of about four hundred armed peasants under the command of a Saxon deserter named Hans Michael Hartmann. Despite his efforts to provide some semblance of military discipline, the peasants fled at the first Austrian volley. Over the next few days, village after village surrendered to the Austrians.[97]

Sickingen's justice was swift and harsh. Five major rebels were executed, among them Gerspach and the deserter Hartmann. Also beheaded were Leonzi Brutschi of Dogern, who had shown great talent as a fund-raiser, and the village headman of Brunnadern, Joseph Lüber.[98] Bläsi Hottinger of Niedergebisbach and Johannes "the Prussian" Marder were returned to hard labor at the fortress in Belgrade; "Gaudihans" Wasmer received a sentence of hard labor at the Outer Austrian fortress of Alt-Breisach. An imperial penal mandate of 29 April 1729 banned on pain of death all unauthorized gatherings and ordered the peasants to surrender the taxes and manumission payments they had withheld since the previous year.[99] As in 1728, moreover, the costs of invasion were borne

---

96. Hostages taken during the campaign were incarcerated in a mill at Tiefenstein on the Alb river in the center of the county; see GLA 65:11426, 82r–83v, "Verzeichnis deren jenigen Sachen wo in der Gemaindt Banholtz den 15ten Mertzen 1739 in der Nacht seindt entraubt wordten, von denen sogenanten unrüohigen sollbetherischen Leüthen undt Harschiereren," and GLA 113:248, B1, Interrogation of Hans Michael "der Saxe" Hartmann of Finsterlingen, 6–25 April 1739.

97. On the Battle of Etzwihl, see GLA 113:253, "Gezimmend und gehorsambe Relation," 26 June 1739; GLA 113:246 is littered with formal submissions. Herrischried held out longest, until 22 March.

98. GLA 113:253, "Gezimmend und gehorsambe Relation," 26 June 1739.

99. GLA 113:240a, 7r–8v; StAFB C1 Landstände 78, Imperial Decree of 29 April 1739. The decree specified the death sentence for unauthorized travel to Vienna; peasants who spoke against the Forest Ordinance would forfeit all property; finally, anyone who entered a sworn rebellious union would lose first his right hand, then his head.

by *salpeterisch* peasants. Unlike Beaurieu, however, Sickingen had nothing to adjudicate: in light of the imperial penal mandate of April, *salpeterisch* grievances were irrelevant. The only changes brought about by the revolt of 1738–39 were two further emancipations, for the serfs of St. Fridolin and a smaller number belonging to Baron Zweyer von Evenbach.[100] In terms of factional politics, the Sickingen Commission simply reimposed the pre-1738 status quo, under which elections were suspended indefinitely and *müllerisch* Octovirs installed for the interim.[101]

Perhaps this explains why *salpeterisch* discontent continued to simmer. Already in August 1739, the Austrian officials detected renewed *salpeterisch* unrest, this time in popular responses to the apocalyptic visions of a twenty-year-old woman in Laufenburg.[102] Another factor was the return to Hauenstein of exiled *salpeterisch* activists, among them Johannes Marder and Bläsi Hottinger, who in 1742 had been amnestied in celebration of the birth of the future emperor Joseph II. The effect of their repatriation showed how fragile the peace of 1739 had been: by March 1743, *salpeterisch* "conventicles" were meeting throughout the county in preparation for Octovir elections on St. George's Day.[103] Although *müllerisch* candidates won in all eight cantons, rumors of a new tax strike spread in August.[104] From the standpoint of Forest Steward Schönau, the exiles could not have returned at a less auspicious moment. Since 1740, the War of Austrian Succession had stretched the Habsburg monarchy's military and fiscal resources to the limit.[105] In Hauenstein, the fiscal burden was extreme: between May and October 1743, for example, Hauensteiners paid out 29,750 gulden in cash, in addition to heavy payments in kind.[106] According to one, probably

---

100. The abbess of St. Fridolin freed her serfs in 1741 in return for 11,500 gulden; see GLA 97:459, no. 1, "Proceß-Acta entzwischen einem fürstl. Stüfft Seggingen und der Graffschafft Hauwenstein puncto der Fahlbarkeit."
101. GLA 65:11223, "Summarischer Außzug."
102. GLA 113:255, 186r–v, "Copia Schreibens ddo Lauffenburg vom 25tn Aug. 1739."
103. GLA 113:255, 5r–v, 13r–v, WVA to VÖRK, 13 March 1743.
104. See, for example, GLA 113:255, 164r–v, Interrogation of Johannes Feldmann, Unteralpfen, 30 August 1743.
105. P. G. M. Dickson, *Finance and Government under Maria Theresia, 1740–1780* (Oxford, 1987), 2:3–5, 114–24.
106. GLA 113:255, 203r–v, "Verzeichnus waß die Graffschafft Hauenstein, von Monath Mayen her 1743 bis den 7tn Dag Weynmonath gelithen haben," 6 October 1743.

exaggerated estimate, the total value of all war levies during the year after April 1743 equaled 215,325 gulden.[107]

In December 1743, the *salpeterisch* faction finally hired legal counsel (a Freiburg lawyer named Kaspar Berger) and formally protested the harsh war imposts. Because the *müllerisch* Eight had been enlisted to collect the exactions, these grievances carried strong overtones of factional resentment.[108] The *müllerisch* Eight realized that war taxes undermined their position and warned that unless Freiburg lowered them, another *salpeterisch* revolt was in the offing.[109] Indeed, popular resentments erupted violently at the earliest opportunity. It came in 1744, when a Franco-Bavarian army invaded Outer Austria, throwing the provincial government into disarray. In the resulting power vacuum, *salpeterisch* leaders took the upper hand and were elected to lead half the cantons in April elections. By August, these magistrates had begun pressuring *müllerisch* peasants to join their cause or suffer persecution.[110] To illustrate the seriousness of their intentions, a group of about a hundred peasants led by Octovir Kaspar Mutter of Rüßwihl arrested the *müllerisch* ex-Speaker, Joseph Tröndle of Rotzel, on the night of 2 August. The Speaker was not harmed and was released when he promised to help gain freedom for imprisoned *salpeterisch* leaders. Five days later, however, Mutter arrested him again, along with the miller Tröndle of Unteralpfen, and replaced both with *salpeterisch* candidates in hastily called elections.[111] The crisis passed when Austrian soldiers liberated the two Tröndles, but a full-scale military suppression of the revolt remained beyond the government's means. In September, the French

107. GLA 113:64, "Specification der Außgaben von Jörg 1743 bis 1744 was hin undt widter Kost in Verwilligungs Gelt, Heü für die Officieren und andteren vill hin und widter lauffen wie bekanth," [end April 1744?].

108. GLA 65:11419, 60r [Nachlaß J. L. Meyer], 4 December 1743, §3; GLA 113:222, 13r–14v, §3. Born in 1705, Berger was attached to the Outer Austrian Fiscal Bureau ("Fiskalamt") and lived in Freiburg; see GLA 113:258, 167r–77v, Interrogation of Johann Kaspar Berger, OÖKR, 25 November 1745.

109. GLA 79:3401, n.p., "Bitt [der] Alt- und Newen Redmann, auch alten Einungsmaister . . . um einer Vorstellung nacher Hof, womit die Aufruhr in besagter Grafschafft gestillt werden möchte" 22 August 1744.

110. GLA 113:255, 97r–v, "Specification der vergangenen Georgi ausgezogener newen Einungs Mäisteren," 29 April 1744.

111. GLA 113:257, "Ohngefehrliche Bericht über diejenige Begebenheithen so sich zue Rozell dn 2tn Augst abens in der Nacht so dan zue Gerwil den 3tn dises zuegetragen"; GLA 113:256, 159r–62v, WVA to VÖRK, 3 August 1744.

drove the provinical government into Swiss exile, and Outer Austria came under a short-lived Bavarian rule.¹¹²

The Franco-Bavarian occupation of Outer Austria temporarily turned the political world of Hauenstein upside down. In the spring, an odd convergence of Austrian war policy and factional politics gave the *salpeterisch* cause the appearance of a patriotic uprising. Within Hauenstein itself, the hapless efforts of *müllerisch* Octovirs to satisfy French war requisitions exposed them to *salpeterisch* accusations of disloyalty to the Habsburg crown.¹¹³ Meanwhile from Innsbruck, an Austrian "Territorial Defense Commission" under the direction of Count Rudolph von Chotek attempted to coordinate anti-French peasant resistance in Outer Austria; apparently unaware of the ongoing struggles in Hauenstein, Chotek responded favorably to a *salpeterisch* plan to muster guerrilla battalions against the French and their allies—who in the rebels' view included the *müllerisch* faction.¹¹⁴ In April 1745, finally, all eight cantons elected *salpeterisch* Octovirs, including the militants Johannes Thoma-ab-Egg and "Gaudihans" Wasmer.¹¹⁵ Once again, the *salpeterisch* agenda became Octovir policy. Armed with Chotek's ill-informed blessings and the legitimizing effect of popular election, Thoma-ab-Egg resumed attacks against the ostensibly "pro-French" *müllerisch* faction.¹¹⁶

This brief inversion of political order inaugurated the bloodiest phase of the "Salpeter Wars." In May 1745, Thoma-ab-Egg mustered the county militia and threatened *müllerisch* peasants with exile and the loss of property if they resisted his authority.¹¹⁷ On 1 May, a force of several hundred peasants entered the city of Waldshut and confiscated a cache of

---

112. On the French conquest of Freiburg on 30 November and subsequent occupation, see [K.u.K. Kriegs-Archiv], *Oesterreichischer Erbfolge-Krieg* (Vienna, 1896–1914), 5:591–96, 690–91; 6:117–19, 162–65. During the occupation, the Outer Austrian government resided in the Swiss town of Klingnau.
113. GLA 113:222, 11r–12v, Joseph Tröndle of Unteralpfen to Joseph Tröndle of Rotzel, 1 March 1745. For accusations of treason, see GLA 113:221, 452r–53v, Interrogation of Joseph Jehle et al., [11 August 1745?].
114. GLA 113:222, 292r–v, Landesdefensionskommission to Hauenstein, 4 April 1745, and 113:263, no. 32, Landesdefensionskommission to Baron von Lüttichau, 13 May 1745.
115. GLA 113:263, n.p., "Ohngefehrliche Beschreibung, waß sich bey der Einungsmeisterwahl am Tag des Hl. Ritters Georgii zugetragen," 28 April 1745.
116. GLA 113:262, n.p., Sickingen to Baron von Zech, 22 May 1745. Sickingen worried that this "misunderstanding" could produce a "real massacre and Peasants' War."
117. GLA 113:263, no. 43, Kaspar Berger to Octovir Martin Bär of Hierholz, 2 May 1745.

weapons there, and during the following weeks, Thoma-ab-Egg, accompanied by "Gaudihans" Wasmer, Martin Mutter of Rüßwihl, two wayward Hungarian cavalrymen, and about forty militiamen confiscated *müllerisch* money, property, and weapons; the total value of these exactions was later estimated at 29,275 gulden.[118] *Müllerisch* peasants who missed the chance to flee Thoma-ab-Egg were bound, beaten, tried, and imprisoned; meanwhile, refugees streamed into nearby towns and cities. On 16 May, Thoma-ab-Egg and small army of eight hundred occupied Laufenburg and Rheinfelden and threatened to raze both towns unless they joined the anti-French insurgence.[119] Thoma-ab-Egg's violent demeanor earned him the nickname "Count of Egg," an epithet which appeared justified when he commanded royal customs officers to stop taxing Hauensteiners.[120] By the end of the month, Count Chotek realized the unforseen consequences of his "Territorial Defense Commission," had Thoma-ab-Egg arrested, and dispersed his partisans.[121]

But "Gaudihans" Wasmer and the other *salpeterisch* Octovirs remained at large. Although French and Bavarian forces had departed in April 1745, Wasmer continued to dominate county politics until winter, mainly because the provincial government remained too weak to intervene. In July, a third imperial commission under Christoph von Ramschwag arrived, but his injunctions to keep "perfect peace" were ignored.[122] Unchecked either by Ramschwag or by provincial authorities, the *salpeterisch* Eight forcibly "converted" *müllerisch* peasants and collected royal taxes with a rigor "contrary to ancient custom," which provoked a *müllerisch* tax strike against them.[123] The *müllerisch* Speaker

---

118. StAWT, Ratsprotokolle, 1 May 1745. On the plunders of May 1745, see GLA 113:231, 48r–49v, "Uhnvorgreifflich kurdzer Extractt über die Ehrlithnusen der jedtzerzeith gehorsambsten Ruohigen," [June? 1745]. These included 717 flintlocks, 91 daggers, and 4,630 gulden in cash; GLA 113:231, 46r–47v, "Specification über die Gewöhr so . . . verlohren und von ihrer Gegenparthey wögg-genohmnen worden," [June? 1745].

119. GLA 65:11223, "Summarischer Außzug."

120. GLA 99:1044, Interrogation of Joseph Jehle and Clemens Thoma, 20 May 1745.

121. GLA 113:240a, 33r–34v, Imperial Patent of 17 May 1745. On the May Terror, see also Haselier, *Streitigkeiten*, 104–5.

122. GLA 113:222, 78r–79v, Imperial Patent of 30 June 1745. For examples of the summer violence, see GLA 113:259, 56r–59v, "Beschreibung nacherstehenden Hergangs . . . zu Waldkirch," 12 July 1745.

123. GLA 113:263, no. 115, Interrogation of Catharina Bienz [?] of Herrischwand, 8 July 1745; GLA 113:259, 114r–v, [Joseph Tröndle of Rotzel], "Notanta," 4 August 1745.

Tröndle of Rotzel and the miller Tröndle of Unteralpfen fled for safety to Waldshut, where they attempted in mid-August to arrange a negotiated peace.[124]

The rebels refused their offers, however, and instead tried to seize the Tröndles by force. The result was open civil war. On 12 November, a *salpeterisch* force of several hundred laid siege to Waldshut and demanded the surrender of the *müllerisch* Octovirs within. A group of about forty broke into the town, but its defenses held, and "Gaudihans" Wasmer was captured during the skirmish. The battle of Schmitzingen, described at the introduction to this book, occurred that evening. On the following day, even more *salpeterisch* peasants, perhaps as many as two thousand, surrounded Waldshut, cut off its water supply, and renewed their demands. Although the siege soon broke, violent clashes continued throughout November.[125] The civil war ended when the provincial president von Stapf (who had witnessed the siege of Waldshut) turned factional conflict against itself by augmenting his regular troops with a force of some eight hundred *müllerisch* refugees.[126] On 26–27 November, three columns invaded Hauenstein to suppress the *salpeterisch* faction, and by 4 December, its resistance had been broken.[127]

The November invasion unleashed a campaign of *müllerisch* vengeance that matched the ferocity of Johannes Thoma-ab-Egg: over a period of four days, *müllerisch* militamen plundered *salpeterisch* households, slaughtered three hundred head of livestock, destroyed fifteen thousand liters of wine, and stole an "indescribable quantity" of money, tools, and bed-linen. Factional violence also exacted a terrible human cost. Several *salpeterisch* women were stripped, robbed, and perhaps raped. The son of a *salpeterisch* Octovir narrowly escaped execution by drowning.[128] This binge of violence ended *salpeterisch* predominance in Hauenstein. It also ended the Salpeter Wars.

124. StAWT Ratsprotokolle, 14 August 1745.
125. StAWT Ratsprotokolle, "Diarium wehrendt der Graffschafft hauensteinischen Unruhe," 12–27 November 1745.
126. GLA 65:11223, "Summarischer Außzug."
127. StAWT Ratsprotokolle, "Diarium," 12–27 November 1745; GLA 113:240a, 48r–49v, "Instruction für die gegen die unruehige Unterthanen ausruckende Commando," 26 November 1745.
128. GLA 65:747, 10r–11v, "Notanta: von deme, was ferners unter Anfiehrung des Bomerers vorgegangen, unterm 27. 28. 29. und 30. 9bris 1745."

For all the bloodletting, however, this last phase of the Salpeter Wars was little more than a boiling over of factional tensions that had stewed for decades. To be sure, the manumission controversy had led certain rebel leaders to articulate a new and fundamental rejection of serfdom in all its aspects. Another peculiarity of this phase was the inversion of alliances between factions and the Austrian state. But otherwise the broad pattern of disagreement between *müllerisch* and *salpeterisch* peasants, both in tactics and in concepts of order, had altered little. Not even the violence was new.

Epilogue

Like that of his predecessor, Ramschwag's main task was to suppress rebellion, not to adjudicate peasant grievances. But where Sickingen had failed, Ramschwag and his adjutant, Stanislas Alois von Vintler, achieved a measure of stability through a combination of force, prosecution, persuasion, and more authoritarian reforms. As for armed force, three cavalry companies were quartered in Hauenstein while the principal *salpeterisch* leaders were tried and banished or imprisoned.[129] Although lesser forms of *salpeterisch* resistance continued throughout the 1740s, this imposed peace held: brief flare-ups in 1747 and 1749 came to nothing, and in 1755, the provincial government preempted another outbreak of rebellion when it deported twenty-seven leading *salpeterisch* families to Timisoara in the newly conquered Banat.[130] Compared with the turmoil of 1725–45, Hauenstein remained quiet for the balance of the century.

Ramschwag's tools were not all made of iron, however. In moves reminiscent of Beaurieu, he and Vintler convened representatives of

129. GLA 113:64, "Entwurff was denen löbl. Donau-Granitzer Hußaren Compagnien so in der Graffschafft Hawenstein einquartiert seynd à dato der Einruckhung ahn Brodt und Pferdt-Porttionen täglichen bebühret," 9 December 1745; Haselier, *Streitigkeiten*, 115–16.

130. On the 1747 unrests, see GLA 113:223, 40r–43v, "Ungeföhrliche Bericht was sich den Früehling 1747 hindurch bis dn 22tn May ihn underschidlichen Sachen bey den . . . unruohigen Underthanen zugetragen." The 1749 disturbance involved a tax strike in Görwihl Canton; see GLA 229:32934, n.p., "Referat wegen Widersetzlichkeiten in Ablegung der herrschaftlichen Abgaben de anno 1749," 28 June 1749. On the 1755 deportations, see GLA 113:272, n.p., "Liquidations-Prothocoll über die von denen in den Banat Temeswar transportierten Hauensteinischen Emigranthen," 1755.

both factions to inspect the content of Hauenstein's "ancient rights" and to persuade *salpeterisch* delegates to "abstain from further conflict."[131] Thereafter, a succession of Forest Stewards continued to consult so-called "Octovirs of the *Salpeterisch Party,*" tacitly recognizing them as a tolerated, permanent opposition.[132] Of course, officials who believed that an excess of democracy had been the chief cause of rebellion would not contemplate restoring Octovir elections.[133] But because effective Austrian rule remained dependent on the active involvement of subjects, abolishing the Eight was equally out of the question. Instead, the imperial government suspended elections year after year until abolition was a *fait accompli,* which vested *müllerisch* leaders with a monopoly on local power as salaried officers appointed for life.[134] In this way, Ramschwag sealed the oligarchical trend of peasant politics.[135]

Thus the turmoil of two decades came to an end. Who had won? For many years, historians of early modern Europe have recognized that as opportunities for peasants to litigate grievances against their lords increased after 1525, so too did the proportion of favorable outcomes of their disputes. The transformation of social tensions into legal disputes, therefore, increased the likelihood that peasants would actually gain satisfaction. In the present case, outcomes beneficial to peasants are easy to identify. The imperial resolutions of the 1730s restricted St. Blasien's juridical rights in the county; and the 1738 manumission treaty emancipated all abbatial serfs; subsequent treaties would abolish serfdom entirely.

But the phenomenon of factionalism complicates this question of benefits. Emancipation, for instance, was both a result of rebellion and the occasion for further unrest. By the same token, factionalism

---

131. GLA 113:266, Vintler to Canton Birndorf, 1 August 1746; GLA 113:266, "Decretum Waldshueth den 4tn 7bris 1746"; Haselier, *Streitigkeiten,* 111.

132. See GLA 113:269, 3r–v, "Copia einer and die . . . Hof-Commission von den Außschuss der unruehigen Hauensteineren unterm 14 Xb. 1751 in Waldshuet ybergebenen Suplic."

133. For example, GLA 113:229, Beaurieu to Charles VI, 11 August 1728; GLA 113:253, 28r–v, "Extract löbl. V:Ö: Weesens Schreiben, so ahn das Waldvogteyambt ergangen," [ca. 11 February 1739].

134. GLA 113:258, 290r–v, Imperial Patent of 14 April 1746; GLA 113:268, 48r–50v, Imperial Patent of 19 April 1747.

135. In Dogern Canton, for example, three men monopolized the post of Octovir from 1768 to 1797; only four served in Birndorf during the same period; see Franz Quarthal and Georg Wieland, *Die Behördenorganisation Vorderösterreichs von 1753 bis 1805* (Bühl, 1977), 308–13.

confounds objective criteria for estimating gain and loss: if asked who profited by the Salpeter Wars, the Hauensteiners themselves would have given two answers, one *salpeterisch,* the other *müllerisch.* From a *salpeterisch* perspective, the Salpeter Wars were an unmitigated disaster. Their faction was excluded from public life, its leaders arrested, imprisoned, impoverished, and exiled. After 1728, not a single *salpeterisch* grievance was satisfied. In 1738, they had paid dearly for freedoms that, they believed, were already their own. Worse, Hauenstein lost the institutions they cherished most: elections and self-rule.

The *salpeterisch* defeat, however, was at best an ambiguous *müllerisch* victory. Superficially, the "obedient" faction profited handsomely: where before 1745 their claim to office had depended on popular election, *müllerisch* leaders now monopolized power by administrative fiat. But they were not so foolish as to think that this monopoly was an undiluted blessing. In the context of factional disagreements over the nature of authority, Ramschwag's reforms created a permanent crisis of legitimacy for the Eight. The *müllerisch* Octovirs-for-life understood this and throughout the remainder of the eighteenth century implored the provincial government to reinstate free elections.[136] For some, the strain of office was too severe. In 1748, for example, Speaker Friedle Baumgartner of Rotzingen asked to be relieved of office, citing the difficulty he encountered in governing a divided polity. For the same reason, the Eight threatened to resign *en masse* one year later, unless elections were reinstated. In both instances, the Outer Austrian government forced them to remain in office.[137] Thus the ideological and tactical conflicts that had originally given rise to factionalism in Hauenstein were not so much resolved as buried. The larger point is that any attempt to gauge favorable outcomes of peasant rebellions must account for peasants' perceptions of those results.

The irony is that in certain respects, the Salpeter Wars were an example of "juridified" social conflict, carried out in conjunction with the strategic application of physical violence. Whether by litigation or supplication, peasants made full use of sanctioned means for the redress

136. GLA 113:268, 138r–39v, Eight to VÖRK, 1 April 1749; GLA 113:268, Eight to VÖRK, 10 April 1750.

137. GLA 113:268, 144r–45v, "Inhibitions-Mandat ahn die sammentliche 8 Einungen," 19 April 1749.

of grievance. At the same time, Hauensteiners also used violence to press their concerns. The fact these two methods were deployed by two mutually hostile factions does not diminish the reality that peasants understood their options broadly and exploited them all to maximum advantage. Nor was this pattern altogether untypical: during a contemporaneous conflict in the Wetterau district of central Germany, for example, severe tensions emerged among peasants over the tactics employed by elected peasant delegates litigating on their behalf.[138] The only difference was that in the Black Forest, factional conflicts did not emerge from litigation, but preceded it.

It is further ironic that one reverse effect of "juridified" social conflict was the destruction of peasant self-governance. This suggests that trends more fundamental than the "juridification" of social conflict were at work in rural Germany during the late seventeenth and eighteenth centuries. The custom of elections—even of the imperfect and limited kind that prevailed in Hauenstein—could not long persist in a wider political world so hostile to autonomous decision-making by "ignorant" and "obstinant" rustics. Indeed, the present case suggests that peasant self-governance contributed to the formation of factions: as pressures from state and seigneur clashed with the obligations of peasant magistrates to their constituents, tactical disputes over proper responses to St. Blasien generated diverging opinions on the conditions of right order.

The combination of an electoral political system with factional strife in the context of struggle against a predatory seigneur brought the ultimate incompatibility of communal and feudal systems of political organization into high relief. As long as conflict did not disrupt it, the uneasy symbiosis of state and seigneurial domination with institutions of autonomous peasant decision-making might have continued indefinitely. But as the Salpeter Wars demonstrated, that symbiosis was all too easily wrecked. The Octovir elections of 1725, 1727, 1738, 1744, and 1745 inverted the normal flow of command, consultation, obedience, and obligation between peasant, seigneur, and prince: an ordinary Hauensteiner could not obey royal or abbatial decrees without

---

138. Werner Troßbach, *Soziale Bewegung und politische Erfahrung: Bäuerlicher Widerstand in hessischen Territorien, 1648-1806* (Weingarten, 1987), 246–56.

contradicting the policies of a duly elected magistracy, nor could the representatives of Emperor Charles enforce his edicts except by relying on the services of peasants who were prepared to defy officials chosen by the majority of their peers.

Yet the mix of interests in the Salpeter Wars was far too complex to sustain an analysis that would define the conflict as a binary opposition of peasant communalism based on popular notions of "ancient law and custom" and a feudal-aristocratic system of political command, justified by divine or some other right. In contrast to contemporaneous rebellions nearby France, for example, the Habsburg state played a decidedly ambiguous role throughout: while their ultimate concern was to enforce peasant obedience, Austrian officials were well aware that upholding at least the trappings of contractual reciprocities were crucial to that end. Much to their chagrin, the commissioners Beaurieu, Sickingen, and Ramschwag were forced to recognize that from the peasants' point of view, an official could no more abrogate electoral customs than a priest could suspend the Ten Commandments. Any attempt to modify Hauenstein's "constitution," if one may call it that, could be accomplished only at the risk of provoking further unrest. Lest they forget it, *müllerisch* Octovirs were ever at hand to remind them. At the same time, the commissioners understood that in the imperial Austrian economy of status and prestige, St. Blasien represented a far greater challenge.[139] It was therefore no coincidence that in 1737, the provincial government allied with *müllerisch* Octovirs in persuading St. Blasien to surrender its rights as serf lord in Hauenstein. To be sure, the state sided more often than not with the abbey. But at bottom, its primary role was that of a referee.

Moreover, political consensus within the peasantry was a dead letter from 1725 on. Hauenstein's governing elites could no more agree to a common political agenda than find a means of enacting it; as the controversy surrounding the session of serf court at Remetschwiel in 1719 revealed, they could not even agree how to distinguish legitimate from illegitimate action. Out of tactical disagreements within Hauenstein's magisterial elite emerged two distinct and largely incompatible articu-

---

139. On the concept of an economy of prestige, see John Spielman, "Status as Commodity: The Habsburg Economy of Privilege," in Charles W. Ingrao, ed., *State and Society in Early Modern Austria* (West Lafayette, Ind., 1994), 110–18.

lations of collective interest and action. That both factions concurred on the need to prevent annexation by St. Blasien was of little consequence in the day-to-day unfolding of events; *salpeterisch* leaders in particular were far too busy denouncing their opponents as traitors to entertain the possibility that a deeper consensus underlay factional differences. The sad irony here is that only the full weight of Austrian regime was sufficient to overcome factionalism.

CHAPTER 3

A House Divided

Dissension and the Geography of Fear

> Every community, every family was rent by partisan strife.   Josef Bader, 1839

How was a person to distinguish friend from foe? At various points during the Salpeter Wars, every peasant confronted this question. Answering it was probably never easy, especially in early stages of the conflict, when distinctions between *salpeterisch* and *müllerisch* were still blurry. By the same token, however, the stakes involved in each decision rose as the lines of factional demarcation hardened and partisan pressures intensified, imposing new and confounding expectations on older patterns of friendship and enmity. Records from the prosecution of *salpeterisch* "ringleaders" and the private correspondence of certain *müllerisch* potentates present a relatively clear picture of how political activists negotiated these hazards. But we know relatively little about how rank-and-file peasants answered the summons to take sides. In the absence of opinion surveys in the modern sense, one is compelled to try to reconstruct attitudes and motivations indirectly from evidence of behaviors as they relate to the flow of events and to structures of everyday life. Of course, this task makes sense only if one assumes that early modern European peasants were capable of articulating their interests in a variety of ways, and that there was no rigid, foreordained prescription for the proper relationship between individual thought or action and the collective interests of the "Whole County." What follows, then, is an attempt to describe the ebb and flow of popular sentiment over time and space, as it was reflected in the documentable favor ordinary Hauensteiners displayed toward one faction or another.

It would be a mistake to reify factions, however. Although the raw material of factional difference was already present in the earliest phases of the Salpeter Wars, the mass of peasants probably did not fully comprehend it until 1728–29, when factional violence and its repression forced the question of factional loyalties onto the consciousness of every Hauensteiner. It seems that neither the Habsburg state nor the abbey of St. Blasien understood the full complexity of public sentiment either; indeed, its very fluidity confounded their preconceived categories of political analysis, organized as they were around demonstrations of deference and obedience. The following exchange between one peasant and an abbatial official who was investigating a rally in which the former had taken part illustrates the confused nature of factions and factional allegiance during these initial stages of the Salpeter Wars. In their discourse we can see the pressures and confusions that emerged when lords and subjects tried to understand new and evolving forms of political identification within older frames of social and political reference. Specifically, confusion emerged from the interrogator's efforts to elicit responses that fit his stereotypes, and from the peasant's struggle to supply the "right answer" while avoiding self-incrimination. The episode shows that in 1726, peasants were still trying to articulate the definitions of collective interests specific to each faction.

This kind of oppressive exchange, multiplied several hundred times over, helped crystallize a pair of well-defined factional identities. Once Hauenstein's political culture had evolved to that point, the problem of categorizing popular sentiment became a little easier: choices and their consequences were clearer. Indeed, there is plentiful data on the popularity of each faction as it varied from canton to canton, from year to year. But the wealth of this evidence should not be permitted to obscure the methodological problems it poses. Many (though not all) of the tallies resulted from artificial attempts to divide and define: these are a series of extensive lists of *müllerisch* and *salpeterisch* peasants, assembled on the authority of imperial or provincial agencies, for the purposes of prosecuting the "rebellious."[1] Although these prosecuting officials strove to spare the "innocent," their punitive objectives required them to reduce a complex continuum of opinion to binary pairs of obedience and rebellion. Guilt brought fines, prison, and other forms of censure, which sharpened the distinction between *salpeterisch* and *müllerisch* even more. Thus factionalism was as much the product of rebellion as its cause.

These circumstances pose a "chicken-and-egg" problem. Did the tallies reveal *actual* divisions or merely a pattern of repression? There are, I think, two answers. One is that the dilemma is false, that it is neither possible nor even desirable to distill the effects of domination from evidence on peasant life. What purpose does it serve, one might ask, to try to erase the effects of domination from the documents of peasant politics, when most of its aspects were conditioned by the fact of subordination? In this connection, David Sabean has suggested that "what is a fact about sources is not necessarily a weakness. . . . There is an irony in the fact that because we cannot get to the peasant except through the lord, our evidence is often a good starting place for considering the relationships which we want to investigate"—namely, those of power and domination.[2] Rebellions, after all, inevitably pertain to power and its distribution. Both the documents of factionalism and the factions themselves share a common origin in the process of domination. The political gulf separating *salpeterisch* from *müllerisch* peasants was no less genuine for the role that repression played in creating it. The second answer flows from the first: the rosters reflect real divisions among peasants *and* a patterned effect of repression. If one conceives of factionalism as an evolu-

---

1. GLA 113:240, 255r–331v, 364r–77v, "Specification der Jenigen so ahn denen in der hauensteinischen Unruohen bis dahin aufgeschollenen 50,000 fl. Unkösten nach dem Steürfueß zu bezahlen haben," [1734]; GLA 65:11426, 98r–100v, "Specification wie von Kais. Kommission die Salpeterer an Geld zu den Unkosten verurtheilt worden 1739"; GLA 113:231, 9r–10v, "Specification wie vill Manschafft in denen 8 Einungen der Graffschafft Hauwenstein sich befindten von 16 Jahren bis auff ds höchste Alter, so von jedter Parthey in drey Classen abgetheilt, ein Theil über 60 Jahr, verheürathet, ein Theill verheürathet undter undt mit 69 Jahren = so den ledigen von 16 Jahren ahn," [1739].

2. David W. Sabean, *Power in the Blood: Popular Culture and Village Discourse in Early Modern Germany* (Cambridge, U.K., 1984), 2–3.

tionary process of conflict and exchange between complex groupings of peasants and lords, the "chicken-and-egg" problem dissolves. The exercise of domination was integral to the formation of factions, just as factions exerted a profound reverse effect on patterns of rule.

Several methodological difficulties remain, however. First, as sources on popular sentiment, the lists contain what modern pollsters call a sampling error: the status, age, and gender characteristics of "respondents" vary from one list to another. Certain tallies, for example, only record peasants with a particular legal status, such as serfdom; others counted only the heads of households, on the demonstrably false assumption that factional unity prevailed *within* each household. To complicate matters further, the tallies vary greatly in precision—some were impressionistic, and some were more systematic, but compiled sloppily and inconsistently. The second problem resembles what modern pollsters might call a framing error: The tallies reflect the responses to a wide variety of "questions." To be sure, tallies gathered on the instructions of imperial commissioners posed the question of loyalties most bluntly; other rosters, however, mirrored responses to more specific questions. Finally, there is no escaping the tendentiousness of rosters that the peasants themselves compiled. Several were assembled on the basis of denunciations by *müllerisch* Hauensteiners of their *salpeterisch* neighbors. Did personal enmities compromise the accuracy of reporting? Probably so, but one can only speculate how much. The only convenient route around these problems is to present the divisions contained in rosters as percentages of the populations they describe.[3] Thus the results should not be taken as exact reflections of factional sympathies; but they *can* offer a general impression of temporal and geographical patterns.

For now, it is enough to emphasize four overriding characteristics of public opinion in eighteenth-century Hauenstein. The first is that despite the pressures that factionalism imposed, the overall popularity

---

3. Where the attitudes of women dependents are documented, I have counted them in the appropriate faction. Otherwise, there is no option but to follow the polltakers' assumptions. The evidence suggests that factional lines often divided households and even nuclear families, separating adult household dependents from their parents or guardians. Here, too, I have recorded such divisions where they are documented. Finally, in the absence of any method to control for the distortions of patronage and personal enmity, there is no recourse but to accept the polltakers' judgment, with the caveat that it was politically tainted.

of either group could vary considerably in the short term. This suggests that the course of events exerted a powerful influence and that peasants followed them closely. The second characteristic, however, is that certain cantons displayed more-or-less stable inclinations toward one faction or the other. Broadly speaking, the central cantons of Görwihl, Dogern, and Birndorf were more likely to support the *salpeterisch* side, while cantons on the northern and southern peripheries of Hauenstein—Wolpadingen, Hochsal, and Murg—displayed stronger *müllerisch* sympathies. The fact that these tendencies correlated most strongly to spatial patterns of domination indicates their effect on the formation of political consciousness among peasants. On balance, these variations point to the influence of long-standing apprehensions over St. Blasien's threat to the institutional integrity of Hauenstein described in Chapter 2. When such fears became manifest in sympathy for the *salpeterisch* cause, they combined with regional networks of sociability to generate pronounced regional patterns, a geography of fear.

This leads to the third point. Viewed in tandem, the twin characteristics of long-term stability and short-term fluctuation suggest patterns of interaction between activist cadres and the rank and file, whose political commitments were less secure. As Chapter 4 will show, both factions drew for leadership on the same elite of relatively well established and wealthy peasants. Arguably it is their influence—in combination with the effects of military repression—that accounts for the stability of regional patterns in aggregate factional loyalties. But neither *müllerisch* nor *salpeterisch* activists could take the sympathies of ordinary Hauensteiners for granted; rather, hearts and minds had to be *won*. The significance of this relationship is that it points to networks of peasant sociability as the vehicle of persuasion.

The fourth and most important point is that almost every village and hamlet in Hauenstein was divided along factional lines. With respect to community as a cultural construct, it is difficult to overstate the significance of such ubiquitous disharmony. Because nearly every locality was split down the middle, it is difficult to sustain the idea that village sociability reinforced a system of communal political values strong enough to generate or enforce consensus. Moreover, the balance of factional sympathies was simply too even to identify either group as intrinsically more congenial to the preservation of communal interests. Were the link to communal interest strong, one would be compelled to conclude that the *müllerisch* agenda expressed it in the south, but not in the central cantons of Hauenstein, and vice versa. Discord, not consensus, was everywhere the norm.

To find a notion of community most relevant to factional discourses, one must look away from the village and toward the "Whole County." The geographical and temporal variations of popular sympathy for the *salpeterisch* cause betokens a widespread consciousness of impending enslavement—a term I use in the metaphorical sense that Hauensteiners themselves deployed to describe St. Blasien's threat to the common weal. A certain liminal quality in the regional distribution of *salpeterisch* strength expressed this sense of doom: the rebel faction was usually strongest just beyond the frontiers of abbatial jurisdiction that crisscrossed Hauenstein. As the events of 1738 would prove, moreover, no topic could reorient factional loyalties like serfdom. Thus popular conceptions of the common interest and destiny were fixed not on villages or parishes, but on cantons and the "Whole County."

Yet even if Hauenstein's peasants were motivated by the common need to preserve and defend collective freedoms, this did *not* translate automatically into consensus. If such notions of community had any effect, it was to sow disunity. Popular fixations with the "Whole County" provided a useful symbolic vocabulary to identify outsiders, but it did not prescribe means to achieve common interests. At the opposite end of the institutional spectrum, villages offered little more than a framework within which competing articulations were fought out. Over time, factions filled this gap: if lines of division were vague at first, the escalating dynamic of rebellion and repression transformed a factional dispute into factional*ism,* a habit of mind that imparted meaning to all political actions and relationships.[4] Thus factions became communities, whose boundaries and identities demanded policing every bit as much as the "Whole County" did.

---

4. See Pierre Bourdieu, *Distinction: A Social Critique of the Judgement of Taste,* trans. Richard Nice (Cambridge, Mass., 1984), 101–2, and *Outline of a Theory of Practice,* trans. Richard Nice (Cambridge, U.K., 1977), 78–95.

Johannes Hilpert and the Inquisitor

Factions were not yet "isms" on Wednesday, 8 November 1726, when Johannes Hilpert, a sawyer from the village of Finsterlingen, was summoned to appear before an inquisitor at the abbatial chancellery.[5] Hilpert's interlocutor wished to discover the significance of a large, unapproved gathering of peasants that had taken place in the village of Waldkirch the previous Sunday afternoon. He correctly assumed that the meeting had concerned the grievances raised by "Salpeter-Hans" Albiez against the Eight and the abbey. Albiez had recently returned from a trip to the imperial court in Vienna where, he reported, Emperor Charles VI had promised that the peasants' grievances would be satisfied.[6] Above all, the inquisitor wanted to know whether the peasantry as a whole agreed with Albiez. His interest was probably heightened by the knowledge that peasants generally thought of Waldkirch as the symbolic center of the county and that at the close of the rally, the attendants had been asked to choose between "the county" *(das Land)* and the ruling college of Octovirs. In framing the question this way, the rally's organizers drew an implicit contrast between the policies of the Eight and the proper means to defend the historic freedoms and privileges of Hauenstein. In a ceremony reminiscent of Octovir elections, those who sided with the "county" were asked to march around a pear tree and be counted.[7] Johannes Hilpert had marched around the pear tree.

To get the unambiguous information he sought, the inquisitor entrapped Hilpert in self-contradiction. "What does it mean," he asked, "to side with the county?" Hilpert reasoned that loyalty to the county signified loyalty to the emperor, an interpretation congenial to anyone. Unsatisfied, the inquisitor asked whether any peasants did *not* side with the county. His question drew Hilpert into the dangerous matter of political differences among peasants; struggling to evade the hazard, Hilpert equivocated. At this point the inquisitor pounced: first, he forced Hilpert to acknowledge the enmity between Albiez and the rul-

---

5. GLA 113:224, 117v–22r, Interrogation of Johannes Hilpert of Finsterlingen, St. Blasien, 8 November 1726.
6. Ibid., 403r–4v, Hans-Friedle Albiez to Conrad Binkert, 9 August 1726.
7. For details on the events at Waldkirch on 3 November, see the interrogation transcripts *(Verhörsprotokolle)* in GLA 113:224, especially 122v–27r (Bläsi Kayser of Neuenmühle) and 127v–36r, 137r–40r (Adam Schmiedle of Niedermühle).

ing Octovirs. Next, he demanded to know with whom the peasantry sided, Albiez or the Eight. Hilpert masked his response with a flourish of deferential protestations: the peasantry, he suggested, adheres to the emperor and the authorities *(Obrigkeit)*, to Hauenstein's ancient privileges, to the Eight, and to the abbot as juridical lord over the canton where Hilpert lived. Unsatisfied, the inquisitor injected a question that drove Hilpert into self-incrimination: "To which side do you adhere?" Hilpert parried with an transparently evasive syllogism: if "the peasantry sides with the emperor and the Eight," and "because I have already confessed that I side with the county," he reasoned, "then it necessarily follows . . . that I belong to the party of the Octovirs." Now it was a simple matter for the inquisitor to ensnare Hilpert in his own self-contradiction:

Inquisitor: How can these things go together, that the peasantry sides with the Eight and with Salpeter-Hans, who are in conflict with one another?

In response Hilpert at first feigned ignorance, but then acknowledged his inconsistency. Trapped, Hilpert played the idiot:

Inquisitor: Is it true that the peasantry sides with Salpeter-Hans [Albiez]?
Hilpert: If I knew which way to speak in order to tell the truth, then I would do it.
Inquisitor: Again, how can these contradictions stand?
Hilpert: That I leave to you.

This transaction summarizes eloquently the elusiveness of factional loyalties during early phases of the Salpeter Wars: neither participant could know that factionalism was quickly emerging as the dominant feature in Hauenstein's political culture, nor were the terms of their respective interpretations of political reality compatible. The inquisitor wished to discover the peasants' political sympathies, but could conceive of them only in terms of subservience or the lack of it: each peasant was either obedient or not, nothing in between. More: the inquisitor also wanted to know where the *whole* peasantry stood, as if complete unanimity among peasants were a reasonable expectation. Only information filtered through his binary oppositions would suffice, even if this meant that Hilpert had to augment his own understanding of political reality to satisfy his interlocutor. For his part, Hilpert was trapped between the actual complexity of peasant politics and the inquisitor's distorting assumptions, for he understood that the least suggestion of sympathy for "Salpeter-Hans" Albiez might be interpreted as disobedience. Hilpert faced a difficult choice: at the risk of self-incrimination, he could vainly assert the variety of political leanings among the peasants, or he could create information that fit the classifications of St. Blasien's agent. At first, he adopted the former tactic, but that created the appearance of dissimulation. Later that same day Hilpert finally succumbed and "admitted" that the peasantry sided with "Salpeter-Hans," pleading that he receive only mild punishments for his "lies."[8]

But Hilpert was *not* lying: there *really was* dissension surrounding Albiez's claims. Not everyone at the Waldkirch rally had marched around the pear tree: among those who did not was Johannes Bächle, an abbatial bailiff from Nöggenschwiel who attended only, it would seem, out of curiosity.[9] In November 1726, factional rivalries among Hauensteiners were as yet in the process of solidifying. Still, the abbatial inquisitor demanded and got the unsubtle characterizations he wanted. As the rebellion evolved, this type of pressure (conveyed through interrogation, military repression, and systematic persecution) separated "rebellious" peasants from their neighbors and polarized their complex quarrels into stark factional oppositions. Similarly, factions became "isms" at the nexus of two conflicts, one among peasants, another between the conflicting assumptions of peasants and lords. Thus Hilpert's confession was the combined product of intimidation and his own dread of persecution. His distress was understandable, but not unique: Hilpert and other abbatial subjects who attended the Waldkirch assembly each received a fine of about 13 gulden for their "crime," which was about what a day

---

8. GLA 113:224, 117v–22r, Interrogation of Johannes Hilpert of Finsterlingen, St. Blasien, 8 November 1726. Such interactions were commonplace; see, for example, GLA 113:224, 114r–17v, Interrogation of Joseph Albiez of Finsterlingen, St. Blasien, 7 November 1726, and GLA 113:224, 136v–37r, Interrogation of Peter Kayser of Bildstein, St. Blasien, 14 November 1726.

9. GLA 13:224, 52r–57v, Interrogation of Johannes Bächle of Nöggenschwiel, St. Blasien. The following May, however, he performed homage to Abbot Franz II, a strong indication of his evolving *müllerisch* sympathies; see GLA 113:229, 71r, "Specification der jenigen Mindergerichtsunterthanen welche zu Wyhlen den 13ten May 1727 das Handgelübt abgelegt haben."

laborer might expect to earn in a month.[10] The sum of these encounters helped generate a geographical pattern of factional sympathies that point to the crucial importance of jurisdictional boundaries in Hauenstein.

Time, Space, and Factions

If factional distinctions were still murky when Hilpert met his inquisitor, the events of 1728 and 1729 would define them far more sharply. As Chapter 2 described, a 1728 imperial commission of investigation headed by Franz Edmund von Beaurieu covered its costs with punitive imposts levied against peasants found guilty of rebellion.[11] That act established important precedents for future imperial interventions: both subsequent commissioners—Ferdinand von Sickingen in 1738–39 and Christoph von Ramschwag in 1744–45—would mimic Beaurieu by penalizing selectively, reinforcing factional divisions in the process. Compiling lists of "rebellious" and "obedient" peasants facilitated both punishment and the further hardening of loyalties.

Imperfect though they are, these lists reveal that already by 1728, certain regional patterns of factional loyalty were emerging. A few cantons, to be sure, exhibited major long-term shifts away from one faction and toward the other: Rickenbach Canton, for example, began as a *müllerisch* stronghold, but grew increasingly *salpeterisch* with each outbreak of turmoil. On the whole, though, the geographical contours of factionalism remained relatively constant. The first glimpse of these emerges from Beaurieu's assessment of fines, which was finally complete in 1734.[12] Unfortunately, the comprehensive lists of peasants upon which these fines were presumably based have not survived; instead, we are left only with lists of penalized Hauensteiners. To complicate matters

---

10. GLA 99:975; the fine for attending the Waldkirch assembly was ten pfund. The ratio between the pfund (lb) and the gulden (fl) was roughly 1 to 0.75; see Jakob Ebner, *Aus der Geschichte der Ortschaften der Pfarrei Birndorf* (Karlsruhe, 1938), 43, and GLA 66:3937.
11. GLA 113:235, 36r–37v, Imperial Patent of 15 April 1728.
12. GLA 113:240, 255r–331v, "Specification der jenigen so ahn denen hauensteinischen Unruohen bis dahin aufgeschwollenen 50,000 fl Unkösten nachdem Steürfueß zu bezahlen haben," [1734].

further, fines were levied against the "guilty" in proportion both to the personal wealth of guilty peasants and to the degree of their culpability. Thus two independent variables, wealth and guilt, determined the severity of individual penalties. One route around this problem is to express *average* fines (the total cash penalty levied against a village divided by the number of fine-paying peasants) as functions of the corresponding *per capita* fines (the total penalty levied against each village divided by its total population) in each village for which data survive. This procedure has the advantage of representing data that pertain only to the *salpeterisch* portion of the population in relation to data measured against total village populations. Total fines for each village are constant between the two data sets. This link enables one to portray, roughly, what proportion of villagers were thought to have supported the rebellion.[13] But again, this method is a compromise with opaque and imprecise data, and its results should not be taken as literal representations.

Still, the 1734 fine register shows a zone of support for *salpeterisch* causes stretching from the western reaches of Görwihl Canton to southern Birndorf Canton and to central districts of Dogern Canton. No single environmental variable united this region, of course, although many of the villages within it were situated on relatively deforested upland plateaus with relatively poor soils. Corresponding to this "rebel belt" are two areas of greater *müllerisch* strength, one in the three southeastern cantons—Rickenbach, Murg, and Hochsal—where soils were generally richer and the climate mild enough to support viticulture, the other in the poor, forest canton of Wolpadingen in the north. Finally, the northeastern canton of Höchenschwand exhibits a confused and patternless jumble of sympathies.

Yet in 1734, neither zone lacks pockets of dissent. Several *müllerisch* outposts punctuate the "rebel belt," such as Unteralpfen in southern Birndorf Canton, where *müllerisch* leader Joseph Tröndle lived, as well as Segeten and Waldkirch in the cantons of Görwihl and Dogern. Similarly, Bergalingen and Hütten seem to have been islands of *salpeterisch*

13. This method also has the virtue of canceling out extreme cases like the hamlets of Steinbach and Egg, which fall outside the normal range of distribution due to their diminutive size. The method enhances villages where both per capita and average fines were high. Conversely, villages that contained small but heavily fined *salpeterisch* minorities appear, appropriately, as relatively "obedient."

activity in an otherwise *müllerisch* sea. Dogern and Birndorf appear to have been the most evenly *salpeterisch* cantons during this early phase: within this region, two clusters of particularly intense *salpeterisch* support emerge, one centered on the villages of Oberalpfen, Bannholz, Ay, and Bierbronnen, the other a string of settlements stretching from Etzwihl through Birkingen to Eschbach. The latter cluster is the densest *salpeterisch* concentration in Hauenstein; their common characteristic was subjection to Austrian jurisdiction in cantons otherwise under the judicial sway of St. Blasien. A third and final cluster of unusually dense *salpeterisch* support appears in the villages of Görwihl Canton that were subject to the jurisdiction of the convent of St. Fridolin in Säckingen.

The content of later, more systematic lists suggest the long-term stability of these patterns. The most exhaustive tally of "rebellious" and "obedient" peasants, compiled in December 1745, reveals an almost identical political geography: once again, a rebel belt appears in the cantons of Görwihl, Birndorf, and Dogern (see Map 4).[14] It also shows *müllerisch* concentrations in the three southern cantons and in Wolpadingen Canton in the north. Even in detail, many patterns reappear. In 1745 no less than in 1734, the rebel belt was punctured by points of *müllerisch* support in Segeten, Burg, Unteralpfen, and Waldkirch. Similarly, both tallies show that *salpeterisch* peasants formed a large majority in the medium-sized villages of central Dogern Canton, but less so in more populous locales at the canton's periphery, such as Nöggenschwiel, Dietlingen, Weilheim, and Dogern. Moreover, the 1745 tally also confirms that the western periphery of Hauenstein was a *salpeterisch* stronghold. Finally, both tallies reveal dense concentrations of *salpeterisch* support in southern Birndorf Canton. These regional patterns seem to have remained relatively fixed for several years after the third rebellion of 1744–45 was finally quelled. The latest surviving data on factional sympathies yield results that differ only slightly from those of 1745. In January 1747, the Ramschwag commission surveyed the political attitudes of married and single males between the ages of eighteen and thirty, which revealed slight gains for the *salpeterisch* faction in the cantons of Rickenbach, Görwihl, Dogern, and Murg, and slight losses in Wolpadingen,

---

14. GLA 113:261 and GLA 113:264; unlike the 1734 register, these records do not combine the separate categories of culpability and wealth.

Höchenschwand, and Hochsal.[15] On the whole, though, the deviations were negligible.

Taken together, these continuities suggest the combined influence of domination and of regional networks of sociability on the formation of factional consciousness. The long-term stability of this geography must not, however, detract from the variability of popular sentiments in the short term, which fluctuated wildly depending on the political issues and pressures of the moment. Scant though it is, the evidence suggests that "Salpeter-Hans" Albiez enjoyed a degree of broad, popular appeal that his following would subsequently lose, as individual fates became more closely tied to those of factions. On the other hand, *salpeterisch* activists displayed a remarkable ability to sway public opinion. Even as late as 1744, the *salpeterisch* faction was able to win four of eight Octovir elections, and then sweep the *müllerisch* faction from office in 1745.[16]

The events of 1738 and 1739 illustrate most vividly the potential of factional sympathies to vary in the short term, depending on the politics of the moment. In those years, the topic that fired passions most was the *müllerisch* proposal to purchase the collective emancipation of all abbatial serfs domiciled in Hauenstein, and the balance of evidence suggests it produced a seismic shift in the balance of factional power. Unfortunately, the tendentiousness of surviving evidence makes it difficult to say exactly where the weight of popular sentiments lay on the eve of the manumission treaty. All we have are three estimates of opinion on the treaty, all of them compiled in February 1738 at the behest of the *müllerisch* Octovirs. They reveal the percentages shown in Table 2 (p. 104).

The first two of these data sets were intended to reassure Austrian and abbatial officials that collecting the manumission fee would proceed without incident and pretended to reflect, first, the attitudes of

---

15. GLA 113:223, 127r–v, "Extract aus denen Beschreibung der acht Einungen . . . wie vill ruohige und ohnruohige verheurathete als ledige von 18 bis auf 30 Jahr sich in jedtem Einung de dato dn 12tn Jenner 1747 . . . befindten, " and 44r–v, 48r, "Notanta," [1747?].

16. GLA 113:258, 54r–55v, "Specification der samentliche new und alten Redtman und Einungsmeisteren," 8 October 1745; GLA 113:255, 97r–v, "Specification der vergangenen Georgi ausgezogener newen Einungsmäisteren," 29 April 1744; GLA 113:263, "Ohngefährliche Beschreibung, waß sich bey der Einungsmeisterwahl am Tag des Hl. Ritters Georgij zugetragen begeben, undt da undt dorthen vor lästerliche Redten außgestossen wordten, undt zwar in der Einung Riggenbach," [28 April 1745].

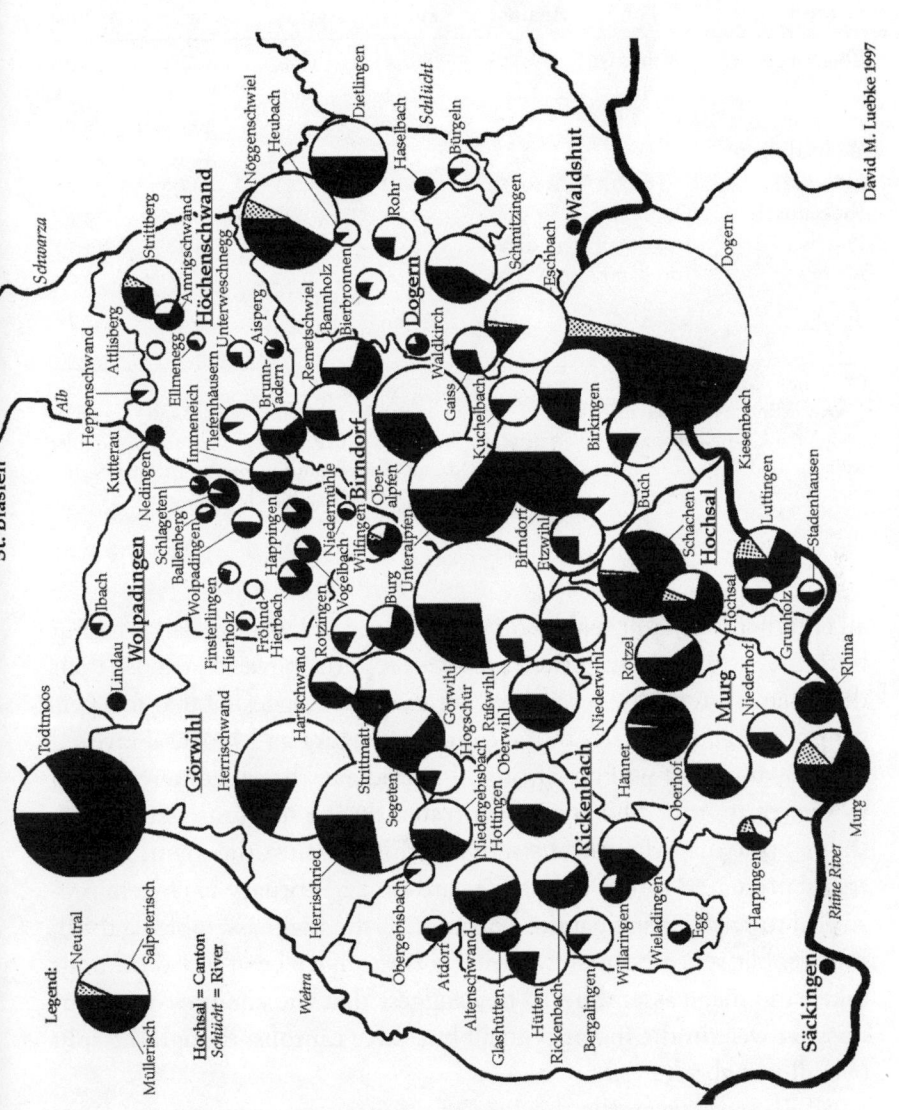

Factional distributions, by village, December 1745

TABLE 2. Peasants for and against the 1738 manumission treaty

Canton:	Estimate 1		Estimate 2		Estimate 3	
	For	Against	For	Against	For	Against
Dogern	98.04	1.96	86.55	13.45	40.94	59.06
Birndoff	84.45	15.55	81.33	18.67	37.68	62.32
Höchenschwand	36.87	63.13	40.46	59.54	30.00	70.00
Wolpadingen	96.61	3.39	100.00	0.00	42.18	57.82
Görwihl	69.07	30.93	76.42	23.58	9.09	90.01
Rickenbach	94.31	5.69	92.59	7.41	70.37	29.63
Hochsal	(no data)	(no data)	100.00	0.00	73.28	26.72
Murg	(no data)	(no data)	100.00	0.00	100.00	0.00
Total	***	***	82.09	17.91	46.87	53.13

(*** = insufficient data)
Source: Estimate 1: GLA 113:116, 50r–55v, "Specification aller ruhigen Burgeren" and "Specification deren Unruhigen," 22 February 1738; Estimate 2: GLA 113:116, 49r–v, "Specification der Ruhigen" and "Specification der Unruhigen," [March? 1738]; Estimate 3: GLA 113:222, 215r–216v, "Specification der ruehig und ohnruehigen Leüthen," [February/March 1738].

all enfranchised adult males *(Bürger)* and, second, of abbatial serfs. But both the results and the criteria of these reports, however, expose their diplomatic intent: the second set, for example, suggested that 100 percent of the abbatial serfs in the cantons of Murg and Hochsal favored emancipation, yet we know from other evidence that discontent existed in the south, too. This optimism rested on the spurious assumption that all peasants who did *not* sign a petition against the manumission treaty presented to the Forest Steward on 22 February 1738 were presumed to *favor* emancipation. Fortunately, the Eight assembled a third, more sober set of estimates, which seem to have been based on polls taken in village assemblies. They suggest that the enemies of manumission were in the majority in all but three cantons, though the split overall was about even.

To be sure, even the third set of estimates was not compiled systematically. But if we take these pessimistic conjectures as broadly accurate, then peasant opinions soon underwent a profound shift. *Salpeterisch* leaders were well aware of the misleading information presented in February and publicly condemned it.[17] In reaction to the manumission treaty, the *salpeterisch* leadership conducted a vigorous campaign to turn popular sentiment against the *müllerisch* faction during the spring and summer of 1738. To judge by a kind of referendum sponsored by *salpeterisch* activists in February 1739, the *müllerisch* faction had been reduced to a minority in every canton. Throughout the county, adult males were asked to endow with plenipotentiary powers of representation a *salpeterisch* delegation that had been organized to petition Emperor Charles VI to rescind the manumission treaty. Individual peasants were given the options of endorsing the proposal, rejecting it, or indicating their neutrality. The referendum revealed a sea change in popular sentiments since a year before.

TABLE 3. Estimates of factional strength (10 February 1739)

Canton:	Enfranchised Males (?)			In Percent		
	müllerisch	*salpeterisch*	neutral	*müllerisch*	*salpeterisch*	neutral
Dogern	130	853	48	12.61	82.74	4.66
Birndorf	82	583	11	12.13	86.24	1.63
Höchenschwand	73	275	0	20.98	79.02	0.00
Wolpadingen	40	254	11	13.11	83.28	3.61
Görwihl	76	918	0	7.65	92.35	0.00
Rickenbach	168	260	0	39.25	60.75	0.00
Hochsal	81	218	0	27.09	72.91	0.00
Murg	(no data)	(no data)	(no data)	(no data)	(no data)	(no data)
Total	650	3361	70	15.93	82.36	1.71

Source: GLA 113:244, 44r–47v. "1739 den 10. Tag Hornung hat das gantze Lant in der Graffschafft Hauwenstein die Vollmacht . . . in allen Einungen, die sich mit Gott und der keisserliche Resoludtion und mit der Gerechtigkeit wollen bleiben haben und legen und halten und mit denen Debitierten"; GLA 113:244, 103r–4v, "Specification oder Beschreibung der jenigen Manschafft in der Graffschafft Hauwenstein welche sich mit dem Berlaten undt allten Einungsmeystern haben und helffen haben und legen und fallen."

17. According to one *müllerisch* informant, *salpeterisch* activists emphatically denied the Octovirs' suggestion that "obedient" peasants outnumbered "rebellious" peasants by a margin of twenty-five to one; GLA 99:1040, 291r–92v, Interrogation of Hans Ebner of Unteralpfen, Unteralpfen, 5 July 1738.

Within a year, the *salpeterisch* faction had gained the upper hand in every canton. *Müllerisch* losses were most severe in the southern cantons of Rickenbach (from 70.37 percent down to 39.25 percent) and Hochsal (from 73.28 percent to 27.09 percent). In the cantons east of the Alb river (Dogern, Birndorf, Wolpadingen, and Höchenschwand), the popularity of the *müllerisch* faction fell an average of 23 percentage points, while Görwihl remained roughly constant. Finally, the tiny percentage of peasants who identified themselves as neutral testified to the degree of intensity that partisan pressures had already achieved by 1739.

These twists and turns of opinion reflected changes in *salpeterisch* rhetoric and organization. On balance, though, such fluctuations must not detract from the larger reality that over the long term, geographical patterns of factional sympathy displayed considerable permanence. This becomes especially clear when one compares data from the early and late phases of the Salpeter Wars. To show the relative stability of opinion beneath periodic shifts, Figure 1 expresses the county-wide percentage of *salpeterisch* peasants in 1738, 1739, 1745, and 1747 as constant (zero), and plots the *salpeterisch* percentage in each canton as a function of it. To be sure, both the constant and cantonal values are based on data that measure different populations—the 1738 and 1739 figures concern only adult males, the 1745 data show the attitudes of all Hauensteiners, while the 1747 numbers represent only the attitudes of males (married and single) between the ages of eighteen and thirty. Despite such "sampling errors," the resulting pattern indicates that certain cantons were consistently more favorable to the *salpeterisch* side: Görwihl Canton, for example, shows a positive result throughout the era of revolt. After Görwihl, a cluster of three cantons (Dogern, Birndorf, and Höchenschwand) fluctuates together, usually above the constant. Wolpadingen Canton varies rather more erratically, but after 1739, it slowly declines as a stable *salpeterisch* base. The three southern cantons of Rickenbach, Murg, and Hochsal remain consistently below the constant, although Rickenbach and Murg grew relatively more *salpeterisch* over time. Hochsal displays a period of "rebelliousness" in 1739, but this trend reverses by 1745 and 1747. On the whole, the graph confirms the relative permanence of regional variations in factional sympathies (Figure 1).

A House Divided ♦ 107

FIGURE I.

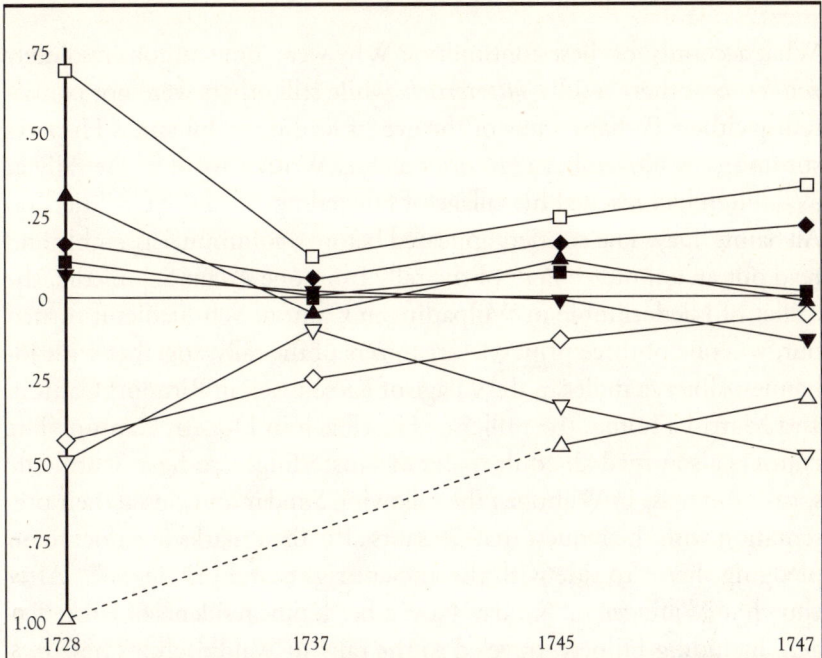

Key:
- ■ Dogern Canton
- ♦ Birnoff Canton
- ▲ Höchenschwand Canton
- ▼ Wolpadingen
- □ Görwihl Canton
- ◇ Rickenbach Canton
- △ Murg Canton
- ▽ HochsalCanton

County-wide *salpeterisch* percentages in each of the four years are taken as a constant (=0). Individual values represent the degree to which the *salpeterisch* percentage for each canton differed from the county-wide percentage for that year.

Sources: GLA 113:222, 215r–16v, "Specification der ruehig und ohnruehigen Leüthen in denen 8 Einungen," [1738?]; GLA 113:244, 44r–47v, "1739 den 10. Tag Hornung hat das gantze Lant in der Graffschafft Hauwenstein die Vollmacht . . . in allen Einungen, die sich mit Gott und der keisserliche Resolludtion und mit der Gerechtigkeit wollen bleiben haben und legen und halten und mit denen Debitierten," and 103r–4v, "Specification oder Beschreibung der jenigen Manschafft in der Graffschafft Hauwenstein welche sich mit dem Berlaten undt alltten Einungsmeystern haben und helffen haben und legen und fallen"; GLA 113:231, 9r–10v, "Specification wie vill Manschafft in denen 8 Einungen der Graffschafft Hauwenstein sich befindten von 16 Jahren bis auff ds höchste Alter, so von jedter Parthey in drey Classen abgetheilt, ein Theil über 60 Jahr, verheürathet, ein Theill verheürathet undter undt mit 69 Jahren = so den ledigen von 16 Jahren ahn," [December 1745?]; GLA 113:223, 44r–v, 48r, "Notanta," [1747?].

Domination, Sociability, and Identity

What accounts for these continuities? Why were some cantons resolutely *müllerisch,* others solidly *salpeterisch,* while still others were not consistently either? Perhaps a few of the events leading to Johannes Hilpert's summons in November 1726 offer a clue. Written word of the rally at Waldkirch had reached his village of Finsterlingen via three couriers on All Saints' Day. The couriers appeared before a communal assembly and read out an announcement of the rally from one Adam Schmiedle, the miller of Niedermühle in Wolpadingen Canton. Schmiedle, it turned out, was one of three principle organizers of the rally, together with Johannes Albiez, a miller in the village of Kiesenbach in Birndorf Canton, and Martin Thoma, the miller of Haselbach in Dogern Canton. The couriers also urged all adult males of Finsterlingen to hear Schmiedle speak after mass in Wilfingen the following Sunday and closed their presentation with the request that peasants affix their marks to a document pledging them "to side with the ancient rights and privileges."[18] After church in Wilfingen on Sunday, November 3, nine residents of Finsterlingen, including Hilpert, traveled to the rally in Waldkirch.[19] These maneuvers indicate social links and networks of communication, most obviously among the three millers—Schmiedle, Albiez, and Thoma— each from a separate canton, who spread word of the coming rally in his own or an adjacent canton.[20] As millers, all of them were in frequent commerce with peasants from many villages and hamlets. Like taverners, blacksmiths, wheelwrights, rent collectors, and peasant magistrates, they were well known to unusually large numbers of ordinary Hauensteiners.

The socioeconomic and kinship ties that bound them to other *salpeterisch* activists, as well as their methods for raising popular consciousness, are subjects for later chapters. For now, it is important to emphasize

---

18. GLA 113:224, 114r–17v, Interrogation of Joseph Albiez of Finsterlingen, St. Blasien, 7 November 1726; GLA 113:224, 127v–41r, Interrogation of Adam Schmiedle of Niedermühle, St. Blasien, 9–12 November 1726.

19. GLA 113:224, 147r–49v, "Actum St Blasien," 14 November 1726.

20. Schmiedle seems to have been responsible for Wolpadingen, while Thoma worked his own canton of Dogern; see GLA 113:224, 127v–41r, Interrogation of Adam Schmiedle of Niedermühle, St. Blasien, 9–12 November 1726, and GLA 113:224, 69r–70v, "Specification der jenigen St. Blasm. Niedergerichts Unterthanen welche auff die vom Mülleren in Haselbach jeglichen Orths beschechene Verkundigung den 3ten 9bris 1726 zu Waldkirch erschinen."

the content of their message and the way it was conveyed. In the first place, the three millers tapped into widely held popular suspicions about St. Blasien's annexationist designs against the county in order pressure the Eight; the fact that some five hundred peasants attended and that they traveled to Waldkirch from at least four cantons testifies to the public interest *salpeterisch* agitation was capable of generating, even in 1726, when the Salpeter Wars had barely started. That public interest, in turn, points to the role played by structures of abbatial domination in the formation of a *salpeterisch* constituency. Second, the millers exploited specific institutional media to get word of the Waldkirch rally out—in this case, communal assemblies and the Sunday Mass. Their labors, in turn, were organized by canton. Each of these units of social organization supplied ready-made audiences of peasants united (or divided) by common concerns—be they local, parochial, or cantonal. The ability of *salpeterisch* organizers to manipulate patterns of peasant sociability, specifically the institutional context of opinion formation, was crucial to their success.

How, then, did the intersection of structures of abbatial domination with peasant sociability create a constituency prone to support the *salpeterisch* cause? Here, too, the Waldkirch rally offers a hint and recommends a distinction. Although the millers exploited the aggregations of peasants that village and parochial assemblies provided, their rhetoric made no mention of village or parochial interests. Rather, their discourse focused entirely on the "Whole County." Even at that level, the millers made little mention of their specific grievances against Octovir policy, but appealed instead to vague fears that the Octovirs had acquiesced to St. Blasien's attempts to diminish the county and its historic freedoms. But it would be a mistake to assume a simple correlation between the experience of abbatial domination and sympathy for the *salpeterisch* cause. We know, for example, that Hilpert's canton of Wolpadingen was only lukewarm to "Salpeter-Hans" and his cause, even though the various forms of abbatial domination overlapped more densely there than in any other canton. Taken in isolation, geographical patterns of domination did not determine the distribution of pro-*salpeterisch* sympathies.

The case is particularly clear with respect to serfdom. In later stages of the Salpeter Wars, no aspect of abbatial domination aroused more popular indignation. As Chapter 1 showed, rules governing the heritability and obligations of serfdom guaranteed that by the time of its abolition in 1738, abbatial serfs comprised a majority of Hauenstein's population and were domiciled in every single village and hamlet within the county. But did these facts automatically create a *salpeterisch* constituency? Perhaps they help explain the ubiquitous factional disharmony in Hauenstein, but the story cannot end there. Among the highest concentrations of serfs were those in the far northern cantons of Höchenschwand and Wolpadingen, but these cantons were less reliably *salpeterisch* than villages located within the "rebel belt." Conversely, the *salpeterisch* constituency was also weak where abbatial serfs were relatively few and where the abbey exercised few seigneurial or juridical powers, the southern cantons of Murg and Hochsal. Rather, the political impact of abbatial serfdom was most potent in cantons under split jurisdiction. Although only the northeastern third of Dogern Canton was subject to abbatial justice, it had the highest percentage of abbatial serfs in Hauenstein. Marriages between serfs and non-serfs had obviously been commonplace for generations, even though servile *formariage* forbade such unions without prior consent. The protocols of abbatial courts record that the abbot did, in fact, enforce this privilege, which suggests that St. Blasien allowed extensive intermarriage between serfs and non-serfs as a means to extend the geographical scope of its influence.[21] As a result, around 90 percent of the canton's population were abbatial serfs by the time of the Salpeter Wars.

That percentage approximates the proportion of enfranchised males who in February 1739 identified themselves with the *salpeterisch* opposition to the manumission treaty (82.74 percent).[22] Of course, serfdom was not the only reason to ally with "Salpeter-Hans." For example, St. Blasien's seigneurial powers in Dogern Canton were greatly increased after 1684, when the abbey acquired the lands of the defunct convent

---

21. Contract protocols, for instance, are punctuated with entries under the rubric of "Erlaubte Hochzeit"; see GLA 61:14160–62. For regional comparisons see Peter Blickle, "Leibherrschaft als Instrument der Territorialpolitik im Allgäu," in Heinz Haushofer and Willi A. Boelcke, eds., *Neue Wege und Forschungen der Agrargeschichte: FS Günther Franz* (Frankfurt, 1967), 51–66.

22. GLA 113:244, 44r–47v, "Vollmacht," 10 February 1739; GLA 113:244, 103r–4v, "Specification . . . welche sich mit dem Berlaten . . . haben," [10 February 1739].

of Königsfelden.[23] The abbey's attempts to increase revenues on the Königsfelden seigneurie provoked a series of local disputes, which found their way into Hauenstein's formal grievances in 1728.[24] Still, the congenital spread of servility threatened to affect Dogern more severely than cantons that were already exposed to more comprehensive abbatial domination: here, the spread of servility might undermine the ability of peasant magistrates to administer royal jurisdiction locally.

A similar dynamic prevailed in the western cantons of Görwihl and Rickenbach, but with an important difference. There, abbatial serfdom also encompassed large numbers of peasants, around 40 percent in Görwihl and 50 percent in Rickenbach Canton. In these cantons, the abbey's seigneurial and juridical powers were even fewer than in Dogern; like it, most of these cantons—indeed, *all* of Rickenbach Canton—were subject to royal jurisdiction. Here too, therefore, any extension of abbatial serfdom threatened to undermine existing structures of self-rule. The difference was that in these cantons, abbatial authorities abutted those of St. Fridolin, with important consequences for the creation of a *salpeterisch* constituency. It was here that double serfdom was most likely to occur; indeed, the census of abbatial serfs taken in 1725 raised conflicts of divided status and obligation so complex that nothing was done to remedy them until 1730.[25] St. Blasien and St. Fridolin habitually resolved such conflicts by trading serfs, but these trades only generated greater conflict between peasants and the abbey. For peasants traded into the harsher, abbatial form of serfdom, such deals were unwelcome: as Chapter 1 showed already, St. Fridolin's dues were not only lighter, but notoriously easy to evade, and none of this was lost on the peasants. For Friedle Hottinger of Niedergebisbach, serf-trading meant

---

23. See GLA 66:7324–26 for lists of the properties involved; see also GLA 229:5664, "Zinß-Ertrag in dem Ambt Waldtshuett, extrahiert auß der Togemer Berain ao 1731, nach Abzug deß Tragerlohns," which summarizes fixed seigneurial revenues from the Königsfelden estate.

24. See §9 of the 1728 grievances of Hauenstein, GLA 113:84. On conflicts concerning the Königsfelden seigneurie, see GAD Urkunden 16, "Beschwerdschrift der Gemeinden Dogern, Espach, Gaiß, Kiesenbach, gegen das Stift St Blasien, die Rechnung des Weinzehends betreffend," 10 September 1729; GAD Urkunden 11, "Verhörsprotokoll, die Berainigung der Grundzinsgüter betreffend," 20 March 1733.

25. GLA 97:462, "Actum Dogern," 19 June 1725; GLA 97:462, St. Blasien to Abbess Maria Magdalena, 4 May 1730.

a harsher subjugation: in 1647 the convent had traded his mother, Maria Huber, to St. Blasien. Hottinger and his sons Bläsi and Michael found this objectionable, and it is no coincidence that all three were among the most active members of the *salpeterisch* faction. For people like the Hottingers, exchanges meant a smaller net return on agricultural labor and smaller inheritances to bequeath.[26] Not that resentment against serf-exchanges invariably transformed into *salpeterisch* sympathies; still, if the presence of *salpeterisch* majorities in the western parts of Görwihl Canton and central Rickenbach Canton are any indication, the problem was vexatious enough to elicit a *salpeterisch* response.

The point of all this is to suggest that the flint of abbatial domination caused sparks where it struck the hammer of peasant sociability: to the extent that cantons provided an institutional context both for opinion-formation and the exercise of peasant self-rule, they provided a frame of reference for evaluating the dangers that abbatial domination posed. As institutions, cantons assembled large numbers of Hauensteiners in the practical affairs of government and justice. Where jurisdictions were divided, cantonal business drew the subjects of royal justice into face-to-face encounters with the realities of life under abbatial jurisdiction and with the possible consequences of its extension. Here again, the example of Görwihl Canton is instructive. On the whole, no single lord held a clearly dominant position, least of all St. Blasien, which drew rents in only a few villages and governed the juridical affairs of only one (Rüßwihl). Although St. Fridolin was a far stronger presence, the largest landowner was the House of Habsburg, and Austrian justice prevailed in 80 percent of the canton's settlements. In practice, therefore, Görwihl Canton was a zone under local jurisprudence.[27] Insofar as the Salpeter Wars concerned the terms of abbatial domination, then, the whole affair should have been of little interest there. Yet Görwihl Canton was perhaps the strongest base of support for the *salpeterisch* faction; no other canton was fined more heavily, and no other canton yielded such consistent *salpeterisch* majorities. Why?

26. The problem also drew the attention of the Eight, who protested as early as 1698 that double serfdom threatened to "ruin the poor countryman"; GLA 97:455, "Extract einer kays. landständ. Commission von sambtl. V:Ö: Landstände übergebenen Gravaminen ao 1698."
27. GLA 113:193, [18th cent.].

A breakdown of factional loyalties by jurisdiction offers a clue. Specifically, the concentration of *salpeterisch* sympathizers in Görwihl Canton points to the fact that most villages with consistently large *salpeterisch* majorities lay *outside* the territorial confines of abbatial lower courts. In Table 4, the exhaustive data on factional sympathies compiled in 1745 are divided up along jurisdictional lines: the first category ("Austria I") shows distributions among all peasants subject to Austrian lower jurisdiction; the fifth ("St. Blasien") shows percentages for those under abbatial justice, the sixth for conventual subjects ("St. Fridolin"), and so on. At first sight, factional distributions appear roughly equivalent between the subjects of royal and abbatial justice: among Austrian subjects, 41.76 percent were "obedient," as opposed to 45.00 percent among St. Blasien's juridical subjects. The similarity is superficial, however, since the zone of Austrian jurisdiction included the two southern cantons that showed only tepid support for scions of "Salpeter-Hans." The second category ("Austria II") shows this pattern clearly: it represents percentages among peasants who were subject to Habsburg justice, but who resided in cantons over which St. Blasien exerted *no* jurisdiction (Rickenbach, Hochsal, and Murg). Among these peasants, the *müllerisch* faction was decidedly the stronger and enjoyed fully 9.38 percentage points more than the average among all Austrian juridical subjects combined. The crucial comparison, however, is between the third and fourth categories. The third category ("Austria III") shows factional distributions among Austrian subjects who lived in cantons under split abbatial and royal jurisdiction: Görwihl, Birndorf, and Dogern. Among the Austrian juridical subjects in these cantons, the popularity of the *salpeterisch* faction approached two-thirds: 65.14 percent, as compared to just over half (53.69 percent) among peasants subject directly to abbatial jurisdiction.

If any group had cause for alarm at the predations of St. Blasien, it was the population of the cantons under split jurisdiction—Görwihl, Dogern, and Birndorf (the category "Austria III"). Here, the abbatial presence compromised the canton's institutional integrity, and any intensification of abbatial power could easily be read as a mortal challenge to cantonal autonomies. If the challenge were not resisted, Görwihl, Dogern, and Birndorf might come to resemble Höchenschwand and Wolpadingen cantons, where the abbot exercised a heavy-handed influence over

TABLE 4. Factional strength by jurisdiction (December 1745)

Juridical Lord:	müllerisch	salpeterisch	neutral
Austria I	41.76	57.26	0.98
Austria II	51.14	47.14	1.72
Austria III	34.22	65.14	0.64
St. Blasien	45.00	53.69	1.31
St. Fridolin	49.00	45.68	5.32
The Eight	83.72	16.28	0.00
Baron Zweyer	62.66	37.34	0.00

Key: Austria I: All subjects of imperial Austrian lower jurisdiction; Austria II: Subjects of Austrian lower jurisdiction domiciled in cantons containing no abbatial courts (Rickenbach, Hochsal, Murg); Austria III: Subjects of Austrian lower jurisdiction domiciled in cantons of split jurisdiction (Görwihl, Birndoff, Dogern); St. Blasien: All subjects of abbatial lower jurisdiction; St. Fridolin: All subjects of conventual lower jurisdiction; The Eight: All subjects of the Octovirs' direct juridical authority (residents of Harpolingen and Willaringen); Baron Zweyer: All subjects of the patrimonial jurisdiction of Baron Zweyer von Evebach (residents of Unteralpfen).

nominations to public office. It made no difference whether the abbot actually possessed the resources to bring about such a change; perceptions were what counted, and peasants found ample reason to distrust St. Blasien. For peasants in the southern cantons, by contrast, St. Fridolin was greater potential threat, but generations of experience had taught them that the convent was easily thwarted. Conversely, peasants in the northern, woodland cantons of Wolpadingen and Höchenschwand had lived under St. Blasien's sway for centuries.[28] Here, shifts in the local distribution of power represented at best a quantitative adjustment on the status quo. A geography of fear, then, coalesced at the *frontiers* of abbatial power.

That fact points to the impact of boundaries on the political consciousness of peasants. Because civil jurisdictions were geographically defined, their effect on peasant politics showed a pronounced "liminal" effect: not juridical domination per se, but a complex, criss-crossing overlap of boundaries between zones of rule influenced the distribution of *salpeterisch* support decisively. To be sure, these speculations are grounded in several assumptions, first, that the majority of peasants perceived in

28. See Heinrich Schwarz, "Der Hotzenwald und seine Freibauern," in Friedrich Metz et al., eds., *Der Hotzenwald: Quellen und Forschungen zur Siedlungs- und Volkstumsgeschichte der Oberrheinlande* (Karlsruhe, 1941), 2:107–9.

St. Blasien the principle threat to Hauenstein's historic freedoms; and second, that peasants under Austrian jurisdiction regarded conditions under abbatial rule to be inferior to their own. Lest there be any doubt about the necessity of these connections, *salpeterisch* activists were ever ready to remind the rank and file. At the Waldkirch rally, the miller Johannes Albiez of Kiesenbach declared that "we juridical subjects [of St. Blasien] must carry a heavy yoke," and warned of dire consequences, should the cause of "Salpeter-Hans" find no support among the peasantry.[29] The fact that Johannes Albiez himself was not a "juridical subject" of the abbey did not dissuade many from "siding with the county" or from joining him in a march on Waldshut to demand the release of *salpeterisch* prisoners held there. Several years later, an anonymous *salpeterisch* partisan characterized a decade of abbatial predations as the advance of captivity: "under false pretenses," he argued, the prelate had conspired to "include us among those in eternal servitude to him." To that end, he had "demanded from the whole county . . . an oath of loyalty and obedience," to which St. Blasien had no more claim than what "the devil may demand of an innocent soul."[30] This peasant verbalized a general fear that all Hauenstein would soon be reduced to an illegitimate enslavement. None of this evidence implies that all peasants responded to perceived dangers equally, or that St. Blasien was the sole source of their anxiety. Rather, it shows how abbatial power heightened consciousness of boundaries in the minds of people living closest to them. It also shows how this shared sense of danger produced identifiable patterns of factional allegiance in time and space.

In the final analysis, however, the implications of one aspect of the Waldkirch rally deserves renewed attention. According to Joseph Albiez of Finsterlingen, perhaps two hundred of the some five hundred peasants in attendance were counted as "siding with the county."[31] In other words, despite all their manipulation of social and institutional networks, the three millers were able to persuade at best half of their audience to

---

29. GLA 113:224, 127v–41r, Interrogation of Adam Schmiedle of Niedermühle, St. Blasien, 9–12 November 1726.

30. GLA 113:241, 106r–10v, "Eine wahr Unterrichtung der *specii factae,* und die Warheit auss der Graffschafft Hauenstein contra Praelaten von St. Blasii," 1 June 1737.

31. GLA 113:224, 114r–17v, Interrogation of Joseph Albiez of Finsterlingen, St. Blasien, 7 November 1726.

pledge themselves publicly. Of course, it would be mistaken to assume that the rest rejected the *salpeterisch* cause: refusal to march around the pear tree did not necessarily imply ideological opposition. Bläsi Kaiser's reasons for refusing were a mixture of tactics and cynicism: under interrogation, he claimed that his reluctance had been grounded in the fear that participation would lead to "heavy costs." "The juridical subjects [of St. Blasien] are always called upon to be counted," he said, but afterward "remain the same as before."[32] Nevertheless, the halfhearted response at Waldkirch indicated the readiness of individual peasants to make their opinions known. As these relatively benign disagreements grew more bitter, disunity became near universal. Thus, despite all the variations of factional sympathy in space and time, Hauenstein's villages were unable to sustain even a semblance of political solidarity. Ultimately, discord underlay every pattern.

32. Ibid., 122v–27r, Interrogation of Bläsi Kaiser of Neuenmühle, St. Blasien, 9 November 1726.

CHAPTER 4

Big Shots versus Little People?

Social Dimensions of Factional Conflict

> I see the poor folk herded together by their opponents, who are roguish knaves, [and how] one binds them with iron chains and shackles, in order to banish them from the land as rebels. . . . I do not mean the poor folk who are daily tortured and burdened, but those poor folk, from whom the Big Shots press the blood of their fingernails and the marrow of their bones, and tear the last morsel of bread from their jaws, even while pretending to be in all ways more pious than the rest.
> From a sermon by Hieronymous Fenard, Niederhofen, 12 October 1755

AT THE TIME OF THE SALPETER WARS, THE CONVENTIONAL WISDOM held that *müllerisch* peasants were wealthier than their *salpeterisch* adversaries. The rebels often described their enemies as "Groß-Hansen"— Big Shots—in contrast to themselves, the "poor and oppressed" of Hauenstein.[1] On those rare occasions when *müllerisch* leaders described the sociology of their own following, they tended to concur.[2] Such self-descriptions implied that factional politics corresponded to divisions of

---

1. GLA 113:99, "Was Hans Meyer der Wagener zue Albffen im Wirtzhaus . . . ausgestossen," 29 March 1732. See also GLA 113:235, 57r–58v, "Freiburg Prisoners" to Charles VI, 25 October 1729; GLA 113:246, 15r–16v, Jacob Albiez of Buch to KK Sickingen, 12 March 1739; and GLA 113:258, 85r–86v, Open letter by Hans Wasmer of Segeten, 3 December 1745.
2. See, for example, GLA 113:241, 292r–93v, Joseph Tröndle of Rotzel to WVA, 5 April 1738. Tröndle assured the Forest Steward that despite popular resentment against the recent emancipation of abbatial serfs, "the best people remain proper" and willing to abide by the manumission treaty.

wealth and status within the peasantry. To some extent this assumption was accurate, though not in the way that contemporaries imagined, for there are many reasons to suspect that neither faction represented the interests of well-defined socioeconomic classes. Chapter 3 showed how factional loyalties varied over time and space—so much so that any simple correlation between factional sympathies and class is tenuous at best: the social composition of both factions was too similar, and the split of factional loyalties too even, for any but the most elastic notion of class to retain its explanatory power.[3]

What role, then, did social and economic forces play among the causes of rebellion and the emergence of factions? Spotty and anecdotal though it is, the surviving evidence suggests that during the first two decades of the eighteenth century, several socioeconomic trends merged with policies of St. Blasien and the behavior of Hauenstein's peasant elite to generate the preconditions of both rebellion and factional dissension. The result was that both factions were dominated by a well-defined elite of officeholders, wealthy farmers, and rural "professionals," such as millers and artisans. The origins of this configuration of power lay in a long-term trend toward greater social differentiation in Hauenstein, which in turn exacerbated oligarchic tendencies in the county's institutional structure. As a result, the tangible benefits of economic and demographic recovery from the catastrophic effects of the Thirty Years' War and the War of Spanish Succession fell principally to elites. Although unequivocal evidence of it is scant, these developments probably increased the dependency for work and protection of day laborers and other rural poor on peasants with large and secure tenancies. The resulting concentration of political power in the hands of rural oligarchs, in turn, magnified the consequences of tactical and ideological disagreements among them. The Salpeter Wars, therefore, were not some mechanical reaction to economic crisis, but emerged from social tensions attending economic recovery; they were not the result of some general immiseration, but of a selective amelioration.

But these trends did not develop in isolation from slow transformations in the structure and practice of domination. St. Blasien was, at the same time, attempting to expand its control over the land market in

---

3. See William M. Reddy, "The Concept of Class," in M. L. Bush, ed., *Social Orders and Social Classes in Europe since 1500: Studies in Social Stratification* (Harlow, U.K., 1992), 13–25.

Hauenstein. Specifically, the abbey sought to counteract the fragmentation of peasant holdings—that deadly result of demographic expansion—and the threat it posed to seigneurial incomes. Its objective was to wrest control over exchanges of real estate, whether through sale, trade, or inheritance. One tool was to extend credit liberally for land purchases: peasant debt would involve the abbey in the property transactions outside the territorial confines of its jurisdictions. Another method was to impose real-estate taxes within the lower courts; a third was St. Blasien's attempt to impose limits on partible inheritance; a fourth was to boost fines for ignoring subpoenas to appear before abbatial courts. Together, these tactics amounted to an attack on ancient inheritance customs and with it, on the peasants' independent ability to regulate property transfers. To be sure, it is not certain that the abbey's exertions bore fruit. But the *perception* of a threat to inheritance custom was just as potent as its reality. To some extent, then, factions coalesced around disagreements over the best way to prevent St. Blasien's triumph.

There are several ironies in this. For all their talk of defending Hauenstein's ancient traditions, the county's peasant elite had few qualms about ignoring inheritance custom when it suited them. As Chapter 1 showed, moreover, administrative confusion at the local level had not only enhanced St. Blasien's concern to install greater controls over land transfers, but *increased* its reliance on village notables, at least temporarily. This suggests that beneath the *salpeterisch* rhetoric of historic liberties lay a deeper struggle over control of the market in land, which in turn betrays their common socioeconomic interest with *müllerisch* leaders to preserve the monopoly of peasant elites on access to public office. A glance at the profiles of leaders on both sides reveals that they were cut from the same social cloth: rural elites, such as millers, innkeepers, manseholders, magistrates, and servants of seigneurial or juridical administration, dominated the leadership cadres of both factions. In its origins, at least, factional politics can be seen as an internecine quarrel within these elite ranks.

These similarities are full of implications. First, they contradict the common suggestion that officeholding peasants were necessarily more "integrated" into structures of domination than their rebellious foes. Leaders of the *müllerisch* faction included a large number of wealthy tenant farmers, millers, blacksmiths, and holders of seigneurial or public office. But these social attributes also describe the *salpeterisch* leadership.

Another implication is that while social differentiation helped create the conditions of factional discord, class did not initially distinguish the social makeup of either faction. By the same token, however, the surviving evidence suggests that faction membership became more biased socially as the turmoil dragged into its second decade. Increasingly, wealthier peasants with secure land tenures cast their lot with the *müllerisch* faction, while poorer folk more often inclined to the cause of "Salpeter-Hans" Albiez and his disciples. This tendency grew more pronounced as the conflict wore on, if only because punitive fines ensuing from the Austrian military interventions of 1728–29, 1739, and 1745 fell so heavily on the purses of individual *salpeterisch* peasants. Here, the causal nexus between class and politics was oddly reversed: class distinctions did not determine factional loyalties so much as politics, in the form of military and judicial repression, reordered factional affiliations along social lines.

If class did not mold factions, then what social forces *did?* I suggest that the social glue of factions was not class, but ties of dependence and kinship. Anecdotal evidence indicates that the leading elites on both sides were often linked by marriage; the result was that a century of increasing oligarchy perpetuated itself in the "dynastic" quality of factional leadership. This, too, is notoriously difficult to reconstruct, and the scarcity of evidence recommends only tentative conclusions. The Salpeter Wars ran their course in a pre-statistical age: village officials possessed neither the skills, the mandate, nor the inclination to keep regular accounts on demographic information and transfers of property, and there were no village notaries to compensate for these deficits.[4] The result is a dearth of postmortem property inventories, which might have offered a complete profile of Hauenstein's social structure.[5]

---

4. The earliest survey of income distributions was compiled in 1761 by the Octovir Johannes Thoma of Haselbach to assist in the collection of property taxes within Dogern Canton; see GLA 229:19644, "Rustical-Fassions-Tabella," [ca. 1761]. The oldest systematic demographic studies date from the era of Theresian and Josephine Reforms in the 1750s and 1760s; see P. G. M. Dickson, *Finance and Government under Maria Theresia, 1740–1780* (Oxford, 1987), 1:24–29. On the absence of notaries, see GLA 113:207, WVA to OÖRK, 9 January 1747.

5. Only a handful of individual inventories survive, but they were collected to levy fines against the patrimonies of *salpeterisch* activists who had either died or fled the county in 1732 and 1739; for example, see GLA 113:240, 52r–59v, "Schuldenbeschreibung Joseph Kolten ab der Haide," [July 1732].

None of this is meant to insinuate that class analysis has no place in the study of early modern peasant rebellions. Far from it: there can be no escaping the fact that virtually all the inhabitants of eighteenth-century Hauenstein—and, for that matter, most other agrarian polities prior to the introduction of rural weaving and other forms of "proto-industrialization"—were united fundamentally by common relationships to the means of cereal and livestock production through the management of the agricultural calendar and of access to communal grazing meadows at the village level.[6] These common bonds also distinguished the peasantry as a whole from urban and aristocratic outsiders. The fact that peasants articulated various means to serve the "common good" must not distract from the fundamental interests uniting them all against predatory lords. On balance, class better explains the broader phenomenon of peasant resistance, in all its forms, than it does the specific social complexion and political content of factionalism. In this sense, the Salpeter Wars were a deadly fight about how best to keep outsiders out.

Recovery and Its Discontents

As Chapter 1 indicated, the Salpeter Wars were preceded by a period of increased social stratification, as southern Germany recovered from the ravages of the Thirty Years' War.[7] During the first decades of the eighteenth century, the German countryside experienced a slow but steady ascent from agrarian depression and a gradual demographic expansion.[8] But these auspicious developments were a mixed blessing. In Hauenstein, they interacted with broadly egalitarian inheritance customs to

---

6. I adopt here E. P. Thompson's understanding of class as a set of socioeconomic relationships, not as a social group of individuals; see his *Making of the English Working Class* (London, 1963), 9–14.

7. Of course, the German peasantry had always known social inequalities, but social divisions deepened in southern and southwestern regions of the empire as the seventeenth century progressed. See Willi A. Boelcke, "Wandlungen der dörflichen Sozialstruktur während Mittelalter und Neuzeit," in Heinz Haushofer and Willi A. Boelcke, eds., *Neue Wege und Forschungen der Agrargeschichte* (Frankfurt, 1967), 80–103.

8. On economic general developments, see Wilhelm Abel, *Agrarkrisen und Agrarkonjunkturen: Eine Geschichte der Land- und Ernährungswirtschaft Mitteleuropas seit dem hohen Mittelalter*, 3d ed. (Hamburg, 1978), 185, 190–91; and on demographic changes, see Michael W. Finn, *The European Demographic System, 1500–1820* (Baltimore, 1981).

reproduce many of the social pressures that had plagued Germany during the fifteenth and sixteenth centuries, specifically, increased social stratification, debt, and the fragmentation of individual peasant landholdings.[9]

The evidence of local trends in grain prices and harvest yields hints that the recovery began in Hauenstein just prior to the first outbreak of rebellion. After erratic fluctuations between 1700 and about 1720, grain prices and harvest yields began a consistent increase, which continued throughout the period of unrest. The slow start was, in all likelihood, a prolonged consequence of the War of Spanish Succession, for as a comprehensive 1739 survey of economic conditions in Outer Austria noted, the Black Forest had been "exposed to the first approach [of troops] in . . . the French wars, through which it has suffered heavily in recent times."[10] In the quarter-century between 1725 and 1750, however, the average price of wheat in the village of Birndorf increased 84.75 percent.[11] Generally speaking, this pattern conformed to price trends throughout southwestern Germany.[12]

The rebellion occurred, therefore, at a time when peasants could expect greater returns from surplus agricultural production—if they were in a position to exploit the opportunity. In fact, the evidence of tithe collection accounts suggest that overall levels of cereal production

---

9. Karl F. Wernet, "Die wirtschaftlichen Verhältnisse der Grafschaft Hauenstein zwischen den Burgunderkriegen und den Salpetereraufständen," *ZGO* 98 (1950): 115–46.

10. GLA 79:3058, "Quaestiones den ganzen Statum der V.Ö. . . . Landen betreffendt," Freiburg, 23 June 1739.

11. GLA 62:34, "Kirchenrechnungen löbl. Gotteßhauß S. Crucis in Birendorf," 1702–51. These trends are confirmed by evidence from the grain market in Waldshut: between 1731 and 1744, the average March price of wheat increased 65.2 percent, that of rye 72.4 percent, and oats fully 81.67 percent; see GLA 227:223.

12. On price movements in the Southwest, see above all François Dreyfus, "Beitrag zu den Preisbewegungen im Oberrheingebiet im 18. Jahrhundert," *VSWG* 47 (1960): 245–46. Evidence from Hauenstein does not fully support Dreyfus's argument. Dreyfus describes low prices throughout the 1720s, followed by a gradual increase in the 1730s and 1740s; the upward turn, he suggests, was slower and later than in nearby France. The comparatively early rise in grain prices in Hauenstein may be attributable to shifts in demand in Basel, the county's primary grain customer. On movements of grain price in Basel, see Auguste Hanauer, *Études économiques de l'Alsace ancienne et moderne* (Strasbourg, 1876–79), 2:82–86, and Wilhelm Abel, *Massenarmut und Hungerkrisen im vorindustriellen Europa: Versuch einer Synopsis* (Hamburg, 1974), 169–78. Compare Alfred Straub, whose findings are closer to those of Dreyfus: Alfred Straub, *Das badische Oberland im 18. Jahrhundert: Die Transformation einer bäuerlichen Gesellschaft vor der Industrialisierung* (Husum, 1977), 41–52.

began to increase at about the same time.[13] To infer harvest levels from tithes assumes, of course, that the latter were consistently proportional, and this was not always the case: more forgiving tithe-lords, for example, often reduced their demands in years of dearth or bad weather.[14] Conversely, increases in tithe receipts might only betray the effects of more effective administration.[15] But in Hauenstein, most lords stuck to an old system of tithe-farming, in which peasants bid for the right to collect on the basis of officially estimated crop yields.[16] The resulting tithe registers suggest that in the 1720s, cereal yields entered a phase of prolonged growth that lasted well into the 1760s.[17] This suggests that at least some Hauensteiners responded actively to the new market conditions created by higher prices.[18] It also points to the exigencies of demographic expansion. Increases in prices and harvest levels dovetailed with a demographic recovery from the calamitous losses of the late seventeenth and early eighteenth centuries; indeed, Wilhelm Abel has argued that this demographic expansion was the driving force behind eighteenth-century agrarian expansion.[19]

But the benefits of recovery might be compromised by inheritance law. Generally speaking, the custom of egalitarian partible inheritance

---

13. GLA 229:9157, "Zehenden-Ertrag in der Pfarr Birendorff wie der Endhalt zeiget" (1695–1792); GLA 66:7283, "Zehendt-Register über die dem löbl. Gottshauß St Blasien . . . über Waldt aigenthumblich zugehörige Zehendten" (1687–1719); and GLA 229:109214, "Waldkirch Zehndrechnungen vom J. 1710 bis auf das J. 1733 einschlüssig."

14. In 1713, for example, the abbey forgave tithes throughout western Hauenstein because of hail damage; see GLA 61:10648 [Hochamtsprotokoll St Blasien], 37, "Gewährter Nachlaß am Zehendbestande [for Birkingen]," 1713.

15. On the use of tithe records as evidence for harvest fluctuations, see Emmanuel Le Roy Ladurie and Joseph Goy, *Tithe and Agrarian History from the Fourteenth to the Nineteenth Centuries: An Essay in Comparative History* (Cambridge, 1982).

16. See, for example, GLA 229:37381, III, "Zehents-Notanta über Waldt," July 1719; GLA 229:9076, "Specification des Zehendten Ertrags . . . ," 1746.

17. To be sure, these trends were punctuated by occasional crop failures—1701, 1704, 1731, and especially 1768–69 produced miserable harvests—but the broader trend held all the same. After 1770, tithe receipts stabilized at the new, higher level. This trend, too, corresponded with patterns found elsewhere in Germany; see Abel, *Agrarkrisen*, 196–219, and *Massenarmut*, 179–80, and Thomas Robisheaux, *Rural Society and the Search for Order in Early Modern Germany* (Cambridge, 1989), 254–56.

18. Abbatial officials voiced concern that grain exports from the Nöggenschwiel and Weilheim jurisdictions threatened to create "great inflation and dearth"; see GLA 61:10549 [Hochamtsprotokoll St Blasien], 22–26, 12 November 1738.

19. Abel, *Agrarkrisen*, 190–91, 196–97. Also compare Robisheaux, *Search for Order*, 254–56.

prevailed in Hauenstein, as it did in wide stretches of the southwestern Germany.[20] Under conditions of demographic expansion, this meant that with each generation, the number of plots under cultivation grew, while their average size shrank. In view of this, royal and seigneurial officials alike worried that in time, the "extraordinary fragmentation of [peasant] holdings" would leave few economically viable plots.[21] The condition of peasant tenancies on a royal manor in the hamlet of Schadenbirndorf gives some idea of just how severe the effects of land fragmentation could become: by 1742, its 57.64 hectares were subdivided into no fewer than 314 parcels; on pasture land, the average parcel size was a mere 0.18 hectares, on the arable only 0.19 hectares.[22] Such fragmentation was not unique to the Black Forest: similar degrees of land fragmentation plagued other parts of Outer Austria as well as the nearby Upper Margraviate of Baden.[23] A side effect of this was overcrowded housing: in Hauenstein, houses were subdivided just like fields, and permission to build new dwellings was often slow to come.[24]

Agrarian expansion, population growth, and inheritance law combined to exaggerate social divisions among peasants. In Hauenstein, the benefits of recovery were unevenly spread: for peasants lucky enough to inherit large, contiguous farmsteads, economic expansion offered the prospect of bigger surpluses and wider markets. But for the majority of rural folk, recovery probably meant more of the same—poverty. In fact, certain indirect evidence suggests that population growth placed many peasants under considerable economic stress. With more mouths to feed, the value of arable land reached a premium; persons unable

20. There were exceptions, of course. Indeed, it is doubtful that a "pure" form of partible inheritance existed anywhere in early modern Europe. See David W. Sabean, "Aspects of Kinship Behavior and Property in Rural Western Europe before 1800," in Jack Goody et al., eds., *Family and Inheritance: Rural Society in Western Europe, 1200–1800* (Cambridge, 1976), 96–111, and Wilhelm Abel, "Schichten und Zonen europäischer Agrarverfassung," *ZAA* 3 (1955): 1–19.

21. GLA 66:7325, "Berainigungs-Prothocoll des . . . Gotteshauß St Blasien," 1731. For contemporary observations on the problem of land fragmentation ("Zerstücklung"), see GLA 229:19642, 158r–59v, WVA to St. Blasien, 5 January 1732.

22. GLA 66:3437, 269–550, "Berainung yber dem Hoff Schaden-Byrndorf Anno 1742."

23. For the Breisgau, see Albrecht Strobel, *Agrarverfassung im Übergang: Studien zur Agrargeschichte des badischen Breisgaus vom Beginn des 16. bis zum Ausgang des 18. Jahrhunderts* (Freiburg, 1972); for the Upper Margraviate of Baden, see Straub, *Badische Oberland*, 28–31.

24. See GLA 67:1726, 485, Abbatial Bailiff Johannes von der Ach of Weilheim to OVA, 23 April 1733.

to gain access to it were forced to seek alternative incomes to satisfy their subsistence needs. For most of the rural poor, this meant wage labor. As Table 5 shows, by 1745 their ranks had swelled to almost 60 percent of the adult male population. Indeed, the laboring poor approached or even exceeded three-quarters of the total population in the more rugged northern and western cantons of Höchenschwand, Rickenbach, and Wolpadingen:

TABLE 5. Peasants and wage laborers in Hauenstein, 1745(?)

Canton:	Peasants	Percent	Laborers	Percent
Dogern	169	48.84	177	51.16
Birndorf	100	35.97	178	64.03
Höchenschwand	48	28.74	119	71.26
Wolpadingen	38	25.17	113	74.26
Görwihl	190	54.60	158	45.40
Rickenbach	59	21.30	218	78.70
Hochsal	98	53.26	86	46.74
Murg	80	43.24	105	56.76
Total:	782	40.39	1154	59.61

Source: StAFB C1 Landstände 90, "Specification der Dritt. Ständ. Städten, Dörffen, Orthschafften," [1745].

The social inequities generated by agrarian recovery were exposed even more starkly in a survey of rural wealth compiled within the relatively fertile canton of Dogern in 1761. There, the wealthiest 10 percent of all "proprietors"—that is, all peasants who tilled even the tiniest parcel of land—in Dogern Canton commanded over 43 percent of all income from land. The poorest 10 percent, meanwhile, disposed of only 0.13 percent.[25] To be sure, these data do not reflect the distribution of wealth from nonagricultural sources; nor do they reflect income from animal husbandry.[26] Most millers and artisans, for example, did not live primarily from tilling the soil; on this scale, they appear deceptively poor. So do the poorest Hauensteiners, who struggled to meet their

25. GLA 229:19644, "Rustical-Fassions Tabella," [ca. 1761].
26. In 1777, for example, Hauensteiners owned 1,723 oxen; see GLA 113:198, "Viehe Beschreibung pro 1777." See also Wernet, "Wirtschaftlichen Verhältnisse," 146.

needs with wage labor.[27] In any case, the register reveals the emergence of a socially and economically dominant peasant elite.

Finally, the recovery brought an increase in rural debt. The impression given by contemporary loan registers suggests that most peasants, even the well-to-do, labored under increasingly heavy financial obligations. The amount of capital loaned from parish coffers in Birndorf, for example, rose 30 percent during the rebellion, from 1,808 gulden in 1727 to 2,319 gulden in 1745.[28] The high rate of truant interest payments suggests, moreover, that large numbers of peasants were overburdened. By 1763, for example, interest on 9,093 gulden in loans from charitable and ecclesiastical foundations in Waldshut had not been paid in three years.[29] The sorry case of Jörg Vogelbacher of Bürgeln may not be paradigmatic, but it shows the extremes peasant debt could reach: when he died in 1740, Vogelbacher owed over 2,556 gulden, which was subtracted from his patrimony, leaving nothing for his heirs.[30] It is impossible to determine the precise extent of rural debt, but the fact that already by 1716, interest on loans may have accounted for 32 percent of St. Blasien's total annual revenues from Hauenstein suggests that it was widespread indeed.[31]

Increasing social stratification was not without political consequences. In view of the enormous responsibilities and paltry compensations of public office, few peasants could afford the investments that election promised. The result was limited access to public office, and as Chapter 2 indicated, the concentration of power in an oligarchic peasant elite was already well under way by the time of the Salpeter Wars. These

---

27. The data may reflect the social effects of rural weaving through the putting-out system, which Swiss entrepreneurs introduced after 1744; see Gerhard Endriß, "Landschaft, Siedlung und Wirtschaft des Hotzenwalds," in Friedrich Metz et al., eds., *Der Hotzenwald: Quellen und Forschungen zur Siedlungs- und Volkstumsgeschichte der Oberrheinlande* (Karlsruhe, 1941), 27–28.

28. GLA 62:34, "Kirchenrechnung . . . in Birendorf," 1727–49.

29. GLA 187:33, no. 3836, "Specification aller derenjenigen in der Grafschafft Hawenstein, welche in die milde Stüfftungen dahier von ihren schuldigen Capitalien mehr dan 3 Zinse mit = 1763 inclus. aufflaufen laßen," 30 January 1764.

30. GLA 229:111414, 46r–47v.

31. GLA 79:2875, "Jährlich-ohngefährlicher Ertrag des Gotteshauß St Blasien sambt dess incorporierten Pfarreyen und Kirchen in dem Oesterreichischen," [1716]. Similar debt levels obtained in the Upper Margraviate, which experienced a severe credit crisis after the failed harvest of 1709; see Straub, *Badische Oberland*, 56–62.

social strains and oligarchic pressures generated the preconditions for rebellion and factional strife, but not the conflicts themselves: absent St. Blasien's responses to land fragmentation, for example, the rebellions might never have occurred. Instead, the conflict erupted when abbatial policies collided with the new, more stratified social environment of peasant politics in the county.

Aristocratic Reactions, Peasant Responses

In many ways, the economic recovery promised to swell St. Blasien's coffers, just as it promised new wealth to well-positioned peasants. Most obviously, bigger harvests generated heftier tithe receipts; a general increase in prosperity might also justify boosting quitrents on abbatial tenancies. Yet other aspects of the recovery were less welcome. The fragmentation of peasant landholdings, in particular, created an administrative nightmare for St. Blasien: the burden of tracking parcels grew with each additional subdivision, and inevitably some parcels were lost to attrition.[32] Large plots of land provided a more efficient tribute base, but if surplus production declined as plots shrank, the weight of fixed dues and services on individual peasants grew. It seems probable, finally, that the increasing number of land-poor peasants found it increasingly difficult to pay rents at all. If seigneurial incomes were to be salvaged, these threats demanded some response. Already in 1692, for instance, the High Steward of Gurtweil had recommended a thorough "renovation" of seigneurial records, because parcels were "all shattered and partitioned."[33] Cadastral surveys of peasant holdings might hold fragmentation in check, and indeed the abbey's seigneurial records were "renovated" in 1709 and 1731.[34] But these were only temporary solutions. A lasting solution would involve tighter legal control over land transfers.

---

32. From the end of the seventeenth century on, the abbey's seigneurial officers regularly informed St. Blasien of the disastrous effects of subdivision on revenues; see, for example, GLA 67:1724, 14 November 1688, case 10; GLA 67:1724, 9 July 1699; and GLA 99:310, "Betrifft die Verstücklung der Häuser und Güter im Zwing und Bahn," [1742].

33. GLA 67:1724, 1692, case 10.

34. GLA 66:7296, "Zinsrodel deß Waldamts," 1709; GLA 66:7325, "Berainigungs-Prothocoll," 1731.

It came in the form of limits on partible inheritance, but the task of implementing them could not succeed except at the expense of peasant autonomy in affairs of property exchange. Local custom safeguarded this independence of action with two provisions, first, the so-called right of withdrawal (*Zugrecht* or *jus retractus,* a custom akin to the French *retrait lignager*),[35] and second, the peasants' traditional freedom in the buying and selling of land. The right of withdrawal enabled siblings to appropriate a portion of lands alienated by sale or trade from family patrimonies: according to the territorial law of 1552, if a peasant sold all his properties to a single heir, the "heir's brother" could legally appropriate half of the lands in question, provided he claimed the right within a month. Similarly, custom allowed heirs to appropriate a share if their father sold part of his lands to a "stranger"—anyone outside the immediate lineage group.[36] Also, male siblings might withhold from lands sold "between brothers of the same parents" *(inter fratres germanos).* Thus the right of withdrawal protected the nuclear family as an intergenerational channel of landed wealth and the social prestige it entailed. Like partible inheritance customs, the right of withdrawal asserted the proprietary rights of lineage groups over individuals and allowed "children to nullify the will of their father."[37] To be sure, it also constrained the ability of peasants to alienate property freely. Yet despite these inconsistencies, these customs provided a set of mechanisms governed, for the most part, by and among peasants.

If customary constraints on the land market were many, however, seigneurial limits had always been few, or so most Hauensteiners believed. In 1723, for example, they complained against abbatial restrictions on partible inheritance, arguing that it had been "always been normal and customary," a claim they repeated in 1728.[38] On the whole, the sale and

---

35. Emmanuel Le Roy Ladurie, "Système de la coutume: Structures familiales et coutume d'heritage en France au XVIe siècle," *AESC* 27 (1972): 825–46.

36. "Landsordnung des Schwartzwalds," 19 December 1552, in Josef Bader, ed., "Nachträge zu den Mittheilungen über die Grafschaft Hauenstein," *ZGO* 12 (1861): 118–22 ["Von Verlassung der Güeter"].

37. This according to the imperial ban against the practice; Decree of Charles VI, 8 August 1731, §1, excerpted in Josef Bader, ed., "Urkundenregeste über die ehemalige sanktblasischen Niedergerichte," *ZGO* 7 (1856): 335.

38. GLA 113:98, Juridical Subjects to Abbot Blasius III, 17 December 1723; GLA 65:11419, 51–61, "Gravamina des Schwarzwaldes," 8 June 1728, §18.

inheritance of peasant lands had proceeded with little official interference.[39] Certainly, tenancy contracts involving abbatial manses constrained the peasants' ability to subdivide their patrimonies without permission, but there is ample evidence that manseholders often ignored bans against partition.[40] Apart from manse contracts, moreover, the terms of tenancy on abbatial lands placed few restrictions on real-estate exchanges. Chapter 1 showed that in addition to manses, St. Blasien in practice recognized only one other form of tenancy—quitrent-estates—which were alienable without permission or compensation to the abbey. Prior to the 1720s, therefore, little in the legal structure of seigneurial domination prevented peasants from disposing of their lands as private property.

One final custom symbolized that autonomy: the ceremonial "purchase of wine" *(Weinkauf)*, a ritual that closed all transactions. At the conclusion of a predetermined period after an agreement to purchase or trade land, buyer and seller closed a deal with a public, ritual toast. During the interval between contract and closure, qualified kin could assert their right of withdrawal. Viewed in isolation from the nexus of peasant-lord relations, the ceremony of *Weinkauf* marked the restoration of harmony after a readjustment in the disposition of property, and the social status it entailed. In the context of seigneurial relations, it signified the peasants' autonomy in real-estate exchanges: the ceremonial pouring of wine, not the official registration of a sale, finalized a deal. The distinction was important: it determined whether the public schedule for asserting the privileges of lineage opened and closed on peasants' time, or the abbot's.[41]

St. Blasien aimed to change all this by subordinating the land market to its own arbitration. In addition to a ban on partitions below a minimum parcel size, the abbey also sought to abolish the right of withdrawal,

---

39. See, for example, official observations in the preamble to GLA 66:7325, "Berainigungs-Prothocoll," 1731.

40. See, for example, GLA 229:9112, no. 2, "Bericht wie der St Blas. Lehen-Frohn-Hoff zu Birndorff seit vor Hundert Jahren hero vertheilet und von welchen Lehen-Leüthen solcher theilbar biß hero besessen worden," 1763; and GLA 229:111412, "Geschlechts-Tafell der Fronhofs Besizeren zu Weilheim von 1550 bis 1781."

41. GLA 99:983, [Joseph Tröndle of Rotzel], "Copia was Hans Fritlin Albüöz der sogenante Salbeter dn 6 Jener 1727 in dem löbl. Regemenz-Haus Freyburg, den Adam Schmitlin Müller von Nitermühle für ein Schreiben . . . hisaugeben hat." Compare also Robisheaux, *Search for Order*, 117.

to impose a one percent sales tax on real estate purchases in excess of 1,000 gulden in value, and to introduce a requirement to register all land transactions—including inheritances and dowries—with abbatial offices.[42] At the same time, abbatial officials reasserted the existing terms of manse contracts.[43] In this, St. Blasien sometimes went so far as to dispossess natural heirs in favor of persons better able to maintain a manse; in this way Jacob Welti acquired a manse in Birndorf, despite the inheritance claims of Christa Eckert.[44] These changes also coincided with increases in the monetized value of certain seigneurial dues and services. For instance, St. Blasien gradually raised the value of certain wine-portage services from 15 gulden to 16 gulden in 1714, and again to 17 gulden in 1715;[45] it also attempted to raise the level of wine tithes in and around the village of Dogern, near Waldshut.[46] In 1710, finally, the abbey increased fines levied against juridical subjects who ignored summonses—the equivalent of 40 kreuzer for the first failure to respond to a subpoena, 1 gulden 20 kreuzer for the second failure, and a hefty 6 gulden 40 kreuzer for the third—as well as the rigor with which these and other dues were collected.[47]

Together, these tactics offered the abbey greater control over peasant economies and, of course, new incomes. They also equipped St. Blasien with a de facto veto over property transactions: unregistered sales and inheritances could be (and often were) declared void.[48] It is difficult to say how effective these policies were; indications are that the abbey's

42. See GLA 229:37293, "Verbott wegen Verstückelung der Lehen- und Zinsgüter in der Herrschafft Gutenburg," 6 July 1731 (which repeated a decree of 1696), and GLA 113:228, 145r–48v, "Copia St Blasm. Taxordnung soviel selbe dessen Mindergerichtl. Unterthanen betrifft," [1728].

43. See GLA 229:37289, "Fundamental-Ursachen des lobl. Gottshaus St Blasien in dem Amt Gutenburg etwelchen Hoff zur Lehen anspreche, welch von denen Inhabern allein für Zinßgüeter gehalten werden," 7–10 January 1671.

44. GLA 67:1724, 599, 13 April 1709.

45. GLA 187:16, "Abrechnung wegen den jährlichen Fuhren, welche von den Besitzern der St Blasianischen Weinmänni-Gütern . . . ao. 1710–1718."

46. GAD Urkunden 16, "Beschwerdeschrift der Gemeinde Dogern . . . des Weinzehents betreffend," 10 September 1729; GAD Urkunden 11, "Rezeß zwischen dem Stifte St Blasien [und] der Gemeinde Togeren . . . des nunmehr abgethanen sogenannten Kübelschwancks betreffend," 28 September 1731.

47. GLA 67:1725, OVA to Speaker of Hauenstein, 9 November 1714.

48. For example, see GLA 61:5776, 6–7, "Null- und nichtig declarierter Kauff," 28 June 1738.

intrusions often failed. But successful or not, the abbey's innovations were perceived as an attack on custom and triggered an allergic political reaction. Throughout the first two decades of the eighteenth century, for example, the Eight bitterly objected to limits on partible inheritance and the right of withdrawal.[49] At the Remetschwiel serf court in 1719, in negotiations surrounding the Accord of Dogern in March 1720, at the homage to Blasius III in 1721, and finally in grievances presented in 1723, the Eight complained that St. Blasien had openly violated the customary structure of real-estate exchange.[50] But the hottest controversy centered on the level of subpoena fines—and by implication, on St. Blasien's ability to enforce its new policies. The Eight protested that the new, higher subpoena fines introduced in 1710 exceeded the maximum allowed by territorial custom.[51] No matter: the Eight lodged formal objections to the new rates in 1719, 1720, 1721, and 1723.[52] Each time St. Blasien rejected the grievance out of hand.

Eventually, St. Blasien's attack on peasant autonomy provided some of the legal stuff of rebellion. Ten of the thirty-nine grievances Hauenstein presented to the Beaurieu commission in 1728, for example, raised objections to St. Blasien's innovations in the land market.[53] From the

---

49. GLA 229:9138, "Bettr. Huldigung â Abt Otto," 22 September 1664; GLA 113:78, "Beschwöhrungs-Puncten von Redtmann undt Einungsmäister, auch denen Nidergerichts Leibfahlbahren, undt Gotteshaus Zinsbahr Underthanen der Graffschafft Hawenstein, wider ... St Blasien," [January 1698]; GLA 65:11419, 5r–6r, "Gravamina des Schwarzwaldes," 8 June 1728.

50. GLA 229:5658, "Puncta welche bey dem Dinggericht zue Remmetschweyll von der Graffschafft Hawenstein eingegeben werden," 14 May 1719; GLA 99:979, "Actum St Blasien," 5 June 1720; GLA 99:428, 229–331, "Huldigungs Prothocoll über eingenomene Huldigung in der Graffschafft Hawenstein," 9–11 September 1721; GLA 99:979 and GLA 113:89, Juridical Subjects to Abbot Blasius III, 17 December 1723.

51. Specifically, the Eight contended that custom set a cumulative maximum of 6 gulden 40 kreuzer on subpoena charges, instead of the cumulative 8 gulden 40 kreuzer levied by St. Blasien. Abbatial officials countered that no single subpoena exceeded the customary amount, and that the customary maximum was not cumulative; GLA 67:1725, 9 November 1714, case 2, and GLA 99:428, 229–331, "Huldigungs Prothocoll," 9–11 September 1721.

52. GLA 229:5658, "Puncta ... der Graffschafft Hawenstein," 14 May 1719; GLA 113:225, 128r–31v, "Protocoll und freundnachbarl. Verabschiedung vom 22. März 1720"; GLA 99:979, "Actum St Blasien," 5 June 1720; GLA 99:428, 229–331, "Huldigungs Prothocoll," 9–11 September 1721; GLA 113:89, Juridical Subjects to Abbot Blasius III, 17 December 1723.

53. Specifically, the peasantry again rejected subpoena rates imposed in 1710, various other taxes (§§ 16–17, 19, 22), and the ban against subdivision (§§ 18, 23); finally, article 21 amounted to a protest against the abbey's right to enforce the terms of lease contracts involving manses; GLA 65:11419, 5r–6r, "Gravamina des Schwarzwaldes," 8 June 1728.

ensuing legal wrangling, St. Blasien emerged the pyrrhic victor. Although an imperial resolution of 1731 voided the abbey's 1710 subpoena schedule, it also abolished the right of withdrawal and established guidelines whereby inheritances might be concentrated in the hands of a single heir.[54] Later, finally, the Reischach Reforms of 1735 prohibited subdivision below the acreage needed to sustain a single head of cattle.[55]

But if these legal squabbles fueled conflict between Hauenstein and the abbey, they were *not* the stuff of factional dissension. As Chapter 2 noted, the process of litigating grievances before the Beaurieu commission was carried out by a joint committee of *müllerisch* and *salpeterisch* representatives, all of them incumbent or former Octovirs. Their complaints, therefore, should not be seen as a transcript of special *salpeterisch* interests, but of the whole peasant elite. Peasant elites on both sides of the factional divide could agree to thwart St. Blasien's attack on custom; however, they could not agree on how to resist the abbey or on the assumptions of right order underlying their choices of method.

A Social Profile of Factional Leadership

There is an irony in this consensus, for those very elites often evaded custom themselves. In conformity with their lease contracts, manseholders often favored single heirs, even though the leases both violated custom and were easily evaded.[56] Others evaded partible inheritance custom by means of sale: in old age, tenants of quitrent-estates often sold their lands to one heir, often at low cost, in exchange for a retirement pension, or *Leibding*. Although heirs were usually obliged to compensate their siblings monetarily, neither the right of withdrawal nor partibility was allowed to interfere.[57] According to the well-informed

---

54. Decree of Charles VI, 8 August 1731, excerpted in Bader, ed., "Urkundenregeste," 335. At the same time, it allowed peasants to dispose of quitrent-estates freely.

55. Decree of Maria Theresa, 28 April 1753, enacting the Reischach Reforms of 26 March 1735, excerpted in J. Bader, ed., "Urkunden und Regeste aus dem Archive der ehemaligen Grafschaft Hauenstein," *ZGO* 11 (1860): 488–89.

56. Georg Thoma bought his father Hans's entire patrimony (a demi-manse) in 1716; GLA 11:4007, 10 October 1718. Georg, in turn, sold these lands to his son Hans Jörg in 1733 and 1738; GLA 11:4008, 16 April 1728, and GLA 61:14160 [Kontraktenprotokoll OVA], 8, 14 June 1738.

57. For examples from the village of Weilheim, see GLA 61:14160 [Kontraktenprotokoll OVA], 301, 20 May 1740, and GLA 61:14161 [Kontraktenprotokoll OVA], 209, 7 January

miller Joseph Tröndle of Unteralpfen, this habit was widespread; the result was an arrangement similar to the inheritance system of "preferential legacy" *(préciput)* that prevailed in parts of northern France.[58] In a related practice, wealthy peasants consolidated their parcels by swapping, but did not allow the right of withdrawal to complicate such deals.[59] Either way, tenants could enlist abbatial bans to serve their personal goals. Thus, while they resisted St. Blasien's intrusions, many elites often pursued strategies of land acquisition that defied custom.

But this did not automatically create a community of interest with the abbey. On the contrary, the matter at stake was principally one of control: peasant elites sought to remove all legal constraints—whatever their origin—on the ability to dispose of property freely. Many of the same manseholders who obeyed their lease contracts also battled to strengthen their autonomous property rights by having their tenancies redefined as quitrent-estates, which would enable them to buy, sell, and subdivide at liberty.[60] In the village of Nöggenschwiel, for example, Hans Jörg Thoma and the abbatial bailiff Johannes Bächle conducted a long-winded legal campaign to redefine their tenancies, until a decision of 3 March 1751 finally ended the matter, albeit without satisfying either plaintiff.[61] Such requests were usually refused, which obliged manseholders to buy and sell lands illegally. Indeed, most tenants did not even trouble to convert their terms of lease and disposed of their properties as they saw fit. In matters of inheritance, at least, peasant elites approached abbatial policy with opportunism.

Of course, not all peasants defied partible inheritance customs. Some fragmentary evidence suggests that factional distinctions within the peasant elite may have reflected individual adherence to inheritance customs. Many peasants who later became prominent *salpeterisch* figures may

---

1743. For examples from Nöggenschwiel, see GLA 61:14160, 8, 14 June 1738; GLA 61:14161, 129, 12 May 1742; and GLA 61:14161, 212, 8 January, 1743.

58. GLA 99:1034, 24r–25v, Joseph Tröndle of Unteralpfen to Marquard Herrgott, 29 January 1732. On *préciput* inheritance in France, see Le Roy Ladurie, "Système de la coutume."

59. For examples from Nöggenschwiel, see GLA 61:14160 [Kontraktenprotokoll OVA], 396, 20 February 1740; GLA 61:14161 [Kontraktenprotokoll OVA], 308–9, 23 August 1743; and GLA 61:14161, 407, 17 October 1744. From Birndorf: GLA 61:14161, 53, 17 December 1738; GLA 61:14161, 23, 8 January 1743; and GLA 61:14162 [Kontraktenprotokoll OVA], 127, 9 December 1749. From Weilheim: GLA 61:14160, 3–4, 14 June 1738; GLA 61:14160, 384, 25 January 1741.

60. GLA 229:37289, "Fundamental-Ursachen," 7–10 January 1671.

61. See GLA 67:1739, 48r, 3 March 1751.

simply have wished to subdivide their patrimonies without restriction; one was "Salpeter-Hans" Albiez himself, who illegally subdivided his manse among his sons in 1727.[62] But the correlation is not ironclad. Albiez's own brother Hans Ulrich had been excluded from inheriting a portion of the family manse, even though it had been illegally subdivided several times since the early seventeenth century.[63] Moreover, not all *salpeterisch* peasants were above adopting the practice of "preferential legacy," even during the rebellion. Martin Eisele, the preeminent *salpeterisch* activist in Nöggenschwiel, passed his lands undivided to his son Hans Peter, who bought out the inheritance claims of his two sisters.[64]

Given the degree of consensus among peasant elites for the need to defend their autonomy in real-estate transactions, it should come as no surprise that the same social milieu supplied the most active personalities of both factions. Like their *müllerisch* enemies, *salpeterisch* leaders included a large number of veteran officeholders, manseholders, and well-to-do rural "professionals," such as blacksmiths, innkeepers, wheelwrights, and millers. Most paradoxical of all is the large number of abbatial functionaries among them. Far from being alien to institutions of domination, many *salpeterisch* leaders were themselves cogs in the machinery of domination.

A few biographical vignettes illustrate the point handsomely. "Salpeter-Hans" Albiez himself was a veteran Octovir and abbatial manseholder who also collected quitrents for St. Blasien in his home village of Buch.[65] As we know, Albiez died in prison in September 1727. His confederate in rebellion, Martin Thoma of Haselbach, was a juror in the abbatial civil court of Weilheim, held his mill from St. Blasien, and continued to collect abbatial quitrents and tithes as late as 1725.[66] Thoma was

62. GLA 67:1739, 43r. See also the case of the *salpeterisch* Joseph Binkert, who in 1743 divided his patrimony with his brother Johannes; see GLA 61:14161 [Kontraktenprotokoll OVA], 270, 20 April 1743, and 276, 24 April 1743; and GLA 229:75492, nr. 1.

63. GLA 113:224, 263r–72v, Interrogation of Hans Ulrich Albiez of Herrischwand, WVA, 9 December 1726.

64. GLA 61:14160 [Kontraktenprotokoll OVA], 364, 22 December 1740.

65. GLA 66:7296, "Zinsrodel deß Waldambts," 1709.

66. Ibid.; GLA 61:13148 [WGP WVA], 2 May 1718; GLA 229:37381, II, OVA to St. Blasien, 23 July 1725; GLA 67:1725, 469–72, Martin Thoma of Haselbach to OVA, 3 December 1725. According to GLA 113:81, "Repartition deren Kösten," 7 July 1728, Thoma possessed a personal worth in excess of two thousand gulden.

sentenced to die by the sword in 1730.⁶⁷ The wealthy blacksmith Conrad Binkert, who financed Salpeter-Hans" Albiez's diplomatic mission to Vienna in 1726, served as headman of Dogern in 1727 and remained an abbatial quitrent collector even after the rebellion had erupted.⁶⁸ Another was Leonzi Brutschi, also of Dogern, whose activities as a *salpeterisch* fund-raiser cost him his head in April 1739. At the time of his death, Brutschi's personal worth lay somewhere between two and three thousand gulden.⁶⁹ And in the western parts of Hauenstein, too, functionaries in the administration of St. Fridolin's estates were enrolled in the *salpeterisch* cause. Johannes Thoma-ab-Egg, who led the rebel Terror of May 1745, owned a large manse and collected quitrents and tithes in southwestern Rickenbach Canton; so vital was Thoma-ab-Egg to the seigneurial administration of the convent of St. Fridolin that in 1746, Abbess Maria Josepha Regina von Liebenfels personally intervened with the Forest Steward to protect his lands from debt foreclosure.⁷⁰ In Herrischried, St. Fridolin's cellarer Joseph Eckert was actively *salpeterisch,* as was his successor, Joseph Sibold.⁷¹

Prosopographical evidence supports the thrust of these anecdotes. A comprehensive source of socioeconomic data on *salpeterisch* leaders survives from 1728, when the Beaurieu commission arrived to identify, audit, and penalize 229 of the "most active" *salpeterisch* peasants.⁷² For the purpose of assessing fines, the commission divided them into three categories of criminal culpability in the recent unrest. Assuming the

---

67. GLA 65:11419, 14r, "Relation über das Strafurtheil," Innsbruck, 4 April 1730.

68. GLA 66:7326, 34r [Renovation in Dogern], 1731; GLA 113:225, 277r–83v, Interrogation of Speaker Joseph Tröndle of Schmitzingen, VÖRK, 30 May 1727.

69. GLA 113:248, A1, Interrogation of Leonzi Brutschi, Vienna, 6–27 April 1739.

70. GLA 61:10507 [Kapitularprotokoll St Fridolin], 224–25, 4 December 1730; GLA 229:6685, "Den sog. Amtszehent zu Bergalingen, Egg u Jungholz betr.," 1556–1785; GLA 229:114349, Abbess Maria Josepha Regina von Liebenfels to Forest Steward Franz Anton von Schönau-Wehr, 16 May 1746.

71. On Sibold, see GLA 229:42659, Abbess Maria Magdalena von Hallwyl to Forest Steward Franz Anton von Schönau-Wehr, 16 February 1732, and GLA 16:1076, "Reverslehenbrief Joseph Sibolds zu Herrischried," 15 April 1726.

72. GLA 113:81, 130r–48v, "Repartition deren Kösten, so auß die Miliz-Commission, auch anderwärtig aufgegangen, und sich ohngefehr ad 10000 fl. Reichswehrl. oder 12000 fl. Raucherwehrl. belaufen, wo Commission pro norma genohmen, das Verbrechen, und dan nebst dem Verbrechen das Vermögen," 7 July 1728; see also GLA 113:225, 102r, "Verzeichnus der jenigen hierunden benambten Rädelsführer, was sie über wissentliche Schuld annoch in Vermögen haben," [1727].

accuracy of its findings, the resulting data show that the most active rebels were also the wealthiest: the average net worth of first-class rebels, the "main ringleaders" *(Haubt-Radl-Füehreren)* who had led the homage boycott in 1727 or who had "abused" public office in service of the *salpeterisch* cause, was 1,791 gulden 50 kreuzer. Second-class ringleaders, "whose crimes approached, but did not equal those of the major ringleaders," averaged 1,233 gulden 45 kreuzer, while the third class of "restless, malicious, and disobedient" subjects were worth only 726 gulden 30 kreuzer. Similarly, the median worth of each group increased with its "culpability," from 400 gulden in class three, to 800 gulden in class two, and to 1,400 gulden in class one.[73] These data also confirm that the *salpeterisch* leadership included numerous officeholders and seigneurial functionaries: among the fifty-one first-class "criminals" were ten ex-Octovirs, three carriers, two cellarers, one tithe-collector, perhaps as many as eight manseholders, and at least two village headmen. Finally, Beaurieu's levy shows that a significant number of *salpeterisch* leaders were rural "professionals," persons who earned their livelihoods from occupations other than agriculture. The same fifty-one first-class "ringleaders" of 1728, for example, included four millers, two innkeepers, two blacksmiths, a glass-maker, a wheelwright, and a shingler.

There is, to be sure, a certain self-fulfilling quality to these figures. In the eyes of imperial commissioners, criminal culpability was all the worse if an accused subject also held seigneurial or public office. Moreover, the commissioners were concerned as much to cover their costs as to prosecute the guilty. On the other hand, the Beaurieu commission's investigation proved remarkably thorough—the 229 defendants may have comprised as much as 10 percent of the adult male population, and perhaps half of all *salpeterisch* males—and when they determined that an officeholder had been only halfhearted in his support of the rebellion, they were prepared to lower the penalty.[74] Although *salpeterisch* activists denied it vehemently, the Beaurieu commission was about as fair-minded an intervention as could be expected from the Habsburg state.

73. GLA 113:81, "Repartition deren Kösten," 7 July 1728.
74. For their willingness to cooperate with the commission, two "ringleaders" (Adam Schmiedle and Conrad Binkert) received reduced sentences; see GLA 65:11419, 14r, "Relation über das Strafurtheil," Innsbruck, 4 April 1730.

The social characteristic uniting this group was their central location in social, economic, and political geographies. As executors of public authority, Octovirs and headmen were the principal brokers of power and information between peasants and representatives of the Habsburg state. As providers of services, millers, innkeepers, and blacksmiths interacted frequently with all the residents of their own and nearby villages. Information flowed through channels of economic and social exchange; the peasants who governed them were also the arbiters of information and, with it, power.[75] Small wonder, then, that in 1746 the Ramschwag Commission considered barring millers from election to the office of Octovir.[76] This recommendation was never implemented, however, perhaps because it would have excluded the services of many *müllerisch* potentates, who, after all, had even named their faction after the profession of its leader, the miller Tröndle. What was true of the *salpeterisch* leadership applied equally well to their *müllerisch* adversaries.

The most active rebels, therefore, formed an economic elite within their faction. The first generation of *salpeterisch* activists, in particular, had long been engaged, socially and economically, with peasants who later became *müllerisch*. The miller Martin Thoma and Georg Fluem of Dietlingen, for example, wound up on opposite sides of the factional fence, even though both had served as executive officers *(Pfleger)* for the Brotherhood of the Rosary, a pious association with members throughout southeastern Hauenstein.[77] Similarly, "Salpeter-Hans" Albiez and his cohort Friedle Hottinger of Niedergebisbach had been Octovirs, on and off, since at least 1715, which placed them in the same social and political circles with such *müllerisch* luminaries as the miller Joseph Tröndle of Unteralpfen and his like-named cousin from Rotzel.[78]

The "clubby" quality of this elite revealed itself in the fact that under the right circumstances, the mutual economic interests of individual

---

75. See David W. Sabean, "The Communal Basis of Pre-1800 Peasant Uprisings in Western Europe," *Comparative Politics* 8 (1976): 355–64.

76. GLA 113:265, "Concept Hauptrelation," [1746].

77. GLA 229:453, 25r, "Specification der Rosencrantz Bruederschafft Einkünfften zu Weilheimb," 4 April 1709, and 12r–15v, "Rechnung löbl. Rosenkrantz Bruderschafft zu Weylen welche Geörg Fluem Ainungs Mr. zue Dietlingen als bisherig gewester Pfleger abgelegt den 9 Marty 1708."

78. See GLA 113:89 [Conference protocol], July 1725; GLA 61:13148 [WGP WVA], 1717; and GLA 66:10170 [RP GH], 1715.

members within it could transcend their political differences. Consider the following example: in August 1742, the leader of the *müllerisch* faction, Joseph Tröndle of Unteralpfen, and Christa Thoma, a miller in the nearby village of Birndorf, jointly lodged a complaint with the abbatial court in Gurtweil about the activities of a third miller, one Johannes Tröndle.[79] The defendant, they charged, had traveled from village to village, collecting grain for his own mill on the banks of the Rhine. In this way he had encroached on the plaintiffs' clientele. The Gurtweil tribunal decided for the plaintiffs.

Two facts make this case significant. The first is that plaintiffs Joseph Tröndle and Christa Thoma were factional enemies. Christa Thoma had been a *salpeterisch* partisan since at least 1726 and was well connected within his faction: his brother was the *salpeterisch* "arch-ringleader" Martin Thoma of Haselbach; his brother-in-law was "Salpeter-Hans" Albiez's financier, the blacksmith Conrad Binkert of Dogern.[80] In 1728, Thoma's misdemeanors had cost him a hefty 250 gulden in fines and deprived him of voting rights until 1734.[81] But factional enmity did not necessarily make for commercial rivalry; though they lived in neighboring villages, Christa Thoma and Joseph Tröndle apparently did not compete for clients. Indeed, their common suit against Johannes Tröndle implied a prior arrangement that delimited the clientele of each miller. When an interloper threatened the profitability of their mills, the plaintiffs overlooked their differences to make common cause.

The second fact is that since 1739 Joseph Tröndle had been involved in a similar quarrel with Adam Schmiedle, the miller of Niedermühle. Like Christa Thoma, Schmiedle had been a prominent *salpeterisch* figure during the early stages of the Salpeter Wars; among other things, Schmiedle had helped organize the November 1726 rally in Waldkirch described in Chapter 3. Christa Thoma's tacit commercial agreement with Joseph Tröndle placed him in conflict with another *salpeterisch* leader (Schmiedle). Here, economic interests undermined factional solidar-

79. GLA 61:5777, 48–52 [Complaint of Joseph Tröndle and Christa Thoma to OVA], 21 August 1742.
80. GLA 113:225, 226r, 127r–31v, "Ausführliche und wahrhofte Lista der Haubträdelführer"; on Christa Thoma and the Birndorf mill, see Jakob Ebner, *Aus der Geschichte der Ortschaften der Pfarrei Birndorf* (Karlsruhe, 1938), 131–37.
81. GLA 113:237, 83r–84v, "Specification deren . . . interessierten Unterthanen," 28 March 1728.

ity. To be sure, Schmiedle had appealed to factional allegiances in order to entice *salpeterisch* customers away from Tröndle, so the battle did not lack political overtones.[82] In a letter to Abbot Franz II Schächtelin, Joseph Tröndle, too, characterized the conflict with Schmiedle as a manifestation of factional strife—despite his common suit with the *salpeterisch* Christa Thoma.[83] In the initial resolution of their dispute, Schmiedle was forbidden to take customers from Tröndle's canton, which also included Christa Thoma's preserve.[84] Commercial interest had driven two *salpeterisch* millers apart.

But it would be misleading to suggest that *salpeterisch* leaders were able to preserve their social and economic standing throughout the Salpeter Wars. On the contrary, the effects of rebellion seriously corroded the economic standing of many *salpeterisch* leaders. Over the course of twenty years, they were subjected to fines, forced labor, and imprisonment, all of which could affect their ability to subsist. For those who took *salpeterisch* solidarity in earnest, political activism carried with it the risk of financial catastrophe. Consider the sorry fate of Bläsi Hottinger of Niedergebisbach, son of the veteran Octovir Friedle Hottinger and a *salpeterisch* activist from 1726 until his death in prison on 19 July 1747. In 1727, Bläsi had an estimated net personal worth of 1,000 gulden.[85] By 1739—after eleven years in prison, forced labor and exile—his worth had fallen about 60 percent to 395 gulden.[86] In 1739 he was exiled to forced labor in the Austrian fortress at Belgrade on the Turkish frontier, from which he returned a pauper in 1745. Hottinger's role in the 1745 uprising led to his final, fatal incarceration.[87]

Activism ruined Bläsi Hottinger utterly, and his was a common fate. In 1744, for example, Hottinger's compatriot Johannes "the Prussian"

---

82. GLA 113:132, no. 9, "Copia Relation was Einungs Meister v Birndorff . . . abgehn laßen," 12 September 1739. Schmiedle had politicized these commercial relations despite the clemency he had received from the Beaurieu commission ten years before.

83. GLA 99:1041, 42r–43v, Joseph Tröndle of Unteralpfen to St. Blasien, 28 January 1739.

84. GLA 113:132, no. 11, Decree of the WVA, 30 September 1739.

85. GLA 113:225, 102r, "Verzeichnus der . . . Vermögen," [1727].

86. GLA 113:254, 96r–98v, 7 October 1739. The value of Hottinger's property was assessed at 3,100 gulden, minus 2,705 gulden in debts. The resulting sum included his wife's properties, which were valued at 197 gulden.

87. GLA 113:258, 302r–14v; GLA 113:268, 53r–v. Empress Maria Theresa pardoned Hottinger in 1743, but because he remained in Vienna to agitate for the *salpeterisch* cause, all his properties were confiscated.

Marder claimed a personal worth of about 1,200 gulden, but testified that he had already lost nearly 1,500 gulden to the twenty-year "affair."[88] In 1728, Marder's fine alone had gobbled up 10 percent of his net personal worth, and his case was not unique: the average fine of first-class rebels in 1730 was about 7 percent of their net personal worth.[89] The wealth of Marder's older brother, Hans Georg, was all but destroyed: from a net worth of about 2,000 gulden in 1739, only 134 gulden remained in 1755.[90] The penalties imposed on *salpeterisch* families deported to the Banat in that year were even more draconian. On average, the sum of debt and deportation costs amounted to 65 percent of their average gross assets; the median burden was higher still, almost 72 percent.[91] It seems likely, then, that the economic position of *salpeterisch* leaders deteriorated drastically as a direct result of their political commitments.

Of course, not all *salpeterisch* peasants were prepared to endure such hardships. The unwilling either absented themselves from politics or switched sides. No less a figure than the blacksmith Conrad Binkert turned against his compatriots, which earned him their lasting enmity.[92] The blacksmith of Birndorf, Caspar Binkert, and even Adam Schmiedle, the miller of Niedermühle, eventually cast their lot with the *müllerisch* faction after early flirtations with the rebels.[93] The most spectacular defection was that of Joseph Tröndle of Schmitzingen. Early on, *this* Joseph Tröndle had been an active *salpeterisch* partisan; as Speaker in 1727, Tröndle had led the homage boycott against Abbot Franz II Schächtelin. Ten years later, he was again an Octovir, but this time as a partisan of the *müllerisch* side; his election in 1737 was all the more remarkable for the fact

---

88. GLA 113:256, 252r–63v, Interrogation of Johannes Marder of Eschbach, Freiburg, 25 August 1744.
89. GLA 113:81, "Repartition deren Kösten," 7 July 1728.
90. GLA 113:250a, D, no. 3, Interrogation of Hans Georg Marder of Waldkirch, 27 April 1739.
91. GLA 113:272, "Liquidations-Prothocoll," [1755].
92. GLA 113:230, 297r–98v, Hans Friedle Gerspach and Michael Tröndle to Conrad Binkert, 6 December 1729.
93. Compare GLA 113:226, "Ausführliche und wahrhafte Lista der Haubt-Rädel-Führer," [1727]; GLA 113:261, 18r–27v, "1745 den 11tn Christ. hat die Gemeint Birndorf auffgesatzt von Haus zue Haus undt Haushaltung mit Namen und Zunamen und wie das Alter und die Ruohige und Unruohige"; and GLA 65:11419, 14r, "Relation über das Strafenurteil," 4 April 1730.

that he had been forever banned from public office in 1730.[94] It is impossible to say, finally, how many people deserted the *salpeterisch* faction in this way. But the ease with which turncoats like Binkert could assume positions of power and authority among their former enemies suggests once again the social similarities of both factions.

Status, Kin, and Factionalism

Even if the social and economic standing of *salpeterisch* leaders declined during the 1730s and 1740s, it is difficult to imagine how factional politics might have taken shape, had the first generation of *salpeterisch* leaders not formed a social elite. The initial strength of their cause, after all, was due in no small part to the prestige enjoyed by its guiding lights, experienced politicians like the veteran Octovir Friedle Hottinger, the cellarer Joseph Sibold of Herrischried, or "Salpeter-Hans" Albiez himself, as brokers between the competing interests of peasants, lords, and the Habsburg state. It also drew strength from the key social location of millers such as Johannes Albiez of Kiesenbach, Hans Georg Albiez of Ibach, Bläsi Huber of Tiefenstein, Martin Thoma of Haselbach, Christa Thoma of Birndorf, Bläsi Kaiser of Neuenmühle, Adam Schmiedle of Niedermühle, and Michael Schmiedle of Kutterau and the innkeepers Georg Freudig of Tiefenhäusern and Hans Brutschi of Dogern. Would the *salpeterisch* appeal have been as great without the support of such providers of finished goods and services as the blacksmiths Conrad Binkert of Dogern, Hans Georg Thoma of Kiesenbach, Thoma Binkert of Remetschwiel, and Caspar Binkert of Birndorf, or the well-endowed glassmaker Joseph Lüber of Glashütten? The *salpeterisch* leadership were hardly the "poor and oppressed" of Hauenstein, but a well-connected elite.

Nor were they politically inexperienced. The agendas and personnel of both factions displayed strong continuities with the Octovirs'

---

94. GLA 66:10170 [RP GH], 1727. For Tröndle's banishment from public office, see GLA 113:237, 83r–84v, "Specification deren jenigen in der letzten vorgewesten. . . . Ohnruhe interessierten Unterthanen welche . . . ddo Wienn den 28tn Mar. von *activâ et passivâ* bey denen Ämbterwahlen perpetuò vel ad tempus priviert." Evidence of his election in 1737 comes from GLA 62:10170 [1737].

struggles over inheritance custom after 1700. Not only were many *salpeterisch* leaders educated by long years of battle against St. Blasien; as vital agents of abbatial and conventual dominion, many of them were acutely aware of the dependence of seigneurs on peasants to rule effectively. The abbey's policies threatened to reduce that dependence, at the expense of peasant elites. Similarly, the Octovirs' resistance to changes in partible inheritance custom reflected the desire of peasant elites to preserve their own indispensability. Seen in this light, the *salpeterisch* faction was heir to a far older struggle over the control of property.

Perhaps it is only coincidental that inheritance custom should have occupied so important a place among the concerns of peasant elites that forged alliances laterally, often through kinship. Inheritance law defined the role of the family as the primary funnel of wealth from one generation to the next. At the very least, St. Blasien's intrusions interfered with peasant autonomy in the making and breaking of alliances through marriage, inheritance, and exchange. It comes as no surprise, then, that the social pattern of factional allegiance shows certain dynastic qualities: each faction seems to have been dominated by a set of families, whose members were often scattered throughout the county. The quintessential example, of course, is that of the miller Joseph Tröndle of Unteralpfen, who with his synonymous cousin, the Speaker of Rotzel, dominated *müllerisch* politics throughout the entire rebellion. After an early affiliation with the *salpeterisch* faction, they were joined by the Speaker's brother Conrad, a resident of Waldkirch and one of Hauenstein's wealthiest peasants.[95] This dynastic tendency was not restricted to the *müllerisch* faction: in the cantons of Birndorf and Dogern, for example, an alliance between the Binkert and Thoma clans dominated the *salpeterisch* scene. There, the brothers Martin, Christa, and Georg Thoma (millers in Haselbach, Birndorf, and Hartschwand, respectively) were related by marriage to Conrad Binkert, the blacksmith from Dogern. Binkert was also allied politically with his stepfather Johannes Hilpert of Schmitzingen.[96] The Albiez family, too, exerted an influence

95. See Jacob Ebner, *Eine Müllerdynastie im Schwarzwald* (Radolfzell, 1908); on Conrad Tröndle's early *salpeterisch* sympathies, see GLA 113:226, 127r–31v, "Ausführliche und wahrhafte Lista der Haubt-Rädel-Führer," [1727]. Conrad's personal net worth was valued at six thousand gulden.

96. See GLA 113:242, 326r–27v, "Verzaichnuß derjenigen hauwenstein. unruhige Undterthannen, welche . . . den 28. Aug. nacher Wien abgegangen."And see GLA 113:230, 293r–v, Interrogation of Christa Thoma of Birndorf, KK Beaurieu, 28 June 1729.

that far outlived its patriarch "Salpeter-Hans"; his son Jacob was described in 1739 as Albiez's "living spirit."[97] In Rickenbach Canton, finally, the Hottinger family of Niedergebisbach—father Friedle and sons Michael and Bläsi—presided over factional politics. The exceptionally militant Johannes Thoma-ab-Egg was the brother-in-law of Hans Friedle Gerspach, a *salpeterisch* organizer *par excellence,* who was executed for his exertions in 1739.[98] There are, to be sure, many documented cases of dissension within families.[99] Still, the weight of evidence suggests that politically, blood was thicker than water.

Such clannishness was replicated within the narrower world of village politics. In the northeastern village of Nöggenschwiel, factional affiliations tended to cohere within kin groups. The *müllerisch* faction, for example, revolved around two families, the Bächles and the Thomas, who shared a common ancestor.[100] The abbatial bailiff, Johannes Bächle, headed the first clan and shared an abbatial manse with the other *müllerisch* patriarch, Georg Thoma. Johannes Bächle bound his fortunes to the *müllerisch* faction, which by his own account earned him nothing but grief from the *salpeterisch* residents of Nöggenschwiel. In his letter of resignation from the office of bailiff in 1751, Johannes remarked that he had "had to endure much aversion and antipathy from the disobedient [peasants]" during the Salpeter Wars, and that while he "had wanted to settle the matter with them," he had "become suspect within the community and all became disobedient, to the shame of the community and the authorities."[101] Like Johannes, all the Bächles were *müllerisch;* so were the Thomas. The *salpeterisch* faction centered on Joseph and Martin Eisele and a different Georg Thoma, a shingler. Their extended families, too, were overwhelmingly *salpeterisch.* The Binkerts and the Brutschis (two families of artisans) were *salpeterisch,* as were the Finks, Schallers,

97. GLA 65:11419 [Nachlaß J. L. Meyer], 36r.
98. GLA 113:241, 83r–92v, Interrogation of Hans Friedle Gerspach of Bergalingen, VÖRK, 12 July 1737. Gerspach was married to Margaretha Thoma, the sister of Johannes Thoma-ab-Egg.
99. A conspicuous case of factional dissent within the family was that of Friedle Tröndle of Rotzel and his father, the Speaker Joseph Tröndle, diarch of the *müllerisch* party. Friedle was elected Octovir in 1727, a year when the *salpeterisch* faction dominated county politics. The extent of Friedle's involvement with the rebellion is unclear, but it was enough to earn him the suspension of his voting rights until 1733.
100. GLA 65:11632, 1r–57r [LB Nöggenschwiel], 1727–30.
101. GLA 229:75480, 3r–4v, Johannes Bächle of Nöggenschwiel to OVA, 20 September 1751.

Schäfers, Villingers, and Vogelbachers. The Fluems, Ganterts, Gersters, Kaisers, and Stigelers were dependable *müllerisch* families. There were exceptions, of course. The Dörflingers, for example, were divided. The Eckerts were mostly *salpeterisch,* except for one named Johannes. Nevertheless, the overall correspondence of kin and faction is clear.[102]

The example of Nöggenschwiel also points to several other social characteristics of factional politics. Despite its reputation as a hotbed of *salpeterisch* agitation, the factional divide bisected the village population evenly, across lines of social distinction.[103] In 1745, for example, just under 52 percent of the villagers identified themselves as rebels, 40 percent as *müllerisch,* and the rest as "neutral."[104] In terms of status, the *müllerisch* side could claim more well-endowed peasants, men like the bailiff Bächle, the manseholder Thoma, and the miller Conrad Gerster. But the well-to-do were not absent from *salpeterisch* ranks. The activist Martin Eisele appears to have possessed substantial acreages and woodlands, as did Joseph Eckert, Steffa Jordan, Johannes Kaiser, and Mathis Leber. The *salpeterisch* faction also included a number of "professionals." In addition to the Binkerts and Brutschis, the rebels included among their numbers the lesser Bächles (who were unrelated to the bailiff): Balthas the innkeeper, Conrad the thatcher, Benedict the shoemaker, Lorenz the fencemaker, and Georg the ropemaker. They also included the black-

---

102. These linkages are based on lists of factional allegiance found in GLA 99:975, "Specification waß vor Mannschafft zuo Waldtkirch erschinen ist," 3 November 1726; GLA 113:225, 147r–v, "Verzeichnuß was für Personen zu Nöggenschwiehl die dem gnetigen Herrn Prelaten nit geholdiget haben," [1727]; GLA 113:229, 71r, "Specification . . . welche . . . das Hand-gelübt abgelegt haben," 13 May 1727; GLA 113:240, 255r–31v, "Specification der jenigen so ahn denen in der Grafschafft Hauensteinischen Unrueh bis dahin aufgeschwollenen 50000 fl. Unkösten nach dem Steürfuß zu bezahlen haben" and "Specificao welche von der Repartition ausgenohmen seindt," [1734]; GLA 113:244, 100r–101v, "Verzeichnuß waß für Manschafft in Neggenschwiell," [February? 1739]; GLA 65:11426, 86r–87v, "Versicherungs Schein für die Unruhige der Gemeindt Nöggenschweyl und Dürthlingen," 23 March 1739; GLA 113:250A, F4–F5 [Labor and fiscal penalties], 29 April 1739; GLA 113:264, "Über die Gemeint Neggenschwiel Man und waibliche Geschlecht der kleinen oder Salbeterschen," [December 1745]; and GLA 113:264, "Der Gemeint Neggenschwiel waß für Rüehige Leüth verheürath, und lethig," [December 1745].

103. GLA 113:250A, I3, "Remonstration über das von der Gemeind Noggenschwihl eingebene Memoria die Eigsmrwahl betreffend von neü und alten Einungsmeister auch Ausschuß der Dogerner Einung," [1739].

104. GLA 113:164, "Über die Gemeint Neggenschwiel Man und waibliche Geschlecht der kleinen oder Salbeterschen" and "Der Gemeint Neggenschwiel waß für Rüehige Leüth verheürath, und lethig," [December 1745].

smiths Joseph Ebner, Georg Thoma, and Thoma Vogelbacher, the coopers Georg and Lorenz Fink, and the weaver Johannes Thoma. While the *müllerisch* clan prevailed in the highest rank of Nöggenschwiel society, the *salpeterisch* side was heavily represented both among wealthier peasants and artisans, who were well placed to control the flow of information.

The social composition of factional leaders and the clannishness of factional allegiance in villages such as Nöggenschwiel suggest that the population at large followed in the train of an elite divided on factional lines. Kin and status often outweighed class in the social formation of factions. Despite the "democratic" quality of Hauenstein's institutional structure, peasant politics in Hauenstein were dominated by a social elite that acted more or less independently of pressures from the rank and file. How is one to explain this? One possibility for the social top-heaviness of peasant politics lies in the formal integration of rural elites in institutions of rule and domination. As Chapter 1 showed, the "club" of political insiders was responsible for almost every aspect of everyday administration. With such powers at stake, magisterial office gravitated to wealthier peasants.

In the final analysis, of course, every Hauensteiner was capable of forming his or her own opinion, even if it contradicted the political pressures of family or economic dependence. Neither clientage nor kinship necessarily caused factional behavior. The argument presented here should not, therefore, be taken to indicate any rigid determinacy of vertical social bonds. Rather, the point is merely that divisions of class were far more important in defining relations between rulers and their subjects as a social whole. On the other hand, the determinants of factionalism—that is, political division among peasants—were more complex. Here, other factors intervened, and perhaps overcame those of economic interest alone. Ultimately, the "economism" implicit in class analysis explains neither the social location nor the material interest of leaders in either faction.[105]

With respect to the role of community in the Salpeter Wars, the data on social patterns presented here suggest that the rebels (both leaders and the rank and file) were no more and no less integrated into hierarchies

---

105. See Pierre Bourdieu, *Outline of a Theory of Practice* (Cambridge, U.K., 1977), 179.

of domination than their *müllerisch* opponents. Neither faction, therefore, can be said to represent a social elite whose political self-interest lay in cooperating with state and seigneurial officials to impose greater controls on village life at the expense of custom and the common material interests of peasants at large. The social similarities between the two factions were simply too great. As the basis of social action, then, the peasants' class interest did not divide communities but unite them. Discord flowed from the competing articulations of competing elites within the peasantry. Moreover, if the example of Nöggenschwiel is any indication, the ties of kin and clientage appear to have outweighed common interests connected with village institutions, and the simple fact that almost every settlement in Hauenstein was torn by factional dissension indicates that Nöggenschwiel's case was far from unique. When peasants formed political opinions and identities, the demands and attachments of village life receded before those of family and the "Whole County."

CHAPTER 5

"Into the Devil's Jaws"

Patrolling the Boundaries of Community

> The days will soon come, and they are not far off, when the just shall attain victory. . . . Innocent blood cries for revenge against the unjust. Then the prisoners will be freed, and the beacon of justice will be ignited. The guilty will be captured, and the innocent will be left alone. God will see to it. Job 3:26.
>
> From a *salpeterisch* flyer circulated in Laufenburg on 5 May 1745

A PEASANT FACTION, LIKE ANY COMMUNITY OF BELIEF AND ACTION, must define what it is and what it is not. Given Hauenstein's homogenous cultural and socioeconomic makeup, this need was especially acute. Moreover, among peasants habituated by custom to expressing their political inclinations through elections, the ideological limits of factional identity required constant adjustment to changing circumstances if rebel leaders were to avoid lapsing into irrelevancy. Maintaining community among the faithful, then, was an ongoing process of patrolling ideological boundaries. Consequently, factional identity was defined as much by what was "out" as by what was "in," a quality social anthropologists describe as the "implicit negativity" of community.[1] Yet in Hauenstein, this negativity was quite explicit.

---

1. See Anthony P. Cohen, *The Symbolic Construction of Community* (Chichester, 1985), 115, and "Of Symbols and Boundaries, or, Does Ertie's Greatcoat Hold the Key?" in Anthony P. Cohen, ed., *Symbolising Boundaries: Identity and Diversity in British Cultures* (Manchester, 1986), 1–19.

This chapter focuses on the rhetoric *salpeterisch* leaders used to distinguish themselves from their rivals and how its evolution exacerbated the depth and ferocity of factional strife. As Chapter 2 already hinted, the *salpeterisch* and *müllerisch* factions emerged in part from growing disunity among peasant elites over the conditions of authority: before these factions coalesced or even had names, the dominant peasant ranks in Hauenstein were divided between those, on the one hand, who tended to equate legality and legitimacy and therefore preferred to litigate grievances through sanctioned channels of judicial appeal, and those who, on the other hand, clung to elastic notions of custom as sacrosanct, of a sovereign incapable of violating it, and who did not shy from extralegal methods to press their point. Factionalism deepened and defined these distinctions. By defining identity negatively, by what it was *not*, *salpeterisch* peasants found a symbolic barrier in the vocabulary of debates over the meaning and nomenclature of serfdom: in brief, *salpeterisch* thinkers identified the *müllerisch* tendency to equate legitimacy and legality with complicity in St. Blasien's plot to undermine Hauenstein's institutional integrity through serfdom. From accusations that peasant magistrates had abetted the imposition of servitude, it was but a short logical step to the conclusion that a *müllerisch* conspiracy had enslaved Hauenstein.

But policing factional identity was not simply a matter of vilifying the other side. There was positive content to *salpeterisch* rhetoric and identity. It is not enough to suggest that *salpeterisch* peasants saw themselves as the guardians of custom, for although "ancient rights" were the subject of incessant talk, it is unclear to perhaps most Hauensteiners exactly what these "ancient rights" actually were. When asked about the content of Hauenstein's "ancient rights," Bläsi Kaiser of Neuenmühle responded that "he wouldn't actually know," that it had something to do with inheritance law and subpoenas, but that "it was all Spanish to him."[2] By the same token, the *salpeterisch* agenda involved much more than a defense of custom. Rather, *salpeterisch* peasants nurtured the positive aspects of their identity through mutually reinforcing myths of origin, images of Emperor Charles VI as Hauenstein's

---

2. GLA 113:224, 122r–27v, Interrogation of Bläsi Kaiser of Neuenmühle, St. Blasien, 9 November 1726.

paternalistic benefactor, and beliefs about the contingency of all domination *(Herrschaft)* on reciprocal, contractual, and exclusive ties. In time, their agenda took on religious significance, as *salpeterisch* leaders linked the restoration of "ancient rights" to the personal and collective salvation of Hauensteiners in heaven.

The implications of these parallel discourses are several. For one, the trajectory of *salpeterisch* logic confounds an old stereotype about the putative "naive monarchism" of early modern peasants, a frame of mind that is supposed to have narrowly constrained the universe of possibility available to them. While it is true that the veneration of monarchs was as stable as any fixture of early modern peasant mentality, the stereotype adds that trust in royal benevolence and idolatrous obsession with "ancient rights" combined to prevent peasants from embracing "revolutionary goals."[3] Before 1789, so the argument goes, the only major exception to this rule was the Peasants' War of 1524–25, when Protestant biblicism and a justificatory vocabulary of "Divine Law" displaced that of ancient custom; equipped with this universalizing terminology, peasants could express their needs "as morally justified demands," which in turn enabled them to transcend the localism of agrarian conflicts before and since.[4] Although memories of the Peasants' War persisted long after 1525, German peasant movements never again crossed this ideological threshold, in part because peasants made use of new avenues to litigate grievances against lords and even sovereigns.

Superficially, *salpeterisch* rhetoric fits this mold; the rebellion remained a strictly local affair, and peasants in neighboring territories

---

3. See, for example, Marc Bloch, *The Royal Touch,* trans. J. E. Anderson (New York, 1961); Hugues Neveux, "Die ideologische Dimension der französischen Bauernaufstände im 17. Jahrhundert," *HZ* 238 (1984): 265–85; George Rudé, "Popular Protest and Ideology on the Eve of the French Revolution," in Ernst Hinrichs et al., eds., *Vom Ancien Régime zur Französischen Revolution—Forschungen und Perspektiven* (Göttingen, 1978), 420–35; Yves-Marie Bercé, *Revolt and Revolution in Early Modern Europe: An Essay on the History of Popular Violence,* trans. Joseph Bergin (New York, 1987), 28–33, and *A History of Peasant Revolts: The Social Origins of Rebellion in Early Modern France,* trans. Amanda Whitmore (Ithaca, 1990), 248–51; Daniel Field, *Rebels in the Name of the Tsar* (Boston, 1976), 1–9; Jerome Blum, *The End of the Old Order in Rural Europe* (Princeton, 1978), 333–35; and Celina Bobinska, "Les mouvements paysans en Pologne aux XVIIIe et XIXe siècles: Problèmes et methodes," *Acta Poloniae Historica* 22 (1970): 136–57.

4. Peter Blickle, *The Revolution of 1525: The German Peasants' War from a New Perspective,* trans. Thomas A. Brady Jr. and H. C. Erik Midelfort (Baltimore, 1981), 155–61, 188.

took no more than a casual interest in it. In terms of the fervor it inspired, moreover, the "naive monarchism" of *salpeterisch* Hauensteiners compared poorly with the universalizing, apocalyptic dreams of contemporary Russian peasants in a "tsar-deliverer" *(tsar-batiushka)* who would someday sweep away all injustices in a grand gesture of paternal benevolence.[5] Rather, most Hauensteiners contented themselves with delusions about the monarch's ignorance of their burdens. In only one recorded instance did anyone suggest that *salpeterisch* rebels were in possession of "Divine Law" *(Göttliches Recht).*[6] To be sure, their belief that only adherence to the cause guaranteed salvation justified social action by indirect reference to divine authority. But the purpose of self-sacrifice always remained the restoration of "ancient rights."

Yet none of this prevented them from elaborating revolutionary goals. Rather, the *salpeterisch* conception of "ancient rights" thrust the burden of legitimation onto those in power: the Eight, the Austrian bureaucracy, and eventually the emperor himself. Indeed, their understanding of legitimate domination embraced so many constraints on its practical exercise that it is difficult to imagine how Charles VI might have behaved to the satisfaction of *salpeterisch* peasants without abdicating all but titular overlordship. Ultimately, even the legitimacy of imperial authority was open to question. Propelled by the tensions borne of military repression, the *salpeterisch* logic of "ancient rights" drove inexorably toward a fundamental repudiation of all existing authority, including the imperial.

The sometimes appeasing gloss on *salpeterisch* arguments should not detract from their revolutionary potential. Arguments with the weightiest political implications—talk of "turning Swiss," for example—were often cloaked in more conciliatory arguments and appeals. Even after twenty years of factional strife, public versions of *salpeterisch* concerns still held open the possibility of peaceful reconciliation; hidden from the gaze of official surveillance, however, the rebels articulated their aspirations in much more radical terms. Much more than its counterpart, *salpeterisch* discourse was a "voice under domination":

5. Field, *Rebels in the Name of the Tsar,* 5–7.
6. GLA 113:239, 370r–79v, Interrogation of Hans Jörg Meyer of Unteralpfen, Unteralpfen, 9 May 1732; GLA 113:99, "Was Hans Meyer der Wagener zue Albffen im Wirtzhaus ausgestossen," Unteralpfen, 29 March 1732.

because the open expression of such beliefs might bring severe punishments, the amount of masking increased with the intensity of threats against speech—but only to a point.[7] When events proved that conciliatory language served no purpose, peasants enunciated their aspirations with fewer constraints. War, the escalation of factional violence, and Austrian military intervention provoked cathartic unmaskings of more defiant sentiments. The upshot is clear: the vocabulary of "ancient rights" veiled a deep-seated desire for liberation from all lords and officials.[8] Like the dispute between Hauenstein and St. Blasien over inheritance law, the issue at stake was peasant autonomy in the regulation of local affairs. To that extent, the rhetoric of "ancient rights" suggests the persistence of ancient reveries about "turning Swiss" and of memories of the Peasants' War of 1524–25 as an object lesson in the liberating potential of collective action to create a world without lords.[9]

These characteristics raise anew the "desideratum of typicality": was the *salpeterisch* rhetoric of factional identity a freakish local exception, or did its emphasis on rights, freedoms, and servitude address more widely held popular concerns? Although research on the political culture of early modern peasants remains sparse, certain evidence suggests that whether in response to the actual experience of servile subjection *(Leibeigenschaft)* or to states of being imagined to exist elsewhere, popular condemnation of serfdom as an intolerable innovation was widespread and on the increase in eighteenth-century Germany. Parallels to the case of Hauenstein suggest that such condemnations blended with notions of individual and collective honor to produce behaviors that are inexplicable in purely economic terms. More important, popular condemnations of serfdom implied new concepts of property. After about 1660, the belief that serfdom implied a general and "unrestricted exposure to the arbitrary dominion of lords" gained currency.[10] This concept resembled nothing more than the Roman legal fiction of absolute ownership

    7. James C. Scott, *Domination and the Arts of Resistance: Hidden Transcripts* (New Haven, 1990), 70–107, 136–82.
    8. Compare Renate Blickle, "Die Tradition des Widerstandes im Ammergau: Anmerkungen zum Verhältnis von Konflikt und Revolutionsbereitschaft," *ZAA* 35 (1987): 138–59.
    9. Thomas A. Brady Jr., *Turning Swiss: Cities and Empire, 1450–1550* (Cambridge, 1985).
    10. Renate Blickle, "Hausnotdurft: Ein Fundamentalrecht in der altständischen Ordnung Bayerns," in Günter Birtsch, ed., *Grund- und Freiheitsrechte von der ständischen zur spätbürgerlichen Gesellschaft* (Göttingen, 1987), 60.

over things *(dominium),* and may reflect the growing popular awareness of sixteenth-century legal doctrine and its tendency to equate serfdom with the slavery of Roman antiquity.[11] Under such redefinitions, serfdom was indistinguishable from slavery in the popular consciousness.[12] Of course, all this was pure speculation. Because their bodies were not owned, Hauensteiners were not slaves, nor could they have imagined the indignities suffered by contemporary African slaves in the American colonies. But at the level of anxieties about the future, the popular equation of serfdom with slavery implied new understandings of freedom and unfreedom. If serfdom meant an inherited state of exposure to arbitrary rule, then emancipation might inaugurate a similarly inherited, unrestricted liberty.

In the final analysis, however, the *salpeterisch* rhetoric of "ancient rights" cannot be fully understood apart from the context of factional politics. Only part of the peasantry adhered to such notions, while the other, *müllerisch* half did not. The founding raison d'être of *salpeterisch* ideology was the need to delimit a factional community. Here, it is striking how *little* of *salpeterisch* rhetoric defamed the behavior of lords, compared to the huge volume of scorn it heaped on *müllerisch* leaders.[13] In 1733, for example, one *salpeterisch* activist confessed under interrogation that "the current prelate [of St. Blasien] is quite a good lord. The Eight alone," he emphasized, "must bear the guilt for this altercation."[14] All masking aside, his language points to a crucial reality of political perception: oppression could be expected from seigneurs like the abbot of St. Blasien, but peasant magistrates could not be forgiven for selling their fellows into slavery. Whatever it meant, "enslavement" was all the worse for its treacherous origin.

A caution should be noted here. The pejorative connotations of the term "ideology" often seem inescapable, or as Terry Eagleton quipped,

---

11. See Werner Troßbach, "'Südwestdeutsche Leibeigenschaft' in der frühen Neuzeit: eine Bagatelle?" *GG* 7 (1981): 86, and Marc Bloch, *French Rural History* (Berkeley, 1966), 105.

12. R. Blickle, "Hausnotdurft," 60.

13. Günther Haselier, *Die Streitigkeiten der Hauensteiner mit ihren Obrigkeiten: Ein Beitrag zur Geschichte Vorderösterreichs und des südwestdeutschen Bauernstandes im 18. Jahrhundert* (Karlsruhe 1940), 61, 62.

14. GLA 113:240, 230r–38v, Interrogation of Joseph Meyer of Au, Vienna, 11 August 1733.

"His thought is redneck, yours is doctrinal, and mine is deliciously supple."[15] Too often, ideology is considered either the disingenuous manipulation or the unconscious distortion of "reality"; but such a conclusion would not be an accurate reflection of the character of popular political discourse in Hauenstein—or perhaps anywhere else, for that matter.[16] First, peasants used symbols selectively, but not to deceive. The *salpeterisch* concept of "ancient rights," for example, made sense of otherwise incomprehensible threats: rooted in ideas of a purer past, it justified defense against an uncertain future. Second, neither faction necessarily interpreted "reality" more accurately than the other. While *müllerisch* leaders had a subtler understanding of legal nuance, *salpeterisch* peasants perceived more keenly the real threat that St. Blasien posed. The point is that for the peasants of Hauenstein, it was the version of reality endorsed by their faction that was persuasive.[17] To understand these worldviews, it is necessary, then, to analyze the "ideology" of each faction in line with Donald Kelley's definition of ideology as a "distinctive and more or less coherent conglomeration of assumptions . . . ideals and goals accepted and perhaps acted upon by a more or less organized group of persons."[18] Here, then, ideology "is a matter of discourse" concerning "the actual uses of language between particular human subjects for the production of specific effects," to wit: patrolling the boundaries of factional community.[19]

The Serfdom Plot Persuasion

Sometime in late 1726 or early 1727, Speaker Joseph Tröndle of Rotzel tried to convince his fellow peasants that his policies had limited the

---

15. Terry Eagleton, *Ideology: An Introduction* (London, 1991).
16. These connotations coincide with what Geertz describes as the "interest" and "strain" theories of ideology; Clifford Geertz, "Ideology as a Cultural System," reprinted in his *Interpretation of Cultures* (New York, 1973), 201–7.
17. See James C. Scott, *Weapons of the Weak: Everyday Forms of Peasant Resistance* (New Haven, 1985), 317–18.
18. Donald R. Kelley, *The Beginning of Ideology: Consciousness and Society in the French Reformation* (Cambridge, 1981), 4.
19. Eagleton, *Ideology*, 9.

relentless spread of serfdom. Serfdom, he argued, was a malady, a corruption of the right order of things, and enumerated his efforts to contain it, such as withholding death duties pending the outcome of several lawsuits.[20] He invited his audience to "consider whether we have sought . . . to promote the common good of the county and to defend it against evil."[21] Judging by his tone, one might assume that Tröndle wished to provoke resistance against St. Blasien, the principle serf lord in Hauenstein. But Tröndle was a prominent *müllerisch* leader, not a rebel; indeed, his words were calculated to distance himself from the *salpeterisch* faction, whose "ambition," he declared, would cause a bloody repeat of the Peasants' War of 1524-25.

Tröndle could advocate such policies because the legality of his means distinguished them from rebellion. For Tröndle, litigation obviated the need for rebellion, let alone direct appeals to Emperor Charles VI. But his preference for approved modes of action also presupposed political norms not shared by all peasants. The two factions disputed the terms of legitimacy, the nature of law, and the proper relationship between rulers and subjects. While Tröndle and other *müllerisch* peasants measured the legitimacy of social action by its legality, notions of "ancient rights, freedoms, and privileges" animated most *salpeterisch* peasants. In part, then, the two factions disagreed over the relationship between written law and unwritten custom: *müllerisch* leaders were often prepared to obey edicts that violated the latter, whereas for *salpeterisch* peasants, a state of "obedience" that violated custom was inconceivable. In response to an official ban against Octovir elections in 1727, for example, the miller Martin Thoma of Haselbach exclaimed—probably within earshot of the Forest Steward—that "the government has no right to order us in electoral matters, and we absolutely won't

---

20. See GLA 97:459, "Prozeß-Acta etzwischen einem fürstl. Stüfft Seggingen, und der Graffschafft Hawenstein puncto der Fahlbarkeit sive den Fahlbezug und Nachjagens-Recht," 1714–42.

21. GLA 113:221, 503r–v, [Joseph Tröndle of Rotzel], "Notanta," [December 1726?]. The evidence for Tröndle's authorship is orthographic. It is possible that Speaker Tröndle's speech was delivered at an assembly held in the village on Hochsal on 17 December 1726; see GLA 113:225, 1r–2v, Bläsi Hottinger of Niedergebisbach to Hans Friedle Albiez of Buch, 17 December 1726.

accept it."[22] About a year later, Thoma explained his remark by suggesting that the elections had proceeded "with imperial approval," even though this was patently not the case.[23] For *müllerisch* partisans, the meaning of obedience was more literal: in the same year 1727, Martin Schneider of Altenschwand phrased the difference with eloquent simplicity when he said, "I am not *salpeterisch,* I obey."[24]

But factional disagreements over the conditions of authority were more complex than that. To begin with, the frontier between written law and custom had never been sharp.[25] Furthermore, the content of custom was always subject to interpretation. For their part, rebels emphasized "ancient customs" selectively: while they prized imperial ratifications of county privilege highly, they often overlooked the requirements of ancient treaties between Hauenstein and various lords—among them St. Blasien's 1467 charter of servile obligations—that ratified forms of subjection they found disagreeable. Finally, *salpeterisch* activists sometimes appealed to transparently counterfeit decrees, one of which was said to absolve Hauenstein from obedience to any authority. At a large assembly in the Görwihl commons on 10 September 1744, for example, Joseph "Glasmännle" Meyer of Au displayed a letter ostensibly in the hand of Queen Maria Theresa, which said that "no one, neither ecclesiastical nor secular authorities, can command you in anything."[26] Neither faction, then, approached the law consistently.

Perhaps no incident epitomized the instrumental elasticity of custom more than the rebels' opposition to the manumission treaty of 1738. Why did *salpeterisch* peasants, otherwise the spirited defenders of local freedoms, reject an opportunity to emancipate themselves from a hated burden? Their reasons were several: first, the manumission treaty had

---

22. GLA 99:985, 70r–71v, "Was der Morte Toma Müller in Haselboch den 4 Tag 9bl. 1727 zuo Dogeren underfangen."

23. GLA 113:232, 138r–81v, Interrogation of Martin Thoma of Haselbach, Freiburg, 16–20 September 1728.

24. GLA 99:976, Interrogation of Martin Schneider of Altenschwand, Unteralpfen, 10 January 1727.

25. Gerald Strauss, *Law, Resistance and the State: The Opposition to Roman Law in Reformation Germany* (Princeton, 1986), 100–101; and see 48–49, 98–101.

26. GLA 113:222, 102r–3v, Interrogation of Bailiff Michael Albiez of Burg and Joseph Rummel of Görwihl, 10 September 1744.

been concluded without popular approval, and second, the price of freedom was oppressive—perhaps as much as five gulden for each and every abbatial serf.[27] More important, however, *salpeterisch* peasants were loath to buy a liberty they thought they owned already. Yet in 1725 the belief in Hauenstein's inherent freedom from servitude was only about seventy years old. In point of law, moreover, the notion of serfdom as a recent innovation was simply mistaken: rather, it had been codified in consensual treaties for nearly half a millennium.[28] Only definitions of custom with the loosest dependence on precedent could support the *salpeterisch* conclusion.

Yet more than any other belief, it was the idea that serfdom was a recent abomination against a historic condition of inherent, corporate freedom that distinguished *salpeterisch* from *müllerisch*. This trope owed its persuasive power and its usefulness to the task of patrolling symbolic barriers between factions in no small part to its very elasticity: the idea of "ancient rights" could encompass and give historical depth to the widest variety of aspirations. It also supplied a ready-made narrative for the origins of factional difference. As Chapter 2 showed, the exertions of Hauenstein's peasant elite to prevent the "eternal perpetuation" of St. Blasien's lease of juridical authorities in the county in 1698–1705 provided *salpeterisch* peasants with the earliest evidence for an Octovir plot to sell Hauenstein into slavery. Thus serfdom was the product of *müllerisch* conspiracy. Moreover, details in the narrative of double-crossing grew more elaborate. Under interrogation in 1726, "Salpeter-Hans" Albiez augmented the myth that the cost of Adam Tröndle's 1704 mission to Vienna was in fact the purchase price of slavery. Adam Tröndle, he said, "had expended many thousands of gulden, and for that reason they now are called serfs."[29] Thus graft amplified betrayal; Albiez later added he had seen "the deed [of sale] and the money" lying "side by side" at a secret place in Waldkirch.[30] Some of the new myths were more prosaic. In 1738, for example, Hans Friedle Gerspach of Bergalingen suggested that back in

---

27. GLA 99:1040, 120r–27v, "Copia Actum Waldshut," 21 February 1738.
28. See, for example, two decrees of the abbatial Forest Bureau, the 1383 *Waldamtsöffnung*, in Josef Bader, ed., "Das ehemalige sankt-blasische Waldamt," *ZGO* 6 (1855): 107–25, and the *Dingrodel* of 26 May 1467, in GLA 21:379, reprinted in Josef Bader, ed., "Urkundenregeste über die ehemaligen sankt-blasischen Niedergerichte," *ZGO* 7 (1856): 235–39.
29. GLA 113:224, 3r, Interrogation of Hans Friedle Albiez, Freiburg, 26–29 October, 1726.
30. GLA 113:222, 7r–10v, Open letter by Hans Friedle Albiez, [ca. 1727].

1704, Adam Tröndle had not observed proper etiquette when presenting a chamois cap *(Gambsbockh)* to the Court Chancellor Bucelleni. This *faux pas,* it was said, had cost Hauenstein its freedom: "If only they had delivered the present in his kitchen, then the word *eigen* would have been stricken, and because of this oversight the word *eigen* has remained to this day."[31]

In time, every conceivable calamity became grist for the mill of factional distance. *Müllerisch* Octovirs were held accountable for the Austrian military interventions of 1729, 1739, and 1745, and of course each imperial commission of investigation was said to have worked unfairly in the *müllerisch* interest.[32] Octovir elections were thought to have been suspended at their behest, although we know from records of *müllerisch* negotiations with the Beaurieu commission that this was not the case.[33] At the same time, *müllerisch* leaders were supposed to be in treasonous cahoots with France: some said they had hired the French army to invade Outer Austria in 1743–44.[34] Indeed, the pejorative epithet "französisch" was applied to *müllerisch* leaders as early as 1727.[35] Three common threads united these often inconsistent accusations: first, that the *müllerisch* Eight had conspired to thwart imperial benevolence through the connivance of officials (whether Austrian or French); second, that these conspiracies were an unjust betrayal of hallowed common rights; and third, that the *müllerisch* Octovirs were conspiring, not only with St. Blasien, but also with mean-spirited Austrian officials for pay.[36]

In the context of such narratives, the *salpeterisch* repudiation of manumission made good sense: by 1739, the belief that Hauenstein was inherently free of serfdom (by *any* name) was fixed in *salpeterisch* minds. And as Chapter 3 showed, the *salpeterisch* interpretation of the manumission treaty produced such a rise in the rebel faction's popularity that

---

31. GLA 113:248, B1, Interrogation of Claus Ebner et al., 22 July 1738. Bucelleni was First Chancellor *(Hofkanzler)* from 1695 to 1704.

32. See, for example, GLA 113:99, "Was Hans Meyer der Wagener zue Albffen im Wirtzhaus . . . ausgestossen," 29 March 1732, and GLA 113:260, 331r–v, Village of Birkingen to Bailiff Hans Peter Schäfer, 18 November 1745.

33. GLA 113:236, 184r–86v, "Actum Togeren den 20ten Aprill 1728."

34. GLA 113:225, 306r–7v, Interrogation of Friedle Stigeler of Dietlingen and Thebus Hupfer of Weilheim, Freiburg, 7 June 1727.

35. GLA 113:221, 452r–53v, Interrogation of Joseph Jehle et al., [11 August 1745?].

36. For this reason, some said, the Eight had not kept accurate financial records since 1701; see GLA 113:221, 452r–53v, Interrogation of Joseph Jehle et al., [11 August 1745?].

by February 1739, nearly 80 percent of all adult males in Hauenstein had repudiated the *müllerisch* proposal. This surge coincided with a radicalization of rebel attitudes. Despite *müllerisch* Octovirs' energetic attempts to advertise the virtues of manumission, most peasants became convinced that emancipation was unnecessary because Hauenstein was free already.[37] Manumission presupposed a legitimate prior unfreedom, which in turn required *salpeterisch* peasants to approve a version of recent history that justified the intolerable.

Indeed, certain *salpeterisch* leaders carried this logic further, arguing that manumission was tantamount to the *purchase* of servitude.[38] As "Gaudihans" Wasmer of Segeten testified in 1739, "Word had it that [as a result of the treaty] we were to acknowledge the prelate of St. Blasien as our liege and serf lord, which words I understood to mean that we were to become serfs."[39] Thus, just as Adam Tröndle's diplomatic exertions in 1704 were reinterpreted as a secret campaign to sell the community into slavery, so the manumission was reinterpreted as its exact opposite. Thus in March 1743, Johannes "the Prussian" Marder of Eschbach and Joseph "Glasmännle" Meyer of Au spread the view that manumission only impoverished the peasants and that, in spite of it all, "we are still serfs . . . just as before." In 1746, Joseph Albiez of Finsterlingen claimed that manumission had "had the sole result that we are now Bohemian serfs."[40] To be sure, such logic was not wholly consistent with the retrospective *salpeterisch* narrative of *müllerisch* betrayal. The reinterpretations of Marder, Meyer, and Albiez made little sense if Hauenstein had been already sold into slavery in 1704. Indeed, *salpeterisch* ideologues seem never to have decided whether "enslavement" was a past injustice, a present-day misdeed, or a future menace. Similarly, they persisted in asserting that Hauenstein was free and always had been. Was the county enslaved or not? Most *salpeterisch* peasants probably collapsed all three chronologies of the slide into slavery—past, present, and future—into one. Thus the timelessness of suspicion imparted an equal urgency to all phases in the *salpeterisch* eschatology of betrayal.

37. GLA 113:79, [Joseph Tröndle of Rotzel], "Ungefehrliche Vorstellung des Fahlbarke[its]-Geschäffts . . . ," [January? 1738].
38. GLA 99:1041, 90r–92, "Copia extract aus denen Aussagen deren Hauensteiner die Einungsmeister betreffend," [February 1739?].
39. GLA 113:248, A4, no. 7, Interrogation of Hans Wasmer of Segeten, 20 April 1739.
40. GLA 113:14, no. 9, Interrogation of Bartle Denz et al., 25 July 1746.

Responses to the manumission treaty were also unexceptional in that *salpeterisch* peasants attributed it to bribery. Just as stories of *müllerisch* perfidy grew in detail, so too did the number and size of payments they were supposed to have received for their nefarious services. One Peter Köpfler alleged that the miller Joseph Tröndle of Unteralpfen had cheated Hauenstein out of 5,000 gulden in the first revolt of 1726–29 and would do it again.[41] In an argument that upended *müllerisch* claims that they had successfully bargained the 1738 manumission tax from 92,000 gulden *down* to 58,000 gulden, Hans Friedle Gerspach accused the Eight of publicizing an emancipation fee 8,000 gulden *higher* than the stipulated price and of embezzling the difference.[42] Such alleged bribes inflated with each year of the turmoil, such that by 1745, Martin Zimmermann of Etzwihl claimed that Hauenstein had been sold for "two tons of coin."[43]

Thus at every turn, the *müllerisch* leadership was accused, in effect, of commodifying non-negotiable, collective freedoms for private gain. Because such deeds violated their oath of office, *müllerisch* Octovirs had perjured themselves and had therefore forfeited their authority— no longer were they "genuine Octovirs," but Hauenstein's true rebels.[44] Moreover, all *müllerisch* peasants were guilty by association of this perjury. Here, individual and collective concepts of honor fused: to the extent that personal reputations were tied to the truthful fulfillment of sacred oaths, individual honor and adherence to the *salpeterisch* construction of "ancient rights" became identical. Thus "a man who does not adhere to the *salpeterisch* [faction] is not an honorable man *[Bittermann]*," as Joseph Zimmerman put it.[45]

It is true that Joseph Tröndle of Unteralpfen occasionally sent presents of trout from his private pond to the abbot of St. Blasien, but such exchanges can hardly be considered any real basis for the accusations leveled against the *müllerisch* leadership.[46] Nor were such courtesies equal

---

41. GLA 99:1041, Interrogation of Domini Widmer and Conrad Tröndle of Remetschwiel, 21 January 1739.

42. See GLA 113:249, B1, and GLA 65:11419, 28r–29v, which contain reports of a rally at Görwihl led by Gerspach on 20 July 1738.

43. GLA 113:259, 75r–v, Interrogation of Hans Jacob Gerteis of Dogern, 26 July 1745.

44. GLA 113:235, 68r–70v, Joseph Tröndle of Unteralpfen to OVA, 14 February 1730.

45. GLA 113:242, Interrogation of Joseph Zimmermann et al., 5 February 1739.

46. GLA 113:239, Abbot Franz II to Joseph Tröndle of Unteralpfen, 12 March 1731 [a letter of thanks].

to the punishments that *salpeterisch* leaders had in mind for them. At a minimum, *salpeterisch* justice dictated that the cost of each calamity should be taken from *müllerisch* purses. But retribution would not stop there: Conrad Ebner of Oberalpfen, for one, thought that all *müllerisch* peasants should be gathered in a field to hear a recitation of the customary privileges they had squandered, then stoned to death if they refused to believe it.[47] These were fierce words, but Ebner still left open the possibility of redemption. More militant rebels were less charitable. Many singled out the *müllerisch* Eight for especially severe censure; already in 1727, for example, two peasants from Nöggenschwiel had suggested that the combative *müllerisch* Octovir Georg Fluem of Dietlingen deserved the dishonorable execution of hanging flanked by two dogs.[48] Together, these penalties mirrored the punishments that *salpeterisch* leaders themselves had experienced at the hands of imperial Austrian investigators—fines, banishments, executions. As such, they amounted to an alternative popular justice warranted, as we shall see, by the requirements of an overriding loyalty to Hauenstein's "ancient rights" and to Emperor Charles as paternal sovereign justiciar.

A final unifying trope in the negative *salpeterisch* discourse on factional difference was that of pollution.[49] To be sure, *salpeterisch* peasants rarely used the vocabulary of filth and purity to describe their opposites. But the *salpeterisch* narrative of betrayal and enslavement, the incompatibility of honor with *müllerisch* sympathies, and *salpeterisch* recipes for retributive justice all were based on a belief in the loss of a bygone purity sullied by serfdom through the mendacity of "disloyal" peasant magistrates. If serfdom by any name polluted the right order of things, then *müllerisch* leaders—not the Benedictines of St. Blasien or the noble sisters of St. Fridolin—were Hauenstein's polluters-in-chief. In articulating their notions of pollution, *salpeterisch* peasants made abundant use of the uterine significations of servile terminology: just as St. Blasien's addition of the prefix *"leib-"* (which in addition to "body" or "belly" could also mean "womb") to older words for serfdom underscored the corporeality and heritability of servile status, the *müllerisch* Eight were said to have sold "the child in its mother's womb" into "eternal serf-

---

47. GLA 113:221, 452r–53v, Interrogation of Joseph Jehle et al., [11 August 1745?].
48. GLA 113:227, 8r–11v, "Actum Gurtweyl," 11 January 1728.
49. On uses of pollution to define and police social arrangements, see Mary Douglas, *Purity and Danger: An Analysis of the Concepts of Pollution and Taboo* (London, 1966), 114–28.

dom."⁵⁰ This connection hid an assumption—common to both Roman and most customary law⁵¹—that status (free or unfree) was a matrilineal inheritance and that the perpetuation of freedom and unfreedom was a function of sexual generation. Although rebels did not use metaphors of rape or emasculation explicitly, by violating the reproduction of a free community, the *müllerisch* faction had, by implication, polluted the generative process and the metaphorical purity of the women of Hauenstein. *Salpeterisch* peasants enacted this connection most vividly through the rituals and ceremonies of Marian pilgrimage.

Moreover, just as honor and factional loyalties were inextricably linked, the *salpeterisch* concept of pollution tied actions to states of being. In a popular, political embellishment on the Roman Catholic cycle of sin, penance, and salvation, factional loyalties became the barometer of personal redemption. The most lurid illustration of this connection was the widespread suspicion that *müllerisch* leaders had consorted with the devil to achieve their ends. The earliest of these associations date from the late 1730s and emerged in response to confessional slanders from the *müllerisch* side. As early as 1726, *müllerisch* Octovir Georg Fluem had smeared *salpeterisch* peasants as "Lutherans" who wished to raze St. Blasien to the ground—a transparent reference to the Peasants' War of 1524–25.⁵² *Salpeterisch* leaders denied the charge vehemently and insisted to the contrary that they were "not fallen from the Catholic faith, as our mendacious antagonists . . . have written."⁵³ From their *salpeterisch* perspective, the opposite was true: the miller Tröndle was considered "worse than a heretic, for a heretic can still obtain the grace of God, which the miller cannot any longer."⁵⁴ In 1739, Martin Thoma demonized Tröndle syllogistically as "a traitor to his country, a scoundrel, and a perjurer, who adheres to the prelate [of St. Blasien], and to the prelate adheres the devil."⁵⁵ Just as the scale of suspected bribes had increased over time, so *salpeterisch* condemnations grew harsher with each new calamity. After

50. GLA 113:99, 1r–2v, "Was Hans Meyer der Wagener zue Albffen im Wirtzhaus . . . ausgestossen," 29 March 1732.
51. Art. "Leibeigenschaft," in Adalbert Erler et al., eds., *Handbuch zur deutschen Rechtsgeschichte* (Berlin, 1971–), 2:1761–72.
52. GLA 113:222, 158r–61v, "Wie sich Johannes Martter dr Preüß und Joseph Mayer seith ihres Arest . . . ihm Lant auffgefüörth," [September 1743?].
53. GLA 113:258, 85r–86v, Open letter by Hans Wasmer of Segeten, 3 December 1745.
54. GLA 113:221, 452r–53v, Interrogation of Joseph Jehle et al., [11 August 1745?].
55. GLA 113:253, 37r, Interrogation of Hans Strittmatter, 8 February 1739.

factional hostilities climaxed in 1743–44, *salpeterisch* peasants denied their adversaries all hope of redemption: *müllerisch* leaders "with all their followers" were damned "for eternity to the abyss of Hell" for having caused the "downfall of women and children, so that God should no longer look upon it."[56] Indeed, some *müllerisch* peasants were "already living in Hell. . . . All are damned who do not adhere to the *salpeterisch* [cause], for God can and will no longer be merciful to them."[57]

His Majesty's Rebels

Condemnations like these had their counterpart in ideas and images that defined *salpeterisch* identity in positive terms. The self-awareness of *salpeterisch* peasants did not depend solely on negative definitions: if the *müllerisch* peasants were lost to the devil, then rebels were the party of God. *Salpeterisch* peasants constructed this dimension of their awareness through a vocabulary of loyalty between Hauenstein and its Habsburg overlord that could legitimate resistance to virtually any source of authority. A higher obligation to defend "ancient rights" outweighed the requirements of written ephemera, including, often, the codified letter of custom itself: as Bläsi Hottinger put it in 1726, the emperor "will protect and guard us and our privileges, and we will not allow chapter and verse *[Punckhten und Buochsteben]* to separate us from our rights."[58] But such vagueness did not prevent *salpeterisch* peasants from ascribing to their cause salvific power, for if *müllerisch* peasants were damned, faith in the *salpeterisch* cause secured one a place in heaven. Indeed, imprecision made the rhetoric of "ancient rights" more effective, permitting individual peasants to supply whatever meaning suited them best. When politics and salvation merged, the elements of *salpeterisch* rhetoric combined to justify a rejection even of the emperor's authority.

56. GLA 113:222, 277r–v, Interrogation of Jacob Ebner of Lochmatt, 1 November 1745.
57. Ibid., 271r–72v, [Joseph Tröndle of Rotzel], "Notanta wegen dem grausamen Scheldten und villen . . . lugenhafften Aussage so vor Gutt undt der ehrbahren Weldt niemahl werdten veranthworthet werden könen," [May 1745?].
58. GLA 113:224, 1r–2r, Bläsi Hottinger of Niedergebisbach to Hans-Friedle Albiez of Buch, 17 December 1726.

At the heart of *salpeterisch* political philosophy lay three main principles: reciprocity, exclusivity, and the contractual character of rule. The idea that domination was based on reciprocal obligations between ruler and ruled was nearly universal among early modern German peasants: in return for obedience, tribute, and military support, the emperor would provide "protection and guardianship" *(Schutz und Schirm),* over the peasants and their ancient customs.[59] This notion pervaded *salpeterisch* rhetoric from the start: already in the summer of 1726, "Salpeter-Hans" Albiez cited an imaginary oath of Emperor Charles VI, who in 1717 had sworn to "guard and protect" the subjects of Hauenstein "in [their] old privileges and customs."[60] But later *salpeterisch* ideologues added two further elements. The first was that domination was also indivisibile: no peasant could be subject to two sovereigns at once, which necessarily precluded homage to St. Blasien. Finally, domination was thought to be contractual in the manner of medieval feudal reciprocities, such that the failure of either liege or vassal to fulfill their respective obligations dissolved the relationship entirely, at least in theory. To be sure, *salpeterisch* peasants traveled a long road to reach that conclusion, but reach it they eventually did.

Popular notions about the reciprocal nature of domination were sustained by a powerful "myth of origin" and by images of the emperor as a caring father-figure. Specifically, *salpeterisch* peasants claimed that Hauenstein had received its "ancient rights" from a benevolent "Good Count Hans" in 1396. The origins of this legend are unclear. Although it appears nowhere before the 1730s, the myth probably rested on an interpretation of genuine historical documents. In 1396, an actual Count Johannes IV of Habsburg-Laufenburg received Hauenstein to rule in bond for loans to the elder, Albertine line of the dynasty and swore at his investiture to sustain the people "in possession of the rights and customs that they have held since ancient times."[61] Perhaps *salpeterisch* peasants were made aware of this "donation" at an assembly held in Hochsal in December 1726,

---

59. See Winfried Schulze, *Bäuerlicher Widerstand und feudale Herrschaft in der frühen Neuzeit* (Bad Canstatt, 1980), 123–24.

60. GLA 113:225, 98r.

61. The oath is reprinted in Josef Bader, ed., "Urkunden und Regeste aus dem Archive der ehemaligen Grafschaft Hauenstein," *ZGO* 10 (1859): 361, and Günther Haselier, *Geschichte des Hotzenwalds* (Lahr, 1973), 35.

when Speaker Joseph Tröndle of Rotzel recited the contents of the county's archive.⁶² In any event, *salpeterisch* peasants fully exploited the vagueness of the pledge. According to Johannes Marder and Bläsi Hottinger, the Good Count Hans had endowed his "forever free county of Hauenstein," eternally and inalienably, with "all its ancient freedoms," in recognition of the peasants' "loyalty" and of three "voluntary" loans.⁶³ Thus the "myth of origins" supplied a symbolic counterpart to their narrative of *müllerisch* betrayal: for Marder and Hottinger, inalienable freedoms were, if not the fruit of outright purchase, then certainly the reward of great financial exertions. Lest there be any doubt about its validity, "Gaudihans" Wasmer claimed to have a copy of Count Hans's oath, which privileged all Hauensteiners, "greater and lesser" alike, in recognition of "services faithfully rendered."⁶⁴

Moreover, the "myth of origins" added that Good Count Hans had established a dynastic benevolence that continued in the paternal love of his modern successors. The *salpeterisch* presumption of Emperor Charles VI's personal concern for Hauenstein was conveyed most vividly by the blacksmith and early *salpeterisch* activist, Conrad Binkert of Dogern, who in 1727 spread the rumor that during an audience with the emperor at his imperial palace in the Vienna, Charles had invited Binkert to sit beside him on the imperial throne to discuss the travails of Hauenstein.⁶⁵ Binkert's story conveyed a sense of grandfatherly goodwill that remained a durable fixture of *salpeterisch* belief throughout the 1730s and 1740s. Nineteen years after Binkert's "encounter," Bläsi Hottinger recalled how Charles had exclaimed, "You my darling children . . . oh my dear sub-

62. GLA 99:980, Bläsi Hottinger to Hans Friedle Albiez, 17 December 1726. See also GLA 65:11223, 58r–69v, Johannes Thoma-ab-Egg and Bläsi Hottinger, "Species facti succincta in sachen Hauenstein. Königl. Cammeralunterthanen auf dem Schwarzwalt ad des Gotteshaus St. Blasii und das Stifft Seckhingen nebst ihren anfang," [1744?], and Haselier, *Streitigkeiten*, 83–84.

63. GLA 65:11223, 58r–69v, "Species facti succincta"; Haselier, *Streitigkeiten*, 81.

64. GLA 113:231, 17r–18v, "Copia Gnaden Brieffs . . . Hansens von Habspurg neben lineo letzten inhaberen . . . der Graffschafft Hauwenstein," n.d.; see also GLA 113:241, 106r–10v, "Eine wahr Unterrichtung der Specii Factae, und die Warheit auss der Graffschafft Hauenstein contra Praelaten von St Blasii," 1 June 1737.

65. According to court testimony of Martin Eisele of Weilheim, Binkert spread word that he had "had to approach the emperor and ascend the throne, and was encouraged to speak freely"; GLA 113:227, 17r–19v, Interrogation of Martin Eisele of Weilheim, OVA, 16 January 1728; see also GLA 113:227, Interrogation of Clemens Dietschi of Weilheim, OVA, 16 January 1728.

jects, you shall have my mercy and you shall be helped in all things, for I do not wish that you should be either *eigen* or *leibeigen* to the monastery of St. Blasien."[66]

The records abound with such "evidence" of imperial benevolence. According to Johannes Thoma-ab-Egg, Emperor Charles in 1732 had sworn "with raised fingers that you ought to be helped."[67] The misunderstandings that arose from such encounters—real and imagined—cannot have been caused by Charles's "habit of trying to please everyone; it was said that anyone who spoke to him came away with the impression that Charles VI thought exactly as he did."[68] More than Charles's personal quirks underlay popular belief in his benevolence. Such perceived expressions of trust did not cease when a woman ascended the throne. Bläsi Hottinger reported that during a "conversation" with Maria Theresa at the coronation of her husband Francis I as Holy Roman Emperor in Frankfurt on 13 September 1745, the monarch clapped her hands in despair and demanded to know why the "Eight have not given the people their ancient privileges, which they received from the first emperors?"[69] Nor were attributions such as these unique to Hauenstein: we know that peasants from other lordships "heard" verbatim words from the emperor or members of his family. In 1712, for example, the Empress-Dowager Eleonora Magdalena von Pfalz-Neuburg "told" peasants from Groß-Raming in Upper Austria that "you, my dear children, shall soon be helped."[70] The veracity of these imperial "quotations" is less important than the fact that peasants believed them and thereby were confirmed in the justice of their struggles.

The sense of direct, personal subjection that these quotes convey superseded all other forms of subjection. All Hauensteiners referred to themselves as "cameral subjects" *(Kameraluntertanen)*, and although the term had a specific legal content, Hans Friedle Gerspach and other *salpeterisch* activists understood it to mean that subjection was collective

---

66. GLA 113:258, 302r–14v, Interrogation of Bläsi Hottinger, Waldshut, 2–7 May 1746.
67. GLA 113:239, 270r–71v, Interrogation of Hans Meyer of Unteralpfen, 24 March 1732.
68. Michael Hughes, *Law and Politics in Eighteenth-Century Germany* (Woodbridge, Suffolk, 1988), 8 n. 6.
69. GLA 113:260, 177r–78v, Interrogation of Joseph Hierholzer of Happingen, 16 November 1745.
70. Quoted in Georg Grüll, *Bauer, Herr und Landesfürst: Sozialrevolutionäre Bestrebungen der oberösterreichischen Bauern von 1650 bis 1848* (Graz, 1963), 11.

and indivisible: as a corporate polity, Hauenstein was subject solely to the emperor and to no other lord.[71] And because the county could have but one ruler, the homage they had sworn to Charles VI in 1717 nullified the homage done to St. Blasien ten years later.[72] *Salpeterisch* peasants could not have been more explicit on this point: in a conversation with Joseph Lüber of Glashütten in May 1727, "Schwarzmichel" Tröndle of Bergalingen explained that "I belong to the emperor, and have sworn loyalty to him. If I were a serf of the abbey, then I could not belong to the emperor, and I would be a knave ... against my wife and children."[73]

Similarly during the homage crisis of 1727, the Speaker Joseph Tröndle of Schmitzingen argued that before any oaths could be rendered, "the emperor himself must release [us]" because "[we] have done homage before the emperor, and wish to pay homage to no other lord."[74] Related to this argument was the tendency to muddle distinctions among the various legal categories of domination, especially with regard to St. Blasien. Changes in the language of homage oaths for St. Blasien's juridical and seigneurial subjects, for example, were thought to undermine Habsburg sovereignty. Conrad Binkert of Dogern implied the same association when he claimed that St. Blasien had "enserfed" its lower courts and so had usurped the "rights of sovereignty."[75] Though such correlations were inaccurate in point of law, they bore a weighty verisimilitude: after all, a long succession of abbots had striven to acquire sovereign rights over Hauenstein and had even claimed to "own" outright their lower courts in the county.[76] But the *salpeterisch* principle of exclusivity did not depend on empirical verification. Potentially, any form of abbatial domination might provide evidence not only of serfdom but also of an involuntary alienation from the imperial patron.

The third, contractual element subverted the status quo even more than the principle of exclusivity did. In the rebels' view, the ongoing

71. GLA 65:11419 [Nachlaß J. L. Meyer], 49v–53r.
72. See Haselier, *Streitigkeiten*, 65. For the protocol of Hauenstein's homage to Charles VI at Luttingen and Dogern on 12 June 1717, see GLA 113:80, A; for homage to Maria Theresa, see StAWT, Ratsprotokolle, 3 October 1741.
73. GLA 113:225, 309r–11v, Interrogation of Michael Tröndle of Bergalingen, VÖRK, 7 June 1727 [Tröndle's remark is translated in the first person].
74. GLA 99:983, Abbatial Bailiff Joseph Schmidt of Todtmoos to Joseph Tröndle of Unteralpfen, 15 June 1727.
75. GLA 113:227, 26r, Interrogation of Friedle Ebner of Steinbach, 16 January 1728.
76. See Haselier, *Streitigkeiten*, 17–22.

legitimacy of subordination depended on the *fulfillment* of reciprocal obligations between ruler and subject, or at least a plausible faith in the emperor's desire to fulfill them. But just as their concept of "ancient rights" was elastic, *salpeterisch* activists described the nature of peasant obligations in minimal terms. By their account, it entailed loyalty and a timely response to musters of the county militia; as for tribute, the militant "Gaudihans" Wasmer was alleged to suggest that a mere 1,500 gulden *per annum* sufficed.⁷⁷ Of course, Hauenstein's annual tax levy far exceeded this amount, so Wasmer's figure could—and did—translate into a justification for tax strikes. Their discourse on reciprocity gives the overwhelming impression that *salpeterisch* peasants considered themselves loyal by definition and that their part of the bargain was negligible. Proof of the pudding, then, was whether the emperor in fact protected custom and privilege. If he did not—and as we have seen, the very existence of *salpeterisch* rhetoric presupposed that "ancient rights" had been lost or stolen—then the terms of legitimate subordination were disrupted. This state of affairs demanded some explanation.

Here, *müllerisch* treachery offered the most convenient explanation. But other authorities came in for similarly harsh opprobrium. Only the emperor seemed immune from suspicion: a corollary to their paternalistic image of the benevolent emperor was the conviction that Charles could not possibly wish them ill. For the most part, *salpeterisch* peasants projected their own aspirations and concepts of justice onto the person of the monarch and could conceive of discord between sovereign and subject only with the greatest difficulty. Imperial patents and decrees that infringed on what they considered "ancient rights," therefore, could not reflect the *bona fide* royal will, but the *ersatz* inventions of unscrupulous bureaucrats conspiring to keep the monarch in ignorance. In 1729, for example, "Schwarzmichel" Tröndle could only rationalize the injustice of his imprisonment by claiming that "the emperor knows . . . not a single word about [my] ordeal." Proof of this, he claimed, was the "fact" that Charles VI had given money to support the rebel cause.⁷⁸ Similarly in March 1732, "Glasmännle" Meyer spread

---

77. GLA 113:255, 265r–68v, Interrogation of Hans Strittmatter of Görwihl, WVA, 7 January 1744; GLA 113:255, 270r–73v, Interrogation of Hans Jacob Sibolt, 7 January 1744.
78. GLA 113:230, 403r–v, Interrogation of Joseph Tröndle of Unteralpfen, Freiburg, 8 December 1729.

the story that Charles VI personally donated fifty gulden, which he "had received . . . from the emperor himself, from his own hand."[79]

If wicked ministers had kept the "well-intentioned" Charles ignorant of Hauenstein's plight, the obvious solution was to remove them.[80] "Schwarzmichel" Tröndle declared frankly that "the emperor should have his scoundrels in Vienna strung up, [and] then things will go better."[81] Amid the mounting frustrations of the 1730s and 1740s, such reveries transformed into the active belief that Charles had actually deposed his ministers, among them First Chancellor Philipp Ludwig von Sinzendorff and Court Councillor Johann Christoph von Bartenstein.[82] Already in 1732, Bläsi Hottinger had hinted that Sinzendorff's name was inscribed "in the emperor's black book," implying that Charles would soon remove him.[83] Nor, of course, were local authorities to be immune from the combined wrath of emperor and peasant. St. Blasien would receive the harshest treatment: at the annual parish festival in nearby St. Peter, the *salpeterisch* exile Johannes Obrist spread the rumor that Emperor Charles, annoyed with the arrogance of his prelates, intended to tax St. Blasien 100,000 gulden or even declare war against the abbey.[84] By 1744, the *salpeterisch* faction had come to deny the legitimacy of local authorities from the Forest Steward to the provincial government in Freiburg.

All this recalled the famous "right of resistance" propounded in Eike von Repgow's thirteenth-century *Sachsenspiegel,* which permitted self-defense against the unjust acts of lords.[85] Eventually, not even the emperor was spared the thrust of its logic. As unrest continued into 1740s,

79. GLA 99:1034, 95r–v, Adam Tröndle of Görwihl to Joseph Tröndle of Unteralpfen, 26 March 1732.

80. GLA 113:221, 35r–36v, Joseph Metzger of Görwihl to Joseph Tröndle of Unteralpfen, 11 December 1738.

81. GLA 113:230, 403r–v, Interrogation of Joseph Tröndle of Unteralpfen, Freiburg, 8 December 1729.

82. GLA 113:258, 180r–81v, Interrogation of Joseph Jehle of Bierbronnen, Innsbruck, 6 May 1746. For the indictments of Sinzendorff and Bartenstein, see GLA 99:1037, 18r–21v, Bläsi Hottinger of Niedergebisbach to Hans Friedle Gerspach, 23 July 1735, and GLA 113:241, 35r–36v, Hottinger to Gerspach, 23 September 1735.

83. GLA 113:241, 35r–36v, Bläsi Hottinger to Hans Friedle Gerspach, Vienna, 23 September 1735.

84. GLA 99:1032, 164r–71v, "Actum St Blasien," 3–5 October 1730.

85. Carl R. Sachße, ed., *Sachsenspiegel* (Heidelberg, 1848), 3:78, §2, p. 297; see also Hans Fehr, "Das Widerstandsrecht," *MIÖG* 38 (1920): 1–38.

evidence mounted that the house of Habsburg had forsaken Hauenstein. Peasants who in 1738 came to regard manumission as the purchase of servitude considered it a fundamental test of the emperor's reciprocal loyalty to Hauenstein. Some recommended that "should the emperor not wish to help [us], we will appeal to a different lord," such as Switzerland, as Johannes Zimmermann of Niederwihl proposed.[86] When that day came, said "Gaudihans" Wasmer, Hauenstein would be as free as their Swiss neighbors across the Rhine.[87] Emperor Charles's death on 20 October 1740 gave an added impetus to speculations about a "reunion" with Switzerland, for Hauensteiners had long been aware that because Charles had no male heirs, a succession crisis was in the offing. Indeed, thirteen years before, the shrewd Martin Thoma had suggested that if Charles died with no sons, Hauenstein would be at liberty to choose a new sovereign.[88]

In fact, by 1738 the idea of "turning Swiss," as a viable alternative to remaining within the Habsburg Crown Lands, was no longer new.[89] Already at the outset of the "Salpeter Wars," Martin Thoma had insisted that before the Reformation, Hauenstein was subject to the canton of Bern, as if to suggest the possibility of someday restoring the tie.[90] But more than any other event, the manumission controversy prompted dreams of restoring a golden age of "Swiss" liberties. In January 1739, for example, Claus Geng of Kuchelbach reminded his neighbors that "in the Swiss War, the peasants attacked, imprisoned, and thoroughly devoured their lords . . . for the peasants said that their lords were the cause of this war."[91] Exactly which "Swiss War" was meant is unclear, but the analogy recommended the possibility of autonomy acquired through force of arms. Others used it to justify secession from Outer Austria: in reaction to war taxes decreed by the provincial Estates in

---

86. GLA 99:988, Interrogation of Abbatial Bailiff Lorenz Baumgartner of Niederwihl, 1 April 1728.

87. GLA 113:258, 184r–v, Interrogation of Jacob Zimmermann of Görwihl, Innsbruck, 11 May 1746.

88. GLA 113:232, 138r–81v, Interrogation of Martin Thoma of Haselbach, Freiburg, 16–20 September 1728.

89. The phrase is borrowed from Brady, *Turning Swiss,* 34–36.

90. GLA 113:232, 138r–81v, Interrogation of Martin Thoma of Haselbach, Freiburg, 16–20 September 1728.

91. GLA 113:242, 205r–6v, Interrogation of Claus Geng of Kuchelbach, [January 1739].

1744, for example, Bläsi Hottinger and Johannes Marder concluded that "all the Estates are scoundrels, and we don't belong to them. Our county is a free one, just like Switzerland."[92] More militant rebels carried this line of reasoning further still. For "Gaudihans" Wasmer, the Austrian military occupation of Hauenstein in June 1745 was proof that Maria Theresa had forfeited her right to rule.[93] To be sure, no one suggested that the county could make do with *no* sovereign overlord. Still, popular assumptions about the contractual reciprocity of domination had justified the rejection of all existing authority. To some, the republican option of "turning Swiss" was doubtless preferable to remaining under the rule of *any* monarch.

If the Swiss option undermined the eighteenth-century structure of domination, so did the quasi-religious urgency that certain *salpeterisch* activists imparted to their mission. Starting in about 1730, *salpeterisch* activists began equating their cause with the salvation of Hauensteiners on earth and in heaven. The first indication of this was a shift in styles of epistolary salutation: prior to 1730, Hauensteiners of both persuasions employed routine forms of greeting in the letters and notes they exchanged, usually "Best Beloved" *(Insonders vielgeliebter)*. Perhaps because of sufferings the Beaurieu Commission had meted out, *salpeterisch* leaders adopted in that year a religiously charged salutation— "Praised Be Jesus Christ" *(Gelobt sei Jesus Christ)*—that implicitly likened their tribulations to those of the Savior.[94] In the gradual formation of factional identities, this was a moment of utmost importance: not only did the new salutation serve to mark its user as a member in the community of the just, it also symbolically inflated the rebel cause to cosmic proportions.

In fact, salvation as a secular metaphor had been an element of the *salpeterisch* rhetoric from the start. Now, however, it acquired overtly religious significance, largely as a means to generate popular support (and

92. GLA 113:259, 127r–v, "Copia Kurzer Bericht," 9 August 1745.

93. At a clandestine meeting in June, Wasmer declared that "now they can make their own laws in the county, just as they please . . . for the Queen cannot impose any authority"; GLA 113:263, interrogation of Adam Tröndle of Görwihl, WVA, 16 June 1745.

94. For an early, transitional example that incorporated both forms of address, see GLA 113:226, 54r–55v, Johannes Marder of Eschbach and Bläsi Hottinger of Niedergebisbach to Hans Georg Marder of Waldkirch, 12 February 1730. The salutation read, "Gelobt sey Jeßus Christ Meinen insunderß villgeliebten Bruoder."

money) for opposition to *müllerisch* ascendancy. Johannes Marder, for one, shamed halfhearted supporters by comparing his trials to Christ's: "Just as no one wants to thank God . . . for His suffering for us," he wrote from prison, "no one thanks us either."[95] Increasingly, the struggle for the restoration of "ancient rights" was presented as an earthly parallel to Christian sanctification: "Show me a shorter route to sanctity," asked "Gaudihans" Wasmer of his fellow parishoners, "than seeking to advance the cause of justice."[96] Thus *salpeterisch* rhetoric bound the eternal salvation of individual Hauensteiners with the fate of *salpeterisch* leaders and their program. But Marder's metaphor introduced the possibility that if justice were not forthcoming on earth, then God himself would decide Hauenstein's grievances. In a similar analogy, Hans Friedle Gerspach warned of divine retribution against the *müllerisch* side: "even if it costs life and limb," he swore, "our affair shall be summoned before the court of God, and on the Third Day all who are guilty shall be called [to account]."[97]

To be sure, such appeals were made *in extremis* and probably fell on deaf ears until the 1740s. Like their notions about the contractual nature of domination, moreover, the *salpeterisch* discourse on salvation was tied at first to a trust in imperial benevolence thwarted by the disloyal machinations of evil ministers. But the eventual denial even of imperial overlordship stretched the legitimating possibilities of *salpeterisch* rhetoric to the limit. On the one hand, the shopworn christological analogies of the 1730s took on a messianic shade as factional tensions climaxed in 1744–45. Edging toward a repudiation of Habsburg overlordship, certain rebels came close to claiming a divine legitimation for themselves. According to one report, for example, "Gaudihans" Wasmer proclaimed himself a deliverer who would throw the *müllerisch* faction "into the jaws of the Devil," where they belonged.[98] On the other hand, the tumults of 1744–45 carried decidedly patriotic pro-Habsburg overtones, nourished by the belief that Baron Chotek's "Territorial

95. GLA 113:236, 54r–55v, Open letter of Johannes Marder of Eschbach et al., 12 February 1730.
96. GLA 113:259, 61r–62v, Interrogation of Bailiff Michael Albiez of Burg and Joseph Rummel of Görwihl, 21 July 1745.
97. GLA 113:241, 66r–67v, Hans Friedle Gerspach of Bergalingen et al. to Joseph Tröndle of Rotzel, 19 April 1737.
98. GLA 113:222, 139r–40v, Interrogation of Joseph Ebner of Segeten, [May 1745?].

Defense Commission" condoned a *salpeterisch* rising against the Franco-Bavarian occupation of Outer Austria. At the moment when *salpeterisch* activists were openly considering the "Swiss" option, the Austrian government seemed openly to endorse their faction. Johannes Thoma-ab-Egg resolved this contradiction by blending patriotism with revolutionary chiliasm: he allegedly claimed to hold special powers from the "king of Hungary" to "depose all secular and ecclesiastical authorities and to impose new ones, as he pleases." *Müllerisch* peasants were now exhorted "to believe in the new Hungarian Apostle and convert."[99] About one year later, the *müllerisch* Speaker Joseph Tröndle of Rotzel reported that *salpeterisch* peasants "make like the Jews and wait for a true Messiah" who would "arrive . . . miraculously from a foreign land to rectify their . . . affairs."[100]

Serfdom, Property, and Honor

We will never know how many peasants shared Wasmer's messianic egotism or the revolutionary patriotism of Thoma-ab-Egg. If the data presented in Chapter 3 are any indication, about half were sympathetic enough to identify themselves as *salpeterisch*. But that proportion compared poorly with the broad opposition rebel leaders mustered against manumission in 1738–39. Nevertheless, the internal logic of "naive monarchism," driven forward by the need to patrol factional differences, ultimately enabled peasants to repudiate the feudal-aristocratic status quo.

For all its sound and fury, this logic signified a great deal about the concerns of ordinary people in early modern Europe. The many points of similarity between *salpeterisch* rhetoric and the political worldview of peasants elsewhere suggest that the logical implications of "naive monarchism" applied well beyond the limits of the Black Forest. Most students of peasant political culture note the near universal veneration of monarchs throughout preindustrial Europe.[101] As the Austrian historian

---

99. GLA 113:262, Interrogation of Michael Gamp, 22–23 May 1745.
100. GLA 113:266, Joseph Tröndle of Rotzel to WVA, 10 November 1746.
101. Bloch, *Royal Touch;* Bercé, *Revolt and Revolution,* 28–33; Field, *Rebels in the Name of the Tsar,* 1–9; Blum, *The End of the Old Order,* 333–35; Bobinska, "Les mouvements paysans en Pologne," 136–57; Neveux, "Ideologische Dimension," 265–85; Rudé, "Popular Protest and Ideology," 428.

Georg Grüll put it, "The relationship of peasant to emperor . . . was still determined by the patriarchal tradition of limitless trust in . . . the monarch, as the father of all subjects," as in France "the king was regarded as the epitome of all that was just and good" (in contrast to that same king's tax collectors).[102] Concerning the oppressive rate of royal taxation, peasant delegates from Quercy in 1662 deluded themselves that "all these abuses and irregularities are taking place against His Majesty's wishes"; nearer to Hauenstein, Bavarian peasants in 1705–6 deployed the rhetoric of Wittelsbach patriotism to legitimate their resistance against an alien Austrian occupation and its collaborators among the Bavarian estates.[103] "Patriotic" legitimations against foreign rule also played important roles in rebellions in the Upper Austrian peasant rebellion of 1626 and the Tyrolean Rising of 1809.[104]

Moreover, just as Hauensteiners venerated the memory of a fourteenth-century "Good Count Hans," French peasants explained the king's fatherly devotion with nostalgic reference to legacies of dynastic benevolence extending centuries into the past. A 1639 text of the Norman *Nu-pieds* expressed a desire to return "to the state in which we were when Louis XII (1498–1515) brought us a golden age"; rebellious Gascons recalled the "golden age" of King Henry IV (1594–1610), "rich as the sea, as charitable as a priest, as brave as a lion, and as good as gold."[105] Examples from England, Spain, Italy, Scandinavia, and Eastern Europe could be added with ease. The point, however, is that throughout Europe, "naive monarchism" and "nostalgia for the golden age . . . would lead the discontented to oppose change, and to demand not innovation, which was detested, but *re-novation,* which would prove miraculous."[106]

Parallels abound within the empire, too. Many German peasants harbored a belief in the return of a "hidden emperor" Frederick, who would rise from his sleep and restore order to human affairs. Similarly, distant memories of the Peasants' War survived among German rustics well into the eighteenth century, just as they did in Hauenstein. In 1660,

102. Grüll, *Bauer, Herr und Landesfürst,* 10, and Bercé, *History of Peasant Revolts,* 248.
103. For Agen: Bercé, *History of Peasant Revolts,* 249; for Bavaria: Richard van Dülmen, "Bäuerlicher Protest und patriotische Bewegung: Der Volksaufstand in Bayern 1705/6," *ZBLG* (1982): 331–61.
104. Klaus Gerteis, "Regionale Bauernrevolten zwischen Bauernkrieg und französischer Revolution: Eine Bestandsaufnahme," *ZHF* 6 (1979): 37–62.
105. Bercé, *History of Peasant Revolts,* 26, 248.
106. Bercé, *Revolts and Revolution,* 25 [emphasis added].

inhabitants of the Hessian county of Wied warned that soon a Peasants' War would erupt, which would be worse than the first one; a few years later in nearby Gründau a peasant named Weigel Fischer declared that "according to the prophesies of the Sibyll, there will be another Peasants' War, which, if it went like the first one, would start down along the Rhine river."[107]

Finally, dreams of "turning Swiss" crop up elsewhere in Austrian lands bordering on the confederation. In 1598, an Outer Austrian peasant declared that "one could live quite well without any authorities *(Oberkeit)* as they do in Switzerland," and in 1664 the rhetorical question of one Vorarlberg peasant expressed similarly autonomist sentiments: "If the peasants stand together as pigs do, who would want to be their overlord?"[108] All these statements suggest the persistence of "dreams of freedom," whether from seigneurs or the early modern state, which if acted upon were potentially as revolutionary as the Peasants' War itself had been.[109] In southern and central Germany particularly, peasants conceived of every battle over a piece of "ancient rights" as part of a broader desire to restore a lost, original state of liberty from taxes, dues, corvées, and outside interference in village affairs.[110]

But what did freedom mean? Was it merely an atavistic reverie, or were more novel ideas at work? One historian has suggested that notions of "mutual and reciprocal obligation" *(mutua et reciproca obligatio)* characterized all peasant thinking about domination.[111] But the *salpeterisch* stress on exclusivity suggests that new ideas about property had invaded the older aspects of the peasant worldview. In the "naive monarchism" of *salpeterisch* peasants, all domination was of a piece: notwithstanding the legal niceties that distinguished sovereign rule from other forms of subordination, Hauenstein could owe allegiance to one lord and no other. Fidelity was indivisible and owed to the emperor.

---

107. Werner Troßbach, *Soziale Bewegung und politische Erfahrung: Bäuerlicher Widerstand in hessischen Territorien, 1648–1806* (Weingarten, 1987), 179–81.
108. Schulze, *Bäuerlicher Widerstand*, 122.
109. On the Peasants' War as a "revolution of the Common Man," see P. Blickle, *Revolution of 1525*, passim.
110. Schulze, *Bäuerlicher Widerstand*, 122–23; see also Rodney Hilton, *Bond Men Made Free: Medieval Peasant Movements and the English Rising of 1381* (New York, 1973), 220–30.
111. Schulze, *Bäuerlicher Widerstand*, 123.

Behind this exclusivity lurked notions about the indivisibility of proprietary relationships generally, whether among people or between people and things.[112] As for the latter, Chapter 4 showed that the *salpeterisch* defense of inheritance custom veiled a larger project to protect the peasants' ability to dispose of their property freely. In this, they resembled their contemporaries in Bavaria, who came to define their hard-won property rights in absolute terms and used the new definition to challenge constructions of divided ownership based on usufruct.[113]

For the former, *salpeterisch* peasants used a vocabulary to describe proprietary claims against their persons as serfs that mirrored the uncompromising terminology of heritability and corporeality embedded in St. Blasien's term for serfdom: *Leibeigenschaft*. The abbatial nomenclature was shot through with the language of outright ownership and no longer signified the limited set of obligations that had comprised medieval serfdom. Redefined as the right of "free and unrestricted disposition over persons," serfdom became indistinguishable from slavery.[114] This understanding of serfdom, too, was not confined to the Black Forest. In 1716, for example, peasants in the Bavarian lordship of Steingaden had "recognized" serfdom as an innovation and concluded that "it involved thoroughly intolerable conditions." Even specific descriptors in the *salpeterisch* lexicon recurred in Steingaden, where it was thought that serfdom would derogate peasants to "slaves" or, at very least, reduce them to "Bohemian servitude."[115] Toward the end of the century, peasants in the Hessian lordship of Sayn-Wittgenstein-Wittgenstein succeeded in freeing themselves from what they called "eternal *Leibeigenschaft* and

---

112. Compare Peter Blickle, "Von der Leibeigenschaft in die Freiheit: Ein Beitrag zu den realhistorischen Grundlagen der Freiheits- und Menschenrechte in Mitteleuropa," in Peter Blickle, ed., *Studien zur geschichtlichen Bedeutung des deutschen Bauernstandes* (Stuttgart, 1989), 213–26; Renate Blickle, "Agrarische Konflikte und Eigentumsordnung in Altbayern, 1400–1800," in Winfried Schulze, ed., *Aufstände, Revolten, Prozeße: Beiträge zu bäuerlichen Widerstandsbewegungen im frühneuzeitlichen Europa* (Stuttgart, 1983), 166–87, and "Leibeigenschaft und Eigentum: Vom Zusammenhang der Erscheinungen in Verfassung und Geschichte des 'Eigens' oder der Hofmark Steingaden," in Sigfrid Hofmann, ed., *Steingadener Chronik* (Steingaden, 1987), 3:966.

113. Renate Blickle, "Nahrung und Eigentum als Kategorien in der ständischen Gesellschaft," in Winfried Schulze, ed., *Ständische Gesellschaft und soziale Mobilität* (Munich, 1988), 88–89.

114. R. Blickle, "Hausnotdurft," 60, and "Nahrung und Eigentum," 88–89.

115. R. Blickle, "Leibeigenschaft und Eigentum," 966.

slavery."[116] And in the bishopric of Speyer, finally, an episcopal official noted in 1797 that the burden of serfdom "looked a lot like slavery and was often enough considered to be the same. . . . The pejorative name [of serf] was hated, more even than the dues [it entailed]. People demanded its abolition, so that the 'eternal lament over the detested *Leibeigenschaft*' would finally come to an end."[117]

Tied to popular redefinitions of serfdom as slavery was the persuasion that it impinged on individual and collective honor. If honor implied membership in a community capable of possessing it, then it also depended on perceptions of the social standing of that community, which in turn was a function of its autonomy.[118] Rebel ideologues made this connection implicitly when they condemned *müllerisch* sympathies as dishonorable; others made the same link when they bargained to purchase their release from serfdom at prices that vastly exceeded the real value of annual returns from servile dues and services. The Hauensteiners themselves eventually paid a fee that exceeded the replacement value of St. Blasien's annual receipts by a factor of seven.[119] And they were not alone. In November 1795, serfs of the Benedictine abbey of St. Gallen in Switzerland agreed to purchase their collective manumission for the princely sum of 161,720 gulden, even though servile dues accounted for only 2.5 percent of St. Gallen's revenues and their replacement value lay in the neighborhood of 17,300 gulden, about one *tenth* the manumission tax.[120] In strictly economic terms, the serfs of both St. Blasien and St. Gallen were far worse off after manumission than before. What they had purchased was release from a social indignity.

116. Werner Troßbach, "Widerstand als Normalfall: Bauernunruhen in der Grafschaft Sayn-Wittgenstein-Wittgenstein, 1796–1806," *Westfälische Zeitschrift* 135 (1985): 102–11.

117. Report to the Speyer Rentkammer, 12 June 1797, quoted in Emil Bühler, "Die Leibeigenschaft im rechtsrheinischen Teil des Fürstbistums Speyer vornehmlich im 18. Jahrhundert," *ZGO* 78 (1926): 14.

118. See Orlando Patterson, *Slavery and Social Death: A Comparative Study* (Cambridge, Mass. 1982), 78–79.

119. St. Blasien's surviving seigneurial records show that over the nine-year period between 1723 and 1732, the abbey collected an annual average of only 395 gulden in servile dues, services, and death duties from its serfs in Hauenstein; see GLA 99:1038, 26r–27v. If one assumes generously that annual revenues approached 400 gulden, then the annual receipt of interest on loans of only eight thousand gulden would have compensated St. Blasien for the loss of all revenues from serfdom in Hauenstein; see David Martin Luebke, "Serfdom and Honour in Eighteenth-Century Germany," *Social History* 18 (1993): 156–57.

120. Wolfgang Müller, *Die Abgaben von Todes wegen in der Abtei St Gallen: Ein Beitrag zur Rechtsgeschichte des sankt-gallischen Klosterstaates* (St. Gallen, 1961), 56.

Where did these new ideas about serfdom and property come from? The importance of servile nomenclature in the construction of *salpeterisch* factional identity recommends a cultural explanation. Within this realm, a plausible answer lies in the diffusion of Roman legal definitions of slavery and property during the sixteenth and seventeenth centuries. Roman law introduced both the legal fiction of absolute ownership over things *(dominium)* and the legal status of slaves as things susceptible to being owned absolutely. To be sure, the old hypothesis that the late medieval "reception" of Roman law in Germany *caused* the revival of serfdom has not stood the test of time. Furthermore, few fifteenth- and sixteenth-century jurists were so unsophisticated as to superimpose Roman slave law on serfdom without qualification.[121] Nevertheless, lords had deployed the Roman definition of slavery as a weapon to reduce the legal defenses of serfs against their masters. Whether these efforts succeeded is less important than the fact that they were attempted, thereby injecting Roman conceptions of freedom and slavery into the vocabulary of debate between lords and subjects.

Ironically, Roman slave law had gone out of jurisprudential fashion well before the eighteenth century.[122] Indeed, in the mid- to late-seventeenth century, interpretations of serfdom lay at the core of controversies between more traditional jurists and proponents of the *usus modernus* such as the Mecklenburger David Mevius (d. 1670), who complained that "it is the unfortunate practice of many . . . legal scholars to refer solely to the ancient rules and regulations made in the Roman Empire when they pass judgment upon customs and practices as they exist in Germany of the present day, and in so doing forget that the ages, and all that goes with them, are transitory."

Mevius specifically cited the odious practice of applying Roman slave law to German serfs without regard for contemporary nuances of social classification, a habit which "gave rise to many excesses, errors, and destructive opinions."[123] Mevius was thinking of lawyers, but within

---

121. Helmut Coing, "Die europäische Privatrechtsgeschichte der neueren Zeit als einheitliches Forschungsgebiet: Probleme und Aufbau," in his *Gesammelte Aufsätze zu Rechtsgeschichte, Rechtsphilosophie und Zivilrecht, 1947–1975* (Frankfurt a.M., 1982), 81–87.

122. See James Q. Whitman, *The Legacy of Roman Law in the German Romantic Era: Historical Vision and Legal Change* (Princeton, 1990), 41–65, and Coing, "Europäische Privatrechtsgeschichte," 81–87.

123. Cited in Gerhard Wesenberg and Gunter Wesener, *Neuere deutsche Privatrechtsgeschichte*, 4th rev. ed. (Vienna, 1985), 121–22.

his frame of reference, the criticism applied equally well to Hauensteiners. Still, the idea that serfs were slaves persisted among social elites, even as it trickled down to the population at large. The old convention still found support, for instance, in the work of eighteenth-century German polyhistors and encyclopedists.[124] Proponents of Enlightenment breathed new life into the notion, this time to disparage human bondage in general. The polemical comparison became a commonplace among social critics such as Voltaire and Montesquieu.[125]

It goes without saying that serfs did not conceive of freedom and servitude in terms so universal as Voltaire's. *Salpeterisch* ideas of serfdom were articulated always with reference to "ancient rights" and to that extent, their outlook remained essentially medieval.[126] Furthermore, *salpeterisch* notions of freedom were conceived primarily in collective, not individual terms. But this should not preclude the possibility that peasants appropriated Roman concepts of slavery and exploited them to their own advantage. Within the confines of specific lordships, popular equations of serfdom with slavery may have implied new understandings of freedom and unfreedom. If indeed peasants had appropriated a Roman-law definition of serfdom, it implied an inherited state of exposure to the unlimited and arbitrary rule of lords. By the same token, emancipation might inaugurate a condition of similarly inherited, unrestricted liberty. In this way, the *salpeterisch* rhetoric of "slavery" and "Bohemian servitude" may have veiled as expansive a notion of liberty as the religiously inspired version articulated during the revolutionary events of 1525.[127]

This peculiar mixture of ideas about serfdom, "ancient rights," freedom, and property helped distinguish *salpeterisch* from *müllerisch*. To be sure, many of the latter would have agreed with particular elements of

---

124. See, for example, "Sclave, Leibeigener, Knecht, Lat. *mancipium, bello captus,* Fr. Esclave, Ital. Sciavo, Holl. Slaof," in Johann H. Zedler, ed., *Zedlers grosses vollständiges Universal-Lexicon aller Wissenschaften und Künste* (Halle, 1732–50), 36:643–45.

125. See Voltaire's "La voix du curé sur le procès des serfs du Mont-Jura", in *Oeuvres complètes de Voltaire* (Kehl, 1784–89), 29:475–86, and Paul Darmstädter, "Die Hörigen im französischen Jura und Voltaires Kampf für ihre Freiheit," *Zeitschrift für Social- und Wirthschaftsgeschichte* 4 (1896): 367–74. On Montesquieu, see Marc Bloch, "Serfs de la Glèbe," in *Slavery and Serfdom,* 193–95.

126. See Klaus Arnold, "Freiheit im Mittelalter," *HJ* 104 (1984): 1–21.

127. See P. Blickle, *Revolution of 1525,* 125–54.

the *salpeterisch* ideology; after all, no less a *müllerisch* luminary than the Speaker Joseph Tröndle of Rotzel publicly declared his personal aversion to serfdom. But the whole ensemble of *salpeterisch* ideas was more than someone so wedded to sanctioned procedures could stomach. Moreover, the structure of *salpeterisch* rhetoric virtually guaranteed that factional hostilities would deepen with each passing year: with so many fundamental issues at stake, the possibility of compromise with the traitorous *müllerisch* side grew ever more remote. After all, the cornerstone of *salpeterisch* thinking was the conviction that fault for Hauenstein's troubles lay at the doorstep of double-crossing *müllerisch* leaders. Together, "naive monarchism" and the plot persuasion informed virtually every action the *salpeterisch* party took.

CHAPTER 6

The Practice of Rebellion

> These are garrulous peasants and have their mouths in the right place.
> Emperor Charles VI, after meeting with delegates from Hauenstein, 1728

IN THE EARLY MODERN COUNTRYSIDE, RESISTANCE WAS DIFFICULT to organize for much the same reason that peasants were hard to govern. The spatially diffuse nature of agricultural production demanded a human geography of many small settlements, just as the requirements of raising crops filled the lives of peasants, male and female, with grinding labor. If under such conditions effective rule required involving peasants in the process of their own domination, so organized resistance was possible only if peasants could manage to coordinate their efforts beyond the narrow confines of the village.

At one time, histories of peasant politics in early modern Europe neglected this process, focusing instead on the violent and the dramatic: movements of armed "hordes" during the German Peasants' War, chateau-razings in France during the turbulent decades of the mid-seventeenth century, food riots in eighteenth-century England, the occasional advent of a false tsar leading armies of desperate Russian serfs. As often as not, this preoccupation with explosive confrontations was meant to illustrate the relative complacency of peasants at all *other* times. But this vision of peasant rebellion as "spasmodic" obscures real continuities between violent outbursts and structures of day-to-day political life. There were, to be sure, armed confrontations aplenty during the Salpeter Wars—the pitched battle with Austrian grenadiers at Etzwihl in March 1739, for example, or the *salpeterisch* siege of Waldshut in November 1745—but in the Black Forest as elsewhere, violence typically *concluded* long processes of opinion-formation, political and financial mobilization, diplomacy, and litigation that were thickly interwoven with the practice of everyday political life.

Thus the dramatic episodes of the Salpeter Wars must be interpreted in the context of less spectacular means by which *salpeterisch* peasants jumped the village fence, as it were, and coordinated their activities county-wide. Such an analysis is needed to uncover, first, how rebel activists mobilized public opinion by appropriating the institutions best suited to transcend village localism. These were not, typically, of the village, but of the canton or the "Whole County." For this reason the Salpeter Wars are better seen as a regional or territorial, not a communal, phenomenon. It is important to stress, however, that this behavior was learned by arduous trial and error. There is an important irony here, too: in learning to appropriate institutions of the "Whole County," rebel organizers adapted to their purposes public political rituals that had for generations served to legitimate the specific policies of elected peasant magistrates. More than once, indeed, the "rebel" organizers were *themselves* elected officials! On closer inspection, then, there was often little that was necessarily "rebellious" in the specific forms of their rebelling.

The second point is that the *salpeterisch* practice of rebellion amounted to a public dramatization of the political cosmos described in Chapter 5. "Naive monarchism" and belief in a "serfdom plot," in particular, informed almost every *salpeterisch* action. Rebel leaders dramatized these twin tenets in a major form of political action—that of diplomatic delegations sent to petition the emperor in Vienna—and suffused these diplomatic delegations with religious significance by uniting them with another kind of pilgrimage, specifically to shrines of the Virgin Mary. This behavior, in turn, implies a different kind of appropriation: if rebellious assemblies of the "Whole County" were adapted from local traditions of ritual legitimation, then the fusion of peasant diplomacy with Marian pilgrimage, in keeping with the monarchism that inspired it, represented a peasant adaptation of imperial Habsburg sponsorship of the cult of the Immaculate Virgin as a barometer of loyalty to the royal dynasty.

These behaviors undercut conventional understandings of "collective action" that stress the necessity of secretive, "defensive" organizing in advance of public demonstrations. The events that *salpeterisch* activists staged were notable for their *publicity;* they were designed as much to *create* constituencies as to show them off. For this reason, most phases of "collective action" transpired in the open; by the same token, most of it was decidedly factional in purpose, designed to score victories over an opposing party. Factionalism, therefore, compromised the very "collectivity" of any action and suggests that it is misleading to distinguish too sharply between processes of mobilization and the projects for which they were intended. Rather, both reinforced the larger rebel aim to discredit opponents.

On balance, the story of *salpeterisch* mobilization is one of failure. Despite some spectacular successes, the ultimate goal of creating political solidarity remained elusive. Indeed, as Chapter 2 showed, factional strife grew increasingly hostile during the late 1730s and early 1740s. There is an irony in this, too. The rebels' mobilization tactics tended to rejuvenate traditional, participatory elements in the institutional structure of the county. To that extent, the rebels' methods countered the oligarchic tendencies that had helped give birth to factionalism in the first place. To that extent, too, the rebels' methods opposed the broad trend in early modern Europe from a system of rule with peasants to one of rule over them. By the same token, however, the practice of rebellion granted free reign to the expression of factional disagreement. Far from achieving political homogeneity, they worsened dissent among the peasants.

Rallies, Rallies, Rallies

Few feats of *salpeterisch* political dramaturgy illustrate the connection between ideology, action, and factionalism so well as a rally that occurred on the feast of Mary Magdalene, 22 July 1738, just outside the village of Görwihl. That morning, a great crowd gathered to hear a report from several *salpeterisch* peasants who had recently returned from a diplomatic mission to Vienna, where they had petitioned Emperor Charles VI to rescind the manumission treaty concluded between the *müllerisch* Eight, St. Blasien, and the provincial government on 15 January. To open the proceedings, one Hans Friedle Gerspach, a native of Bergalingen who had also traveled to Vienna, enjoined all who were loyal to "God, the emperor, and the rights of Hauenstein," to recite an *Ave Maria* and the Lord's Prayer. Then Gerspach gave a speech that was meant to prove Emperor Charles VI's opposition to the servile condition of most Hauensteiners. Although manumission remained the emperor's wish, he argued, *serfdom itself* had originated in the traitorous greed of *müllerisch* Octovirs, as if to imply that Charles, by favoring manumission, opposed the *müllerisch* faction. The manumission fee should therefore be kept to a minimum. From the standpoint of Austrian officials, presumably, this was wishful thinking at best, face-saving dissimulation at worst: in fact, Gerspach's delegation had failed to persuade the emperor and his ministers to rescind the manumission treaty. Nevertheless, Gerspach's rhetorical damage-control was so persuasive that according to one *müllerisch* spy, "even the most peaceful person would have fallen into the fire of rage." Finally, the assembly elected some two hundred delegates to present to Forest Steward von Schönau their demand that he confirm in office four rebels who had been elected Octovir the previous April. Before it disbanded, the group swore "no longer to follow the old *[müllerisch]* Octovirs."[1]

The rally, therefore, served an explicitly factional purpose: while Gerspach's ultimate objective was peasant unity against emancipation, his method was to involve the largest possible number of peasants in sworn opposition to the governing elite of *müllerisch* Octovirs. Gerspach's rhetoric, moreover, fused the themes of "naive monarchism" and the "serfdom plot" outlined in the previous chapter: despite its conciliatory tone, his speech recapitulated the shopworn motifs of a benevolent emperor and of domestic treason as the origin of serfdom. The religious overtones and the ritual structure of this assembly—a ceremonial progression from prayer to sermonizing to oath-taking—implied the importance of taking sides. In terms of its sheer size, too,

---

1. The confrontation with Schönau occurred as planned on the following day. After many hours of argument, however, the Forest Steward held firm, and the delegates dispersed without achieving a thing; GLA 113:242, 105r–10v, WVA to VÖRK, 24 July 1738.

the gathering was a big success. If the lowest contemporary estimate of eight hundred participants is accurate, roughly five percent of the total population was in attendance. But Gerspach's broader goal of uniting the peasantry behind the *salpeterisch* cause proved elusive: despite the organizational triumph of 22 July 1738, the rebels did *not* suppress factional divisions, let alone erase them. Rather, factional tensions escalated to open violence the following spring.

The rally was also indicative of a rebel taste for politics of scale. Only mammoth organizational exertions could have produced so large a gathering, given both the *müllerisch* obstructionism and the dispersed human geography of Hauenstein. To be sure, the rally of 22 July registered the largest recorded attendance of any *salpeterisch* assembly. But it was not unique: similar gatherings had often drawn hundreds of attendees.[2] Indeed, throughout the Salpeter Wars, rebel activist leaders preferred the mass rally as their principal method of mobilizing the resources of labor, money, and opinion they needed for costly undertakings, such as diplomatic missions to Vienna. Hans Friedle Gerspach, like other political impresarios before and after him, was an adept practitioner of mass politics.

All in all, it is possible to identify ninety-six contentious *salpeterisch* gatherings between 1726 and 1745. Of these, fully twenty-six—including the rally of 22 July—were billed as assemblies of the "Whole County" *(Landsgemeinde)*, convocations of the entire body politic. In so doing, rebels appropriated a traditional forum of decision-making in common: although it is doubtful that "Assemblies of the Whole County" ever enjoyed a formal, legislative function, they *were* linked with a popular expectation that major decisions of the Eight required general endorsement. Another 30 percent of *salpeterisch* gatherings transpired in the context of parish and canton assemblies. Fewer than half were limited to single villages. These figures cannot, of course, account for the presumably large number of communal assemblies for which no evidence survives. Moreover, these figures also exclude the numerous official assemblies that rebels turned to their own advantage. On 2 May 1728, for example, rebels transformed an assembly of the Weilheim pa-

---

2. Only three weeks earlier, for example, Gerspach had attracted a crowd of over five hundred to Görwihl; GLA 113:242, 71r–72v, Interrogation of Georg Ebner of Bannholz, 9 July 1738.

rish into an illegal Octovir election: the *müllerisch* ex-Octovir Georg Fluem had convened the meeting to convince the parishioners of the legal precedent for serfdom, but when he had finished, the militant Martin Thoma of Haselbach prevailed upon the cantonal tax collector, Hans Meyer of Rohr, to authorize an impromptu election. The assembly then chose Thoma—illegally, because Octovir elections were forbidden by decree of the Forest Steward.[3] On the other hand, it is unlikely that even communal assemblies might easily have escaped the surveillance of *müllerisch* spies, who regularly supplied the royal and abbatial authorities with detailed reports on *salpeterisch* activities.

How did the rebels come to prefer such grandstanding, and why? One likely answer is that the practice of rebellion was learned behavior that built on the experience of peasant magistrates who joined the rebel cause early on. The veteran Octovirs among them, such as Friedle Hottinger of Niedergebisbach, Hans Friedle Baumgartner of Rotzingen, and "Salpeter-Hans" Albiez himself, modeled their behavior on familiar precedents. They preserved, for example, the living memory of the homage controversies at the turn of the century, when the Eight had convened several "Assemblies of the Whole County" to gain support for their lawsuit against St. Blasien over the odious nomenclature of serfdom.[4] One practical consequence of their leadership was that the rebels' earliest attempts to mobilize popular opinion were carried out within familiar and conventional bounds. When in 1727, as a result of a *salpeterisch* victory in Octovir elections, the rebels' policy of refusing homage to Abbot Franz II became the official policy of the Eight, rebel mobilization became one with official modes of communication.

These qualities of precedent and routine made for some conspicuous propagandizing. In the autumn of 1726, for example, "Salpeter-Hans" Albiez launched an ambitious, one-man campaign of village assemblies in Görwihl Canton. As Chapter 2 described, his campaign culminated on 18 October at the Görwihl village tavern with a gathering timed to

3. GLA 113:229, 195r–97v, Interrogation of Georg Fluem of Dietlingen, Waldshut, 29 July 1728.
4. GLA 67:1809, 192–97, "Instruction vor die von Redmann undt Einungsmeister aus gantzer Gemeindt der Graffschafft Hawenstein nacher Wienn deputierte Adam Tröndle von Underalpffen, Balthasar Hueber von Riggenbach, undt Adam Schmidle von Waldkirch," 20 November 1705.

coincide with a session of the Forest Steward's weekly court, which was being held in the upper room of the same building. Thus Albiez's agitations took place within full view of authority. Indeed, the large crowd Albiez drew (about two hundred) disrupted the judicial business upstairs, an effect he surely intended.[5]

Albiez's campaign is notable for two reasons: in the first place, he exhibited confidence in the utility of village assemblies as an effective communication tool, which he used in the conventional manner: to convey information of general interest and concern. Because factional distinctions were still fluid and allegiances weak, Albiez had little to fear from the obstructions of hostile village headmen and elders. As factional divisions deepened and hardened, *salpeterisch* organizers learned to base their estimates of the utility of village assemblies more on the sympathies of village elders and less on the public functions of communal institutions as such. By the time of Gerspach's rally in July 1738, communal solidarity was already so chimerical that village assemblies often presented little consensus to build upon.

Second, the brazen publicity of Albiez's campaign contradicts the reigning interpretation of "collective action" among early modern European peasants. According to this view, poor and relatively powerless groups tended to mobilize defensively against threats from the "outside" and to "pool their resources to fight off the enemy."[6] In this initial, "defensive" stage, mobilizers are supposed to have acted with the utmost secrecy to seal themselves off from both ideological and military intervention. Secrecy, in turn, required a united front of disobedience that broke down communication between rulers and ruled. During the "defensive" stage, finally, communes attempted to impose internal political unanimity, because dissent threatened to rend the "thinly woven net of a growing movement." Only after the movement was secure against these dangers could rebels "go public," as it were, and promote their interests "offensively."[7]

---

5. See Albiez's own account of his campaign in GLA 113:224, 1r–26v, Interrogation of Hans Friedle Albiez of Buch, Freiburg, 26–29 October 1726; for the official version, see GLA 99:979, WVA to VÖRK, 26 July 1726.
6. Charles Tilly, *From Mobilization to Revolution* (New York, 1978), 73.
7. Werner Troßbach, *Soziale Bewegung und politische Erfahrung: Bäuerlicher Protest in hessischen Territorien, 1648–1806* (Weingarten, 1987), 47. In "offensive" collective action, accord-

The tactics of "Salpeter-Hans" Albiez, however, present a different picture. There was nothing secretive about them, and for good reason. Albiez was merely replicating habits of public communication he had practiced throughout his long career in politics. Moreover, his success depended on a *publicity* designed less to protect a "peasant syndicate" than to create a constituency, and this was best done out in the open. As subsequent events would prove, *salpeterisch* leaders acted "defensively" only when they had to—usually in the *aftermath* of military intervention. To be sure, Albiez himself paid a heavy price for his bravado (he died in prison). But that did not drive his followers "underground." Indeed, they made the *salpeterisch* movement even more public. Five days after Albiez's arrest, Hans Georg Thoma of Kiesenbach sent couriers into villages throughout Hauenstein to announce what turned out to be the first *salpeterisch* "Assembly of the Whole County," held in Waldkirch on Wednesday, 8 November 1726. Significantly, Thoma claimed to be acting under the "command of the government in Freiburg," an appropriation of authority that acknowledged the function of village assemblies as vehicles of official communication.[8] In using village assemblies to advertise a more general convocation, however, Thoma departed from Albiez's tactics and established an organizational style that would remain one of the most persistent features of *salpeterisch* mobilization throughout the 1730s and 1740s.

The circumstances of *salpeterisch* mobilization changed dramatically in May 1728, when the Austrian state intervened militarily to enforce homage to Abbot Franz II. Nevertheless, *salpeterisch* activists adapted to the new dangers with remarkable agility, and with only a few days' preparation, were able to muster their first show of military strength. To meet the emergency of invasion, two rebel organizers—Martin Thoma and Johannes Marder "the Prussian" of Eschbach—cobbled together a two-stage approach, consisting first of canton assemblies to proclaim a subsequent "Assembly of the Whole County," to be held in conjunction

---

ing to Tilly, "a group pools resources in response to opportunities to realize its interests." It is most often organized from the top down, "by leaders and agitators," in contrast to "defensive" forms, which are more often organized from the bottom up; *From Mobilization to Revolution*, 73–74.

8. GLA 113:224, 30r, Hans Georg Thoma of Kiesenbach to Martin Thoma of Haselbach, [1 November 1726].

with religious services on Pentecost.[9] Early in the morning on 16 May, Thoma's couriers distributed an open letter to local organizers, instructing them to hold canton assemblies throughout the day.[10] These rallies were to proclaim an "Assembly of the Whole County" in Dogern on 17 May.[11] Village institutions played only a minor role in this process; instead, Marder and Thoma relied on the propagandistic potential of the canton assembly, a strategy which proved highly successful: the turnout was five to six hundred adult males, many of them armed.[12] By 1729, the principal features of this two-stage stratagem were firmly established. Typically, an inner circle of *salpeterisch* leaders would agree on a program of action; couriers would then fan out to announce upcoming convocations of canton or county. On a few occasions, these assemblies consisted of elected village representatives; at other times the invitation was general. In the main, however, village assemblies served as vehicles of communication in the context of mobilization on a regional scale. Any decisions were reached at the bigger assemblies.

Rebel organizers went underground only in the aftermath of military intervention. During the *müllerisch* ascendancy of the 1730s they learned to distrust village institutions: most village assemblies seem to have fallen under solid *müllerisch* control, and as far as we know, *salpeterisch* cadres avoided them.[13] Most *salpeterisch* gatherings met in secret places, such as Friedle Hottinger's house in Niedergebisbach or the back room of a tavern in Herrischried.[14] But if these "defensive" measures were intended to prevent infiltration, they were not terribly successful:

---

9. On the morning of 15 May, Thoma and Marder sent word to key rebels in each canton that "everyone, great and small," should assemble in Dogern the same evening. But notice was too short, and only a small number appeared; GLA 113:232, 73r–v, Martin Thoma of Haselbach to Michael Schmiedle of Kutterau, [15 May 1728], and GLA 113:229, 7r–8v, Martin Thoma of Haselbach to Joseph Sibold of Herrischried, 15 May 1728.

10. GLA 113:229, 21r–v, Martin Thoma to Conrad Tröndle of Waldkirch, 16 May 1728, and 4r, Martin Thoma to "the honorable, good, and dear friends and neighbors below the Alb river," 16 May 1728.

11. These canton assemblies were obvious replications of electoral assemblies, which had been held only two weeks before. Martin Thoma had been among the illegally elected Octovirs; GLA 113:232, 138r–81v, Interrogation of Martin Thoma of Haselbach, Freiburg, 16–20 September 1728; see also GLA 113:229, 180r–v, "Prothocollum Informativum," 24 July 1728.

12. GLA 113:229, 47r–50v, Interrogation of Johannes Wasmer of Todtmoos, 18 May 1728.

13. For an example, see GLA 113:221, 118r–v, [A resolution of Görwihl Canton], 11 June 1733.

14. See GLA 113:235, 81r–85r, WVA to VÖRK, 22 February 1730; GLA 113:235, 92r–102r, WVA to VÖRK, 5 March 1730; GLA 113:240, 152r–58v, Interrogation of Johannes Jehle of Haide, Waldshut, 13 April 1733.

it is a testament to the thoroughness of *müllerisch* snooping that the names of individual peasants attending were recorded and passed on to provincial authorities.[15] Once the opportunity presented itself, however, rebel organizers escalated their tactics of public agitation to produce the most effective manipulation of village communes they had ever achieved. Beginning in the spring of 1738, *salpeterisch* leaders began to organize rallies in series, using each assembly to advertise the next, even bigger gathering. Rebel organizers filled the time between meetings by agitating in the villages and parishes. This escalation produced rallies of unprecedented scale—including Gerspach's rally of 22 July.

The occasion for such a rally arose in January 1738, when news of the *müllerisch*-inspired manumission treaty began to circulate. In February and March, rebel activists decided to sabotage the treaty by sending a delegation of peasants to petition Charles VI. As Martin Thoma's couriers had done in 1728, now Joseph Eckert of Herrischried and Hans Friedle Gerspach traveled from village to village, holding assemblies to elect delegates for an "Assembly of the Whole County" to be held on Annunciation Day (25 March) in the hamlet of Etzwihl.[16] The seventy or so delegates agreed to gather the signatures of peasants who opposed the manumission treaty, which would be presented to the provincial government in Freiburg. To collect them, the assembly authorized another series of local meetings.[17] Again in early April, two teams of organizers held "unauthorized" communal assemblies to collect signatures in the cantons of Birndorf, Höchenschwand, Dogern, Rickenbach, and Görwihl.[18] The campaign was especially effective in Rickenbach Canton,

---

15. GLA 113:236, 163r–69v, Interrogation of Michael Sibold of Herrischried, Waldshut, 11 February 1730; GLA 113:236, 170r–77v, Interrogation of Joseph Eckert of Herrischried, Waldshut, 17 February 1730; GLA 113:236, 236r–42v, Interrogation of Joseph Lüber of Rütte, Waldshut, 28 February 1730.

16. GLA 113:249, B1, Interrogation of Conrad Fricker of Luttingen, Waldshut, 11 April 1739.

17. GLA 113:241, 269r–v, "Datum Anno 1738 dem 25tn Tag Mertzen haben mir zuo Etwihl ein Außschutz zuogehalten undt haben vier Debudierte auff Freiburg geshichkht."

18. Jacob Albiez of Buch and Joseph Kalt of Haide began on 31 March in Höchenschwand Canton, where they held an unapproved assembly at Tiefenhäusern. On 1 April they turned back into Birndorf Canton, holding informal village assemblies in Remetschwiel and Bannholz; on 2 April they proceeded to Nöggenschwiel, Weilheim, and Schmitzingen in Dogern Canton; GLA 113:242, 10r–11v, Joseph Tröndle of Unteralpfen to Joseph Tröndle of Rotzel, 2 April 1738. Meanwhile west of the Alb river, the other team "ran . . . day and night from village to village"; GLA 113:241, 290r–91v, Andreas Thoma of Altenschwand to Joseph Tröndle of Rotzel, 2 April 1738.

where "in all villages the majority [was] infected."[19] It paid electoral dividends as well: on St. George's Day, *salpeterisch* candidates were elected Octovir in four cantons, and in mid-June another county-wide assembly resolved to withhold taxes from incumbent *müllerisch* Octovirs.[20] Finally, the need to raise money for diplomatic missions prompted yet another series of rallies in July. Once again, rebel couriers called canton assemblies to announce a general convocation at Görwihl on 8 July.[21] The result was the largest gathering to date: *müllerisch* spies reported an attendance of around five hundred, who agreed that "the old Octovirs must be driven from office."[22] This was followed by an "Assembly of the Whole County" at Görwihl after mass on Sunday, July 20, where it was resolved to reassemble in two days' time: the result, of course, was the assembly of eight hundred on 22 July.[23]

It should be stressed that most rallies were not ends in themselves, but means of amassing the popular favor, donations, and signatures for delegations to Vienna. These were especially costly: quite apart from the personal hazards they entailed, the expenses of clothing, travel, room, board, fees, and bribes were beyond the ability of most peasants to sustain. Formulaic letters of petition had to be written up by court scriveners, who charged a fee.[24] If they were imprisoned, delegates bore the costs of their own incarceration.[25] We possess little evidence of the total sums an average delegation spent, but a ledger of expenses compiled by Leonzi Brutschi of Dogern in April 1739 gives a rough indication of the costs involved (see Table 6).

19. GLA 113:241, 278r–v, 285r–87v, 292r–94v, WVA to VÖRK, 14 April 1738.
20. GLA 113:242, 34r–41v, WVA to VÖRK, 19 June 1738.
21. GLA 113:242, 105r–10v, WVA to VÖRK, 24 July 1738; GLA 113:249, B1, Interrogation of Hans Friedle Gerspach of Bergalingen, 14–25 April 1739.
22. GLA 113:242, 71r–72v, Interrogation of Georg Ebner, 8 July 1738.
23. GLA 113:242, 121r–22v, Joseph Tröndle of Unteralpfen to WVA, 24 July 1738.
24. See Helfried Valentinisch, "Advokaten, Winkelschreiber und Bauernprokuratoren in Innerösterreich in der frühen Neuzeit," in Winfried Schulze, ed., *Aufstände, Revolten, Prozeße: Beiträge zu bäuerlichen Widerstandsbewegungen im frühneuzeitlichen Europa* (Stuttgart, 1983), 188–201.
25. This expense could be considerable. "Salpeter-Hans" Albiez's year-long incarceration cost him about 225 gulden in local currency; GLA 113:241, 5r–14v, Freiherr von Reischach to VÖRK, 5 September 1734.

TABLE 6. Costs in gulden of a Delegation to Vienna (1739)

Clothing	25
Travel	164
Board	43
Alms	17
Other	49

Source: GLA 113:248, A1, Interrogation of Leonzi Brutschi of Dogern, 6–27 April 1739.

Judging by Brutschi's figures, the cost of travel alone approached two hundred gulden; room and board would vary with the duration of a delegate's stay, and whether it was passed in taverns or prisons. Most delegations, moreover, included several members. In 1727, Hauenstein dispatched five delegates, and five again in 1728. Six traveled to Vienna in 1737. The largest delegations were the two dispatched in 1738, which included twenty and twenty-three delegates each. All in all, Hauenstein sent almost seventy individual delegates to Vienna, and at two hundred gulden apiece, their cumulative travel costs alone must have approached fourteen thousand gulden.[26] The combined burdens of room, board, bribes, and court costs might well have doubled this total.

To meet these expenses, large "contentious gatherings" proved to be especially effective. An assembly at Görwihl on 7 February 1739, for example, resolved to raise 1,000 gulden for Leonzi Brutschi's trip (although in the end only 404 gulden were actually collected).[27] Likewise, Gerspach's summer campaign in 1738 brought in about 1,000 gulden.[28] An indication of the value of rallies as fund-raising vehicles emerges from the years of *müllerisch* ascendancy in the mid-1730s, when large "contentious gatherings" were too risky to hold. During that period, the

---

26. Evidence of the 1727 delegation suggests even higher average costs. That four-man delegation alone cost a total of 1,400 gulden—a cost, in other words, of 350 gulden per person. The *salpeterisch* Octovirs of 1727 allocated 800 gulden of that amount from public funds; another 600 gulden came in the form of a public loan; GLA 113:241, 5r–14v, Reischach to VÖRK, 5 September 1734.

27. GLA 113:248, A1, Interrogation of Leonzi Brutschi, 6–27 April 1739.

28. GLA 113:242, 34r–41v, WVA to VÖRK, 19 June 1738; GLA 113:242, 304r–v, WVA to VÖRK, 29 August 1738; GLA 113:248, B1, Interrogation of Hans Friedle Gerspach of Bergalingen, Waldshut, 14–25 April 1739.

rebels' ability to finance expeditions was so curtailed that the four missions dispatched between between 1730 and 1737 were funded entirely by the delegates themselves. Consequently, the size of delegations was kept to a minimum, and one of them was aborted for lack of cash.[29]

In the process of assembling money and signatures, village assemblies played a subordinate role, even in 1738, when rebel organizers exploited them so heavily. The reasons are simple: most obviously, "Assemblies of the Whole County" had the potential to reach audiences far larger than any village assembly could. Generating a favorable climate of opinion was crucial for two main reasons. Most generally, it enhanced the probability that the *salpeterisch* leadership could actually marshal the material resources pledged to it.[30] More practically, it increased the rebels' chances of winning elections to public office, which Jacob Albiez equated with victory over the *müllerisch* side: "If [we] can collect and unite the majority of votes," he told Franz Meyer in 1738, "then [we] have won the quarrel."[31] Faced with the combined constraints of time, money, human geography, and official obstruction, the *salpeterisch* leadership sought and found an efficient means to generate support: the mass rally.

Another reason why village assemblies were not the primary vehicle of *salpeterisch* propagandizing is that village headmen and elders were often unreliable. Because the balance of factional power made some villages sympathetic but others hostile, the utility of communal assemblies depended largely on the loyalties of individual headmen, and mass rallies enabled *salpeterisch* leaders to minimize their dependence on them. Predictably, *müllerisch* leaders faced the same set of advantages and drawbacks. Just as the great sequence of rebel rallies was gearing up in April 1738, for example, the *müllerisch* Eight tried their own campaign of communal assemblies for the purpose of thwarting *salpeterisch* criticism against the manumission treaty. It was not especially successful: Forest Steward von Schönau reported that the "holding of communal assemblies" had not hindered the spread of popular

29. GLA 113:235, 81r–85v, WVA to VÖRK, 22 February 1730; GLA 113:235, WVA to VÖRK, 5 March 1730; GLA 113:236, 190r–217v, Interrogation of Friedle Hottinger of Niedergebisbach, Waldshut, 20 February–13 March 1730.

30. Tilly, *From Mobilization to Revolution*, 52–97. Tilly's definition of "resources" emphasizes the material to the neglect of "normative" varieties, such as favorable public opinion, which he identifies as an organizational precondition of mobilization.

31. GLA 113:243, 8r–9v, Interrogation of Franz Meyer of Buch, Waldshut, 12 October 1738.

hostility to manumission. Nevertheless, Schönau and the *müllerisch* Eight continued to use communal assemblies to counteract rebel propaganda throughout the 1730s and 1740s.[32]

Not surprisingly, then, the outcomes of such assemblies usually reflected the shifting balance of local factional loyalties. In July 1727, for example, an assembly in the divided village of Hänner, called to discuss the homage controversy, ended in "dissension" *(Cunfusion)*.[33] Similarly in September 1743, the juror Conrad Ebner convened the commune in Oberalpfen to whip up support for a *salpeterisch* tax strike. The result reflected a breakdown of communal solidarities: about half of the villagers followed Ebner, the rest did not.[34] On the whole, communal institutions stood in an ambivalent relationship to rebel mobilization. Indeed, two decades of factional strife played such havoc with the smooth running of village assemblies that in at least one village, factional opponents of the headman simply stopped attending them. Ironically, the "Whole Honorable Commune" of Etzwihl resolved in 1747 to remedy the "ubiquitous disunity and slanders and swearing" that had engulfed the village by making attendance at communal assemblies compulsory.[35] This injunction was probably no more effective than earlier attempts to achieve unity. Factional strife undermined the usefulness of communal institutions as tools for forging a single political will.

Diplomats, Virgins, and Propaganda

A total of twelve diplomatic expeditions were sent from Hauenstein to Vienna between 1725 and 1750, each with the intention of achieving a personal encounter with the reigning Habsburg dynast or some other form of royal intercession; another delegation departed in 1745 to meet

32. GLA 113:241, 278r–v, 285r–87v, 294r–v, WVA to VÖRK, 14 April 1738. For examples of communal assemblies that opposed the rebels, see GLA 113:242, 369r–v, Interrogation of Headman Joseph Völlin of Oberalpfen, Unteralpfen, 30 December 1738; GLA 99:1041, 172r–v, Abbatial Bailiff Hans Friedle Jehle to OVA, 6 March 1739; and GLA 113:256, 104r–6v, Joseph Tröndle of Unteralpfen to WVA, 1 May 1744.

33. GLA 99:984, 34r, Joseph Tröndle of Rotzel to Joseph Tröndle of Unteralpfen, 18 July 1727.

34. GLA 113:256, 104r–6v, Joseph Tröndle of Unteralpfen to WVA, 1 May 1744.

35. GLA 229:13845, 16 July 1747.

with Queen Maria Theresa at the coronation of her imperial husband, Francis Stephen of Lorraine, in Frankfurt; a fourteenth delegation went to Wetzlar, in hopes of provoking the intervention of the Imperial Chamber Court *(Reichskammergericht)* seated there, despite the fact that the RKG was incompetent to judge cases emerging from the Habsburg Crown Lands (see Appendix 3).[36] In Vienna, delegates tirelessly pursued the chance for an imperial audience and to get it, they solicited such lofty persons as the empress-dowager and Charles VI's confessor, Veit Georg Tönnemann.[37] They also sought out such magnates as Prince Eugene of Savoy and his *protégé*, Crown Prince Charles Alexander of Württemberg. On several occasions, delegates actually obtained audiences with Charles VI: "Salpeter-Hans" Albiez had a hearing with Charles probably on 1 August 1726; Conrad Binkert, in 1727.[38] When the emperor was absent from the capital, delegates pursued him. On 1 December 1731, "Glasmännle" Meyer approached the emperor's carriage during a hunt near Raab and presented a list of grievances; the tactic worked again for Hans Friedle Gerspach and "Schwarzmichel" Tröndle near Laxenburg in 1737.[39]

Just as *salpeterisch* rallies failed to overcome factional divisions, however, these diplomatic efforts were dismal flops: although delegates sometimes achieved their immediate goal of contact with the sovereign, such interactions were ill-suited to produce the kind of royal intervention that the peasants found welcome. Only one *salpeterisch* delegation attained its goals even partially: the 1727 delegation brought about a slight revision of homage formulas. But even this small triumph was not to the liking of *salpeterisch* peasants, and in any case, the government was more concerned to thwart an affront to imperial dignity posed by the

36. The twelve missions include two (both in 1730) that did not reach their destination and a third (1738) that was diverted to Hochau in pursuit of Charles VI. The total also excludes the 1704 delegation, which is listed in Appendix 3 as a precedent for the rest.
37. In 1737, the delegates sought the financial assistance of the empress-dowager; GLA 113:241, 200r–203v, "Copia Relationis oder Attestati," 23 April 1737. Contacts with Tönnemann date from at least 1728; see GLA 113:236, 329r–v, Open letter of Johannes Marder (?), 7 April 1728.
38. GLA 113:224, 403r–04v, Hans Friedle Albiez to Conrad Binkert, 9 August 1726; GLA 99:985, 171r–v, Interrogation of Joseph Wagner of Unteralpfen, 7 December 1727.
39. Joseph "Glasmännle" Meyer reportedly approached the emperor during mass, perhaps in December 1731; GLA 113:240, 230r–38v, Interrogation of Joseph Meyer of Au, Vienna, 11 August 1733.

oaths.⁴⁰ On every other occasion, the delegations failed completely, in part because the peasants' wishes were beyond the ability, much less the desire, of any tribunal to fulfill. Instead, delegates were typically rewarded with imprisonment combined with instructions to litigate grievance through regular channels for the simple reason that strictly speaking, *direct* appeals to the Imperial Chancellery had been forbidden since at least 1710.⁴¹ When in 1727 the Chancellery forbade any future *salpeterisch* delegations, it was merely reiterating existing law.⁴²

Why, then, did the rebels persist in such behavior? The question looms even larger when one considers that indulging it ruined the lives of several *salpeterisch* delegates. Suffering and feelings of abandonment shout from letters the delegates wrote from prison. Writing home from his imprisonment in Komárom, Hungary, delegate Martin Eisele chided his halfhearted fellows back home that "we must all go under if you dear friends and neighbors give us no succor. Remember what you promised us all when you sent us out of the county . . . realize that we risked our entire wealth, our wives and children, yes even our own lives for you and did what we, as honest delegates, were obligated to do."⁴³

Thus by any standard of political economy, delegations made no sense. In the context of factional politics and ideology, however, delegations were altogether more reasonable. They had, for example, the potential to legitimate the prestige of rebel leaders at times when conventional sources of authority, such as elective office, were unavailable to them.⁴⁴ Few peasants could claim a distinction so weighty as direct, personal contact with imperial majesty, as "Salpeter-Hans" Albiez, "Glassmännle"

---

40. GLA 113:235, 28r–30r, Imperial Resolution of 28 June 1727. On negative peasant reactions, see GLA 113:229, 192r–95v, Interrogation of Hans Peter Schäfer of Birkingen, Waldshut, 26 July 1728, and GLA 113:232, 138r–81v, Interrogation of Martin Thoma of Haselbach, 16–20 September 1728.

41. GLA 79:3431, Imperial Resolution of 12 March 1710. This decree banned the delivery of petitions without the signatures of the parties to the conflict, or their representatives. In 1717, the imperial government extended the ban to include any and all delegations to Vienna which lacked the prior approval of provincial authorities; GLA 79:3431, Imperial Resolution of 28 August 1717.

42. GLA 113:221, 32r–33v, 6 October 1727.

43. GLA 99:1043, Martin Eisele of Nöggenschwiel to Joseph Eisele of Nöggenschwiel, 7 June 1740.

44. Werner Troßbach made a similar finding in the case of Hessian peasant delegations to the *Reichshofrat;* see his *Soziale Bewegung,* 230–56.

Meyer, Hans Friedle Gerspach, and "Schwarzmichel" Tröndle could. The practically minded Conrad Binkert exploited the distinction of an audience with Emperor Charles to cajole money from his fellows back home.[45] Certainly no *müllerisch* leader could match the prestige such encounters imparted. More generally, the informal title of *Deputierter* was an honor peasants carried for life, and in 1745, Johannes Thoma-ab-Egg used it to win the Octovir election in his home canton of Rickenbach.[46]

So well did the *salpeterisch* practice of diplomacy accord with central precepts of their ideology that it is difficult to imagine a plausible alternative. The link to "naive monarchism" was obvious. As the previous chapter showed, the delegates' tendency to project their own political aspirations onto the monarch justified a suspicion of all intervening authorities, from the Imperial Chancellery to the *müllerisch* Eight, and generated the imaginary community of interest between sovereign and subject that Hans Friedle Gerspach articulated so laboriously at his "Assembly of the Whole County" of 22 July 1738. But again, the truth of the delegates' claims about imperial benevolence is less important than the fact that they were made at all. Without fail, each imperial encounter confirmed delegates in their "naive" belief that the emperor wished only to help them. This was the information delegates brought home, information which justified any expense. It is only a small exaggeration to suggest that it was the whole point of sending delegations to gain personal access to the emperor. From this perspective, delegations were peasant monarchism in practice.

45. Writing home from Vienna, Binkert reportedly claimed that as a result of his audience, the Upper Austrian government in Innsbruck had already washed its hands of the entire affair. Binkert then asked for the considerable sum of seven hundred gulden; GLA 99:985, 171r–v, Interrogation of Joseph Wagner of Unteralpfen, Unteralpfen, 7 December 1727.

46. Johannes Marder, Bläsi Hottinger, Joseph Meyer, Hans Friedle Gerspach, Johannes Thoma-ab-Egg, and Hans Wasmer all used the title of *Deputierter* to distinguish themselves; see GLA 113:231, 5r, Marder to "Ihro Durchleücht," [1729?]; GLA 113:236, 54r–55v, Marder and Hottinger to Hans Georg Marder, 12 February 1730 [written from prison in Belgrade]; GLA 99:1034, 137r–v, Marder and Hottinger to "guette Freünd," 5 April 1732 [also written from a Belgrade prison]; GLA 99:1035, 104r–5v, Thoma-ab-Egg to "Schwager," 16 November 1733 [written from prison in Vienna]; GLA 99:1037, 18r–21v, Marder and Hottinger to Gerspach, 2 July 1735 [written from prison in Vienna]. On the election of Thoma-ab-Egg, see GLA 113:263, "Ohngefehrliche Beschreibung, waß sich bey der Einungsmeisterwahl am Tag des hl. Ritters Georgii zugetragen . . . und zwar in der Einung Riggenbach," 28 April 1745.

From the same point of view, the quick fix of direct appeals made good financial sense. If delegations were expensive, the process of formal litigation threatened to inflate the costs attending redress of grievance even more. The slothful pace of eighteenth-century justice required decades of perseverance, and in the end, the Austrian government was unlikely to satisfy complaints directed against policies of its own making.[47] If only the emperor could be induced to intervene, the costs of litigation would be saved. And in any case, official injunctions to litigate through normal channels contradicted the rebels' belief in a structure of domination based on direct, mutual, and reciprocal obligation between lord and subject.

Finally, the *salpeterisch* practice of rebellion resonated with their belief in the existence of a "serfdom plot," a belief that reduced collective ills to serfdom and laid blame for them at the doorstep of corrupt and treasonous *müllerisch* Octovirs. Specifically, a twofold shift in the content of Hauenstein's formal grievances reflected the increasingly factional essence of *salpeterisch* delegations (see Appendix 4). To be sure, a disparity between concrete and transcendent demands had characterized *salpeterisch* grievance lists from the start; requests for relief from fiscal burdens, for example, or for modifications in the legal construction of domination—the usual stuff of peasant litigation—were also few and far between.[48] Still, concrete demands increasingly gave way to more vague

47. Werner Troßbach's study of Hessian protest movements provides vivid examples of the huge expenditures of time and money involved in litigating "by the book"; see his *Bauernbewegungen im Wetterau-Vogelsberg-Gebiet, 1648–1806: Fallstudien zum bäuerlichen Widerstand im Alten Reich* (Darmstadt, 1985). See also Peter Blickle, "Bäuerliche Rebellionen im Fürststift St Gallen," in P. Blickle, ed., *Aufruhr und Empörung? Studien zum bäuerlichen Widerstand im Alten Reich* (Munich, 1980), 215–95; Claudia Ulbrich, "Bäuerlicher Widerstand in Triberg," in P. Blickle, ed., *Aufruhr und Empörung?* 146–214; and Renate Blickle, "Agrarische Konflikte und Eigentumsordnung in Altbayern, 1400–1800," in Schulze, ed., *Aufstände, Revolten, Prozeße,* 166–87.

48. Initially, such demands centered on St. Blasien's fiscal claims; after 1737, fiscal concerns shifted to the "Waldordnung," which burdened their "own private forests" ("ihren eygenen Waldtungen beschwert"); GLA 113:221, 99r–100v, 9 June 1738. See also GLA 99:1040, 120r–27v, "Copia Actum Waldshut," 21 February 1738, and GLA 113:244, 112r–13v, "Allerdurchleüchtigster . . . Landsfürst etc. wir Deputierte der Graffschafft Hauenstein bitten fusfällig um Gottes Barmherzigkeit Willen dies wenige doch gnädig zu durchlesen," [1739]. Complaints against seigneurial burdens were lacking entirely. Concerning the terms of domination, the 1727 delegation demanded the restoration of impartible inheritance customs;

requests for formal recognition as the emperor's "immediate" subjects and for ratification of Hauenstein's corporate "rights and privileges."[49] The second shift in *salpeterisch* grievances was toward a preoccupation with factional politics, as complaints against the venality of *müllerisch* Octovirs and requests for the release of *salpeterisch* prisoners became more common. During the summer delegation of 1738, this shift caused a falling-out between delegates Hans Friedle Gerspach, Joseph Eckert, and Joseph Ebner of Hottingen, who wanted Hauenstein's grievances to include more accusations against the Eight. Ebner returned home in a huff, but the trend was in his favor.[50]

The content of *salpeterisch* grievances did not, however, exhaust the relationship between delegations and factional politics. On the contrary: *salpeterisch* activists draped their missions in a thick cloak of ritual and ceremony, whose symbolic language described the rebels' conception of right order and of the forces arrayed against it. Specifically, delegates often inaugurated their treks to Vienna with mass processions to nearby shrines of the Virgin Mary. These pilgrimages were carefully staged to demonstrate the higher purpose of the *salpeterisch* cause—and the mendacity of those who would deny the validity of their endeavor. Thus the ritualization of delegations imparted a propagandistic function to them all. To

---

GLA 113:225, 396r–98v, "Copia memorialis," [1727]. Similarly in 1726, Albiez had complained against serfdom "of the baser hand"; GLA 113:224, 1r–26v, Interrogation of Hans Friedle Albiez, 26–29 October 1726.

49. GLA 113:224, 180r–85v, [Hans Friedle Albiez of Buch], "Memoriale ad Imperatorem von dem hawenstein. Tumultanten eingegeben in Wien," [1726]; GLA 113:225, 396r–98v, "Copia memorialis an ihro Röm. Kay. und König. Cath Mth. . . v[on] denen 4 deputierten Cameralunterthanen von der Grafschafft Hauwenstein," [1727]; GLA 99:978, 9r–10v, "Copia ad Augustissimum allerunterthgste Remonstraon und Bitt Redmann, Einungsmeistern und gesambter Unterthanen der Cameral-Graffschafft Hawenstein," [1729]; GLA 113:244, 112r–13v, "Wir Deputierte der Graffschafft Hauenstein bitten fusfällig," [1739]; GLA 65:11223, 58r–69v, "Species facti succincta in Sachen hauenstein. könig. Cameralunterthanen auf dem Schwarzwald ad das Gotteshaus St Blasii und das Stifft Seckhingen nebst ihren Anfang," [1744?]. For the demand that Hauenstein be recognized as an "immediate subject" of the emperor, see also GLA S IV 737, Stiftsarchiv St Paul im Lavantal, Kloster St Blasien Handschriften 166/2, "Diaria R. P. Marquardi Hergots über seine Wienner Geschäfften de Anno 1728/1729" [hereafter Diaria Marquardi Hergots], entry for 14 March 1728. Similarly with respect to serfdom, the earliest grievances were concerned mostly with servile terminology in homage oaths and manumission contracts; by 1729, the demand had inflated to encompass serfdom as such.

50. See GLA 113:242, 361r–62v, Interrogation of Joseph Ebner of Hottingen, Rotzel, 7 December 1738, and 380r–81v, Interrogation of Martin Albiez and Jacob Widmer, Unteralpfen, 20–23 December 1738.

some extent, therefore, the instrumental utility of delegations lay in the terrain of factional politics back home in Hauenstein. In this connection, it is well to note the anthropologist Simon Roberts's reminder that

> People go to court-like agencies for a wide variety of purposes: for reasons of honor, to publicize some established position which requires no court ruling, or just to make life difficult for an enemy. The very notion of "dispute" may not be apposite if the court is just being used as a platform from which to tell people something. In cases of this sort, the objective may not lie in terms of judgment at all.[51]

As with *salpeterisch* rallies, the most elaborate examples of this practice date from 1738. In late April, for example, "Schwarzmichel" Tröndle, Leonzi Brutschi, Joseph Eckert, Hans Friedle Gerspach, and sixteen others departed for the capital, there to persuade Emperor Charles to release imprisoned delegates from earlier missions and to establish a "nonpartisan" imperial commission to investigate St. Blasien's right to collect servile dues and services.[52] The larger purpose of these demands, however, was to prevent the manumission treaty of January 1738: if Charles could agree with the *salpeterisch* view that abbatial serfdom had no legal or historical basis, then emanicpation would be moot and its high price unnecessary. To underscore the importance of their diplomatic efforts to the peasantry as a whole, the four delegates inaugurated their journey with a pilgrimage in the company of 111 "young girls" or "virgins" *(Jungfrauwen)* to the Marian shrine at Einsiedeln in Switzerland. There, the pilgrims prayed for Emperor Charles's military victory over "the Turk," as well as "for the success of their own undertaking," a rhetorical device that succeeded in equating seditious acts with loyalty and "obedience" with apostasy.[53] From Einsiedeln, the delegates traveled by boat across Lake Constance, thence overland to the Danube, then by river to

---

51. Simon Roberts, "The Study of Dispute: Anthropological Perspectives," in John Bossy, ed., *Disputes and Settlements: Law and Human Relations in the West* (Cambridge, U.K., 1983), 23.

52. GLA 113:242, 69r–70v, 197r–98v, Interrogation of Hans Ebner of Unteralpfen, Unteralpfen, 5 July 1738; GLA 113:249, B1, Interrogation of Hans Friedle Gerspach, Waldshut, 14–25 April 1739.

53. GLA 65:11419, 48r–49v [Biographical sketch of Leonzi Brutschi], April 1739.

Vienna, where they met with failure.[54] In a decree of 9 June 1738, Charles flatly dismissed their demands.[55] On his return to Hauenstein in mid-June, Gerspach launched the campaign of contentious gatherings that would culminate in the mass rally of 22 July 1738.

Already in August of the same year, yet another delegation departed for Vienna, this time accompanied by five hundred peasants (according to one, probably exaggerated account), including another hundred *Jungfrauwen*. Like its predecessor, this mass pilgrimage required plenty of advance planning and fund-raising, and indeed a handwritten note survives, listing the quota of virgins each parish in Dogern Canton was required to supply, plus an admonition for all to donate cash: according to this scheme, Dogern Canton was to supply twenty-one virgins, six from the village of Dogern itself, seven from the villages of Schmitzingen, Gais, and Waldkirch, and a further eight from the parish of Weilheim, including the village of Nöggenschwiel.[56] Again as in the previous spring, the crowd of pilgrims traveled to Einsiedeln, where they prayed for the emperor's health and for "peace in their land." According to interrogation protocols assembled after the fact, the maidens had been dressed in white and marched holding candles—a combination of symbols calculated, it would seem, both to demonstrate the delegates' penitential purity and humility and to expose the putative treachery of peasants who disputed the legitimacy of their project. The participants remained to pray in Einsiedeln for a few days and even obtained a certificate documenting their pilgrimage to the shrine.[57]

All told, about half of the *salpeterisch* delegations included pilgrimages to Marian shrines, most often to Einsiedeln; in at least two other recorded instances, group pilgrimages were undertaken without diplomatic missions to plead for the Virgin to intercede, as it were, in a factional dispute.[58] The full slate of Marian destinations included shrines

54. GLA 113:242, 44r–54v, 96r–99v, Interrogation of Michel Tröndle of Bergalingen, Freiburg, 7–21 June 1738.

55. GLA 113:221, 160r–61v, "Copia . . . Decreti ahn die ahnwesender Hauwensteiner," Laxenburg, 23 May 1738; GLA 113:221, *Salve conducto,* Laxenburg, 9 June 1738.

56. GLA 113:224, 6r–v, Joseph Sibold of Kuchelbach to [?], 30 August 1738.

57. GLA 113:246, 32r–v, "Attestatum," Einsiedeln, 5 September 1738.

58. See GLA 113:237, 253r–57v, Interrogation of Georg Schlachter of Herrischried, Waldshut, 13 May 1730, and GLA 113:223, 40r–43v, "Ungeföhrliche Bericht was sich den Früehling 1747 bis dn 22.tn May ihn underschidlichen Sachen bey den . . . unruohigen Underthanen zugetragen," [1747].

at Maria Stein in Lower Austria, Maria Zell in Styria, and a Loreto shrine in Hungary (probably Stotzing), as well as the less distant sites of Marian veneration in Todtmoos and Triberg.

Rebel ideology was encoded in virtually every element of these pilgrimages. To the extent that their propagandistic manipulations of pilgrimage appropriated the political significations of Habsburg Marian piety, the delegates replicated in the providential sphere their imagined pact of mutual and reciprocal obligation with the Austrian dynasty. Since 1600, a succession of Habsburg dynasts had associated the fortunes of the Crown Lands symbolically with Marian protection through sponsorship of the cult of the Immaculate Virgin. Symptomatic of this program was Emperor Ferdinand III's designation of the Virgin as patron saint of Austria and the Habsburg dynasty in 1647.[59] As a result, Marian veneration became not only a yardstick of Catholic orthodoxy, but one of loyalty to the house of Habsburg as well.[60] Under Leopold I, Marian pilgrimage assumed enormous symbolic importance: his nine pilgrimages to Maria Zell were stage-managed as acts of public supplication on behalf of all Austrian subjects.[61] When the Hauenstein delegates combined their missions with prayers to Mary for the emperor's well-being, arguably, they were merely returning the favor. Perhaps it would be stretching the formal parallel between missions and pilgrimages to suggest that peasants endowed the emperor with the same ontological status in secular affairs as the Virgin possessed in her sphere. Nevertheless, the delegates informed their manipulation of rituals and symbols connected with imperial *pietas mariana* with the assumption of sovereign benevolence and, with it, sovereign antipathy toward their enemies. Given the degree to which sovereigns politicized pilgrimage, finally, should we be surprised that subjects reciprocated in kind?[62]

---

59. Anna Coreth, *Pietas austriaca: Osterreichische Frömmigkeit im Barock* (Munich, 1982), 51–52; Ludwig Hüttl, *Marianische Wallfahrten im süddeutsch-österreichischen Raum* (Cologne, 1985), 128.

60. Coreth, *Pietas austriaca*, 45.

61. Ibid., 54–64; Hüttl, *Marianische Wallfahrten*, 141–42, 148–53. The Marian emphasis of *pietas austriaca* did not end with Leopold I. Charles VI, revived it after a brief lapse under Leopold's successor Joseph I. Maria Theresa continued the tradition, albeit with less enthusiasm.

62. On official, propagandistic manipulations of saint veneration, see most recently Philip M. Soergel, *Wondrous in His Saints: Counter-Reformation Propaganda in Bavaria* (Berkeley, 1993), especially 159–216.

Yet functional and structural explanations such as this do not explain why the delegates chose to link their journey with *Marian* veneration and not, say, that of St. Blaise, the patron saint of Hauenstein, or St. Fridolin, whom certain peasants recognized as Hauenstein's patron saint.[63] One is tempted to invoke popular appropriations of royal Marian propaganda and leave it at that. Another possibility is that sponsorship of Marian shrines by the post-Tridentine church, at the expense of sites devoted to the veneration of local saints, left few alternatives to the Virgin. But the *salpeterisch* preoccupation with a "serfdom plot" suggests that the choice of Mary was neither symbolic action by default nor simply a matter of mimicry. The rebel belief in a state of bygone purity sullied by serfdom with the collusion of "disloyal" peasants identified the latter as Hauenstein's principal polluters. As the previous chapter showed, the accusation that *müllerisch* leaders had sold "the child in its mother's womb" into "eternal servitude" expressed the assumption that freedom or unfreedom was inherited from mothers at childbirth, and that the perpetuation of both was therefore a sexual function.[64] The *salpeterisch* ideology of a "serfdom plot" implied a shaming intervention that violated the metaphorical purity of Hauenstein's women in the generation of a free community. Small wonder, then, that in symbolizing their goal of defending Hauenstein against the "purchase" of wrongfully alienated freedoms, the delegates invoked a complex of symbols that managed to link purity with a process of sexual generation, just as the figure of *Maria Immaculata* did. Processions of *Jungfrauwen* to Einsiedeln achieved the same link between purity (white robes and candles signifying penitential humility) and generation ("virgins" symbolizing the community's biological potential for procreating its free status into the future) in an act of supplication for the well-being of the polity as a whole.[65] At bottom, then, the procession of *Jungfrauwen* symbolized the possibility of restoring a lost, original state of liberty in a world free of lords and officials—and of treasonous *müllerisch* peasants!

---

63. EAF Bistum Konstanz Specialia, Pfarrei Birndorf, Hans Ebner of Birndorf et al. to Johann Erhard Leicker, Deacon in Waldshut, 29 January 1735.

64. The quotation is from GLA 113:99, 1r–2v, "Was Hans Meyer der Wagener zue Albffen im Wirtzhaus . . . ausgestossen," 29 March 1732.

65. For a fuller discussion, see David M. Luebke, "The Seditious Uses of 'Naive Monarchism' and Marian Veneration in Early Modern Germany," *PP* (forthcoming).

Conclusion

The death of Emperor Charles VI in October 1740 and the ensuing War of the Austrian Succession put an effective end to *salpeterisch* delegations. There were a few more, to be sure, such as Bläsi Hottinger's fruitless trip with Martin Mutter of Rüßwihl to Francis Stephen's imperial coronation in Frankfurt.[66] But military events and the bloody escalation of factional conflict inside Hauenstein itself diverted rebel energies to other tasks.

What can be learned from the *salpeterisch* practice of rebellion? For one thing, it compromises the argument that the forms and patterns of rebel mobilization arose primarily from the sum of local, material interests. According to this reasoning, rebellions crystallize around the combined material interests of several, even hundreds of village polities. Furthermore, peasants could not hope to mobilize resources between villages unless they *first* created solidarities within each commune that obscured "the responsibility of individual peasants behind the collective responsibility of the village commune."[67] Thus rebellions retained their "communal" character, even after they became regional in extent. But this view begs the question of collective interest and its potentially multiple articulations. More than that, it begs the question of how public opinion forms in the first place: even if unanimity had prevailed in the villages and hamlets of Hauenstein, who would have translated their interests into collective action? Who would have distilled a common set of grievances from the mass of local interests? Mobilization implies the conscious and coordinated actions of individuals in many villages, and the *salpeterisch* practice of rebellion, like any political movement, was artificial, the product of human creativity.

But Hauenstein's villages were *not* united, and the specific practices of the rebellious faction reflected this reality. Through trial and error, *salpeterisch* activists learned that big rallies were the simplest, least expensive way to summon the resources of opinion and funds needed to support costly projects like sending delegations to Vienna. More to the point, rallies freed them from the need to navigate the turbulent

---

66. GLA 113:258, 302r–14v, Interrogation of Bläsi Hottinger, 2–7 May 1746.
67. Andreas Suter, *"Troublen" im Fürstbistum Basel (1726–1740): Eine Fallstudie zum bäuerlichen Widerstand im 18. Jahrhundert* (Göttingen, 1985), 124.

waters of village politics. The constraints of local politics, as well as the pattern of *salpeterisch* mobilization itself, indicate the crucial role of activists, identifiable "faces in the crowd" that reappeared in rally after rally, delegation after delegation. The example of Hans Friedle Gerspach squarely contradicts George Rudé's suggestion that, prior to the French Revolution, the leaders of "crowds" enjoyed a "purely temporary" authority and, consequently, that there was little or no continuity of leadership between one contentious gathering and the next.[68] Rather, strategies of mobilization and collective action were devised within a network of *salpeterisch* leaders and executed from the top down. Although this style was more inclusive than that of their opponents, it is difficult to imagine how it might have been otherwise. David Sabean notes correctly that no rebellion as lengthy as the Salpeter Wars could have been sustained unless activists had somehow taken local action on a regional scale.[69] "Contentious gatherings" and delegations were the main public expressions of this process, and both show that the mental horizons of rebel leaders extended far beyond the narrow confines of the village fence. Thus mobilization was "supracommunal" in character from the outset; narrow local or parochial interests in no way inhibited the development of a county-wide movement. By the same token, the huge distances delegates traveled to reach Vienna show that the mental geography of *salpeterisch* leaders was anything but village-bound. Though Hauensteiners may have been ignorant of nearby Württemberg, they could claim reasonably detailed knowledge of life in a capital city many hundreds of miles distant.

Salpeterisch delegations and their ritual construction, moreover, recommend some anthropological variations on the theme of early modern social conflict in the "juridified" mode. If, as the evidence presented here suggests, Hauenstein's delegates to Vienna acted out an essentially familial conception of their subordination to the emperor that was incompatible with litigation through regular channels of administrative appeal, then it is difficult to see how social conflict in Hauenstein was

68. George Rudé, *The Crowd in History: A Study of Popular Disturbances in France and England, 1730–1848*, rev. ed. (London, 1981), 251–52.
69. David W. Sabean, "The Communal Basis of Pre-1800 Peasant Uprisings in Western Europe," *Comparative Politics* 8 (1976): 355–64.

in any sense "juridified." From the rebels' point of view, obtaining a face-to-face encounter with Charles VI was to place domination and subordination in its proper context.[70] This, of course, meant side-stepping the officially sanctioned route of judicial appeal that *müllerisch* leaders preferred to exploit. Rebels complained bitterly against the excessive costs of litigation through channels, and to that extent, "juridification" did not smother the fires of dissension but fanned them.[71] To the rebellious onlookers, the Austrian judicial juggernaut was part of the problem, and the emperor's personal intervention would spare them the huge expenses of formal lawsuits. Of course, litigation was not everywhere as divisive as it proved to be in Hauenstein. Still, the *salpeterisch* practice of rebellion suggests a basic incompatibility between "juridified" social conflict and paternalistic conceptions of rule and authority.

Parenthetically, it is worth noting that the responses of Imperial Chancellery officials to the *salpeterisch* practice of direct appeals to the emperor exposed equivocal attitudes toward their own apparatus of judicial review. By its own regulations, the Chancellery would have been well within its rights to forbid such direct appeals. Until the mid-1730s, however, it did not prevent Hauenstein's delegates even from gaining personal access to Charles VI, and an explanation may lie in the crown's competition for social dignity with intermediate lords—in this case, St. Blasien. In 1728, Abbot Franz II's emissary in Vienna, the priest and genealogist Marquart Herrgott, encountered a strong "anti-abbot" faction among councillors in the Imperial Chancellery, including Johann Christoph von Bartenstein; the peasants' strongest champion was the young state secretary *(Staatssekretär)* Anton von Buol.[72] Apparently, the principal reason for their antipathy was that the homage formulas St. Blasien's juridical subjects were required to deliver contained language that suggested abbatial pretensions to sovereignty in Hauenstein. Such formulas injured imperial dignity, and to that extent, "peasant-friendly"

---

70. Compare David Sabean, "A Prophet in the Thirty Years' War: Penance as a Social Metaphor," in his *Power in the Blood: Popular Culture and Village Discourse in Early Modern Germany* (Cambridge, U.K., 1984), 61–93, and 22.

71. GLA 113:242, 380r–81v, Interrogation of Martin Albiez and Jacob Widmer, 20 December 1738.

72. Diaria Marquardi Hergots, 11r, entry for 22 March 1728.

attitudes in Vienna reflected worries over the abbey's attempts to disrupt the Habsburg "economy of privilege" at the very bottom of the hierarchy,[73] in addition to genuine concerns over the causes of Hauenstein's ongoing unrests.[74] The point is that when peasant grievances touched on the economy of privilege, the Chancellery found itself undermining the authority of its own provincial justice system. In such cases, "peasant-friendly" policies could *subvert* the integrity of institutions designed to transform social conflicts into legal disputes.[75]

Be that as it may, attempts to bypass systems of judicial review were hardly limited to Black Forest peasants. Georg Grüll documented almost identical patterns of belief and action in the Upper Austrian lordships of Wildeneck, Groß-Raming, the Lower Mühlviertel, the Hausruckviertel, Molln, Hollstein, and Göstling, as well as Reit in Lower Austria, during the period between 1649 and 1712.[76] Delegations were sent from other lordships in Outer Austria as well, such as Pfirt (1511), Schwarzenberg-Kastelberg (1598), and Triberg (1706).[77] In seventeenth- and eighteenth-century Vienna, the steady flow of delegations generated lively business for "peasant attorneys" and freelance petition-writers.[78] Such enactments of "naive monarchism," if such they were, did not limit themselves to peasant delegations. On a royal visit to Transylvania, Emperor Joseph II was bombarded with almost 19,000 supplications for royal intervention into local legal squabbles.[79] Similar attempts to provoke sovereign intercession against royal bureaucracies have been described in Württemberg

---

73. John P. Spielman, "Status as Commodity: The Habsburg Economy of Privilege," in Charles Ingrao, ed., *State and Society in Early Modern Austria* (West Lafayette, Ind., 1992), 110–18.

74. See, for example, Marquard Herrgott's account of his audience with Prince Eugene of Savoy on 17 March 1728; Diaria Marquardi Hergots, 6r–7v.

75. Schulze tends to see institutions of judicial review and "peasant-friendly" policies as complementary; see his "'Geben Aufruhr und Aufstand Anlaß zu neuen heilsamen Gesetzen': Beobachtungen über die Wirkungen bäuerlichen Widerstands in der Frühen Neuzeit," in Schulze, ed., *Aufstände, Revolten, Prozeße*, 274–80.

76. Georg Grüll, *Bauer, Herr und Landesfürst: Sozialrevolutionäre Bestrebungen der oberösterreichischen Bauern von 1650 bis 1848* (Graz, 1963), 9–11, 129–34, 250–55, 270–75, 361–62.

77. Claudia Ulbrich, "Der Charakter bäuerlichen Widerstands in vorderösterreichischen Herrschaften," in Schulze, ed., *Aufstände, Revolten, Prozeße*, 215 n. 80, and "Bäuerlicher Widerstand in Triberg," 181–82.

78. Helfried Valentinisch, "Advokaten, Winkelschreiber und Bauernprokuratoren in Innerösterreich in der frühen Neuzeit," in Schulze, ed., *Aufstände, Revolten, Prozeße*, 183–201.

79. Jerome Blum, *The End of the Old Order in Rural Europe* (Princeton, 1978), 335.

and Saxony (to say nothing of eastern Europe and Scandinavia).[80] These appeals and delegations remain inexplicable unless peasants considered them at least minimally efficacious, which they did, despite overwhelming evidence to the contrary.

By the same token, the *salpeterisch* manipulation of Marian pilgrimage points to a neglected aspect of religious observance in Catholic Europe, namely the seditious uses of saint veneration. In Hauenstein, Marian pilgrimage was a form of collective action in the service of overtly political objectives. *Salpeterisch* delegates adapted well-established rites and symbols of Marian veneration to illustrate the significance of their undertaking to the whole peasantry. In this respect, they resembled the bulk of baroque pilgrimages—paraliturgical, communal processions, usually to a nearby shrine, undertaken with the explicit intention of maintaining communal well-being by binding it to a reciprocal pact with some saint or the Virgin.[81] The specific practice of festive communal pilgrimages in the company of white-clad, crowned, and candle-bearing women was already well-established in southern Germany by 1500 or so.[82] Thus baroque pilgrimage functioned as a rite of communal solidarity—whether the ritual was designed to create solidarity or merely to confirm it. The cases under discussion here were of the former variety:

80. On Württemberg: Sabean, "Prophet in the Thirty Years' War," 61–93. On Saxony: Willi A. Boelcke, *Bauer und Gutsherr in der Oberlausitz* (Bautzen, 1957), 230. On Denmark: Thomas Munck, *The Peasantry and the Early Absolute Monarchy in Denmark, 1660–1708* (Copenhagen, 1979). On Poland: Bobinska, "Les mouvements paysans en Pologne aux XVIIIe et XIXe siècles: Problèmes et methodes," *Acta Poloniae Historica* 22 (1970): 136–57.

81. Wolfgang Brückner, "Zur Phänomenologie und Nomenklatur des Wallfahrtswesens und seiner Erforschung: Wörter und Sachen in systematisch-semantischem Zusammenhang," in Dieter Harmening et al., eds., *Volkskultur und Geschichte: Festgabe für Josef Dünninger zum 65. Geburtstag* (Berlin, 1970), 411. Elsewhere, Brückner suggests that the "will to communal well-being" *(Gemeinschaftswille)* was characteristic of baroque pilgrimage, a function carried out principally by pious fraternities *(Bruderschaften);* see his *Verehrung des Heiligen Blutes in Walldürn* (Aschaffenburg, 1958), 175–79. See also Klaus Guth, "Geschichtlicher Abriß der marianischen Wallfahrtsbewegungen im deutschsprachigen Raum," in Wolfgang Beinert and Heinrich Petri, eds., *Handbuch der Marienkunde* (Regensburg, 1984), 737, and Hüttl, *Marianische Wallfahrten,* 39, 65–83.

82. The practice was especially common in Bavaria, where white-clothed female pilgrims were known as *Weißprangerinnen.* On the penitential iconography of white clothing in Marian pilgrimage, see Hüttl, *Marianische Wallfahrten,* 13–14, and Irmgard Gierl, *Bauernleben und Bauernwallfahrt in Altbayern: Eine kulturhistorische Studie aufgrund der Tuntenhausener Mirakelbücher* (Munich, 1960), 115–16.

by fusing diplomacy and Marian pilgrimage, the delegates symbolically identified their sectarian agenda with the transcendent good of the whole. Pilgrimage thus exerted a powerful legitimating influence on one party in a fractious polity.[83]

All this suggests that pilgrimage was what cultural anthropologists describe as a site of competing symbolic discourses.[84] Traditionally, anthropologists of pilgrimage have been divided between Durkheimians, who view it as a vehicle for reinforcing existing social structures, and others, such as Victor and Edith Turner, who see it as a "liminal" experience of "unmediated egalitarian association" *(communitas),* "which betokens the partial, if not complete abrogation" of those structures.[85] Broadly speaking, the evidence presented here suggests that these views are contradictory only in isolation: taken together, they aptly describe the competition between elite and popular discourses over the meaning of sacred space.[86] On the one hand: royal manipulations of Marian veneration and pilgrimage served the dual purposes of self-aggrandizement and of undergirding hegemonic claims of rule. On the other hand: popular appropriations of that royal practice were designed both to exculpate rebellious behaviors and to help forge solidarities among peasants.

Of course, it would be silly to refract the whole of rebellious practice and Marian veneration in early modern Germany through the prism of Hauenstein. Nevertheless, the rebels' seditious use of pilgrimage was not unique. For one thing, it had precedent: the first recorded mission from Hauenstein that was inaugurated by a procession to Einsiedeln occurred in 1704. There, delegates promised further pilgrimages for the emperor Leopold's benefit as the *quid pro quo* of his assistance.[87] For

83. Compare Peter Burke, "The Virgin of the Carmine and the Revolt of Masaniello," *PP* 99 (1983): 14–15, 18.

84. See John Eade and Michael J. Sallnow, "Introduction," in Eade and Sallnow, eds., *Contesting the Sacred: The Anthropology of Christian Pilgrimage* (London, 1991), 5.

85. I borrow the summary descriptions of Eade and Sallnow, "Introduction," 4–5. For Turner, see Victor W. Turner and Edith Turner, *Image and Pilgrimage in Christian Culture: Anthropological Perspectives* (New York, 1978), 1–39.

86. See Rebekka Habermas, *Wallfahrt und Aufruhr: Zur Geschichte des Wunderglaubens in der fruhen Neuzeit* (Frankfurt: Campus, 1991), 45–49, 76–78.

87. GLA 67:1809, 323–84, Abbot Augustine to Emperor Leopold, 1704. Again in 1728, an imprisoned delegate named Johannes Marder pledged pilgrimages on behalf of Hauenstein and the emperor to Rome, Tiengen, and Einsiedeln, where he would also sponsor a mass; see GLA 113:232, 91r–117v, Interrogation of Johannes Marder, Freiburg, 22–23 September 1728.

another, it had parallels: in July 1712, for example, a peasant delegate from Groß-Raming inadvertently evaded arrest by combining his mission to Vienna with a pilgrimage to the shrine of Maria Taferl in Lower Austria.[88] A more striking example of peasants fusing saint veneration with social conflict comes from eighteenth-century Switzerland. In 1781, the rural subjects of the Catholic city-state of Fribourg rebelled against official infringements on local autonomies.[89] On 3-4 May, some three thousand armed peasants laid siege to Fribourg, but were defeated in the attempt. During the confrontation their commander, one Pierre Nicolas Chenaux, a well-to-do peasant from La Tour-de-Trême, was captured and beheaded. In the aftermath of the so-called "Chenaux Affair," peasants adapted the rituals of saint veneration to the political ends of articulating grievance in a popular "canonization" of their deceased leader: for many years after 1781, Chenaux's skull, impaled on the city ramparts, became the object of popular, chiliastic pilgrimage. In this case, peasants adapted the practices of saint veneration to articulate not only their grievances, but distinctions between themselves and their enemies as well. In a similar case from Bavaria, an established Marian pilgrimage at Preißenberg provided the symbolic material of conflict between the Augustinian abbey of Rottenbuch and its Ammergau subjects.[90] Starting in the 1610s, Rottenbuch abbey began sponsoring the Preißenberg *Wallfahrt* in order to enhance both its incomes and social standing. The peasants, however, displayed greater interest in a Marian shrine of their own making in the village of Peiting. Throughout the mid-seventeenth century, Preißenberg flagged while Peiting flourished, despite official discouragement and the absence of liturgical support. In 1650, the abbatial provost of Rottenbuch left no doubt that the Peiting pilgrimage represented a direct challenge to the

88. Grüll, *Bauer, Herr und Landesfürst*, 270.
89. François-Ignace de Castella, "La chronique scandaleuse des misères qui ont agité la magistrature, la bourgeouisie, les terres anciennes, et la majeure partie des bailliages du canton de Fribourg en 1781 et 1782," reprinted in *Archives de la société d'histoire du canton de Fribourg* 6 (1899): 397–478; Paul Hugger, "Kommentare zum freiburgischen Chenaux-Handel von 1781: Ein Beitrag zur Geschichte der chiliastischen und nativistischen Strömungen in der Schweiz," *SZG* 23 (1973): 324–40, reprinted in Hugger, *Sozialrebellen und Rechtsbrecher in der Schweiz: Eine historisch-volkskundliche Studie* (Zürich, 1976), 9–28; and Pierre Felder, "Ansätze zu einer Typologie der politischen Unruhen im schweizerischen Ancien Régime," *SZG* 26 (1976): 363–69.
90. Habermas, *Wallfahrt und Aufruhr*, 35–44.

abbey's authority and prestige. It is probably no coincidence that the Peiting pilgrimage emerged toward the close of a long-winded and violent rebellion against a 50 percent increase in manorial dues.[91] Nor is it impossible that in their sponsorship of Peiting, Ammergau peasants sought to avail themselves of a new ideology of Marian veneration then being forged in Munich and reflected principally in Wittelsbach's sponsorship of the Marian shrine at Altötting.[92] If that is the case, then Ammergau peasants were capable of manipulating Marian veneration in much the same way that Hauensteiners did.

These examples suggest that the cultural hegemony of elites was "paper-thin."[93] The rebels' borrowing from precedent and elite example suggests that the state cult of *Maria Immaculata* was exposed to forms of popular cultural appropriation that ran at political cross-purposes to its original intent. Thus official sponsorship determined little more than a menu of officially sanctioned symbols and icons available for popular manipulation. Still, it is unlikely that peasants outside Hauenstein made seditious use of Marian pilgrimage in exactly the same way. But if one assumes the multivocality of specific practices, then it is essential to understand the contexts that imparted meaning to them. Taken in isolation, no single aspect of *salpeterisch* rebellious practice was unique; most Marian pilgrimages, moreover, were simply pious in motivation, and *salpeterisch* activists could hardly have exploited the practice unless it also remained popular for pious reasons. The steady, eighteenth-century crescendo of communions received at the few remaining sites of transregional Marian pilgrimage indicates just this.[94] Removed from political

---

91. Renate Blickle, "'Spenn und Irrung' im 'Eigen' Rottenbuch: Die Auseinandersetzungen zwischen Bauernschaft und Herrschaft des Augustiner-Chorherrenstifts," in *Aufruhr und Empörung?* 95–114; Habermas, *Wallfahrt und Aufruhr*, 34.

92. Hüttl, *Marianische Wallfahrten*, 95–124; Habermas, *Wallfahrt und Aufruhr*, 33; Robert Bauer, *Die Bayerische Wallfahrt Altötting* (Munich, 1970); Olivia Wiebel-Fanderl, *Die Wallfahrt Altötting: Kultformen und Wallfahrtsleben im 19. Jahrhundert* (Passau, 1982), 6–10. On the Bavarian *pietas mariana*, see Soergel, *Wondrous in His Saints;* and Gerhard P. Woeckel, *Pietas Bavarica: Wallfahrt, Prozession, und Ex-Voto-Gabe im Hause Wittelsbach im Ettal, Wessobrunn, Altötting und der Landeshauptstadt von der Gegenreformation bis zur Säkularisation und der "Renovatio ecclesiae"* (Weissenhorn, 1992).

93. See James C. Scott, *Domination and the Arts of Resistance: Hidden Transcripts* (New Haven, 1990), 82–85.

94. At Maria Hilf ob Passau in Bavaria, for example, the number of communions grew from a few thousand in 1640 to over 100,000 in 1700. At Maria Zell in Austria, communions

context, however, the popular meanings of these pilgrimages remain virtually undiscernible: one can only wonder how many of them were also seditious.

It is a tragic irony that the *salpeterisch* practice of rebellion was indeed more inclusive than that of the *müllerisch* side. But if rebel activists thought that their rallies and delegations would create political unanimity, events proved them wrong. *Salpeterisch* efforts produced amazingly large crowds and electoral majorities, but never generated a homogenous political will in Hauenstein. In the long run, moreover, the character of political discourse was such that the notion of a "loyal opposition" was (or became) oxymoronic. Ultimately, neither faction could abide an adversary. In part, the factional mayhem of 1744–45 represented a final, fatal *salpeterisch* attempt to enforce with violence a "communal" consensus that rallies and delegations had failed to produce.

---

grew from 61,000 in 1689 to 188,000 in 1725, and Einsiedeln experienced a similar surge in popularity. On Maria Hilf, see Walter Hartinger, *Mariahilf ob Passau: Volkskundliche Untersuchung der Passauer Wallfahrt und der Mariahilf-Verehrung im deutschsprachigen Raum* (Passau, 1985), cited in R. Po-chia Hsia, *Social Discipline in the Reformation: Central Europe, 1550-1750* (London: Routledge, 1989), 158, figure 5.8; on Maria Zell, see Franz Jantsch, *Mariazell: Das Heiligtum der Gnadenmutter Österreichs* (Graz, 1952), 109, cited in Hüttl, *Marianische Wallfahrten*, 48.

CONCLUSION

Peasant Factions in the Holy Roman Empire

THE STORY OF THE SALPETER WARS RECORDS A FAILURE OF PEASANTS to unite against lords who sought to expand their authorities at the expense of local autonomies. Long-term social forces that had concentrated wealth and local power within a relatively small peasant elite, despite an institutional structure designed to prevent oligarchy, combined with these external pressures to produce political factions. To be sure, the political "insiders" who benefited from these trends had disputed the tactics best suited to thwart the annexationist abbey of St. Blasien long before "Salpeter-Hans" Albiez launched his fateful campaign to restore the "ancient rights" of Hauenstein in 1725. The process of resistance itself deepened these disagreements to such an extent that communal solidarity proved unenforceable. As these quarrels became more ideologically charged, the leaders of each faction conscripted their kin groups and clienteles into factional struggle. The result was a factional politics that by 1745 had escalated to the point of civil war. After some twenty years of often bloody feuding, lawsuits, three Austrian military invasions, and half a dozen rebel attempts to provoke the emperor's personal intervention, the Salpeter Wars resulted in the destruction of precisely those autonomies that Hauenstein's peasant elites had labored for generations to defend.

What can these conflicts tell us about the state of popular politics and culture in early modern Europe more generally? Was the breakdown of communal solidarities widespread? Was factionalism its symptom, and if so, how often? Of course, no case study can portray the entirety of the broader phenomenon it purports to represent; yet, the institutional context of these conflicts was not so unusual that comparative analysis is impossible.[1]

At the risk of oversimplifying, we can say that the pattern of peasant rebellion between 1525 and 1800 was characterized by three main shifts. One was a geographical expansion: the unrest and instability that had persisted in regions that had been epicenters of rebellion in 1525, such as the Allgäu, Upper Swabia, and the Black Forest, spread to previously unaffected territories, especially the eastern portions of the Holy Roman Empire (Silesia, Lusatia), as well as parts of central and northern Germany (the Palatinate, Hessen, Saxony).[2] The Habsburg lands, in particular, were plagued by peasant unrest of disproportionate magnitude.[3] Second, the institutional context of rebellion reflected the broad division of German states into large and small principalities. The latter were relatively slow to centralize bureaucratically and were more exposed to judicial interference from the two principal imperial tribunals, the Imperial Chamber Court and the Imperial Aulic Council.[4] The insatiable fiscal hunger of the larger states added princely taxation to the long list of seigneurial burdens that continued to supply cause for revolt in all regions, while their exemptions from exposure to imperial jurisdiction ensured that litigation of peasant grievance was contained *within* the institutions of the territorial state.[5] In territories

1. Richard van Dülmen, "Formierung der europäischen Gesellschaft in der frühen Neuzeit: Ein Versuch," *GG* 7 (1981): 5–41.
2. One region—Alsace—that had been embroiled in the Peasants' War of 1525, however, experienced no major revolts afterward; Peter Bierbrauer, "Bäuerliche Revolten im Alten Reich: Ein Forschungsbericht," in Peter Blickle, ed., *Aufruhr und Empörung? Studien zum bäuerlichen Widerstand im Alten Reich* (Munich, 1980), 1–69.
3. Ibid., 52; Georg Grüll, *Bauer, Herr und Landesfürst: Sozialrevolutionäre Bestrebungen der oberösterreichischen Bauern von 1650 bis 1848* (Graz, 1963).
4. Werner Troßbach, "Bauernbewegungen in deutschen Kleinterritorien zwischen 1648 und 1789," in Winfried Schulze, ed., *Aufstände, Revolten, Prozeße: Beiträge zu bäuerlichen Widerstandsbewegungen im frühneuzeitlichen Europa* (Stuttgart, 1983), 233–85.
5. Tom Scott, "Peasant Revolts in Early Modern Germany," *HJ* 28 (1985): 457; see also Thomas Robisheaux, "Peasant Revolts in Germany and Central Europe after the Peasants' War: Comments on the Literature," *CEH* 17 (1984): 384–403.

both large and small, however, peasants seeking redress of grievance won greater access to appellate tribunals.[6]

Third, peasant rebellions also exhibited several qualitative changes over time. The violence of peasant uprisings, for example, appears to have decreased after the Thirty Years' War, in part because the Imperial Diet in 1654 checked the attempts of territorial lords to limit peasants' access to imperial judicial tribunals. Apart from a few notable exceptions, such as the "moonlight slaughter" *(Mondschlacht)* at Sendlingen during the Bavarian rising of 1705–6 or the "Kuckshäger War" in Schaumburg-Lippe in 1797, comparatively few rebellions escalated to the point of open, armed confrontations.[7] Another qualitative change was the increased localism of rebellions, a phenomenon which some historians explain by the tendency of social conflicts to transform into legal disputes: placing conflict in the discursive context of law and precedent undermined the material and ideological conditions of collective action *across* jurisdictional boundaries. Be that as it may, transregional revolts diminished in number. Although the late sixteenth and early seventeenth centuries produced a few transregional rebellions, these all but vanished after 1648. Only in a few instances, finally, did rebellions yield criticisms of the existing sociopolitical order as fundamental as those of 1525, a trend that might also have reflected the "juridification" of social conflict, especially in smaller principalities.

The causes of these rebellions varied greatly, of course. In contrast to the sixteenth-century revolts, few after 1600 involved religious controversy, and most of these were confined to the archibishopric of Salzburg and the archduchy of Austria, zones of intense Counter-Reformation activity.[8] Similarly, personal serfdom no longer incited as much peasant unrest as it had in the late Middle Ages, although it continued to spark rebellion in Outer Austrian lordships such as Triberg and Hauenstein.[9]

---

6. Jürgen Weitzel, *Der Kampf um die Appellation ans Reichskammergericht: Zur politischen Geschichte der Rechtsmittel in Deutschland* (Cologne, 1976).

7. For Bavaria, see Richard van Dülmen, "Bäuerlicher Protest und patriotische Bewegung: Der Volksaufstand in Bayern von 1705/06," *ZBLG* 45 (1982): 331–61; on the "Kuckshäger War," see Carl-Hans Hauptmeyer, "Bäuerlicher Widerstand in der Grafschaft Schaumburg-Lippe, im Fürstentum Calenberg und im Hochstift Hildesheim: Zur Frage der qualitativen Veränderung bäuerlicher Opposition am Ende des 18. Jahrhunderts," in Schultze, ed., *Aufstände, Revolten, Prozesse*, 217–32, here 223.

8. Bierbrauer, "Bäuerliche Revolten," 54.

9. Ibid., 55; Werner Troßbach, "'Südwestdeutsche Leibeigenschaft' in der frühen Neuzeit:

A form of serfdom associated with a *corvée* labor—based system of seigneurial domination *(Gutsherrschaft)*, however, continued to incite rebellions in Bohemia, Silesia, and Lusatia.[10] Nevertheless, certain perennial causes of revolt persisted. Not least among these were the effects of pan-European subsistence crises in the 1650s, 1698–99, 1709, and 1756–57, usually in combination with other stresses.[11] For the period after 1648, for example, Werner Troßbach has identified five great waves of peasant revolts in the small principalities (1650–60, 1700–1716, 1725–33, 1752–56, and 1767–73), three of which seem to have been connected with subsistence crises.[12] The nature of "other stresses" was determined in large part by distinctions between large and small territories. Taxation figured among the causes of only a quarter of all rebellions between 1525 and 1789, the bulk of them in smaller principalities that were poorly equipped to enforce imperial levies or cope with the unrest they sometimes ignited.[13] The second, third, and fourth waves of revolt in smaller territories were sparked by the temporary weight of imperial war levies.[14] In larger states, rebellions against seigneurial imposts were more common, especially in the Habsburg lands, where these burdens were exacerbated by the crown's habit of mortgaging its estates and authorities to raise funds, a practice called "lien administration."[15] For lessees, the profitability of "lien administration" depended on their ability to increase imposts above

---

eine Bagatelle?" *GG* 7 (1981): 69–90. On the role of serfdom in Triberg, see Claudia Ulbrich, "Bäuerlicher Widerstand in Triberg," in P. Blickle, ed., *Aufruhr und Empörung?* 189.

10. Hartmut Harnisch, "Landgemeinde, feudalherrlich-bäuerliche Klassenkämpfe und Agrarverfassung im Spätfeudalismus," *ZfG* 26 (1978): 887–97.

11. See Wilhelm Abel, *Massenarmut und Hungerkrisen im vorindustriellen Europa: Versuch einer Synopsis* (Hamburg, 1974).

12. Troßbach, "Bauernbewegungen," 253.

13. Bierbrauer, "Bäuerliche Revolten," 52–53; Winfried Schulze, "Europäische und deutsche Bauernrevolten in der frühen Neuzeit: Probleme der vergleichenden Betrachtung," in Schulze, ed., *Europäische Bauernrevolten in der frühen Neuzeit* (Frankfurt, 1982), 10–20. On the weight of imperial levies, see Winfried Schulze, *Bäuerlicher Widerstand und feudale Herrschaft in der frühen Neuzeit* (Bad Canstatt, 1980), 66–69.

14. Troßbach, "Bauernbewegungen," 234–35.

15. Bierbrauer, "Bäuerliche Revolten," 53. In several Habsburg territories, landlords attempted to transform a rent-based seigneurial system into one that more resembled the *corvée* labor-based system of *Gutswirtschaft;* see Alfred Hoffman, "Zur Typologie der Bauernaufstände in Oberösterreich," in *Der oberösterreichische Bauernkrieg 1626: Ausstellung des Landes Oberösterreich* (Linz, 1976), 15–22. On the practice of "lien administration," see Hermann Rebel, *Peasant Classes: The Bureaucratization of Property and Family Relations under Early Habsburg Absolutism, 1511-1636* (Princeton, 1983), 25–28. See also Claudia Ulbrich, "Agrarverfassung und bäuerlicher Widerstand im Oberrheingebiet," *ZAA* 30 (1982): 149–67.

the costs of lease, sparking violent peasant responses, most notably in the "Upper Austrian Peasants' War" of 1626. Finally, imperial politics often figured prominently among the causes of rebellion, especially in smaller territories. The first of Troßbach's "waves," for example, came in response to an Imperial Diet resolution of 1654 that codified the right of princes to levy imperial taxes without the prior approval of territorial estates.[16]

Inevitably, the Salpeter Wars conformed with some of these patterns, but not all. St. Blasien's leases of juridical authorities in Hauenstein were an example of "lien administration," although the extra fiscal burdens they posed no longer figured prominently among peasant grievances after the abbey's final, "perpetual" lease of juridical authorities in 1705. Subsistence crises played no discernible role; on the contrary, as Chapter 4 showed, Hauenstein's revolts erupted in the midst of economic recovery and generally improving crop yields. To the extent, however, that the Salpeter Wars were a defense of peasant autonomies, they shared much with other revolts. As Troßbach has noted, even subsistence crises did not produce rebellion unless the fiscal burdens attending intensifications of seigneurial or state power prevented peasants from compensating for harvest deficits. Thus in Germany, even revolts born of hunger acquired an "antifeudal orientation," especially in smaller territories.[17] Blickle goes further, arguing that in political terms, *all* early modern rebellions amounted to "confrontation[s] between the developing territorial state and rural societies defending their communal rights."[18] To that extent, the bulk of German peasant revolts were, like the Salpeter Wars, "defensive" in nature.[19]

The social environment of rebellion in Hauenstein resembled that of other regions as well. Virtually every region of Germany studied so far has confirmed a long-term, Europe-wide trend toward greater social stratification in the village, beginning in the mid-sixteenth century.[20]

16. Troßbach, "Bauernbewegungen," 241.
17. Ibid., 244.
18. Peter Blickle, "Auf dem Weg zu einem Modell der bäuerlichen Rebellion—Zusammenfassung," in P. Blickle, ed., *Aufruhr und Empörung?* 296–308.
19. Bierbrauer, "Bäuerliche Revolten," 56; see also Klaus Gerteis, "Regionale Bauernrevolten zwischen Bauernkrieg und französischer Revolution: Eine Bestandaufnahme," ZHF 6 (1979): 37–62.
20. In general, see Thomas Robisheaux, "The World of the Village," in Thomas A. Brady Jr. et al., eds., *Handbook of European History, 1400–1600: Late Middle Ages, Renaissance,*

This tendency was not uniform, of course, nor everywhere as severe in its effects. In extreme cases, such as that of Mecklenburg, the expansion of aristocratic *latifundia* at the expense of peasant holdings brought more immiseration than elsewhere. More typical of eastern Germany was Upper Lusatia, where in one lordship the expansion both of *latifundia* and a small number of large peasant farms caused the smallholder class to grow 25 percent between 1536 and 1629. Similarly, the number of middling peasants in the lordship of Königsbrück decreased by half between 1560 and 1777, as smallholders and the landless *(Gärtner* and *Häusler)* combined grew from 18.7 to 52.6 percent of the total population.[21] This bifurcation of rural society also prevailed outside the region of *Gutsherrschaft*. In sixteenth-century Austria, a policy of "bureaucratic capitalism," involving the creation of large, inheritable leases, tended to concentrate wealth among peasant elites.[22] Even in the economically backward principality of Hohenlohe, the gradual integration of peasant producers into regional grain markets polarized villages

---

and Reformation, vol. 1, *Structure and Assertions* (Leiden, 1994), 93–99, and Willi A. Boelcke, "Wandlungen der dörflichen Sozialstruktur während Mittelalter und Neuzeit," in Heinz Haushofer and Willi A. Boelcke, eds., *Neue Wege und Forschungen der Agrargeschichte: FS Günther Franz* (Frankfurt, 1967), 80–103. For particular regions, see Rebel, *Peasant Classes;* Rudolf Endres, "Sozialer Wandel in Franken und Bayern auf der Grundlage der Dorfordnungen," in Ernst Hinrichs and Günter Wiegelmann, eds., *Sozialer und kultureller Wandel in der ländlichen Welt des 18. Jahrhunderts* (Wolfenbüttel, 1982), 211–27; Gerd Wunder, "Bäuerliche Oberschichten im alten Wirtenberg," in Kuno Ülshofer, ed., *Bauer, Bürger, Edelmann: Ausgewählte Aufsätze zur Sozialgeschichte von Gerd Wunder* (Sigmaringen, 1984), 132–46; Thomas Robisheaux, *Rural Society and the Search for Order in Early Modern Germany* (Cambridge, U.K., 1989), especially 68–91; Franz Irsliger, "Gross- und Kleinbesitz im westlichen Deutschland vom 13. bis 18. Jahrhundert: Versuch einer Typologie," in Péter Gunst and Tamás Hoffmann, eds., *Grand domaine et petites exploitations en Europe au Moyen Age et dans les temps modernes: Rapports nationaux* (Budapest, 1982), 33–59; Diederich Saalfeld, "Stellung und Differenzierung der ländlichen Bevölkerung Nordwestdeutschlands in der Ständegesellschaft des 18. Jahrhunderts," in Ernst Hinrichs and Günter Wiegelmann, eds., *Sozialer und kultureller Wandel in der ländlichen Welt des 18. Jahrhunderts* (Wolfenbüttel, 1982), 229–50; Josef Mooser, "Gleichheit und Ungleichheit in der ländlichen Gemeinde: Sozialstruktur und Kommunalverfassung im östlichen Westfalen vom späten 18. bis in die Mitte des 19. Jahrhunderts," *ASG* 19 (1979): 231–62; and Karlheinz Blaschke, "Soziale Gliederung und Entwicklung der sächsischen Landbevölkerung im 16. bis 18. Jahrhundert," *ZAA* 4 (1956).

21. Boelcke, "Wandlungen," 90; William W. Hagen, however, has recently questioned the success of Prussian *Junkers* to transform themselves "into masters of large-scale demesne farms geared to market production . . . worked by an enserfed peasantry"; see his "How Mighty the Junkers? Peasant Rents and Seigneurial Profits in Sixteenth-Century Prussia," *PP* 108 (1985): 80–116.

22. Rebel, *Peasant Classes,* 28–32, 142–69.

into rich and poor. In the Langenburg district of Hohenlohe, for example, the top 10 percent of households increased their share of total taxable income from 44 percent in 1528 to 62 percent fifty years later. In 1599, angry cottagers protested that "a number of our tenant farmers have so much more than they actually need for the household's subsistence, but we need every scrap to stock up our barns and to supply our small households."[23] When the economic upswing that had fueled stratification came to a halt in the early seventeenth century, competition for scarcer resources heightened political tensions born of social trends, and in general, stratification appears to have increased again with economic and demographic recovery in the early eighteenth century, when the Salpeter Wars erupted.[24] A study of land cadastres in eighteenth-century Hesse shows that by 1726 over half of all peasant land in one district was under the control of fifty households, about 15 percent of the total.[25] The extent of stratification was about the same in Hauenstein, where in one canton the wealthiest decile commanded 43 percent of all income from land.[26]

These increasingly uneven distributions of wealth emerged in tandem with concentrations of political power, usually with the encouragement of state bureaucracies in the form of absolutist "village and police ordinances" *(Dorf- und Polizeiordnungen)*. Heide Wunder has argued that after the Thirty Years' War, the territorial states gradually transformed village institutions into instruments of domination, a process that brought "rationalizing" professional administrators into daily contact (and conflict) with the villagers concerned to preserve their traditions. Generally speaking, the state gradually stripped the village of most autonomous juridical and legislative authority, and communal

---

23. Robisheaux, *Rural Society*, 84.

24. On the eighteenth-century demographic expansion, see Peter Kriedte, *Peasants, Landlords, and Merchant Capitalists: Europe and the World Economy, 1500–1800* (Cambridge, U.K., 1983), 101–5.

25. Thomas Fox, "Land Tenure, Feudalism and the State in Eighteenth-Century Hesse," in Richard Herr, ed., *Themes in Rural History of the Western World* (Ames, 1993), 122. The jurisdiktion in question was Ebsdorf. See also Robert von Friedeburg, "Bauern und Tagelöhner: Die Entwicklung gesellschaftlicher Polarisierung in Schwalm und Knüll im Gewand der traditionellen Dorfgemeinde, 1737–1855," *ZAA* 39 (1991): 44–68.

26. See Chapter 4 and GLA 229:19644, "Rustical-Fassions-Tabella," ca. 1761.

forms of political organization atrophied as a result.²⁷ To be sure, this process was no more uniform than that of social stratification. In the large principalities of lower Saxony, for example, sovereigns often helped to *defend* local autonomies against landed aristocrats. There, princes had been able to rule only through a fiscal, military, and administrative reliance on nobles and large monasteries. Saxon nobles, like nobles everywhere, lived by extracting a share of surplus peasant production; but Saxon princes had to protect their villagers against excessive exploitation if they were to preserve their own tax base. Only in the eighteenth century did Saxon princes acquire the bureaucratic means to intervene in the regulation of village life—with rebellions the result.²⁸ In the east, by contrast, princes were more concerned to integrate nobles and their estates into military and administrative bureaucracies, largely at the expense of independent rural communities.²⁹ On balance, the decay of local autonomies was well advanced by the eighteenth century.

Wunder's analysis captures the disruptive force of state intervention in local affairs. Equally important, however, was the degree to which subjects shared, as Thomas Robisheaux put it, "in the process of their own domination, the way in which village society shaped the structure of the early modern state."³⁰ Before the Thirty Years' War, the regulation of internal, village affairs had been largely beyond the reach of princes;

---

27. Heide Wunder, *Die bäuerliche Gemeinde in Deutschland* (Göttingen, 1986), 80–113; see also her "Die ländliche Gemeinde als Strukturprinzip der spätmittelalterlich-frühneuzeitlichen Geschichte Mitteleuropas," in Peter Blickle, ed., *Landgemeinde und Stadtgemeinde in Mitteleuropa: Ein struktureller Vergleich* (Munich, 1991), 385–402.

28. Carl-Hans Hauptmeyer, "Entstehen und Verlust lokaler Autonomien im ländlichen Raum: Die deutsche Tradition der Gemeindereformen," *Essener Geographische Arbeiten* 15 (1986): 1–13; "Dorf und Territorialstaat im zentralen Niedersachsen," in Ulrich Lange, ed., *Landgemeinde und frühmoderner Staat: Beiträge zum Problem der gemeindlichen Selbstverwaltung in Dänemark, Schleswig-Holstein und Niedersachsen in der frühen Neuzeit* (Sigmaringen, 1988), 217–35; and "Aufklärung und bäuerliche Opposition im zentralen Niedersachsen des ausgehenden 18. Jahrhunderts," in Rudolf Vierhaus, ed., *Das Volk als Objekt obrigkeitlichen Handelns* (Tübingen, 1992), 197–217.

29. Hartmut Harnisch, "Die Landgemeinde im ostelbischen Gebiet (mit Schwerpunkt Brandenburg)," in P. Blickle, ed., *Landgemeinde und Stadtgemeinde*, 309–32. Harnisch stresses, however, that the Prussian state strove to keep villages "capable of [administrative] function" (funktionsfähig). See also Otto Büsch, *Militärsystem und Sozialleben im alten Preußen, 1713–1807: Die Anfänge der sozialen Militarisierung der preußisch-deutschen Gesellschaft* (Berlin, 1962).

30. Robisheaux, *Rural Society,* 258.

instead, village institutions were tied far more closely to those of seigneurial domination *(Grundherrschaft)*. In sixteenth-century Württemberg, for example, the ducal administration proved unable to enforce its decrees without the help of village elites.[31] The power to elicit obedience could be secured only through villagers enlisted into state service.[32] In territories where local officeholders were appointed from above, the state itself provided peasants a route to power in the village. Where offices were elective, property qualifications or custom could transform them into the de facto patrimonies of wealthy families—although this, too, varied from region to region.[33] In their studies of southern German villages, for example, Renate Blickle and Peter Bierbrauer have found little evidence of oligarchy, at least in the sixteenth century.[34] A study of rebellion in the upper Swabian county of Hohenzollern, however, reveals that in one village, 29 persons filled 143 public offices assigned between 1579 and 1582, most of whom held large tenancies, for an average of 4.9 offices per oligarch.[35] If evidence from seventeenth- and eighteenth-century central Germany is any indication, oligarchic trends prevailed.[36] Finally, the development of "quasi-feudal" relations between tenant farmers and the swelling ranks of landless or land-poor laborers reinforced an oligarchic trend in peasant politics.[37] As a result, wealth, rank, and

31. R. W. Scribner, "Police and the Territorial State in Sixteenth-Century Württemberg," in E. I. Kouri and Tom Scott, eds., *Politics and Society in Reformation Europe* (London, 1987), 103–20; see also James Allen Vann, *The Making of a State: Württemberg, 1593–1793* (Ithaca, 1984), 58–88.

32. Wunder notes that the state often exerted its influence through "leading village representatives"; *Bäuerliche Gemeinde*, 95. For an instructive example of how difficult government could be in the face of passive peasant resistance, even in the eighteenth century, see David W. Sabean, *Power in the Blood: Popular Culture and Village Discourse in Early Modern Germany* (Cambridge, U.K., 1984), 144–73.

33. Rudolf Endres, "Ländliche Rechtsquellen als sozialgeschichtliche Quellen," in Peter Blickle, ed., *Deutsche Ländliche Rechtsquellen: Probleme und Wege der Weistumsforschung* (Stuttgart, 1977), 161–84.

34. Peter Bierbrauer, "Die ländliche Gemeinde im oberdeutsch-schweizerischen Raum," in P. Blickle, ed., *Landgemeinde und Stadtgemeinde*, 188; Renate Blickle, "Besitz und Amt: Bemerkungen zu einer Neuerscheinung über bäuerliche Führungsschichten," *ZBLG* 40 (1977): 277–90.

35. Eberhard Elbs, "Owingen 1584: Der erste Aufstand in der Grafschaft Hohenzollern," *Zeitschrift für hohenzollerische Geschichte* 17 (1981): 44–47.

36. Werner Troßbach, "Die ländliche Gemeinde im mittleren Deutschland (vornehmlich 16.–18. Jahrhundert)," in P. Blickle, ed., *Landgemeinde und Stadtgemeinde*, 263–88.

37. Wunder, *Bäuerliche Gemeinde*, 96; Mooser, "Gleichheit und Ungleichheit," 231–62.

power tended to concentrate in the hands of the village elites.[38] As a practical matter, it is likely that the intrusions of sovereigns and seigneurs *increased* their dependence on the cooperation of village elites; such, at least, was the case in Hohenlohe as well as Hauenstein.

These social and political transformations call into question the "communal" nature of peasant rebellion in early modern Germany and, by extension, in western Europe as a whole. With respect to Hauenstein, the implication is clear: in an institutional culture that both stressed the necessity of communal decision-making and furnished a wide variety of tactical options for pursuing the redress of grievance, social stratification and oligarchic trends among peasants combined with seigneurial intrusions on local autonomies to undermine communal solidarities, with peasant factionalism the result. As a defense of local autonomies in a sociopolitical environment of increasing inequity among peasants, therefore, the Salpeter Wars typified the rebellions of its age. But what about the bitter factional dissension that characterized the Salpeter Wars throughout their twenty-year course? The regional studies of Robisheaux and Hermann Rebel have exposed bitter social tensions beneath outward appearances of solidarity in seventeenth-century Hohenlohe and Upper Austria;[39] in eighteenth-century Württemberg, intravillage strife between tenant farmers and day laborers over access to common pastures generated a twenty-year lawsuit before the ducal administration.[40] But cases of socially charged legal bickering are one thing, rebellions characterized by factional dissension, such as the Salpeter Wars, quite another.

To find them does not require much digging. The strongest parallels arose, like the Salpeter Wars, in the heart of that zone of central Europe where "communal-cooperative" institutions were most fully developed—southwestern Germany, Switzerland, and the North Sea littoral. The introduction to this book already cited the parallel of the *Craichies,* a

---

38. See the essays in Günther Franz, ed., *Bauernschaft und Bauernstand, 1500–1970: Büdinger Vorträge, 1971–1972* (Limburg a.d. Lahn, 1975). For French comparisons, see Yves-Marie Bercé, *Revolts and Revolutions in Early Modern Europe: An Essay on the History of Political Violence* (New York, 1987), 70–72, 84–85.

39. Robisheaux, *Rural Society,* 175–98; Rebel, *Peasant Classes,* 199–29.

40. Wolfgang Kaschuba, "Kommunalismus als sozialer 'common sense': Zur Konzeption von Lebenswelt und Alltagskultur im neuzeitlichen Gemeindegedanken," in P. Blickle, ed., *Landgemeinde und Stadtgemeinde,* 72 (the community in question was Nehren, on the Swabian Alb).

dissenting faction that emerged during peasant rebellions in the Swiss episcopal canton of Basel, where village institutions were strong despite the continuation of seigneurial domination. But there were others as well. Between 1701 and 1708, for example, the Swiss forest canton of Schwyz was riven by factional conflict between the ruling oligarchy and a reform movement led by one Joseph Anton Stadler.[41] Roughly during the period of *müllerisch* ascendancy in Hauenstein, the Swiss canton of Zug split between competing "soft" *(Lind)* and "hard" *(Hart)* parties (1728–35), while in Appenzell the "Sutter Affair" divided the peasants into competing factions. Schwyz and Zug both heated up again in 1764–65, when a "hard" faction rebelled against the ruling "soft" families, who supported the reorganization of Swiss companies in French service.[42] But the closest parallel to the Salpeter Wars, however, were a series of conflicts in Toggenburg, part of the canton of St. Gallen. Although the Benedictine abbey of St. Gallen held sovereign rule over that canton, an assembly of enfranchised Toggenburgers elected a common governing council *(Landrat),* which ran the canton's internal affairs. In the early eighteenth century, however, the attempts of Abbot Leodegar Burgrisser to centralize his authority generated resentment among the Toggenburg peasantry, especially its Protestant members.[43] Tensions reached a crisis in 1707, when the assembly in effect overthrew the abbot and installed itself in his place. But frictions quickly developed between the moderate, mostly Catholic "soft" faction and the militant, Protestant peasants of the "hard" faction. When a number of "soft" villages restored ties to St. Gallen in 1711, the "hard" faction occupied them by force and banished members of the opposing group.[44] In time, factionalism escalated to violence; in 1734, elected

---

41. Ulrich Im Hof, "Ancien Régime," in *Handbuch der Schweizer Geschichte* (Zürich, 1975–77), 2:691. See also Pierre Felder, "Ansätze zu einer Typologie im schweizerischen Ancien Régime, 1712–1789," *SZG* 26 (1976): 324–89, and Rudolf Braun, *Das ausgehende Ancien Régime in der Schweiz: Abriß einer Sozial- und Wirtschaftsgeschichte des 18. Jahrhunderts* (Göttingen, 1984).

42. Felder, "Ansätze," 341–42; Im Hof, "Ancien Régime," 762–73; Dominik Schalter, "Geschichte der Linden und Harten in Schwyz," *Der Geschichtsfreund* 21 (1866): 345–96; 22 (1867): 162–208.

43. In 1704, the Toggenburg peasants elected magistrates that were unacceptable to Leodegar, with the result that many offices remained unoccupied; see Peter Blickle, "Bäuerliche Rebellionen im Fürststift St Gallen," in *Aufruhr und Empörung?* 252. On the complex institutional structure of Toggenburg, see his *Landschaften im alten Reich: Die staatliche Funktion des Gemeinen Mannes in Oberdeutschland* (Munich, 1973), 76–86.

44. Factional conflict eventually escalated into a civil war between coalitions of Protestant and Catholic cantons throughout Switzerland. In the resulting "War of the Twelve"

peasant magistrates of the "hard" faction persecuted "soft" peasants with a gruesome "lynch-justice."[45] Parallels to the *salpeterisch* terror of May 1745 could hardly be more obvious.

Similar conflicts along the North German coast suggest such feuding was not unusual. At the time of "Salpeter-Hans" Albiez's trip to Vienna, East Frisia was in the grips of the "War of the Resisters" (*Renitentenkrieg*, 1725–27), a classic confrontation between territorial Estates, led by the city of Emden, and a prince with absolutist pretensions; caught between these forces, the East Frisian peasantry split in two.[46] The institutional structure of East Frisia was such that elected peasant delegates represented their constituent villages in the territorial diet. In 1725, these delegates, and their villages with them, divided into roughly equal groups of "resisting" and "obedient" peasants. But as in Hauenstein, this nomenclature was misleading: though they sided with the prince against Emden, "obedient" peasants were not necessarily more compliant than their *müllerisch* contemporaries. Peasant militiamen fought on *both* sides in the pitched battle between the troops of the Estates and the prince on 2 February 1725; moreover, "obedient" peasants vigorously combated taxes imposed by the "resisting" Estates. And after "resisting" delegates were expelled from the diet in 1727, "obedient" representatives proved themselves to be lively defenders of the Estates' rights against their erstwhile ally, the prince.[47] To be sure, the "War of the Resisters" engulfed peasants in conflicts beyond their control. Still, forces of communal cohesion could not prevent the development of factional rifts.

Each of these factional struggles exposed the effects of social stratification and state intrusion in the countryside. In most of the Swiss examples, "partisan struggles" pitted the followers of oligarchic ruling families against the adherents of "communal democracy," consisting

---

(1712), the Protestant alliance prevailed and imposed a new treaty of confederation for Switzerland; P. Blickle, "Fürststift St Gallen," 253–55; Im Hof, "Ancien Régime," 694–700.

45. P. Blickle, "Fürststift St Gallen," 255.

46. Bernd Kappelhof, *Absolutistisches Regiment oder Ständeherrschaft? Landesherr und Landstände in Ostfriesland im ersten Drittel des 18. Jahrhunderts* (Hildesheim, 1982); Michael Hughes, *Law and Politics in Eighteenth-Century Germany* (Woodbridge, Suffolk, 1988).

47. The "resisting" Estates encountered so much difficulty keeping "obedient" peasants in line that in late 1726, 150 soldiers were dispatched to exact a thirty thousand gulden penalty from one hinterland district; Kappelhoff, *Absolutistisches Regiment*, 251–55, 325–26, 374–76.

typically of poor and middling peasants who resented the dominant families' monopoly over access to elective office.[48] Here, factional and social divisions overlapped. In East Frisia, factional divisions reflected divisions in the religious and social geography of the region: most "resisting" villages were highly stratified and Calvinist, while "obedient" peasants were Lutheran and more uniformly poor.[49] That said, the Frisian case differed from the Swiss in that the social glue of both factions was mainly kinship and clientage, not class.[50] Similarly in Toggenburg, factional divisions reflected confessional ones: "hard" Protestants were far less willing to accommodate the abbot than their "soft" Catholic fellows. But it would be misleading to leave it at that. Among the determinants of factional allegiance, political and tactical criteria sometimes outweighed those of religion, especially after 1711, when the willingness to negotiate with St. Gallen decided factional loyalties. Like the *salpeterisch* faction, "hard" Toggenburgers were distinguished primarily by their refusal to tolerate abbatial rule.[51]

It is probably mere coincidence that the majority of these instances of factional conflict emerged near the summit of that "broad mountain" of "communal-cooperative" peasant institutions. Elsewhere, a number of rebellions amounted to a defense of well-to-do peasants and their interests, both against interference from outside the peasant community and against the demands of the growing number of land-poor or landless peasants. David Sabean argues that such internal conflicts figured prominently among the causes of rebellion as early as the late fifteenth

---

48. The "democratic" movements were usually led by ambitious social climbers, such as Kaspar Jodok von Stockalper vom Thurm in Wallis (to 1678), Joseph Anton Stadler in Schwyz (to 1708), and Joseph Anton Sutter in Appenzell Innerrhoden (1760); Felder, "Ansätze," 341, 343. On peasant elites in Switzerland, see Albert Hauser, "Soziologische Struktur eidgenössischen Bauerntums," in Franz, ed., *Bauernschaft und Bauernstand*, 65–85.

49. See Jörg Engelbrecht, *Die reformierte Landgemeinde in Ostfriesland im 17. Jahrhundert* (Frankfurt, 1982).

50. Kappelhoff, *Absolutistisches Regiment*, 311–12, 320, 331–32; on the political structure of rural East Frisia see Egbert Koolmann, *Gemeinde und Amt: Untersuchungen zur Geschichte von gemeindlicher Selbstverwaltung und landesherrlicher Amtsverwaltung im südlichen Ostfriesland* (Aurich, 1969). On rural social structure see Friedrich Swart, *Zur friesischen Agrargeschichte* (Leipzig, 1910), 263–70, 307–23.

51. P. Blickle, "Fürststift St Gallen," 290. A similar overlay of confessional and political divisions appears to have characterized peasant politics in the Thurgau in the years before 1712; see Hans Bühler, *Der Thurgau im zweiten Villmerger Krieg und beim Vollzug des vierten Landfriedens* (Frauenfeld, 1968), 13–14.

and sixteenth centuries.[52] His sample has been criticized as too narrow; but Hermann Rebel's discovery of similar dynamics in the Habsburg Crown Lands throughout the late sixteenth century suggests that it was widespread well before the absolutist dismantling of village autonomies had reached its full extent.[53] Even amid the relative unanimity of 1525, tactical divisions emerged between competing peasant factions. In Upper Austria, Rebel writes,

> The 1525 uprising . . . took the form of quarrels among the peasants over what were the crucial issues . . . .The radical party among the peasants tended toward violent disruptions of meetings where they issued such public demands as a rollback in the price of oats . . . the abolition of labor services and of the lords' practice of using the peasant farms as feedlots for their own cattle [etc.] . . . .The moderate party, on the other hand, powerful and dominant in an alliance of rural parishes, contented itself with submitting grievances to the emperor, negotiating with imperial authorities at meetings in Innsbruck, and demanding political recognition and institutional status for the subject population as a whole.[54]

In the seventeenth century, this uneasy coalition fell apart. Archaeological evidence uncovered at one battle site of the "Upper Austrian Peasants' War" of 1626, for example, has revealed that a large proportion of peasant combatants were women, children, and old people. Abandoned by the "politically active" peasant leadership, resistance was carried on into the 1630s by "roving bands" of the poor and disenfranchised, preaching a "political program . . . of revolutionary suicide, religious hallucinations, and millennial faith in the return of the legendary Frederick Barbarossa."[55] In Hohenlohe, finally, a storm of protest against labor services during the 1590s reflected the effort of village elites to shore up their hold on status and property against a new burden that threatened to undo their dominance in village life.[56]

52. David W. Sabean, *Landsbesitz und Gesellschaft am Vorabend des Bauernkrieges: Eine Studie der sozialen Verhältnisse im südlichen Oberschwaben in den Jahren vor 1525* (Stuttgart, 1972).
53. Rebel, *Peasant Classes*, 3–10.
54. Ibid., 4–5.
55. Ibid., 9.
56. Robisheaux, *Rural Society*, 187–88.

On balance, then, social polarization and the intensification of state and seigneurial rule undermined solidarity among peasants, and if historians seek the causes of their disagreements, they typically find it in the social and institutional transformations I have been describing. But the evidence of this book adds that these changes had a cultural dimension with profound consequences for the construction of peasant beliefs and actions. In the domain of cultural history, scholars have disagreed over the power and progress of hegemony as it affects the texture of peasant culture. Proponents of the "acculturation thesis" insist that peasants were objects of an elite cultural domination that resulted in the destruction of an autonomous popular culture.[57] By a gradual and forcible indoctrination, peasants were "acculturated" to the norms and outlooks of elites. Opposed to this view are those who place equal emphasis on popular resistance in the process of cultural change,[58] and those who regard peasants and other subaltern groups either as active participants in cultural interactions or as the progenitors of cultural change in their own right. Peter Blickle, for example, has argued that no less a transformation than the Protestant Reformation had an autonomous source of origin in the long-term efforts of villagers to assert communal control over parish appointments.[59]

The evidence offered in Chapter 6 suggests that cultural exchange across social barriers was anything but passive. Rather than absorbing new elements of elite culture passively and without resistance, Hauenstein's rebels adapted them to their *own* purposes. Their appropriation of the imperial cult of the Virgin Mary, for example, may have appeared as a perfect instance of acculturation, but closer inspection shows that its subjective meanings contradicted the intent of royal propagandists at nearly every turn. If this was "acculturation," so be it; but it was not uni-

---

57. Robert Muchembled, *Culture populaire et culture des élites dans la France moderne* (Paris, 1978); Pierre Chaunu, *Le temps des Réformes: Histoire religieuse et système de civilisation* (Paris, 1975); Jean Delumeau, *La peur en occident* (Paris, 1978).

58. See, for example, Marc Forster, *The Counter-Reformation in the Villages: Religion and Reform in the Bishopric of Speyer, 1560–1720* (Ithaca, 1992).

59. Peter Blickle, *Gemeindereformation: Die Menschen des 16. Jahrhunderts auf dem Weg zum Heil* (Munich, 1985), and "Communal Reformation and Peasant Piety: The Peasant Reformation and Its Late Medieval Origins," *Central European History* 20 (1987): 216–28. See also the case studies in "Communal Reformation" and in P. Blickle, ed., *Zugänge zur bäuerlichen Reformation* (Zürich, 1987).

formly successful as a hegemonic device or as an instrument of reinforcing domination by cultural means. Moreover, if education and literacy were the principal vehicles of acculturation, as some have suggested, then I have found little evidence that they were very effective.[60] Indeed, this book would be unthinkable had not peasants on both sides of the factional divide written down their thoughts, often with the confidence that their words would be read and disseminated by other peasants. One rebel activist—Johannes Marder of Eschbach—even knew a smattering of Latin! Finally, the persistence of "naive monarchism" and the eighteenth-century revival in Hauenstein of ancient desires to "turn Swiss" suggest that in the realm of political culture, at least, the effect of hegemony was minimal.

But that is not the whole story. The Salpeter Wars suggest that "acculturation" was not uniform and had the potential to sow dissension *among* peasants. I have argued throughout this book that the cultural difference between factions was one of conflicting concepts of order, in which *müllerisch* leaders accepted elite definitions of social conflict in legalistic terms, while their opponents rejected them in favor of vaguer and more elastic notions of "ancient rights" that were informed by an essentially medieval, reciprocal conception of rule. In practice, this difference was expressed in conflicting attitudes toward the relationship of statute to "custom": because the *müllerisch* faction absorbed official definitions of right, they were prepared to accept the supremacy of statute when it clearly documented the emperor's will. *Salpeterisch* peasants could never bring themselves to do this; for them, custom was an indissoluble bond of mutual obligation between lord and subject. They therefore tended to interpret *any* violation of it as evidence of some unjust interference. In cultural terms, then, *müllerisch* leaders were "acculturated" to elite norms as they pertained to the definition of sociopolitical relationships. To that extent, the progress of acculturation destabilized the cultural bases of solidarity among peasants.

It should be noted, however, that this was not a uniform process. As Chapter 6 demonstrated, the number of *salpeterisch* grievances that pertained to specific terms of seigneurial or juridical domination *diminished*

---

60. See, for example, Karl Vocelka, "Public Opinion and the Phenomenon of *Sozialdisziplinierung* in the Habsburg Monarchy," in Charles Ingrao, ed., *State and Society in Early Modern Austria* (West Lafayette, Ind., 1994), 119–38.

over time, while the number of demands relating principally to factional politics increased. Similarly, as Chapter 3 showed, the popularity of each faction varied considerably over space and time, even as factional loyalties rigidified. Together, these variations suggest that the factionalization of peasant politics widened the gap between peasants "acculturated" to elite norms and those who were not. Still, it would be misleading to suggest that this trend indicated a fundamentally atavistic mentality on the part of *salpeterisch* peasants. Their notion of "custom" was creative; *salpeterisch* peasants derived new meanings of custom by "reading between the lines" of medieval charters and treaties. This fluidity gave their rhetoric of "ancient rights" its revolutionary potential: carried to their logical conclusions, *salpeterisch* assumptions about "ancient rights" contained the claim to freedom from aristocratic rule. In the mouths of fiery militants like "Gaudihans" Wasmer and Johannes Thoma-ab-Egg, their "backward-looking" rhetoric justified demands for a full-blown transformation of existing social and political conditions.[61]

This complex pattern of culturation transactions recommends a recasting of Winfried Schulze's argument about the "juridification" of social conflict.[62] On the whole, the tactics of *müllerisch* peasant magistrates avoided hostile confrontation in favor of litigation through regular channels of judicial appeal, and in this sense their behavior conformed with Schulze's description of "juridified" social action. The *salpeterisch* side, in contrast, adopted a more belligerent stance even though, as Chapter 2 showed, several of its policies (including the homage boycott of 1727–28) repeated tactics used in earlier, seventeenth-century conflicts between the Eight and St. Blasien. The point is that factional divisions overlapped with tactical choices, just as the degrees of acculturation appear to have done. Was the willingness of peasants to litigate symptomatic of acculturation? Were hierarchies of judicial appeal themselves hegemonic tools of acculturation? The balance of evidence presented here suggests that the answer to both questions is yes. It also suggests that expanded opportunities for litigating grievances could destabilize peasant solidarity just as acculturation might, generating a crisis of too many choices. Hermann

61. Compare Perez Zagorin, *Rebels and Rulers, 1550–1660* (Cambridge, U.K., 1982), 1:23.
62. Winfried Schulze, "Die veränderte Bedeutung sozialer Konflikte im 16. und 17. Jahrhundert," in Hans-Ulrich Wehler, ed., *Der Deutsche Bauernkrieg, 1524–1526* (Göttingen, 1976), 277–302.

Rebel's analysis of the behavior of peasant elites in Upper Austria also supports this view. There, he argues, peasants "were both pacified and reduced to individual action in courts," where they "learned to accept and act within the narrow bounds of . . . state politics."[63] As the preceding chapter suggested, the *salpeterisch* practice of appealing directly to Emperor Charles amounted to a rejection of "juridified" conflict as yet another means for seigneurs to despoil Hauenstein of its "ancient rights."

Conflict in the "juridified" mode, however, rarely meant forsaking more violent, demonstrative resistance methods—in the Black Forest or anywhere else. Even though Hauenstein's factions differed sharply in tactical style, *müllerisch* leaders were savvy enough to appreciate the diplomatic uses of a hotheaded domestic enemy. In their dealings with St. Blasien and the Austrian state, the very existence of an unruly opposition strengthened the bargaining position of *müllerisch* magistrates. On several occasions, their Cassandra-like warnings of renewed *salpeterisch* unrest yielded official acquiescence to *müllerisch* demands—not least among them the abolition of personal serfdom from Hauenstein. The upshot is clear: it would be misleading to characterize the acculturating effects of litigation as inevitably hegemonic in nature.[64] To be sure, litigation brought Hauenstein's upland rustics into direct and regular contact with well-educated scriveners, assessors, even imperial councillors. But as the fruits of *müllerisch* politicking showed, such contacts merely educated them in modes of self-defense more effective than violent confrontation alone.

Be that as it may, the larger point remains that "acculturation" added to the destabilizing consequences for peasant solidarity of social polarization and the intensification of rule. In view of the divisive conflicts they provoked, it is paradoxical that most historians emphasize the

---

63. Rebel, *Peasant Classes*, 6.

64. I allude here to Gerhard Oestreich's concept of "social discipline" *(Sozialdisziplinierung)* in early modern Europe, to the extent that it involved the introduction of certain disciplinary practices intended to create obedient subjects; see his "Structure of the Absolutist State," in his *Neostoicism and the Early Modern State* (Cambridge, U.K., 1982), 258–73. See also R. Po-Chia Hsia, *Social Discipline in the Reformation: Central Europe, 1500–1700* (London, 1989), though it is limited to "social discipline" in the spheres of religion and morality. This estimation of "juridification" agrees with Schulze's; see Winfried Schulze, "'Geben Aufruhr und Aufstand Anlaß zu neuen heilsamen Gesetzen': Beobachtungen über die Wirkungen bäuerlichen Widerstands in der Frühen Neuzeit," in Schulze, ed., *Aufstände, Revolten, Prozeße,* 280–81.

ongoing vitality of the community as the social and ideological basis of peasant revolt. As Tom Scott put it, "At first glance, [this] emphasis on the community . . . might seem incompatible with [the] widespread social and economic stratification of village life," which "ought to have impeded collective action."[65] The usual explanation of Scott's paradox, that internal village conflicts remained latent until the nineteenth century, when the social dislocations of capitalist integration finally dissolved political solidarity among peasants, simply begs the question of factional strife.[66] The evidence of this book suggests a different scenario, that political tensions had undermined communal solidarities ever since the late Middle Ages, when social differentiation began to erode the demographic dominance of midlevel peasants. To that extent, even the most "communal" of rebellions were exposed to the hazard of internal dissension and remained "communal" only if it could be repressed. Thus throughout the early modern era, peasant solidarity was a "compulsory collectivity" *(Zwangskollektiv)*.[67] Moreover, the Salpeter Wars suggest that communal institutions, too, were losing their power to impose solidarity much earlier than is usually imagined. The combined effect of social polarization from within and intensified rule from without were expressed in ways as various as their institutional context was diverse. But the impact was ubiquitous and tended to corrode solidarities historically based on a large and vital midlevel peasant class.

Did this mean that peasants ceased to think of themselves as political unities? Did their sense of community corrode at the same pace as their ability to enforce solidarity? The evidence of the Salpeter Wars suggests otherwise. Throughout this book, I have emphasized that peasants of both factions continued to identify themselves with "Whole County," its customs, institutions, and history. By the same token, I have argued that it is misleading to interpret peasant factions solely by a simple, sociopolitical arithmetic that equates the beliefs and actions of wealthy officeholders with the interests of sovereigns and seigneurs, and conversely, the beliefs and actions of the poor and disenfranchised with the "collective" interests of the whole. As Chapter 4 showed, there

65. T. Scott, "Peasant Revolts," 463.
66. Ibid.; Schulze, "Europäische und deutsche Bauernrevolten," 40–42.
67. Claudia Ulbrich, "Die Inzlinger Rebellion (1600–1613)," *Badische Heimat* 2 (1991): 287–96.

was no simple correlation between wealth, status, and faction; rather, the peasantry was divided vertically, between competing groups of similar social composition. Similarly, while the two peasant factions defined their county's proper relationship with external political forces in various and incompatible ways, neither group retreated from the overriding need to protect and preserve "ancient rights."

The upshot is that factional dissension was altogether *compatible* with the ongoing vitality of collective consciousness among peasants. To be sure, peasant solidarity was impossible in the absence of shared identity and common purpose; but the reverse does not hold. Indeed, the *salpeterisch* rhetoric of factional identity was so permeated with the language of betrayal, and *müllerisch* leaders so pained to show how their actions benefited the common good, that it is difficult to explain the intensity of factional antipathies in the *absence* of a strong, collective identity. The Salpeter Wars, then, are an ironic testament to the durability of a common sense of history and purpose that continued to define belief and action for factions whose very existence, in the long run, subverted peasant self-rule.

APPENDIX I

Lords and Officeholders in Eighteenth-Century Hauenstein

The Eight
(*Italics* = Speaker; **Bold** = *salpeterisch*)

Year	Name	Village of Residence	Canton
1704	Hans Baumgartner	Amrigschwand	Höchenschwand
	Hans Denz	Wolpadingen	Wolpadingen
1710	Peter Geng	Brunnadern	Höchenschwand
	Hans Denz	Wolpadingen	Wolpadingen
1714	Hans Ebner	Tiefenhäusern	Höchenschwand
	Hans Denz	Wolpadingen	Wolpadingen
1715	Adam Schmiedle	Waldkirch?	Dogern
	Hans Friedle Albiez	Buch?	Birndorf
	Peter Geng	Brunnadern	Höchenschwand
	Friedle Albiez	Wilfingen	Wolpadingen
	Conrad Schmidt	?	Görwihl
	Balthas Huber	Rickenbach?	Rickenbach
	Conrad Fricker	Luttingen?	Hochsal
	Hans Jacob Bächle	Murg?	Murg
1716[1]	Georg Fluem	Dietlingen	Dogern
	Joseph Tröndle	Unteralpfen	Birndorf
	Hans Jehle	Amrigschwand	Höchenschwand
	Hans Denz	Wolpadingen	Wolpadingen
	Hans Friedle Baumgartner	Rotzingen	Görwihl
	Andreas Ebner	Hottingen	Rickenbach

1. GLA 113:239, 262r–63v, [1716].

Year	Name	Village of Residence	Canton
1716, (cont.)	Michael Tröndle *Joseph Eckert*	Hochsal Hänner	Hochsal Murg
1717	Joseph Tröndle Hans Friedle Albiez *Peter Geng* Friedle Albiez Jacob Malzacker Friedle Hottinger Caspar Böhler Hans Gerteis	Dogern Buch Brunnadern Wilfingen Strittmatt Niedergebisbach Hochsal Bünzgen	Dogern Birndorf Höchenschwand Wolpadingen Görwihl Rickenbach Hochsal Murg
1718	Adam Schmiedle Hans Meyer Georg Baumgartner Joachim Böhler Michael Sibold *Balthas Huber* Joseph Tröndle Joseph Eckert	Waldkirch Ay Unterweschnegg Nedingen Schellenberg Rickenbach Rotzel Hänner	Dogern Birndorf Höchenschwand Wolpadingen Görwihl Rickenbach Hochsal Murg
1719	Georg Fluem Friedle Ebner *Peter Geng* Hans Denz Joseph Eckert Caspar Böhler Hans Jacob Bächle	Dietlingen Steinbach Brunnadern Wolpadingen Herrischried Hochsal Murg	Dogern Birndorf Höchenschwand Wolpadingen Görwihl Hochsal Murg
1720	Friedle Binkert Joseph Tröndle Hans Jehle Friedle Albiez Michael Sibold Hans Jacob Huber Joseph Tröndle *Joseph Eckert*	Dogern Unteralpfen Amrigschwand Wilfingen Schellenberg Atdorf Rotzel Hänner	Dogern Birndorf Höchenschwand Wolpadingen Görwihl Rickenbach Hochsal Murg

Year	Name	Village of Residence	Canton
1726	Joseph Tröndle	Dogern	Dogern
	Joseph Tröndle	Unteralpfen	Birndorf
	Hans Jehle	Amrigschwand	Höchenschwand
	Hans Denz	Wolpadingen	Wolpadingen
	Hans Jacob Scheuble	Schellenberg	Görwihl
	Andreas Thoma	Altenschwand	Rickenbach
	Joseph Tröndle	Rotzel	Hochsal
	Hans Jacob Döbele	Murg	Murg
1727	**Joseph Tröndle**	**Schmitzingen**	**Dogern**
	Hans Friedle Albiez	**Buch**	**Birndorf**
	Hans Jacob Sibold[2]	**Kuchelbach**	**Birndorf**
	Michael Schmiedle	**Kutterau**	**Höchenschwand**
	Lorenz Scheuble	**Fröhnd**	**Wolpadingen**
	Joseph Eckert	**Herrischried**	**Görwihl**
	Michael Hottinger	**Niedergebisbach**	**Rickenbach**
	Friedle Tröndle	Rotzel	Hochsal
	Joseph Jehle	**Hänner**	**Murg**
1728	**Martin Thoma**[3]	**Haselbach**	**Dogern**
	Hans Friedle Jehle	Weilheim	Dogern
	Joseph Tröndle	Unteralpfen	Birndorf
	Hans Ebner	Tiefenhäusern	Höchenschwand
	Benedict Jehle	Hierholz	Wolpadingen
	Friedle Baumgartner	Rotzingen	Görwihl
	Andreas Ebner	Hottingen	Rickenbach
	Joseph Tröndle	Rotzel	Hochsal
	Hans Gerteis	Bünzgen	Murg
1730[4]	Joseph Gerteis	Dogern	Dogern
	Friedle Ebner	Steinbach	Birndorf
	Peter Geng	Brunnadern	Höchenschwand
	Hans Denz	Wolpadingen	Wolpadingen

2. Sibold was elected to stand in for the imprisoned Hans Friedle Albiez of Buch.
3. According to Thoma's testimony of 16–20 September 1728, he was elected Octovir at an illegal election in Weilheim; GLA 113:232, 138r–81v; see also 60r–v and GLA 113:229, 180r–v, "Prothocollum informativum," 24 July 1728.
4. GLA 65:11634, Fallbarkeitsregister, 19 September 1730.

Year	Name	Village of Residence	Canton
1730, (cont.)	Adam Tröndle	Görwihl	Görwihl
	Andreas Thoma	Altenschwand	Rickenbach
	Caspar Ebner	Rotzel	Hochsal
	Hans Jacob Döbele	Murg	Murg
1733–34	Joseph Gerteis	Dogern	Dogern
	Joseph Tröndle	Unteralpfen	Birndorf
	Hans Jehle	Amrigschwand	Höchenschwand
	Benedict Jehle	Hierholz	Wolpadingen
	Friedle Baumgartner	Rotzingen	Görwihl
	Andreas Thoma	Altenschwand	Rickenbach
	Joseph Tröndle	Rotzel	Hochsal
	Joseph Jehle	Hänner	Murg
1737	Joseph Tröndle	Schmitzingen	Dogern
	Joseph Tröndle	Unteralpfen	Birndorf
	Hans Ebner	Tiefenhäusern	Höchenschwand
	Benedict Jehle	Hierholz	Wolpadingen
	Baptist Zimmermann	Hartschwand	Görwihl
	Andreas Thoma	Altenschwand	Rickenbach
	Joseph Tröndle	Rotzel	Hochsal
	Joseph Jehle	Hänner	Murg
1738[5]	**Jacob Hilpert**	**Bürgeln**	**Dogern**
	Friedle Ebner	Steinbach	Birndorf
	Michael Höffler	Oberweschnegg	Höchenschwand
	Hans Georg Albiez	**Ibach**	**Wolpadingen**
	Balthas Eckert	**Herrischried**	**Görwihl**
	Joseph Völkle	Atdorf	Rickenbach
	Joseph Gerteis	Bünzgen	Hochsal
	Conrad Fricker	**Luttingen**	**Murg**
1738–39[6]	Joseph Tröndle	Schmitzingen	Dogern
	Joseph Tröndle	Unteralpfen	Birndorf
	Hans Ebner	Tiefenhäusern	Höchenschwand
	Benedict Jehle	Hierholz	Wolpadingen

5. GLA 113:241, 319r–21v, 324r–26v, WVA to VÖRK, 25 April 1738.
6. GLA 113:251, 13r, 9 March 1739.

Year	Name	Village of Residence	Canton
1738–39 (cont.)	Heinrich Matt	Strittmatt	Görwihl
	Andreas Thoma	Altenschwand	Rickenbach
	Joseph Tröndle	*Rotzel*	*Hochsal*
	Joseph Jehle	Hänner	Murg
1742	Johannes Thoma	Haselbach	Dogern
	Joseph Tröndle	Unteralpfen	Birndorf
	Johannes Albiez	Amrigschwand	Höchenschwand
	Benedict Jehle	Hierholz	Wolpadingen
	Jacob Baumgartner	Rotzingen	Görwihl
	Andreas Thoma	Altenschwand	Rickenbach
	Joseph Tröndle	*Rotzel*	*Hochsal*
	Joseph Jehle	Hänner	Murg
1743	*Hans Jacob Bächle*	Birndorf	Birndorf
1744[7]	**Hans Georg Marder**	**Waldkirch**	**Dogern**
	Conrad Ebner	**Oberalpfen**	**Birndorf**
	Joseph Freudig	**Tiefenhäusern**	**Höchenschwand**
	Michael Denz	Wolpadingen	Wolpadingen
	Joseph Völkle	Atdorf	Rickenbach
	Caspar Mutter	**Rüßwihl**	**Görwihl**
	Joseph Tröndle	*Rotzel*	*Hochsal*
	Martin Fricker[8]	**Hochsal**	**Hochsal**
	Friedle Bäumle	**Murg**	**Murg**
1745	*Georg Ebner*	**Birndorf**	**Birndorf**
	Joseph Jehle	**Bierbronnen**	**Dogern**
	Michael Jehle	**Oberweschnegg**	**Höchenschwand**
	Martin Bär	**Hierholz**	**Wolpadingen**
	Hans Wasmer	**Segeten**	**Görwihl**
	Johannes Köpfler[9]	**Görwihl**	**Görwihl**

7. GLA 113:255, 97r–v, "Specification der vergangenen Georgi ausgezogener newer Einungsmäisteren," 29 April 1744, and 110r–110v, "Bericht von Fritz Gerteiß Vogten zu Rotzell," 10 August 1744.

8. Fricker assumed Joseph Tröndle's office when the latter fled into exile in Waldshut.

9. Köpfler was elected by *salpeterisch* peasants to replace Hans Wasmer of Segeten after the latter's arrest; GLA 113:260, 41r–42v, interrogation of Michael Albiez of Burg, 8 December 1745.

Year	Name	Village of Residence	Canton
1745 (cont.)	Friedle Baumgartner[10]	Rotzingen	Görwihl
	Johannes Thoma-ab-Egg	**Egg**	**Rickenbach**
	Johannes Schlachter[11]	**Hornberg**	**Rickenbach**
	Friedle Strittmatter	Luttingen	Hochsal
	Martin Fricker[12]	**Hochsal**	**Hochsal**
	Friedle Döbele	Murg	Murg
1746	Johannes Thoma	Haselbach	Dogern
	Johann Michel Tröndle[13]	Unteralpfen	Birndorf
	Johannes Albiez[14]	Amrigschwand	Höchenschwand
	Michael Denz	Wolpadingen	Wolpadingen
	Friedle Baumgartner[15]	Rotzingen	Görwihl
	Joseph Tröndle[16]	Rotzel	Hochsal
	Friedle Espach[17]	Grünholz	Hochsal
	Joseph Jehle	Hänner	Murg

"Sich nennend Reedmann und Einungs Meister"
[Those calling themselves Speakers and Octovirs][18]

Year	Name	Village of Residence	Canton
1746	Joseph Jehle	Bierbronnen	Dogern
	Georg Ebner	Birndorf	Birndorf
	Michael Jehle	Oberweschnegg	Höchenschwand
	Martin Bär	Hierholz	Wolpadingen
	Martin Fricker	Hochsal	Hochsal
	Friedle Döbele	**Murg**	**Murg**
1751	Johannes Thoma	Haselbach	Dogern
	Johann Michel Tröndle	Unteralpfen	Birndorf

10. *Müllerisch* peasants in Görwihl canton chose Baumgartner to replace the imprisoned Hans Wasmer of Segeten; GLA 113:260, 92r–93v, WVA to VÖRK, 15 December 1745.

11. Schlachter acted as Octovir in the place of Johannes Thoma-ab-Egg, after Thoma-ab-Egg was arrested and imprisoned.

12. According to the testimony of Hans Georg Marder on 11 May 1746, *müllerisch* Friedle Strittmatter was elected on St. George's Day, but did not appear at Görwihl to be sworn into office, whereupon the *salpeterisch* Martin Fricker was promptly elected and invested.

13. Johann Michel was the son of Joseph Tröndle of Unteralpfen.

14. Albiez filled out the remainder of Joseph Tröndle of Rotzel's term as Speaker from September 1747 to March 1748.

15. Baumgartner was elected Speaker at the rigged 1748 "elections."

16. The aged Speaker Joseph Tröndle died during the 1747 electoral term, on 13 September.

17. Espach filled out the term of Joseph Tröndle's term as Octovir of Hochsal Canton.

18. GLA 113:266.

Year	Name	Village of Residence	Canton
1751 (cont.)	Johannes Albiez	Amrigschwand	Höchenschwand
	Michael Denz	Wolpadingen	Wolpadingen
	Friedle Baumgartner	Rotzingen	Görwihl
	Joseph Völkle	Atdorf	Rickenbach
	Friedle Espach	Grünholz	Hochsal
	Joseph Jehle	Hänner	Murg

"Einungsmeister der Unruhigen"

Year	Name	Village of Residence	Canton
1751	**Hans Georg Marder**	**Waldkirch**	**Dogern**
	Georg Ebner	**Birndorf**	**Birndorf**
	Conrad Ebner	**Oberalpfen**	**Birndorf**
	Martin Bär	**Hierholz**	**Wolpadingen**
	Johannes Schlachter	**Hornberg**	**Rickenbach**
	Martin Fricker	**Hochsal**	**Hochsal**
	Friedle Döbele	**Murg**	**Murg**
1768[19]	Johannes Thoma	Haselbach	Dogern
	Johann Michel Tröndle	Unteralpfen	Birndorf
	Johannes Albiez	Amrigschwand	Höchenschwand
	Michael Denz	Wolpadingen	Wolpadingen
	Johannes Sibold	Herrischwand	Görwihl
	Andreas Thoma	Altenschwand	Rickenbach
	Joseph Strittmatter	Schachen	Hochsal
	Joseph Eckert	Hänner	Murg

Abbots of St. Blasien[20]

Augustin Fink	1695–1720
Blasius III Bender	1720–1727
Franz II Schächtelin	1727–1747
Cölestin Vogler	1747–1749
Meinrad Troger	1749–1764
Martin II Gerbert	1764–1793
Mauritius Ribbele	1793–1801

19. Franz Quarthal and Georg Wieland, *Die Behördenorganisation Vorderösterreichs von 1753 bis 1805* (Bühl, 1977), 308–13.

20. *Das Tausendjährige St Blasien: 200jähriges Domjubiläum,* ed. Christa Römer and Ernst Petrasch, 2v (Karlsruhe, 1983), 1:375–79.

Abbesses of St Fridolin[21]

Maria Regina von Ostein	1693–1718
Maria Barbara von Liebenfels	1718–1730
Maria Magdalena von Hallwyl	1730–1734
Maria Josepha Regina von Liebenfels	1734–1753
Helena von Roggenbach	1753–1755
Anna Maria von Hornstein-Göffingen	1755–1781

Forest Stewards[22]

Georg Reinhard von Kageneck	1693–1714
Franz Leopold Beck von Willmendingen	1715–1728
Franz Anton von Schönau-Wehr	1729–1748
[Vacant]	1748–1752
Franz Anton Fidel von Schönau-Wehr	1752
[Vacant]	1752–1760
Joseph Xavier Tröndle von Greiffenegg	1760–1765
Joseph Freiherr von Landsee	1766–1782
Franz Edler von Spaun	1783–1788

Habsburg Dynasts

Leopold I	1690–1705
Joseph I	1705–1711
Charles VI	1711–1740
Maria Theresa	1740–1780
Joseph II	1780–1790

21. Otto Bally, "Das Damenstift Säckingen," *Vom Jura zum Schwarzwald* 1 (1884): 119–47, 161–67.

22. Günther Haselier, *Geschichte des Hotzenwalds* (Lahr, 1973); Quarthal and Wieland, *Behördenorganisation*.

APPENDIX 2

St Blasien's Annual Revenues from the Forest Bureau (ca. 1716)

Source of income	Gulden	%
1. **Revenues deriving from juridical authority:**		
Court fees	119	1.49
Licenses	42	0.53
Other	10	0.12
Subtotal:	171	2.14
2. **Seigneurial incomes:**		
Rents	1160	14.51
Corvées	260	3.25
Subtotal:	1420	17.76
3. **Revenues from parish patrimony:**		
Tithes	1990	24.90
Blood tithes	269	3.37
Straw tithes	32	0.40
Other	45	0.56
Subtotal:	2336	29.23
4. **Revenues from serfdom:**		
Mainmorte	658	8.23
Manumissions	231	2.89
Shrove chickens	66	0.83
Subtotal:	955	11.95
5. **Other sources of revenue:**		
Interest on loaned capital of 53,010 gulden	2600	32.53
Miscellaneous	511	6.39
Subtotal:	3111	38.92
Total:	7993	100.00

Source: GLA 79:2875, "Jährlich-ohngefährlicher Ertrag des Gotteshauß St Blasien . . . in dem Oesterreichischen," ca. 1716.

APPENDIX 3

Rebel Delegations and Pilgrimages

Year	Destination(s)	Description
1704	Einsiedeln, Vienna	A deputation led by **Adam Tröndle** of Unteralpfen proceeds to Vienna via the Marian shrine at Einsiedeln in Switzerland. In Vienna, Tröndle seeks and wins an audience with the empress. An audience with Emperor Leopold I follows on 11 March. The deputation members also pledge to send "women, widows, and orphans" to Marian shrines in Einsiedeln, Todtmoos, and Triberg, and to request that "His Majesty the Emperor, Her Majesty the Empress, King Joseph, and King Charles should receive all that they demand *(verlangen)* of all-merciful God . . . and that we need not be[come] serfs of the prelate [of St. Blasien]."
1726	Vienna	In May, **Hans Friedle Albiez** travels with two compatriots from the lordship of Schönau and Todtnau to Vienna, where he obtains an audience with Emperor Charles VI on 1 August. After several orders to return home, Albiez departs for Hauenstein in September.
1727	Vienna	**Conrad Binkert**, **Bläsi Hottinger**, **Adam Schmiedle**, and **Michel Baumgartner** travel to Vienna equipped with a signed petition list bestowing plenipotentiary powers of representation on his delegation. Binkert claims later to have enjoyed a fifteen-minute audience with Emperor Charles. The delegates return in the spring.

Year	Destination(s)	Description
1728	Einsiedeln, [Vienna]	In May, **Martin Thoma** of Haselbach launches an abortive mission to Vienna, via the Marian shrine at Einsiedeln. In Einsiedeln, Thoma is joined by **Johannes Thoma-ab-Egg**, **Michel Tröndle**, and **Hans Friedle Gerspach**, but the delegation does not proceed to its intended destination.
1728	Vienna	During the summer months, **Martin Thoma** of Haselbach, **Johannes Marder**, **Johannes Thoma-ab-Egg**, **Michel Tröndle**, **Hans Friedle Gerspach**, **Georg Baumgartner** of Rotzingen, and **Johannes Albiez** of Kiesenbach travel to Vienna via Schaffhausen, Lindau, and the Danube by boat; Baumgartner returns early. Once in Vienna, the delegates gain the intercession of Prince Eugene of Savoy; but the deputation is arrested and returned to Freiburg. While in prison, Marder pledges to make pilgrimages to Tusenbach in Alsace, Rome, Einsiedeln, and Tiengen; Marder also pledges to offer a holy mass at Einsiedeln.
1729	Vienna	In the late spring, **Georg Thoma** of Hartschwand departs on a mission to Vienna with the aim of gaining the release of his brother, Martin Thoma of Haselbach, from prison in Freiburg. Thoma receives assurances from "a lord in Vienna" that his brother will be freed and returns to Hauenstein. Once home, Thoma discovers that he has been deceived and flees to Switzerland to escape arrest.
1730	Bludenz [Vienna]	In February, an attempt to dispatch a petition via third parties in Bludenz (Vorarlberg) fails; the project entails the dispatch of **Joseph Meyer** of Au to Bludenz.
1730	Einsiedeln [Vienna]	In May, an abortive mission to Vienna proceeds first to Maria Einsiedeln in the company of "a hundred virgins with crowns," there to pray on the emperor's behalf and for the release of Hauensteiners imprisoned in Vienna and Freiburg.

Year	Destination(s)	Description
1730	Maria Stein Einsiedeln Tusenbach Wetzlar	**Michel Tröndle** of Bergalingen and **Hans Friedle Gerspach** travel secretly to the Imperial Chamber Court in Wetzlar. The mission is preceded by several pilgrimages, first to Maria Stein near Basel, second, to Maria Einsiedeln, and third, to Tusenbach in Alsace.
1731–32	Vienna, Laxenburg	In the summer of 1731, **Joseph Meyer** of Au and **Johannes Thoma-ab-Egg** travel via Vienna to the Imperial residence at Laxenburg, where they achieve two encounters with Emperor Charles; Thoma and Meyer are arrested and kept in the Vienna *Rumorhaus*.
1737	Vienna, Laxenburg Lanzendorf Maria Loreto Eisenstadt	**Michel Tröndle** of Bergalingen, **Hans Friedle Gerspach**, **Joseph Eckert** of Herrischried, **Michel Schmidt** of Hierbach, **Bläsi Hottinger**, **Verena Zimmermann**, and **Joseph Meyer** of Au depart on 15 April 1737 for Vienna and Laxenburg; after reaching Vienna, the group went on pilgrimage to Loreto and Eisenstadt in Hungary. Gerspach and Tröndle claim to have received audiences with the emperor and the prince of Lorraine.
1738	Einsiedeln Vienna, Laxenburg	In the spring, **Michel Tröndle** of Bergalingen, **Leonzi Brutschi**, **Joseph Eckert**, **Hans Friedle Gerspach** and sixteen others depart for Vienna and Laxenburg. The mission is inaugurated by a pilgrimage to Einsiedeln in the company of a hundred virgins and twenty to thirty young males, where they pray for the emperor's military success against the Turk. In Vienna, the group seeks help from Chancellor von Sinzendorff, but to no avail. In May, the delegates approach Emperor Charles at Laxenburg, who orders their return to Hauenstein.
1738	Einsiedeln Maria Zell Hochau	In late August a group of perhaps five hundred Hauensteiners (by one account), including one hundred virgins, departs for Vienna led by **Johannes Thoma-ab-Egg**. The mission is

Year	Destination(s)	Description
1738 *(cont.)*		inaugurated with a pilgrimage to Einsiedeln. Though the majority return from Einsiedeln, a core group continues via Linz, Styria, and Maria Zell to Hochau, where they approach Emperor Charles "on the hunt"; the delegates also seek the intercession of the Imperial Confessor Veit Georg Tönnemann, who gives them money for the return trip to Hauenstein.
1739	Vienna	**Leonzi Brutschi** departs after Ash Wednesday for Vienna, in order to achieve the release of deputation members there. In Vienna, Brutschi seeks the intercession of Imperial Confessor Veit Georg Tönnemann, but is arrested nonetheless.
1745	Frankfurt	**Bläsi Hottinger** of Niedergebisbach and **Martin Mutter** of Rüßwihl travel to the coronation of Emperor Francis Stephen in Frankfurt, in an attempt to petition them on behalf of Hauenstein. They remain in Frankfurt from October 3 to 16.

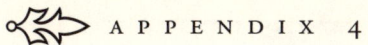 APPENDIX 4

A Synopsis of Rebel Grievances, 1726–1743

V = Grievance or demand presented to the imperial court in Vienna
F/I = Grievance or demand presented to the provincial governments in Freiburg and Innsbruck

Grievances	1726	1727	1729	1737	1738	1739	1743
Against serfdom:							
Abolition of patrilineal serfdom	F/I						
Reduction of monetized servile dues	F/I						
Abolition of servile homage oaths	V	V					
Abolition of servile manumission formulas	F/I						
Abolition of the 1738 Manumission Treaty						F/I	V
Against abbatial justice:							
Reduction of abbatial court subpoenas	F/I						
Restoration of the "Weinkauf"	F/I						
Restoration of partible inheritance	F/I						
Abolition of the 1720 Dogern Accord	F/I	V					
Against the Eight:							
Restoration of free Octovir elections						V	F/I
Relief from venality of *müllerisch* Octovirs					F/I	V	F/I
Satisfaction for *müllerisch* slanders						V	F/I
Release of *salpterisch* prisoners					V	V	
Restitution of confiscated *salpeterisch* property				F/I		V	

247

Grievances	1726	1727	1729	1737	1738	1739	1743
General Demands:							
Abolition of serfdom				V	F/I		
Abolition of abbatial jurisdiction						V	
Restoration of imperial privileges	F/I	F/I	F/I		F/I	F/I	F/I
Establishment of a nonpartisan imperial investigation				V			
Release from abbatial tyranny					F/I	F/I	
Personal intervention of the emperor					F/I		
Other Demands:							
Abolition of the "Waldordnung"					F/I	V	
Reduction of immigration restrictions						V	

Select Bibliography

Archives

Generallandesarchiv Karlsruhe (GLA)
11 St Blasien
16 Säckingen
21 Vereinigte Breisgauer Archive
61 Protokolle
62 Rechnungen
65 Handschriften
66 Beraine
67 Kopialbücher
79 Akten Breisgau Generalia
97 Akten Säckingen Stift, Stadt und Amt
99 Akten St Blasien
113 Akten Hauenstein
187 Akten Waldshut Amt
227 Akten Waldshut Stadt
229 Specialakten der kleineren Ämter und Städte und der Landgemeinden

Stiftsarchiv St Peter im Lavantal
Kloster St Blasien Handschriften (on microfilm in GLA)

Erzbischöfliches Archiv Freiburg im Breisgau (EAF)
Bistum Konstanz Handschriften: Ha 78 Acta visitationum
Bistum Konstanz Specialia: Pfarreien

Stadtarchiv Freiburg im Breisgau (StAFB)
C1 Landstände

Stadtarchiv Waldshut-Tiengen (StAWT)
Ratsprotokolle

Gemeindearchiv Dogern am Rhein (GAD)
Gemeindebuch
Urkunden

Published Sources

Bader, Josef, ed. "Das ehemalige sankt-blasische Waldamt." *ZGO* 6 (1855): 96–125.
———, ed. "Das ehemals sanktblasische Amt Gutenburg." *ZGO* 3 (1852): 355–84.
———, ed. "Josef Tröndlin: 'Grundlicher Bericht von dem in der Gravschaft Hauenstein entstandenen Unruhenhandel von 1720 bis 1730." In Josef Bader, *Briefe über dem badischen Oberland*. Freiburg, 1833.

———, ed. "Nachträge zu den Mittheilungen über die Grafschaft Hauenstein." *ZGO* 12 (1861): 101–27.
———, ed. "Das Stift St Blasien und seine hauensteinischen Unterthanen." *ZGO* 7 (1856): 99–127.
———, ed. "Urkunden und Regeste aus dem Archive der ehemaligen Grafschaft Hauenstein." *ZGO* 10 (1859): 353–84; 11 (1860): 465–90.
———, ed. "Urkundenregeste über die ehemaligen sankt-blasischen Niedergerichte." *ZGO* 7 (1856): 228–56, 328–50.
"Beschreibung der Österreichischen Vorlande (ca. 1780)." In F. Metz, ed., *Vorderösterreich*.
Ebner, Jakob, ed. "Bericht des Redmanns Josef Tröndle von Rotzel über einen Besuch in St Blasien am 24. und 25. Juni 1732." *Badische Heimat* 19 (1932): 188–91.
Lugo, Alphons Johann. "Statistik der k.k. Vorlande (30 May 1797)." In F. Metz, ed., *Vorderösterreich*. Scheffel, Joseph Viktor. "Aus dem Hauensteiner Schwarzwald (1853)." In *J. V. von Scheffels Gesammelte Werke*, ed. Johannes Proelß, vol. 3. Stuttgart: A. Bonz, 1907.
"Stiftungsbuch von S. Blasien, vom Abte Caspar I. von 1323 bis 1571." In Franz J. Mone, ed., *Quellensammlung der badischen Landesgeschichte*, vol. 2. Karlsruhe: Macklot, 1854.

Books and Articles

Abel, Wilhelm. *Agrarkrisen und Agrarkonjunkturen: Eine Geschichte der Land- und Ernährungswirtschaft Mitteleuropas seit dem hohen Mittelalter*. 3d ed. Hamburg: Parey 1978.
———. *Geschichte der deutschen Landwirtschaft von frühen Mittelalter bis zum 19. Jahrhundert*. 3d ed. Stuttgart: Fischer, 1978.
———. *Massenarmut und Hungerkrisen im vorindustriellen Europa: Versuch einer Synopsis*. Hamburg: Parey, 1974.
———. "Schichten und Zonen europäischer Agrarverfassung." *ZAA* 3 (1955): 1–19.
Anderson, Benedict. *Imagined Communities: Reflections on the Origin and Spread of Nationalism*. London: Verso, 1983.
Arnold, Klaus. "Freiheit im Mittelalter." *HJ* 104 (1984): 1–21.
Bader, Josef. "Die ehemalige Grafschaft Hauenstein und ihre Bewohner." *Badenia* 1 (1839): 19–30.
———. "Geschichte des Gotteshauses St Blasien." *Badenia* 1 (1839): 171–91.
———. *Über die Unruhen im Hauensteinischen*. Freiburg: Wagner, 1833.
Bader, Karl S. *Der deutsche Südwesten in seiner territorialstaatlichen Entwicklung*. Stuttgart: Koehler, 1950.

———. "Dorf und Dorfgemeinde im Zeitalter von Naturrecht und Aufklärung." In Wilhelm Wegener, ed., *FS Karl Gottfried Hugelmann*, vol. 1. Aalen: Scientia, 1959.
———. *Dorfgenossenschaft und Dorfgemeinde: Studien zur Rechtsgeschichte des mittelalterlichen Dorfes*. 2 vols. Cologne: Böhlau, 1957–62.
———. "Grundlagen dörflichen Verfassungslebens im südwestdeutschen Raum." In Wolfgang Müller, ed., *Landschaft und Verfassung: Beiträge zur ländlichen Verfassungsgeschichte im deutschsprachigen Südwesten*. Bühl: Konkordia, 1969.
———. "Zur Tal-, Dorf- und Stadtverfassung des Schwarzwaldes." In Ekkehard Liehl and Dieter Sieck, eds., *Der Schwarzwald: Beiträge zur Landeskunde*. Bühl: Konkordia, 1980.
Bercé, Yves-Marie. *Croquants et nu-pieds: Les soulèvements paysans en France du XVIe au XIXe siècle*. Paris: Gallimard/Julliard, 1974.
———. *Fête et révolte: Des mentalités populaires du XVIe au XVIIIe siècle: Essai*. Paris: Hachette, 1976.
———. *Revolt and Revolution in Early Modern Europe: An Essay on the History of Political Violence*. Trans. Joseph Bergin. New York: St Martin's, 1987.
Bérenger, Jean. *Finances et absolutisme autrichien dans la seconde moitié du XVIIème siècle*. 2 vols. Lille: Atelier reproduction des thèses, Université Lille III, 1975.
Berkner, Lutz. "Inheritance, Land Tenure and Peasant Family Structure: A German Regional Comparison." In Goody et al., eds., *Family and Inheritance..*
Bierbrauer, Peter. "Bäuerliche Revolten im Alten Reich: Ein Forschungsbericht." In P. Blickle, ed., *Aufruhr und Empörung?*
———. "Das Göttliche Recht und die naturrechtliche Tradition." In Peter Blickle, ed., *Bauer, Reich, und Reformation: FS Günther Franz*. Stuttgart: Ulmer, 1982.
———. "Die ländliche Gemeinde im oberdeutsch-schweizerischen Raum." In P. Blickle, ed., *Landgemeinde und Stadtgemeinde*.
———. "Die oberländer Landschaften im Staate Bern." *Berner Zeitschrift für Geschichte und Heimatkunde* 44 (1982): 145–62.
Birtsch, Günter, ed. *Grund- und Freiheitsrechte von der ständischen zur spätbürgerlichen Gesellschaft*. Göttingen: Vandenhoeck & Ruprecht, 1987.
Blaschke, Karlheinz, "Dorfgemeinde und Stadtgemeinde in Sachsen zwischen 1300–1800." In P. Blickle, ed., *Landgemeinde und Stadtgemeinde*.
———. "Soziale Gliederung und Entwicklung der sächsischen Landbevölkerung im 16. bis 18. Jahrhundert." *ZAA* 4 (1956).
Blickle, Peter. "Auf dem Weg zu einem Modell der bäuerlichen Rebellion—Zusammenfassung." In P. Blickle, ed., *Aufruhr und Empörung?*
———. "Bäuerliche Rebellionen im Fürststift St Gallen." In P. Blickle, ed., *Aufruhr und Empörung?*
———. "Bauern und Reformation: Positionsbestimmungen." In Peter Blickle, ed., *Zugänge zur bäuerlichen Reformation*, vol. 1, *Bauer und Reformation*. Zurich: Chronos, 1987.

———. "The Criminalization of Peasant Resistance in the Holy Roman Empire: Toward a History of the Emergence of High Treason in Germany." *JMH* 58 Suppl. (1986): S88–S97.

———. *Deutsche Untertanen: Ein Widerspruch.* Munich: Beck, 1981.

———. *Gemeindereformation: Die Menschen des 16. Jahrhunderts auf dem Weg zum Heil.* Munich: Oldenbourg, 1987.

———. "Kommunalismus: Begriffsbildung in heuristischer Absicht." In P. Blickle, ed., *Landgemeinde und Stadtgemeinde..*

———. "Kommunalismus, Parlamentarismus, Republikanismus." In P. Blickle, *Studien.*

———. *Landschaften im alten Reich: Die staatliche Funktion des Gemeinen Mannes in Oberdeutschland.* Munich: Beck, 1973.

———. "Leibherrschaft als Instrument der Territorialpolitik im Allgäu." In Haushofer and Boelcke, eds., *Neue Wege und Forschungen.*

———. "Die politische Entmündung des Bauern: Kritik und Revision einer These." In P. Blickle, ed., *Revolte und Revolutionen in Europa.*

———. *The Revolution of 1525: The German Peasants' War from a New Perspective.* Trans. Thomas A. Brady Jr. and H. C. Erik Midelfort. Baltimore: Johns Hopkins University Press, 1981.

———. "Die staatliche Funktion der Gemeinde—die politische Funktion der Bauern: Bemerkungen aufgrund von oberdeutschen ländlichen Rechtsquellen." In P. Blickle, ed., *Deutsche Ländliche Rechtsquellen.*

———. *Studien zur geschichtlichen Bedeutung des deutschen Bauernstandes.* Stuttgart: Fischer, 1989.

———. *Unruhen in der ständischen Gesellschaft, 1300–1800.* Munich: Oldenbourg, 1988.

———. "Von der Leibeigenschaft in die Freiheit: Ein Beitrag zu den realhistorischen Grundlagen der Freiheits- und Menschenrechte in Mitteleuropa." In P. Blickle, *Studien.*

———, ed. *Aufruhr und Empörung? Studien zum bäuerlichen Widerstand im Alten Reich.* Munich: Beck, 1980.

———, ed. *Deutsche Ländliche Rechtsquellen: Probleme und Wege der Weistumsforschung.* Stuttgart: Klett-Cotta, 1977.

———, ed. *Landgemeinde und Stadtgemeinde in Mitteleuropa: Ein struktureller Vergleich.* Munich: Oldenbourg, 1991.

———, ed. *Revolte und Revolutionen in Europa: Referate und Protokole des internationalen Symposiums zur Erinnerung an den Bauernkrieg 1525.* Munich: Oldenbourg, 1975.

Blickle, Renate. "Agrarische Konflikte und Eigentumsordnung in Altbayern, 1400–1800." In Schulze, ed., *Aufstände, Revolten, Prozeße.*

———. "Hausnotdurft: Ein Fundamentalrecht in der altständischen Ordnung Bayerns." In Birtsch, ed., *Grund- und Freiheitsrechte.*

———. "Leibeigenschaft und Eigentum: Vom Zusammenhang der Erscheinungen in Verfassung und Geschichte des 'Eigens' oder der Hofmark Steigaden." In Sigfrid Hofman, ed., *Steingadener Chronik*, vol. 3. Steingaden: Verlag der Gemeinde Steingaden, 1987.

———. "Nahrung und Eigentum als Kategorien in der ständischen Gesellschaft." In Winfried Schulze, ed., *Ständische Gesellschaft und soziale Mobilität*. Munich: Oldenbourg, 1988.

———. "'Spenn und Irrung' im 'Eigen' Rottenbuch." In P. Blickle, ed., *Aufruhr und Empörung?*

———. "Die Tradition des Widerstandes im Ammergau: Anmerkungen zum Verhältnis von Konflikt- und Revolutionsbereitschaft." *ZAA* 35 (1988): 73–93.

Bloch, Marc. *French Rural History: An Essay on Its Basic Characteristics*. Trans. Janet Sondheimer. Berkeley: University of California Press, 1966.

Blum, Jerome. *The End of the Old Order in Rural Europe*. Princeton: Princeton University Press, 1978.

———. "The European Village as Community: Origins and Functions." *Agricultural History* 45 (1971): 157–78.

———. "The Internal Structure and Polity of the European Village Community from the Fifteenth to the Nineteenth Century." *JMH* 43 (1971): 541–76.

Bobinska, Celina. "Les mouvements paysans en Pologne aux XVIIIe et XIXe siècles: Problèmes et methodes." *Acta Poloniae Historica* 22 (1970): 136–57.

Boelcke, Willi A. "Neuerungen in der Wirtschaft am Oberrhein während des 18. Jahrhunderts." In Volker Press et al., ed., *Barock am Oberrhein*. Karlsruhe: Braun, 1985.

———. "Wandlungen der dörflichen Sozialstruktur während Mittelalter und Neuzeit." In Haushofer and Boelcke, eds., *Neue Wege und Forschungen*.

Bourdieu, Pierre. *Distinction: A Social Critique of the Judgment of Taste*. Trans. Richard Nice. Cambridge: Harvard University Press, 1984.

———. *Outline of a Theory of Practice*. Trans. Richard Nice. Cambridge: Cambridge University Press, 1977.

Brady, Thomas A., Jr. *Turning Swiss: Cities and Empire, 1450–1550*. Cambridge: Cambridge University Press, 1985.

Braubach, Max. *Prinz Eugen von Savoyen*. 5 vols. Munich: Oldenbourg, 1963–65.

Burke, Peter. *Popular Culture in Early Modern Europe*. New York: Harper, 1978.

Burmeister, Karl-Heinz. "Genossenschaftliche Rechtsfindung und herrschaftliche Rechtssetzung: Auf dem Weg zum Territorialstaat." In P. Blickle, ed., *Revolte und Revolutionen in Europa*.

Buszello, Horst. "Gemeinde, Territorium, und Reich in den politischen Programmen des deutschen Bauernkriegs, 1525/26." In Wehler, ed., *Der Deutsche Bauernkrieg 1524–1526*.

Cohen, Anthony P. "Of Symbols and Boundaries, or, Does Ertie's Greatcoat Hold the Key?" In Anthony P. Cohen, ed., *Symbolising Boundaries: Identity and Diversity in British Cultures*. Manchester: Manchester University Press, 1986.

———. *The Symbolic Construction of Community*. Chichester: Ellis Horwood, 1985.

Cohen, Anthony P., and John L. Comaroff. "The Management of Meaning: On the Phenomenology of Political Transactions. In Bruce Kapferer, ed., *Transaction and Meaning: Directions in the Anthropology of Exchange and Symbolic Behavior*. Philadelphia: Institute for the Study of Human Issues, 1976.

Dickson, P. G. M. *Finance and Government under Maria Theresia, 1740–1780*. 2 vols. Oxford: Clarendon Press, 1987.

Dreyfus, François G. "Beitrag zu den Preisbewegungen im Oberrheingebiet im 18. Jahrhundert." *VSWG* 47 (1960): 245–56.

Dülmen, Richard van. "Bäuerlicher Protest und patriotische Bewegung: Der Volksaufstand in Bayern von 1705/06." *ZBLG* 45 (1982): 331–61.

———. "Formierung der europäischen Gesellschaft in der frühen Neuzeit: Ein Versuch." *GG* 7 (1981): 5–41.

Eagleton, Terry. *Ideology: An Introduction*. London: Verso, 1991.

Ebner, Jakob. *Aus der Geschichte der Ortschaften der Pfarrei Birndorf*. Karlsruhe: Wetzel, 1938.

———. *Aus der Geschichte des Hauensteiner Dorfes Unteralpfen*. Karlsruhe: Wetzel, 1925.

———. *Aus der Geschichte von Görwihl und des Görwihler Berges*. 1952.

———. *Eine Müllerdynastie im Schwarzwald*. Radolfzell, 1908.

———. *Geschichte der Ortschaften der Pfarrei Hochsal*. [Unteralpfen], 1958.

———. *Geschichte der Ortschaften der Pfarrei Niederwihl im Hotzenwald*. [Unteralpfen, 1955].

———. *Geschichte der Ortschaften der Pfarrei Waldkirch bei Waldshut*. Waldshut: Pressverein Waldshut, 1933.

———. *Geschichte der Salpeterer im 18. Jahrhundert*. 2 vols. Unteralpfen, 1953–55.

———. "Die Salpeterer im 19. Jahrhundert." *Badische Heimat* 19 (1932): 192–204.

Elbs, Eberhard. "Owingen 1584: Der erste Aufstand in der Grafschaft Zollern." *ZfHG* 17 (1981): 9–127.

Endres, Rudolf. "Ländliche Rechtsquellen als sozialgeschichtliche Quellen." In P. Blickle, ed., *Deutsche Ländliche Rechtsquellen*.

———. "Sozialer Wandel in Franken und Bayern auf der Grundlage der Dorfordnungen." In Hinrichs and Wiegelmann, eds., *Sozialer und kultureller Wandel*.

———. "Stadtgemeinde und Landgemeinde in Franken." In P. Blickle, ed., *Landgemeinde und Stadtgemeinde*.

Endriß, Gerhard. "Landschaft, Siedlung und Wirtschaft des Hotzenwaldes." In F. Metz et al., eds., *Der Hotzenwald*.

Evans, R. J. W. *The Making of the Habsburg Monarchy, 1550–1700: An Interpretation*. Oxford: Clarendon Press, 1979.

Farr, Ian. "'Tradition' and the Peasantry: On the Modern Historiography of Rural Germany." In R. J. Evans and W. R. Lee., eds., *The German Peasantry: Conflict and Community in Rural Society from the Eighteenth to the Twentieth Centuries.* London: Croom Helm, 1986.
Fehr, Hans. "Das Widerstandsrecht." *MIÖG* 38 (1920): 1–38.
Felder, Pierre. "Ansätze zu einer Typologie der politischen Unruhen im schweizerischen Ancien Régime." *SZG* 26 (1976): 324–89.
Fellner, Thomas, and Heinrich Kretschmayr. *Die österreichische Zentralverwaltung,* pt. 1, *Von Maximilian I. bis zur Vereinigung der österreichischen und böhmischen Hofkanzlei (1749).* 3 vols. Vienna: Holzhausen, 1907.
Field, Daniel. *Rebels in the Name of the Tsar.* Boston: Houghton Mifflin, 1976.
Flinn, Michael W. *The European Demographic System, 1500–1820.* Baltimore: Johns Hopkins University Press, 1981.
Franz, Günther. *Der deutsche Bauernkrieg.* 2 vols. Berlin: Oldenbourg, 1933–35.
———. *Der Dreissigjährige Krieg und das deutsche Volk.* 3d rev. ed. Stuttgart: Fischer, 1961.
Geertz, Clifford. "Ideology as a Cultural System." In Clifford Geertz, *The Intepretation of Cultures.* New York: Basic Books, 1973.
———. "Local Knowledge: Fact and Law in Comparative Perspective." In Clifford Geertz, *Local Knowledge: Further Essays in Interpretive Anthropology.* New York: Basic Books, 1983.
———. "Studies in Peasant Life: Community and Society." *Biennial Review of Anthropology* 1961: 1–41.
Gerteis, Klaus. "Regionale Bauernrevolten zwischen Bauernkrieg und französischer Revolution: Eine Bestandaufnahme." *ZHF* 6 (1979): 37–62.
Goody, Jack. "Inheritance, Property, and Women: Some Comparative Considerations." In Goody et al., eds., *Family and Inheritance.*
Goody, Jack, et al., eds. *Family and Inheritance: Rural Society in Western Europe, 1200–1800.* Cambridge: Cambridge University Press, 1976
Gothein, Eberhard. "Der Breisgau unter Maria Theresia und Joseph II." *NJBHK* 10 (1907).
———. "Die Hofverfassung auf dem Schwarzwald, dargestellt an der Geschichte des Gebiets von St Peter." *ZGO* 39 (1886): 257–316.
———. "Die oberrheinische Lande vor und nach dem dreißigjährigen Krieg." *ZGO* 39 (1886): 1–45.
———. *Wirtschaftsgeschichte des Schwarzwaldes und der angrenzenden Landschaften.* Strasbourg: Trübner, 1892.
Grube, Walter. "Dorfgemeinde und Amtsversammlung in Altwürttemberg." *ZWLG* 13 (1954): 194–219.
Grüll, Georg. *Bauer, Herr und Landesfürst: Sozialrevolutionäre Bestrebungen der oberösterreichischen Bauern von 1650 bis 1848.* Graz: Hermann Böhlaus Nachfolger, 1963.

Harnisch, Hartmut. "Landgemeinde, feudalherrlich-bäuerliche Klassenkämpfe und Agrarverfassung im Spätfeudalismus." *ZfG* 26 (1978): 887–97.

———. "Die Landgemeinde im ostelbischen Gebiet." In P. Blickle, ed., *Landgemeinde und Stadtgemeinde*.

Haselier, Günther. *Geschichte des Hotzenwalds*. Lahr: Schauenburg, 1973.

———. *Die Streitigkeiten der Hauensteiner mit ihren Obrigkeiten: Ein Beitrag zur Geschichte Vorderösterreichs und des südwestdeutschen Bauernstandes im 18. Jahrhundert*. Karlsruhe: Südwestdeutsche Druck- und Verlagsgesellschaft, 1940.

Hauptmeyer, Carl-Hans. "Aufklärung und bäuerliche Oppositionen im zentralen Niedersachsen des ausgehenden 18. Jahrhunderts." In Rudolf Vierhaus, ed., *Das Volk als Objekt obrigkeitlichen Handelns*. Tübingen: Niemeyer, 1992.

———. "Die Bauernunruhen in Schaumburg-Lippe 1784–1793." *NJLG* 49 (1977): 149–207.

———. "Dorf und Territorialstaat im zentralen Niedersachsen." In Ulrich Lange, ed., *Landgemeinde und frühmoderner Staat: Beiträge zum Problem der gemeindlichen Selbstverwaltung in Dänemark, Schleswig-Holstein und Niedersachsen in der frühen Neuzeit*. Sigmaringen: Thorbecke, 1988.

———. "Die Landgemeinde in Norddeutschland." In P. Blickle, ed., *Landgemeinde und Stadtgemeinde*.

Haushofer, Heinz, and Willi A. Boelcke, eds. *Neue Wege und Forschungen der Agrargeschichte: FS Günther Franz*. Frankfurt: DLG-Verlag, 1967.

Heilingsetzer, Georg. *Der oberösterreichische Bauernkrieg 1626*. Vienna: Heeresgeschichtliches Museum, 1976.

Heitz, Gerhard. "Agrarstruktur, bäuerlicher Widerstand, Klassenkampf im 17. und 18. Jahrhundert." In Schulze, ed., *Aufstände, Revolten, Prozeße*.

Heitz, Gerhard, and Günter Vogler. "Bauernbewegungen in Europa vom 16. bis zum 18. Jahrhundert." *ZfG* 28 (1980): 1060–78.

Henning, Friedrich-Wilhelm. *Dienste und Abgaben der Bauern im 18. Jahrhundert*. Stuttgart: Fischer, 1969.

Heydendorf, Walther E. "Vorderösterreich im Dreißigjährigen Kriege: Der Verlust der Vorlande am Rhein und die Versuche zu deren Rückgewinnung." *MÖS* 12 (1959): 74–142.

Hinrichs, Ernst, and Günter Wiegelmann, eds. *Sozialer und kultureller Wandel in der ländlichen Welt des 18. Jahrhunderts*. Wolfenbüttel: Herzog August Bibliothek, 1982.

Hobsbawm, Eric. *Primitive Rebels: Studies in Archaic Forms of Social Movement in the 19th and 20th Centuries*. New York: W. W. Norton, 1959.

Hughes, Michael. *Law and Politics in Eighteenth-Century Germany*. Woodbridge, Suffolk, 1988.

Ingrao, Charles W., ed. *State and Society in Early Modern Austria*. West Lafayette, Ind.: Purdue University Press, 1994.

Irsliger, Franz. "Gross- und Kleinbesitz im westlichen Deutschland vom 13. bis 18. Jahrhundert: Versuch einer Typologie." In Péter Gunst and Tamás Hoffmann, eds., *Grand domaine et petites exploitations en Europe au Moyen Age et dans les temps modernes: Rapports nationaux*. Budapest: Akadémiai Kiadó, 1982.
Jehle, Fridolin. *Die Geschichte des Stiftes Säckingen*. Säckingen: Bürgermeisteramt, 1969.
Kageneck, Alfred Graf von. *Das Ende der vorderösterreichischen Herrschaft im Breisgau: Der Breisgau von 1740 bis 1815*. Freiburg: Rombach, 1981.
Kaplan, Steven L. *The Famine Plot Persuasion in Eighteenth-Century France*. Philadelphia: American Philosophical Society, 1982.
Kappelhoff, Bernd. *Absolutistisches Regiment oder Ständeherrschaft? Landesherr und Landstände in Ostfriesland im ersten Drittel des 18. Jahrhunderts*. Hildesheim: Lax, 1982.
Kaschuba, Wolfgang. "Kommunalismus als sozialer 'common sense': Zur Konzeption von Lebenswelt und Alltagskultur im neuzeitlichen Gemeindegedanken." In P. Blickle, ed., *Landgemeinde und Stadtgemeinde*.
Kelley, Donald R. *The Beginning of Ideology: Consciousness and Society in the French Reformation*. Cambridge: Cambridge University Press, 1981.
Kettering, Sharon. "The Historical Development of Political Clientelism." *Journal of Interdisciplinary History* 18 (1988): 419–47.
———. *Patrons, Brokers, and Clients in Seventeenth-Century France*. New York: Oxford University Press, 1986.
Le Roy Ladurie, Emmauel. "Family Structures and Inheritance Customs in Sixteenth-Century France." In Goody et al., eds., *Family and Inheritance*.
———. *The Peasants of Languedoc*. Trans. John Day. Urbana: University of Illinois Press, 1976.
———. "Révoltes et contestations rurales en France de 1675 à 1788." *AESC* 29 (1974): 6–22.
Link, Edith M. *The Emancipation of the Austrian Peasant, 1740–1798*. New York: Columbia University Press, 1949.
Ludwig, Theodor. *Der badische Bauer im 18. Jahrhundert*. Strasbourg: Trübner, 1896.
Luebke, David Martin. "Community and the Politics of Discord: A Case Study of Peasant Rebellion in Early Modern Germany." Ph.D. dissertation, Yale University, 1990.
———. "Factions and Politics in Early Modern Germany." *Central European History* 25 (1992): 281–301.
———. "Serfdom and Honour in Eighteenth-Century Germany." *Social History* 18 (1993): 143–61.
Lütge, Friedrich. *Geschichte der deutschen Agrarverfassung vom frühen Mittelalter bis zum 19. Jahrhundert*. 2d ed. Stuttgart: Fischer, 1967.
Lutz, Robert H. *Wer war der Gemeine Mann? Der dritte Stand in der Krise des Spätmittelalters*. Munich: Oldenbourg, 1979.

Mannheim, Karl. *Ideology and Utopia: An Introduction to the Sociology of Knowledge.* Trans. Louis Wirth and Edward Shils. New York: Harcourt Brace, 1952.
Martini, R. "Die ländliche Siedlungsgestalt im Schwarzwald." *ZGO* 45 (1931): 266–303.
Merk, Joseph. "Geschichte des Ursprunges, der Entwickelung und Einrichtung der Hauensteinischen Einung im Mittelalter." *Jahrbücher der Geschichte und Staatskunst* 2 (1833): 126–57.
Metz, Friedrich, ed. *Vorderösterreich: Eine geschichtliche Landeskunde.* 2d rev. ed. Freiburg: Rombach, 1967.
Metz, Friedrich, et al., eds. *Der Hotzenwald: Quellen und Forschungen zur Siedlungs- und Volkstumsgeschichte der Oberrheinlande.* Karlsruhe, Südwestdeutsche Druck- und Verlagsgesellschaft, 1941.
Metz, Rudolf. *Geologische Landeskunde des Hotzenwalds.* Lahr: Schauenburg, 1980.
Meyer, Elard Hugo. *Badisches Volksleben im neunzehnten Jahrhundert.* Strasbourg: Trübner, 1900.
Meyer, Josef Lukas. *Geschichte der Salpeterer auf dem südöstlichen Schwarzwald.* Freiburg: Waißenegger, 1837.
———. "Die Wiedertäuferlehre im Hauensteinischen." *Badenia* 2 (1840): 276–300.
Mooser, Josef. "Gleichheit und Ungleichheit in der ländlichen Gemeinde: Sozialstruktur und Kommunalverfassung im östlichen Westfalen vom späten 18. bis in die Mitte des 19. Jahrhunderts." *ASG* 19 (1979): 231–62.
Mousnier, Roland. *Fureurs paysannes: Les paysans dans les révoltes du XVIIe siècle (France, Russie, Chine).* Paris: Calmann-Lévy, 1967.
———. "Recherches sur les soulèvements populaires en France avant la Fronde." *Revue d'Histoire Moderne et Contemporaine* 5 (1958): 81–113.
Müller, Wolfgang. "Wurzeln und Bedeutung des grundsätzlichen Widerstands gegen die Leibeigenschaft im Bauernkrieg von 1525." *SVGBU* 93 (1975): 1–41.
Mullett, Michael. *Popular Culture and Popular Protest in Late Medieval and Early Modern Europe.* London: Croom Helm, 1987.
Nagel, Helmut. *Die Siedlungen des Hotzenwaldes: Ein Beitrag zur Siedlungsgeographie des südlichen Schwarzwaldes.* Karlsruhe, 1930.
Neustädter, Max. "Der erste Salpetererkrieg von 1728 bis 1732 im Lichte der Tagebücher vom Pater Marquard Herrgott." *Badische Heimat* 19 (1932): 175–85.
Neveux, Hughues. "Die ideologische Dimension der französischen Bauernaufstände im 17. Jahrhundert." *HZ* 238 (1984): 265–85.
Oldendorf, Karl-Heinrich. "Der vorderösterreichische Breisgau nach dem Dreißigjährigen Kriege und seine Bedeutung für das Haus Österreich." Ph.D. dissertation, Freiburg i.B., 1957.
Ortner, Josef P. *Marquard Herrgott (1694–1762): Sein Leben und Wirken als Historiker und Diplomat.* Vienna: Böhlau, 1972.
Ott, Hugo. *Die Klostergrundherrschaft St Blasiens im Mittelalter.* Stuttgart: Kohlhammer, 1969.

———. "St Blasien." *Germania Benedictina* 5 (1975): 146–60.
———. *Studien zur Geschichte des Klosters St Blasien im hohen und späten Mittelalter.* Stuttgart: Fischer, 1970.
Pillorget, "Genèse et typologie des mouvements insurrectionnels d'apres une étude regionale (la Provence de 1596 à 1715)." *Francia* 4 (1977): 365–89.
———. *Les mouvements insurrectionnels de Provence entre 1596 et 1715.* Paris: A. Pedone, 1975.
Prasse, Max. "Die Agrarverfassung des Schwarzwaldes vor der Bauernbefreiung: Wirtschaftsgeschichtliche Studien." Ph.D. dissertation, Basel, 1937.
Press, Volker. "Französische Volkserhebungen und deutsche Agrarkonflikte zwischen dem 16. und 18. Jahrhundert." *Beiträge zur historischen Sozialkunde* 7 (1977): 173–200.
———. "Stadt- und Dorfgemeinden im territorialstaatlichen Gefüge des Spätmittelalters und der frühen Neuzeit." In P. Blickle, ed., *Landgemeinde und Stadtgemeinde.*
Quarthal, Franz. "Die habsburgischen Landstände in Südwestdeutschland." In Günther Bradler and Franz Quarthal, eds., *Von der Ständeversammlung zum demokratischen Parlament: Die Geschichte der Volksvertretung in Baden-Württemberg.* Stuttgart: Theiss, 1982.
Quarthal, Franz, and Georg Wieland. *Die Behördenorganisation Vorderösterreichs von 1753 bis 1805.* Bühl: Konkordia, 1977.
Rabe, Hannah. *Das Problem Leibeigenschaft.* Wiesbaden: Steiner, 1977.
Rebel, Hermann. *Peasant Classes: The Bureaucratization of Property and Family Relations under Early Habsburg Absolutism, 1511–1636.* Princeton: Princeton University Press, 1983.
Roberts, Simon. "The Study of Dispute: Anthropological Perspectives." In John Bossy, ed., *Disputes and Settlements: Law and Human Relations in the West.* Cambridge: Cambridge University Press, 1983.
Robisheaux, Thomas. "Peasant Revolts in Germany and Central Europe after the Peasants' War: Comments on the Literature." *CEH* 17 (1984): 384–403.
———. *Rural Society and the Search for Order in Early Modern Germany.* Cambridge: Cambridge University Press, 1989.
Rösener, Werner. *Bauern im Mittelalter.* Munich: Beck, 1986.
———. "Die spätmittelalterliche Grundherrschaft im südwestdeutschen Raum als Problem der Sozialgeschichte." *ZGO* 127 (1979): 17–69.
Rudé, George. *The Crowd in History: A Study of Popular Disturbances in France and England, 1730–1848.* Rev. ed. London: Lawrence & Wishart, 1981.
———. "Popular Protest and Ideology on the Eve of the French Revolution." In Ernst Hinrichs et al., eds., *Vom Ancien Régime zur Französischen Revolution—Forschungen und Perspektiven.* Göttingen: Vandenhoeck & Ruprecht, 1978.
Rumpf, Joachim. "Die Salpetererbewegung im 19. Jahrhundert." *Badische Heimat* 57 (1977): 377–89.

Saalfeld, Diederich. *Bauernwirtschaft und Gutsbetrieb in der vorindustriellen Zeit.* Stuttgart: Fischer, 1960.

———. "Stellung und Differenzierung der ländlichen Bevölkerung Nordwestdeutschlands in der Ständegesellschaft des 18. Jahrhunderts." In Hinrichs and Wiegelmann, eds., *Sozialer und kultureller Wandel.*

Saarbrücker Arbeitsgruppe. "Die spätmittelalterliche Leibeigenschaft in Oberschwaben." *ZAA* 22 (1974): 17–69.

Sabean, David W. "Aspects of Kinship Behavior and Property in Rural Western Europe before 1800." In Goody et al., eds., *Family and Inheritance.*

———. "The Communal Basis of Pre-1800 Peasant Uprisings in Western Europe." *Comparative Politics* 8 (1976): 355–64.

———. "Family and Land Tenure: A Case Study of Conflict in the German Peasants' War (1525)." *PSN* 3 (1974): 000–00.

———. *Landbesitz und Gesellschaft am Vorabend des Bauernkrieges: Eine Studie der sozialen Verhältnisse im südlichen Oberschwaben in den Jahren vor 1525.* Stuttgart: Fischer, 1972.

———. "Markets, Uprisings and Leadership in Peasant Societies: Western Europe, 1381–1789." *PSN* 2 (1973): 17–19.

———. *Power in the Blood: Popular Culture and Village Discourse in Early Modern Germany.* Cambridge: Cambridge University Press, 1984.

———. *Property, Production and Family in Neckarhausen, 1700–1870.* Cambridge: Cambridge University Press, 1990.

Sablonier, Roger. "Das Dorf im Übergang vom Hoch- zum Spätmittelalter: Untersuchungen zum Wandel ländlicher Gemeinschaftsformen im ostschweizerischen Raum." In Lutz Fenske et al., eds., *Institutionen, Kultur und Gesellschaft im Mittelalter: FS Josef Fleckenstein.* Sigmaringen: Thorbecke, 1984.

Sahlins, Peter. *Boundaries: The Making of France and Spain in the Pyrenees.* Berkeley: University of California Press, 1989.

Schiff, Otto. "Die deutschen Bauernaufstände von 1525 bis 1789." *HZ* 130 (1924): 189–204.

Schlageter, Albrecht. "Die ungehorsamsten Untertanen Vorderösterreichs." *Das Markgräflerland,* n.s., 8 (1977): 2–19.

Schmale, Wolfgang. *Bäuerlicher Widerstand, Gerichte und Rechtsentwicklung in Frankreich: Untersuchungen zu Prozessen zwischen Bauern und Seigneurs vor dem Parlament von Paris (16.–18. Jahrhundert).* Frankfurt:Klosterman, 1986.

Schülin, Fritz. "Die Grundherrschaft des Klosters St Blasien im Markgräflerland." *Das Markgräflerland* 34 (1972): 155–93.

Schultz, Helga. "Bäuerliche Klassenkämpfe zwischen frühbürgerlicher Revolution und Dreissigjährigem Krieg." *ZfG* 20 (1972): 156–73.

Schulze, Winfried. "Der bäuerliche Widerstand und die 'Rechte der Menschheit.'" In Birtsch, ed., *Grund- und Freiheitsrechte.*

———. *Bäuerlicher Widerstand und feudale Herrschaft in der frühen Neuzeit.* Bad Canstatt: Frommann-Holzboog, 1980.

———. "Herrschaft und Widerstand in der Sicht des 'gemeinen Mannes' im 16./17. Jahrhundert." In Winfried Schulze and Hans Mommsen, eds., *Vom Elend der Handarbeit: Probleme historischer Unterschichtsforschung.* Göttingen: Vandenhoeck & Ruprecht, 1981.

———. "'Geben Aufruhr und Aufstand Anlaß zu neuen heilsamen Gesetzen': Beobachtungen über die Wirkungen bäuerlichen Widerstands in der Frühen Neuzeit." In Schulze, ed., *Aufstände, Revolten, Prozeße.*

———. "Die veränderte Bedeutung sozialer Konflikte im 16. und 17. Jahrhundert." In Wehler, ed., *Der Deutsche Bauernkrieg 1524–1526.*

———. "Der Windische Bauernaufstand von 1573: Bauernaufstand und feudale Herrschaft im späten 16. Jahrhundert." *Südostforschung* 33 (1974): 15–61.

———, ed., *Aufstände, Revolten, Prozeße: Beiträge zu bäuerlichen Widerstandsbewegungen im frühneuzeitlichen Europa.* Stuttgart: Klett-Cotta, 1983.

Schwarz, Heinrich. "Der Hotzenwald und seine Freibauern." In F. Metz et al., eds., *Der Hotzenwald.*

Scott, James C. *Domination and the Arts of Resistance: Hidden Transcripts.* New Haven: Yale University Press, 1990.

———. *The Moral Economy of the Peasant: Rebellion and Subsistence in Southeast Asia.* New Haven: Yale University Press, 1976.

———. *Weapons of the Weak: Everyday Forms of Peasant Resistance.* New Haven: Yale University Press, 1985.

Scott, Tom. "Peasant Revolts in Early Modern Germany." *HJ* 28 (1985): 455–68.

———. "Reformation and Peasants' War in Waldshut and Environs: A Structural Analysis." *ARG* 69 (1978): 82–102; 70 (1979): 140–68.

Spielman, John P. "Status as Commodity: The Habsburg Economy of Privilege." In Ingrao, ed., *State and Society in Early Modern Austria.*

Spittler, Gerd. "Staat und Klientelstruktur in Entwicklungsländern: Zum Problem der politischen Organisation von Bauern." *Archives européennes de sociologie* 18 (1977): 57–83.

———. *Verwaltung in einem afrikanischen Bauernstaat: Das koloniale Französisch-Westafrika, 1919–1939.* Freiburg: Atlantis, 1981.

Steuer, Peter. "Der vorderösterreichische Rappenkrieg (1612–1614)." *ZGO* 128 (1980): 119–65.

Straub, Alfred. *Der badische Oberland im 18. Jahrhundert: Die Transformation einer bäuerlichen Gesellschaft vor der Industrialisierung.* Husum: Matthiesen, 1977.

Strauss, Gerald. *Law, Resistance and the State: The Opposition to Roman Law in Reformation Germany.* Princeton: Princeton University Press, 1986.

Strobel, Albrecht. *Agrarverfassung im Übergang: Studien zur Agrargeschichte des badischen Breisgaus vom Beginn des 16. bis zum Ausgang des 18. Jahrhunderts.* Freiburg: K. Alber, 1972.

Suter, Andreas. "Die Träger bäuerlicher Widerstandsaktionen beim Bauernaufstand im Fürstbistum Basel 1726–1740: Dorfgemeinde—Dorffrauen—Knabenschaften." In Schulze, ed., *Aufstände, Revolten, Prozeße*.
———. *"Troublen" im Fürstbistum Basel (1726–1740): Eine Fallstudie zum bäuerlichen Widerstand im 18. Jahrhundert*. Göttingen: Vandenhoeck & Ruprecht, 1985.
Tacke, Jürgen. "Studien zur Agrarverfassung der oberen badischen Markgrafschaft im 16. und 17. Jahrhundert." *Das Markgräflerland* 2 (1956).
Thompson, E. P. "The Moral Economy of the English Crowd in the Eighteenth Century." *PP* 50 (1971): 76–136.
Tilly, Charles. "Food Supply and Public Order in Modern Europe." In Charles Tilly, ed., *The Formation of National States in Western Europe*. Princeton: Princeton University Press, 1975.
———. *From Mobilization to Revolution*. New York: Random House, 1978.
———. "Hauptformen kollektiver Aktionen in Westeuropa, 1500–1975." *GG* 3 (1977): 153–63.
———. *The Vendée*. Cambridge: Harvard University Press, 1964.
Troßbach, Werner. "Bauernbewegungen in deutschen Kleinterritorien zwischen 1648 und 1789." In Schulze, ed., *Aufstände, Revolten, Prozeße*.
———. *Bauernbewegungen im Wetterau-Vogelsberg-Gebiet, 1648–1806: Fallstudien zum bäuerlichen Widerstand im Alten Reich*. Darmstadt: Historische Kommission für Hessen, 1985.
———. "Bauernprotest als 'politisches' Verhalten: Zu den Agrarkonflikten im Wetterau-Vogelsberg-Gebiet zwischen 1648 und 1806." *Archiv für hessische Geschichte und Altertumskunde*, n.s., 42 (1984): 65–106.
———. "Die ländliche Gemeinde im mittleren Deutschland (vornehmlich 16.–18. Jahrhundert)." In P. Blickle, ed., *Landgemeinde und Stadtgemeinde*.
———. *Soziale Bewegung und politische Erfahrung: Bäuerlicher Widerstand in hessischen Territorien, 1648–1806*. Weingarten: Drumlin, 1987.
———. "'Südwestdeutsche Leibeigenschaft' in der frühen Neuzeit: eine Bagatelle?" *GG* 7 (1981): 69–90.
Ulbrich, Claudia. "Agrarverfassung und bäuerlicher Widerstand im Oberrheingebiet." *ZAA* 30 (1982): 149–67.
———. "Bäuerlicher Widerstand in Triberg." In P. Blickle, ed., *Aufruhr und Empörung?*
———. "Der Charakter bäuerlichen Widerstands in vorderösterreichischen Herrschaften. In Schulze, ed., *Aufstände, Revolten, Prozeße*.
———. "Freiheit und Eigenschaft in spätmittelalterlichen ländlichen Rechtsquellen des Oberrheins." In P. Blickle, ed., *Deutsche Ländliche Rechtsquellen*.
———. *Leibherrschaft am Oberrhein im Spätmittelalter*. Göttingen: Vandenhoeck & Ruprecht, 1979.

Valentinisch, Helfried. "Advokaten, Winkelschreiber und Bauernprokuratoren in Innerösterreich in der frühen Neuzeit." In Schulze, ed., *Aufstände, Revolten, Prozeße.*

Vann, James Allen. *The Making of a State: Württemberg, 1593–1793.* Ithaca: Cornell University Press, 1984.

Vierhaus, Rudolf. *Germany in the Age of Absolutism.* Trans. Jonathan B. Knudsen. Cambridge: Cambridge University Press, 1988.

———. *Staaten und Stände: Vom westfälischen Frieden bis zum hubertusberger Frieden, 1648 bis 1763.* Berlin: Propyläen, 1984.

Vocelka, Karl. "Public Opinion and the Phenomenon of *Sozialdisziplinierung* in the Habsburg Monarchy." In Ingrao, ed., *State and Society in Early Modern Austria.*

Vogler, Günter. "Bäuerlicher Klassenkampf als Konzept der Forschung." In Schulze, ed., *Aufstände, Revolten, Prozeße.*

Walker, Mack. *German Home Towns: Community, Estate, and General Estate, 1648–1871.* Ithaca: Cornell University Press, 1971.

Walter, Thomas. *Die Geschichte der österreichischen Zentralverwaltung in der Zeit Maria Theresias (1740–1780).* Vienna: Holzhausen, 1938.

Wehler, Hans-Ulrich, ed. *Der Deutsche Bauernkrieg 1524–1526.* Göttingen: Vandenhoeck & Ruprecht, 1976.

Weitzel, Jürgen. *Der Kampf um die Appellation ans Reichskammergericht: Zur politischen Geschichte der Rechtsmittel in Deutschland.* Cologne: Böhlau, 1976.

Wernet, Karl F. "Die Bevölkerung der Grafschaft Hauenstein." *ZGO* 104 (1956): 245–57.

———. "Die finanzielle Leistungsfähigkeit der Grafschaft Hauenstein." *ZGO* 100 (1952): 753–61.

———. "Der Hauensteiner Landfahnen: Entstehung, Entwicklung, und Bedeutung der Hauensteiner Wehrorganisation bis zum Begin der Unruhen in der Grafschaft im Jahre 1726." *ZGO* 95 (1943): 301–97.

———. "St Blasiens Versuche, sich der Grafschaft Hauenstein pfandweise zu bemächtigen." *ZGO* 107 (1959): 161–82.

———. "Die Stellung St Blasiens im vorderösterreichischen Staatsverband." *ZGO* 99 (1951): 621–25.

———. "Der Umfang der Grafschaft Hauenstein." *ZGO* 104 (1956): 423–54.

———. "Die wirtschaftlichen Verhältnisse der Grafschaft Hauenstein zwischen den Burgunderkriegen und den Salpereraufständen." *ZGO* 98 (1950): 115–46.

———. "Der Zwing und Bann St Blasiens." *Mein Heimatland* 22 (1940): 149–77.

Wrightson, Keith. "Aspects of Social Differentiation in Rural England, 1580–1660." *JPS* 5 (1977): 33–47.

———. "Two Concepts of Order: Justices, Constables and Jurymen in Seventeenth-Century England." In John Brewer and John Styles, eds., *An Ungovernable People: The English and Their Law in the Seventeenth and Eighteenth Centuries.* New Brunswick: Rutgers University Press, 1980.

Wunder, Gerd. "Bäuerliche Oberschichten im alten Wirtenberg." In Kuno Ülshofer, ed., *Bauer, Bürger, Edelmann: Ausgewählte Aufsätze zur Sozialgeschichte von Gerd Wunder.* Sigmaringen: Thorbecke, 1984.

Wunder, Heide. "'Altes Recht' und 'göttliches Recht' im Deutschen Bauernkrieg." *ZAA* 24 (1976): 54–66.

———. *Die bäuerliche Gemeinde in Deutschland.* Göttingen: Vandenhoeck & Ruprecht, 1986.

———. "Die ländliche Gemeinde als Strukturprinzip der spätmittelalterlich-frühneuzeitlichen Geschichte Mitteleuropas." In P. Blickle, ed., *Landgemeinde und Stadtgemeinde.*

———. "Peasant Communities in Medieval and Early Modern Germany." In *Les communautés rurales/Rural communities,* vol. 5. [Recueils de la Société Jean Bodin pour l'Histoire Comparative des Institutions, 40–46]. Paris: Dessain et Tolra, 1987.

———. "Zur Mentalität aufständischer Bauern: Möglichkeiten der Zusammenarbeit von Geschichtswissenschaft und Anthropologie, dargestellt am Beispiel des Samländischen Bauernaufstandes von 1525." In Wehler, ed., *Der Deutsche Bauernkrieg 1524–1526.*

Zagorin, Perez. *Rebels and Rulers, 1500–1660.* 2 vols. Cambridge: Cambridge University Press, 1982.

Index

acculturation. *See* domination: cultural aspects of
agricultural economy: animal husbandry and, 16, 125; cereal production and, 16–17, 122–23; expansion of, 10, 118, 121–24, 216, 218, 230; forestry and, 16; harvest yields in, 122–24, 216; market relationships of, 16, 124, 230; subsistence crises of, 123, 215–16; viticulture and, 100, 130
Albiez, Johannes (Kiesenbach), 108, 115, 141
Albiez, "Salpeter-Hans" Friedle (Buch), 3, 102, 134–35, 141, 163, 212; election of, 55; as Octovir, 63–67, 137; as political activist, 185–87, 194–95
"ancient rights," concepts of, 63, 88, 96, 148–65, 167, 198, 227–29, 231; and manumission, 75, 156–59, 178; salvation and, 171
artisans, rural, 108–9, 118–19, 121, 125, 134–37, 141, 144

Bächle, Johannes (Nöggenschwiel), 98, 133; on village strife, 143–44
Baden-Durlach, margraviate of, 51, 124
Bavaria: electorate of, 175, 209–10; peasant rebellions in, 173, 209–10, 214
Beaurieu, Franz Edmund von, 68; as imperial commissioner, 70–72, 88, 99
Bierbrauer, Peter, 19–20
Binkert, Caspar (Birndorf), 140–41
Binkert, Conrad (Dogern), 135, 138, 166, 196; as delegate, 67–68, 164, 194; as turncoat, 140–42

Birndorf: canton, 34, 37, 43, 78, 94, 100–101, 106, 113–14, 142, 189; village, 46, 122, 126, 130
Blasius III Bender, abbot (1720–27), 66, 131
Blickle, Peter, 5, 19, 50–51, 216, 226
Blickle, Renate, 220
Bloch, Marc, 15
Brutschi, Leonzi (Dogern), 78, 135, 199; as fund-raiser, 190–92

cantons. See Hauenstein: political institutions of
Charles VI, emperor (1711–40), 29, 62, 163–69, 183, 199–200, 229; peasant encounters with, 65, 96, 164, 168, 194, 196, 205
chiliasm, 170–72, 205
class interest, 23–24, 118, 131, 136–37, 145–46, 224; articulations of, 9, 22–24, 203; and community, 13, 52, 146, 203; and peasant rebellions, 9, 23, 121, 136–41, 145–46
community, 13–14, 94–95, 147, 202–3, 207–8, 211, 221, 230–31; factions as, 11–12, 14, 66, 90–91, 95, 98, 147–49, 152, 156, 162, 178–79, 231; and peasant rebellions, 5–9, 12, 15, 17, 19–21, 143–45, 182; villages as, 5, 12–13, 70, 193
corruption, accusations of, 34–35, 64, 156–57, 159, 161, 198
courts of law, 49, 199; appellate, 32, 46, 62, 73; burdens imposed by, 40, 62, 64, 130–32; imperial, 22, 28–29, 58, 194; and land market, 11, 37,

265

courts of law *(cont.)*
   47, 73, 118–19, 129–31; local, 10, 26, 30–32, 37, 46, 62, 95, 112–15, 134; and peasant debt, 37, 40, 46, 73, 119; and social control, 21–23, 46, 58, 73, 85–87, 110, 112–13, 119, 130–31, 141, 204–6, 213–14, 221, 228–29. See also Habsburg state: as juridical lord; St. Blasien: as juridical lord; St. Fridolin: as juridical lord

"divine law", 149–50, 171
Dogern: canton, 37, 43, 69, 77, 94, 100–101, 106, 110–11, 113–14, 125, 142, 189, 200; village, 18, 47, 69, 77, 101, 130, 135, 200
domination, 2, 15, 26–27, 49–52, 87, 177–78, 182, 218–19, 230; cultural aspects of, 12, 23, 66–67, 70–71, 73, 88, 91, 93–94, 96–99, 102, 109, 112–16, 148, 151–52, 201–2, 208–9, 226–29. *See also* peasant elites

Eagleton, Terry, 152–53
Eckert, Joseph (Herrischried), 135, 189, 198–99
Einsiedeln, Marian shrine, 199–200, 202, 208
Einung, Einungsmeister. See Hauenstein, political institutions of
Eisele, Martin (Nöggenschwiel), 134, 143–44, 195
espionage, factional, 73, 93, 183, 185, 188–90

faction rosters, 90–94, 99–116, 135–36
factions, 2–5, 20–21, 54, 85–87, 90–91, 152–53, 178–79, 211–13, 221–31; and elections, 9, 53, 69, 71, 76–77, 79–81, 102, 222–24; formation of, 10–11, 14, 23–24, 52, 54–55, 62–72, 87–88, 90–93, 95–99, 102, 109–16, 148, 182, 212, 221–28; kinship and, 11, 120, 128, 133, 142–45, 212, 224; membership in, 90–116, 145, 157–58, 172, 184, 192–93; nomenclature of, 3, 4, 148, 222–24; religious aspects of, 149, 161–62, 170–72, 181, 183, 188–89, 198, 200–202, 207, 210; ritual aspects of, 72, 75, 79, 91, 96, 115–16, 148, 161, 181, 183, 188, 198–202, 207–8; social composition of, 6, 94, 117–20, 134–46, 204, 230–31; strategies of, 7, 55, 69, 71–74, 77, 79, 86–89, 96, 154, 181–82, 185, 187, 189, 190–202, 204, 210–11, 223, 228–31. *See also* order, concepts of
Fluem, Georg (Dietlingen), 137, 160–61, 185
Forest Steward: office of, 27, 31–36, 59, 73, 168; Franz Anton von Schönau as, 76–77, 79, 192–93; Franz Leopold von Beck as, 65, 185–86
France, 27, 157; peasant rebellions in, 173, 180
Francis I Stephen, emperor, 165, 194, 203
Franz II Schächtelin, abbot, 66–67, 139–40, 185, 187

Gerichtsherrschaft. See courts of law; Habsburg state: as juridical lord; St. Blasien: as juridical lord; St. Fridolin: as juridical lord
Gerspach, Hans Friedle (Bergalingen), 143, 156–57, 159, 165, 171, 204; as delegate, 194, 198–200; as rally organizer, 77–78, 183–84, 191
"Good Count Hans", 163–64, 173
Görwihl: canton, 37, 45, 94, 100–101, 106, 111–14, 185, 189; village, 30, 65, 155, 182–85
Grundherrschaft. See seigneurial regime

Habsburg Crown Lands, 22, 27–28, 165, 194; aristocracy of, 48–50; peasant delegations in, 206–7; peasant estates in, 29–30, 49–51; peasant rebellions in, 213–16, 225, 229
Habsburg dynasty, 3, 27–29; devotion to, 6, 25, 63, 148–49, 160, 162–68, 183, 195–96, 200–201, 204–5; and marian veneration, 182, 193, 201, 210, 226; repudiation of, 150, 168–70
Habsburg state, 25–29; Court Chancellery of, 29, 49, 55, 65, 68, 195–96, 205–6; as juridical lord, 101, 111–14; as landlord, 30, 40, 49, 112; and "lien administration," 32–33, 58–60, 62–63;

Habsburg state *(cont.)*
military interventions of, 11, 55–56, 68–69, 77–78, 80, 82–84, 120, 151, 157, 160, 170, 187, 212; and peasant factions, 54, 56, 71–72, 74, 78–79, 81, 83–84, 86–87; "peasant-friendly" policies of, 49, 205–6; and St. Blasien, 48–50, 58–59, 68, 74–75, 88, 194–95, 205–6; role in "Salpeter Wars," 54–55, 67–68, 70–81, 83–85, 88–89, 91–92, 99, 120, 131–32, 136, 151, 157, 170, 194, 205–6
Hauenstein, 2, 3, 26, 25–53, 69; elections in, 64, 66, 68–69, 72, 76–77, 79–81, 87, 102, 157, 185, 190, 192, 197, 211; electoral customs of, 30–35, 53, 72, 85–88, 137, 147, 154; finances of, 32, 35, 76–77, 79–81, 167; judicial institutions of, 32, 73; military institutions of, 31, 57, 77–78, 81–82, 187; origins myth of, 25, 148, 163–64; political institutions of, 19, 25–35, 57, 69, 85–87, 145, 184; in popular awareness, 6, 11, 24, 35, 33, 63, 69, 75, 95–96, 108–9, 115–16, 146, 154–66, 169–70, 181, 184, 198, 230–31; population of, 17, 118–19, 121, 123–25; rebellious tradition of, 55–62, 169; and St. Blasien, 57–58, 60–62, 64, 156, 228; as serf lord, 75; social structure of, 17, 43, 45, 47, 102, 108–10, 112, 118, 120–21, 124–26, 145, 186
heresy, accusations of, 161
Herrgott, Marquard, 68, 205
Herrschaft. See domination
Hessen, 174–76, 214, 218; peasant rebellions in, 21–22, 87
High Steward, office of, 46–47, 127, 138
Hilpert, Johannes (Finsterlingen), 96–99, 108
Höchenschwand, canton, 34, 37, 43, 46, 100, 102, 106, 110, 113–14, 125, 189
Hochsal: canton, 40, 94, 100, 102, 106, 110, 113–14; village, 163–64
Hohenlohe, 217–18, 221, 225
Holenstein, André, 66–67
Holy Roman Empire, 2, 22–25, 28, 48, 66; estates of, 28–29; peasant rebellions in, 213–16, 221, 223–29

homage boycotts, 59–61, 66–70, 140, 163, 166, 185, 187, 228
honor, concepts of, 151–52, 159–61, 166, 176, 195–96
Hottinger, Bläsi (Niedergebisbach), 71, 78–79, 111–12, 139, 143, 162, 164–65, 168, 170, 203
Hottinger, Friedle (Niedergebisbach), 111–12, 141, 143, 188; as Octovir, 63, 137, 185

ideology, 147, 152–53. *See also* order, concepts of; political culture
inheritance customs, 5, 10, 41–42, 70–71, 119, 121–24, 128–29, 142, 175; subversion of, 10–11, 119, 128–34, 142
inn-keepers, 108, 119, 136–37, 141

Joseph II, emperor (1780–1790), 49, 79, 206
juridification. *See* courts of law: and social control

Kaiser, Bläsi (Neuenmühle), 116, 141, 148
Kuckshäger War (1797), 214

Landesherrschaft. See Habsburg state
land fragmentation, 119, 122–24, 129, 132
Leibeigenschaft, Leibherrschaft. See Hauenstein: as serf lord; St. Blasien: as serf lord; St. Fridolin: as serf lord; serfdom
Leopold I, emperor (1690–1705), 61, 65, 201, 208
Lüber, Joseph (Glashütten), 141, 166

Marder, Johannes "the Prussian" (Eschbach), 71, 78–79, 139–40, 158, 164, 170–71, 227; as rally organizer, 187–88
Marian veneration, 198–202, 206–10, 226
Maria Theresa, queen (1740–1780), 34, 49, 155, 165, 170, 194
Meyer, Joseph "Glasmännle" (Au), 155, 158, 167–68; as delegate, 194–96
millers, 108–9, 118–19, 125, 134, 136–39, 141
mobilization, 12, 180–82, 186, 203–4; strategies of, 12, 22, 72–73, 77–79, 102, 105, 108–9, 170–71, 181–204, 207–8, 210–11

müllerisch faction. *See* factions
Murg: canton, 40, 100–101, 104, 106, 110, 113–14; village, 37

"naive monarchism", 6, 149–50, 172–74, 179, 181, 183, 196, 206–7, 227
Nöggenschwiel: factions in, 143–46; village, 45–46, 101, 133–34, 200

Obervogt. See High Steward, office of
Octovirs. *See* Hauenstein: political institutions of
order, concepts of, 4, 44, 48, 76, 81, 88–89, 148–74, 177–79, 181–82, 193–205, 226–28, 229–31
Outer Austria, 3, 27–28, 32–33, 124, 189; estates of, 19, 29–30, 49, 51–52, 170; Franco-Bavarian occupation of, 56, 80–83, 157, 172; peasant rebellions in, 57, 168–70, 174, 213–14
Outer Austrian government, 27–28, 73; role in "Salpeter Wars," 65–66, 80, 82, 86

parishes, 42; and mobilization, 108–9
patrimonial jurisdiction. *See* courts of law: local; St. Blasien: as juridical lord; St. Fridolin: as juridical lord
peasant battles, 1, 57, 69, 77–78, 82–84, 180–81, 214, 223; at Etzwihl, 78, 181; at Schmitzingen, 1, 83, 200. *See also* Kuckshäger War
peasant debt, 119, 122, 126, 140
peasant delegations, 60–62, 65, 67–68, 73, 77, 96, 105, 154, 156–58, 181, 183–84, 189–209, 229; costs of, 190–92. *See also* Charles IV, emperor (1711–40): peasant encounters with
peasant elites: as "brokers," 27, 36, 52–53, 64, 69, 71–72, 80, 87, 137, 141–43, 159; and domination, 8–10, 24–27, 30, 33, 46–52, 55–56, 69, 85–87, 118–20, 218–20, 223–24; and Habsburg state, 2, 8–10, 18, 23–24, 35–36, 29–33, 49–53, 85, 137; and office-holding, 7–8, 21–24, 34–35, 51–52, 126, 220–21, 230; and peasant rebellion, 7, 9, 21, 23, 108, 132–34, 137–39, 204, 223–25, 230–31; and seign-eurial regime, 8, 26–27, 30, 47–48, 87, 119, 123, 132–36, 142–43, 220. *See also* entries for individual peasants
peasant litigation, 49, 58–59, 62, 64, 70–71, 80, 111, 131–32, 156, 185, 197, 205, 212, 228–29. *See also* courts of law: and social control
peasant rebellions, 4, 5, 19–22, 54–55, 149–51, 173–74, 180–81, 206, 208–10, 213–15, 221–25, 227–31; factions and, 5, 15, 53, 71–73, 85–86; punishments for, 71–73, 78–79, 84, 86, 92, 94, 98–100, 116, 120, 135–36, 138–40, 160, 187, 195. *See also* Kuckshäger War; Peasants' War; Upper Austrian Peasant's War; War of the Penny; War of the Resisters; *and entries for individual regions*
Peasants' War (1524–25), 4, 22–23, 57, 149, 174, 178, 180, 225; popular memories of, 58, 149, 151, 154, 161, 173–74
perjury, accusations of, 159
pilgrimage, 161, 181, 198–202, 207–11
political culture, 10–13, 25, 33, 90–91, 93–94, 213, 227–29; and factions, 11–12, 53, 55, 75–76, 90–91, 93–94, 148
pollution, concepts of, 160–61, 202
property, concepts of, 151–52, 175–77

rallies, political, 12, 91, 96–99, 108–9, 115–16, 138, 155, 163–64, 182–93, 200, 203–4, 211. *See also* mobilization: strategies of
Ramschwag, Christoph von, as imperial commissioner, 82, 84, 88, 99, 101, 137
Rebel, Hermann, 221, 225, 228–29
Reichskammergericht, Reichshofrat. See courts of law: imperial
Remetschwiel, serf court in, 44, 62–63, 88, 131
Rickenbach, canton, 45, 77, 99, 101, 106, 111–14, 125, 189–90
Robisheaux, Thomas, 48, 219, 221
Russia, peasant rebellions in, 150, 180

Sabean, David W., 13, 92, 204, 224–25
Säckingen. *See* St. Fridolin

salpeterisch faction. *See* factions
salvation, concepts of, 161–62, 170–72, 202
satanism, accusations of, 161–62
Schmiedle, Adam (Niedermühle), 108, 138–41
Schulze, Winfried, 21–23
seigneurial regime, 5–6, 8, 35, 40, 45–47, 49, 128–29, 219–20; burdens imposed by, 30, 41–42, 47, 111, 130, 213, 215–16, 219, 221; complaints against, 49, 55, 57, 110–11, 197–98, 227–28. *See also* Habsburg state: as landlord; St. Blasien: as landlord; St. Fridolin: as landlord
serfdom, 3, 15, 31, 42, 45, 50, 75, 95, 151, 155, 161, 175–78, 183, 202; burdens imposed by, 43–45, 50, 62–64, 70, 111–12, 155; census of, 63–64; complaints against, 31, 42, 50, 57, 59, 62–66, 75–76, 78, 84, 109–10, 115, 154, 156, 199; "double," 42–43, 50, 111–12; legal disabilities imposed by, 44–45, 62–63, 70, 76; manumission from, 73–79, 85, 102, 104–5, 152, 155–59, 169, 176, 183, 189, 199, 202, 229; nomenclature of, 60–61, 63, 66, 68, 148, 157, 160, 165, 175, 185; "of the baser hand," 42–43, 50; and peasant rebellion, 15, 31, 74–77, 95, 110–12, 115, 214–15; popular awareness of, 42, 60–66, 68, 148, 151, 154–58, 178–79, 202; as "slavery," 61, 63, 76, 95, 115, 152, 158, 160–61, 166, 169, 175–78, 202, 229; and social control, 43–45, 110–11. *See also* St. Blasien: as serf lord; St. Fridolin: as serf lord
Sickingen, Ferdinand Sebastian von, as imperial commissioner, 77–79, 84, 88, 99
social stratification, 10–11, 24, 118, 121–22, 124–26, 216–21; political effects of, 11, 34–35, 52–53, 85, 118–20, 126–27, 182, 212, 221, 223–26, 230
St. Blasien, 35–36, 48–49; administrative practices of, 10–11, 45–48, 118–19, 127, 141; expansionism of, 58–59, 61, 68, 94, 108, 115, 118, 148, 153, 166, 205, 212; incomes of, 40, 42, 44, 48, 119, 126–27, 130; as juridical lord, 3, 10, 18, 33–34, 37, 40–42, 45–46, 49–50, 58–60, 62, 85, 95, 101, 111–14, 118–19, 129–32, 156, 166, 205, 216; as landlord, 3, 40–42, 47, 49, 110–11, 119, 127, 129–30, 134; role in "Salpeter Wars," 54, 65–68, 74–75, 96–99, 115, 166; as serf lord, 3, 10, 31, 42–45, 50, 57–62, 64–65, 74–75, 85, 88, 109–11, 148, 154
St. Fridolin, 36–37, 40, 52–53; as juridical lord, 37, 40–42, 101, 113–14; as landlord, 41–42, 112, 135; as serf-lord, 44–45, 79, 111
Suter, Andreas, 7
Switzerland, 3, 16, 19–20, 25, 27, 51–52, 66, 176, 221–24; peasant rebellions in, 20–21, 209, 221–24. *See also* "turning Swiss," concept of

tax strikes, 77–78, 82, 167, 193
Thirty Years' War (1618–1648), 27–29, 60, 118, 121, 214, 218–19
Thoma, Christa (Birndorf), 138–39, 141–42
Thoma, Martin (Haselbach), 71, 108, 134, 137–38, 141–42, 154–55, 161, 169; election of, 185; as rally organizer, 187–88
Thoma-ab-Egg, Johannes, 135, 143, 165, 172, 228; election of, 196; and "May Terror," 81–83
Thompson, E. P., 7, 22
tithes, 42, 122–23, 127, 130
treason, accusations of, 63–64, 77, 81, 148, 156–57, 160–61, 164, 179, 181, 183, 197–98, 200, 231
Tröndle, Adam (Unteralpfen), 60–62, 65, 156–58
Tröndle, Joseph (Rotzel), 80, 82–83, 137, 142, 172, 179; as Speaker, 74, 153–54
Tröndle, Joseph (Schmitzingen), 140–41, 166
Tröndle, Joseph (Unteralpfen), 4, 23, 53, 55, 67, 80, 82–83, 133, 142, 159, 161; as miller, 137–39; as Octovir, 62–65, 72–73
Tröndle, "Schwarzmichel" (Bergalingen), 73, 166–68; as delegate, 194, 196, 199

Troßbach, Werner, 215–16
Turner, Victor, and Edith Turner, 208
"turning Swiss," concept of, 11–12, 30, 150–51, 169–74, 227
Tyrol, 19, 27, 29, 51; peasant rebellions in, 173

Upper Austrian Peasants' War (1626), 173, 216, 225

villages, 2, 5, 11–13, 20, 70, 94–95, 109, 116, 143–45, 180–81, 186, 193, 203; assemblies of, 5, 7, 12–13, 17–18, 104, 108–9, 184–90, 192–93; and social control, 8, 18–21, 26–37, 47–48, 56, 69, 94–95, 116, 181, 186, 186–89, 192–93, 203; types and structure of, 18–21, 180
violence, factional, 1–2, 56, 67, 78, 80–84, 151, 184, 211, 212, 222–23; threats of, 160, 171–72
Vorarlberg, 19, 27, 29, 51, 174
Vorderösterreich. See Outer Austria

Waldkirch, village, 96–98, 100–101, 106, 115–16, 138, 156, 187, 200
Waldshut, 75–76, 115, 126; seige of, 1, 81–83, 181
Waldvogt. See Forest Steward
War of Austrian Succession (1740–1748), 56, 79, 80–84, 151, 203
War of the Penny (1612–1614), 57
War of the Resisters (1725–1727), 221, 223–24
War of Spanish Succession (1698–1714), 10, 59, 62, 118, 122–23
Wasmer, "Gaudihans" (Segeten), 76, 78, 81–83, 158, 164–65, 169–72, 228
"wicked ministers", 150, 167–73, 196
Wolpadingen, canton, 34, 37, 43, 46, 94, 100–101, 106, 108–10, 113–14, 125
Wunder, Heide, 2, 218–19
Württemberg, 16, 25, 49–51, 204, 206–7, 220–21

Zweyer von Evenbach, Baron, 36, 79
Zwing und Bann, district of, 36, 48, 58–59